always up to date

The law changes, but Nolo is always on top of it! We offer several ways to make sure you and your Nolo products are always up to date:

1 **Nolo's Legal Updater**

We'll send you an email whenever a new edition of your book is published! Sign up at **www.nolo.com/legalupdater**.

2 **Updates @ Nolo.com**

Check **www.nolo.com/update** to find recent changes in the law that affect the current edition of your book.

3 **Nolo Customer Service**

To make sure that this edition of the book is the most recent one, call us at **800-728-3555** and ask one of our friendly customer service representatives. Or find out at **www.nolo.com**.

please note

We believe accurate and current legal information should help you solve many of your own legal problems on a cost-efficient basis. But this text is not a substitute for personalized advice from a knowledgeable lawyer. If you want the help of a trained professional, consult an attorney licensed to practice in your state.

2nd edition

Getting Permission

How to License & Clear Copyrighted Materials Online & Off

by Attorney Richard Stim

Second Edition	SEPTEMBER 2004
Editor	STEPHANIE BORNSTEIN
Cover Design	TONI IHARA
Cover Elements	WAYDE NISHIMURA, RICH STIM, DENIS CLIFFORD
Book Design	TERRI HEARSH
Production	MARGARET LIVINGSTON
Proofreading	ROBERT WELLS
CD-ROM preparation	ANDRÉ ZIVKOVICH
Index	MICHAEL FERREIRA
Printing	DELTA PRINTING SOLUTIONS, INC.

Stim, Richard.
    Getting permission : how to license & clear copyrighted materials online & off / by Richard Stim.– 2nd ed.
        p. cm.
    Includes index.
    ISBN 1-4133-0074-X (alk. paper)
    1. Copyright licenses--United States--Popular works. 2. Trademark licenses--United States--Popular works. I. Title.

KF3002.Z9S75 2004
346.7304'82--dc22

                                                          2004049534

Acknowledgments

Thanks to those who provided me with helpful information in various chapters, including: Bobby Neel Adams, Paula Berinstein, Bruce Blank, Denise D'Ambrosia, Mary Goljenboom, Phillip Greenspun, Bill Hammons, Joan Menschefreund, Robert Panzer, Cheryl Pickerell, and Richard Vittenson.

About the Author

Richard Stim is an attorney and editor at Nolo. He is the author of several Nolo books, including *Music Law: How to Run Your Band's Business, Patent Pending in 24 Hours*, and *Patent, Copyright & Trademark: An Intellectual Property Desk Reference*.

Table of Contents

4 Getting Permission to Use Artwork

5 Getting Permission to Use Music

11 Art and Merchandise Licenses

12 Releases

13 Copyright Research

14 After Permission Is Granted

15 Assignments and Works Made for Hire

16 Help Beyond This Book

Appendixes

A How to Use the CD-ROM

B Forms

Text Permission Worksheet

Text Permission Letter Agreement

Text Permission Agreement

Photo Permission Worksheet

Photo Permission Agreement

Artwork Permission Agreement

Agreement to Use Artwork in Motion Picture

Lyric Permission Letter Agreement

Notice of Intention to Obtain Compulsory License for Making and Distributing
  Sound Recordings

Music Synchronization and Videogram License Agreement

Master Use and Videogram License

Linking Agreement

APS/CCC Coursepack Agreement

Coursepack Permission Request Form

Coursepack Permission Agreement

Basic Permission to Use a Trademark in a Book or Magazine

Basic Permission to Use a Trademark in a Movie

Basic Permission to Use a Trademark in a Photograph or Artwork

Trademark License Agreement

Merchandise License Agreement

Merchandise License Worksheet

Short-Form Merchandise License Agreement

Unlimited Personal Release Agreement

Index

1

Introduction to the Permissions Process

From the Indies to the Andes, what a mission.
Stopping only now and then to do some fishing
And he went without a copyright permission
What a very daring thing to do.

"From the Indies to the Andies in His Undies" by
Lawrence Royal, Ernie Burnett, and William E. Faber
© Rialto Music Publishing.

These whimsical song lyrics, written more than 50
years ago, express a basic truth about copyright
law: Using someone's creative work without permission can be a very daring thing to do. An unhappy
copyright owner may sue you, seeking monetary
damages, preventing you from publishing your
work, or both. On the other hand, by simply obtaining permission, you gain lawsuit-free access to
the work you need.

This book is intended to reduce your risks by
guiding you through the permissions process and
explaining how to obtain the appropriate rights
when using other people's creative work. Information is provided about locating copyright owners,
asking for permission, assessing the conditions of
the permission agreement, and avoiding potential
disputes.

This chapter offers an overview of the whole
process, explaining the purpose and legal basis for
permission, as well as the potential risks of operating without permission. It also serves as a guide to
using this book.

A. Permission: What Is It and Why Do I Need It?

Obtaining copyright permission is the process of
getting consent from a copyright owner to use the
owner's creative material. Obtaining permission is
often called "licensing"; when you have permission,
you have a license to use the work. Permission is
often (but not always) required because of intellectual property laws that protect creative works such
as text, artwork, or music. (These laws are explained in more detail in the next section.) If you
use a copyrighted work without the appropriate
permission, you may be violating—or "infringing"—
the owner's rights to that work. Infringing someone
else's copyright may subject you to legal action. As
if going to court weren't bad enough, you could be
forced to stop using the work or pay money damages to the copyright owner.

As noted above, permission is not always required. In some situations, you can reproduce a
photograph, a song or text without a license. Generally, this will be true if the work has fallen into
the public domain, or if your use qualifies as what's
called a "fair use." Both of these legal concepts involve quite specific rules and are discussed more
fully in subsequent chapters. In most cases, however, permission is required, so it's important to
never assume that it's okay to use a work without
permission.

Many people operate illegally, either intentionally or through ignorance. They use other people's
work and never seek consent. The problem with
this approach—besides its questionable ethics—is
that the more successful the project becomes, the
more likely that a copyright owner will learn of the
use. Therefore, if you want your project to become
successful, unauthorized use becomes an obstacle.

Some people avoid getting permission because
they don't understand the permissions process or
consider it too expensive. However, the process is
not difficult and the fee for use of common text,
photo, or artwork is commonly under $200 per use.
In some cases, it's free. On the other hand, the legal
fees for dealing with an unauthorized use lawsuit
can easily cost ten to 50 times the average permission expense—or more!

B. The Basics of Getting Permission

This section outlines the basic steps for obtaining
permission. Subsequent chapters provide more detailed information about this process for each type
of permission you may be seeking, whether for text,
photographs, music, or artwork.

In general, the permissions process involves a simple five-step procedure:

1. Determine if permission is needed.
2. Identify the owner.
3. Identify the rights needed.
4. Contact the owner and negotiate whether payment is required.
5. Get your permission agreement in writing.

Each step is described in more detail below.

1. Determine If Permission Is Needed

The first step in every permission situation is to determine whether you need to ask for permission. In other words, do you need an agreement or can you use the work without permission? Determining whether to ask for permission depends on two questions:

- Is the material protected under law?
- Would your use of the material violate the law?

Unfortunately, it is not always possible to answer these questions with a definitive "yes" or "no." Sometimes, you may have to analyze the risk involved in operating without permission. Below are some basic legal principles you'll need to know. Subsequent chapters explore these principles in more depth.

a. Is the Material Protected Under Intellectual Property Law?

You should always start with the presumption that, if the creative work you want to use was first published after 1922, U.S. copyright law protects it. There are only two ways that a work published after 1922 is not protected: Either the owner of the work made a mistake (such as failing to renew the copyright) or the work does not meet the minimum standards for copyright protection. Later chapters on the permission rules for particular types of creative works provide guidelines to determine if the work you intend to use is protected.

A work that isn't protected by intellectual property laws is in the public domain and can be used without asking for permission. Most works that fall into the public domain do so because of old age. Public domain status may also be due to other reasons discussed in Chapter 8.

EXAMPLE: Bill wants to include his recording of the song "Give My Regards to Broadway" on his website. Because the song was first published in 1904, it is in the public domain and Bill can use it without obtaining permission.

b. Would Your Use of the Material Constitute a Violation of Law?

If a creative work is protected under intellectual property laws, your unauthorized use may still be legal. This is because there are exceptions to each of the laws protecting creative work—situations in which authorization is not required. For example, under copyright law, a principle known as "fair use" permits you to copy small portions of a work for certain purposes such as scholarship or commentary. Under the fair use doctrine, you could reproduce a few lines of a song lyric in a music review without getting permission from the songwriter (or whoever owns the copyright in the song). Chapter 9 discusses fair use in greater depth.

c. What Is the Risk of Not Asking for Permission?

The goal of this book is to minimize your risk of being sued. As explained in each chapter, the risk of being sued depends on not only your particular use, but on factors such as the likelihood that the use will be spotted, whether you are a "worthy" target for litigation, or whether the other side is inclined to sue.

This book recommends a conservative approach. Unless you are certain that the material is in the public domain or that your use is legally excusable, seeking permission is worth your time. If you are not sure, you'll have to either make your own risk assessment or obtain the advice of an attorney knowledgeable in copyright or media law.

EXAMPLE: I wanted to use the lyrics from the song "From the Indies to the Andies in His Undies," featured at the beginning of this chapter. I located information about the writers of the song from a compilation recording of country music. Then, I located the name of the publisher (Rialto Music, Inc.) from the American Society of Composers, Authors, and Publishers (ASCAP), who informed me that the owner had ended its affiliation with the organization in 1975. I searched to no avail for the songwriters and Rialto Music on the Web using a search engine. I also checked the online Library of Congress records but found no reference, either because the song was never registered or the song was written before the date their online computer records began. I contacted the Harry Fox Agency, another agency that controls rights, who gave me a reference for Rialto in Providence, Rhode Island. I tried using operator assistance but could find no listing. I decided to proceed without permission because my limited use of the lyrics (four lines) for purposes of commentary, combined with my good-faith attempt to find the owner, probably qualifies as a fair use.

2. Identify the Owner

Identifying the owner of the work you want to use is crucial to obtaining permission. Sometimes, this task is simple. Often, you may be able to locate the rights owner just by looking at the copyright notice on the work. For example, if the notice reads "Copyright 1998, Jones Publishing," you would start by finding the Jones Publishing company. Sometimes, more detailed research is required. Copyright ownership may have passed through several hands since your copy of the work was published.

In addition, some kinds of art, such as film and recorded music, can involve multiple owners, each with a separate right to different underlying works. For example, in order to use a Johnny Cash recording, you would have to obtain permission from the record company, the music publisher (the owner of the song), and, in some cases, from Mr. Cash's estate.

You'll find that the method of identifying owners differs from industry to industry. For example, photographic reproduction rights are often owned by stock photo organizations, while many music performance rights are owned by performing rights societies. Subsequent chapters on the permission rules for particular types of creative works will advise you on how to locate owners. In addition, Chapter 13 discusses the process of searching for owners in Copyright Office records.

3. Identify the Rights You Need

The next step in getting permission is to identify the rights you need. Each copyright owner controls a bundle of rights related to the work, including the right to reproduce, distribute, and modify the work. Because so many rights are associated with copyrighted works, you must specify the rights you need. This can be as simple as stating your intended use—for example, you want to reproduce a photograph in your magazine or display a cartoon in your PowerPoint presentation.

Asking for the proper rights can be a balancing act. You don't want to pay for more than you need, but you don't want to have to return for a second round of permissions. Sometimes this requires negotiating with the rights owner to find a middle ground for fees.

Besides identifying the type of intended use, you'll need to figure out some other details of your use of the material. Specifically, your permissions agreement will need to deal with three common variables: exclusivity, term, and territory.

a. Exclusive or Nonexclusive

All permission agreements are either exclusive or nonexclusive. A permission agreement is exclusive if you are the only person who has the right to use the work as described in the agreement. For example, if you enter into an agreement with the owner of a photograph for the exclusive use of the photograph in a cookbook, no one else could use the photograph in another cookbook. Exclusivity can be as narrow or as broad as you choose. For example, you could expand the exclusivity of your permission agreement by obtaining the exclusive right to print the photo in any book, not just any cookbook.

Most permission requests are nonexclusive, meaning others can use the material in the same way as you. For example, if you have a nonexclusive agreement to use a photo in your cookbook, the same photo could be used in someone else's cookbook (provided permission was granted). The permission agreements included throughout this book offer you the option to choose exclusive or nonexclusive rights.

b. Term of Use

The length of time for which you are allowed to use a work is often referred to as the "term." Your rights under a permission agreement will often be limited in duration. For example, if you are licensing the right to display a photograph on a website, the copyright owner may limit the length of your use to one year. Alternatively, you might obtain what's called a "one-time use," meaning you can only use the material in one edition of a magazine, not in subsequent editions. If there is no express limitation on the use, you are allowed to use the material for as long as you want or until the copyright owner revokes the permission. Some agreements prohibit the copyright owner from revoking rights by granting permission "irrevocably." Sometimes an agreement states that it is "in perpetuity," which means that rights are granted without time limits. In reality, the copyright owner can only grant permission for as long as the owner's copyright protection lasts. After that, anyone can use the material without permission.

c. Territory

Your rights under a permission agreement may be limited to a geographic region referred to as the "territory." For example, the copyright owner of a book may grant you permission to reprint a chapter only in the U.S. and Canada.

As you go through the various chapters, this book will advise you on how to shape your permission agreement so that you obtain the rights you need for your purposes.

4. Plan Ahead for Permission

Expect getting permission to take anywhere from one to three months. Permission should be obtained before you complete your work. It is sometimes more difficult and more expensive to obtain permission after a book, film, or recording is complete. If the copyright owner becomes aware that you have a vested interest in obtaining permission (for example, your book is already in production), the price may rise. In addition, if you can't obtain permission, you'll have to re-do the work, which is expensive and time consuming. The best policy is to start seeking all required permissions as soon as possible.

5. Negotiate Whether Payment Is Required

The primary issue that arises when seeking permission is whether you will have to pay for the permission you seek. Sometimes, the owner of the work will not require payment if the amount you wish to use is small, or if the owner wishes to contribute to an educational or nonprofit effort. In some cases, an artist or musician eager for exposure may agree to suspend payment unless the work becomes profitable, or may condition payment on other factors.

EXAMPLE: Sam is making a low-budget documentary film in which he wants to include photographs of vintage accordions. He contacts the copyright owner of the photographs who, in return for a credit at the end of the film, signs an agreement allowing use of the photographs in the film. However, the agreement also provides that, if Sam uses the photographs in a poster or advertisement for the film, he must make an additional one-time payment of $1,500.

Although many uses are free, expect to pay at least $100 or more for each copyright permission. Some types of permission almost always require payment. For example, using a photo owned by a stock photo agency usually requires a payment of $200 or more. Using a song in a commercial usually requires a payment of several thousand dollars.

Generally, permission fees are linked to the size of the audience your work will reach. A large metropolitan newspaper will have to pay more to use a photograph than a small town newspaper. Commercial uses, such advertisements, cost more than nonprofit or educational uses. The fees for website uses may depend upon on the number of visitors to the site. In each chapter, we will discuss the likelihood of payment and the current rates for common uses. However, these figures can vary widely, as the copyright owner has discretion when charging a fee.

6. Get It in Writing

Relying on an oral agreement or understanding is almost always a mistake. You and the rights owner may have misunderstood each other or remembered the terms of your agreement differently. This can lead to disputes. If you have to go to court to enforce your unwritten agreement, you'll have difficulty proving exactly what the terms are. Get written permission agreements—do not rely on oral agreements.

That said, an oral permission may be legally enforceable if it qualifies as a contract under general contract law principles. Moreover, even if you have no explicit oral agreement, you may still have a right to use a work if permission can be inferred from the conduct of the parties.

EXAMPLE: Sam is writing a book and asks for permission to reproduce Tom's photo. Tom quotes Sam a fee of $100, which Sam sends to Tom. After receiving the payment, Tom sends the photograph to Sam. Although they never put an agreement into writing, a permission agreement may be inferred from Tom's conduct.

What If You Hire Someone to Create a Work?

Most of the situations described in this book deal with obtaining permission to use an existing work. However, it's possible that you may hire an artist or other creative person to create the work for you. If the creative person qualifies as your employee, you will automatically own all rights to the work he or she creates on your behalf, and no permission is required. The Supreme Court has established standards for determining whether a creative person is an employee. These standards include factors such as whether the person is given weekly or monthly payments (instead of being paid by the job), whether you withhold employee taxes for the person, and whether the person receives employee benefits.

If the person creating the work is not an employee, he or she is an independent contractor. In this event, your ownership of the person's work is not automatic. To guarantee your ownership of an independent contractor's work, you should use either a work-for-hire agreement (if your commission meets the requirements) or an assignment. Chapter 15 addresses these agreements. For a thorough analysis of acquiring rights from independent contractors, see *The Copyright Handbook*, by Stephen Fishman (Nolo).

C. Overview of Intellectual Property Laws

A wide body of federal and state laws protect creative property such as writing, music, drawings, paintings, photography, and films. Collectively, this body of law is called "intellectual property" law, which includes copyright, trademark, and patent laws, each applicable in various situations and each with its own set of technical rules. When obtaining permission to use creative works, you're concerned primarily with copyright law. However, trademarks, trade secrets, and publicity and privacy rights sometimes come into play when permission to use certain types of works is sought. Below is a summary of the various types of intellectual property laws that are relevant to the permissions process. Later chapters provide more details as needed.

- **Copyright.** Original creative works such as paintings, writing, architecture, movies, software, photos, dance, and music are protected by federal copyright law. A work must meet certain minimum requirements to qualify for copyright protection (discussed in Chapters 8, 9, and 13). The length of protection also varies depending on when the work was created or first published. (See Chapter 8 for an explanation of copyright duration.)
- **Trademark.** Brand names such as Nike and Avis, as well as logos, slogans, and other devices that identify and distinguish products and services are protected under federal and state trademark laws. Unlike copyrighted works, trademarks receive different degrees of protection depending on numerous variables including the consumer awareness of the trademark, the type of service and product it identifies, and the geographic area in which the trademark is used. (See Chapter 10.)
- **Right of Publicity.** The image and name of a person are protected under a patchwork of state laws known as the right of publicity. These laws protect against the unauthorized use of a person's name or image for commer-

cial purposes—for example, the use of your picture on a box of cereal. The extent of this protection varies from state to state. (See Chapter 12.)
- **Trade Secrets.** State and federal trade secret laws protect sensitive business information. An example of a trade secret would be a confidential marketing plan for the introduction of a new software product or the secret recipe for a brand of salsa. The extent of trade secret protection depends on whether the information gives the business an advantage over competitors, is kept secret, and is not known by competitors. (See Chapter 10.)
- **Right of Privacy.** Although not part of intellectual property laws, state privacy laws preserve the right of all people to be left alone. Invasion of privacy occurs when someone publishes or publicly exploits information about another person's private affairs. Invasion of privacy laws prevent you from intruding on, exposing private facts about, or falsely portraying someone. The extent of this protection may vary if the subject is a public figure—for example, a celebrity or politician. (See Chapter 12.)

D. Permission Tools: Licenses and Releases

Obtaining permission to use a protected work requires entering into an agreement with the owner of that work. Your agreement may give you the right to use the work (a "license") or it may be a promise that the owner will not sue you for an unauthorized use (a "release").

1. Licenses and Clearances

A license is the legal right to do something that you would not otherwise be permitted to do. For example, you need a driver's license to give you the right to drive a car. The owner of a copyrighted work can authorize someone else to use the work by granting a license to the user. For example, the owner of a photograph copyright can grant a license to someone else who wants to reproduce the photograph on a greeting cards. If no license has been given, the copyright owner can sue for the unauthorized use of the work, referred to as "infringement."

The terms "license" and "permission agreement" are often used interchangeably. You may also find that, in some situations, a license or permission agreement is referred to as a "clearance agreement." "Clearance" is a general term used to describe the process by which permission is granted.

> **EXAMPLE:** Don is writing a book on British horror films and wants to reproduce an image from a 1950s film. Don must obtain a license to reproduce the image from the owner of rights in the film.

2. Releases

A release is an agreement by which someone releases you from legal liability for a particular activity. In essence, the person is agreeing ahead of time to give up (or release) any right to sue you that may arise from a specific situation. Releases are often used to avoid lawsuits involving someone's right of privacy (the right to be left alone) or right of publicity (the right to control how one's image, voice, or persona will be used to sell things). A release may also protect against claims of defamation (a false statement that injures someone's reputation). Releases are discussed in more detail in Chapter 12.

> **EXAMPLE:** *Makeover* is a TV show in which audience members are selected for beauty and fashion makeovers. Any audience member selected must sign a release before appearing on the show. The release protects the TV show from any potential lawsuits by disgruntled participants who are unhappy with the results of

their makeovers and seek damages for legal claims such as infliction of emotional distress or defamation.

⚠ **Don't rely on the title of an agreement.** In many cases, licenses and releases overlap. For example, a release agreement may contain license language and vice versa. Despite what it says at the top of the agreement, either type of agreement can be used to grant rights or to prevent lawsuits. Because of this overlap, the title of an agreement is less important than the content. Always review any agreement carefully (and compare it to the model agreements in this book) before assuming what rights it covers.

E. How to Use This Book

The information in this book deals with three basic issues involved in the permissions process:

- **Whether permission is necessary.** If permission isn't needed, you can save yourself time and money.
- **What type of work you want to use.** The permissions process often varies according to what type of work you want to use—photographs, text, artwork, music, trademark, or a person's image.
- **How you plan to use the work.** Obtaining permission also depends on how you plan to use the work—whether in an article, on T-shirts, on a website, in a video or film, or in an academic publication.

Depending on which issue you're dealing with, you may want to focus on different chapters of this book as outlined below.

1. Whether Permission Is Necessary

Permission is not always necessary before you can use creative materials. The following chapters discuss how to evaluate whether permission is necessary in various contexts.

- **Academic permissions.** Chapter 7 explains when permission is not required for academic and library uses.
- **The public domain.** Chapter 8 deals with materials that are not protected by copyright law and fall into what's called the "public domain."
- **Fair use.** Chapter 9 provides information about "fair use," the copyright principle that enables limited uses of materials without permission.
- **Releases.** Chapter 12 discusses when permission is needed to use a real person's image.
- **Copyright research.** Chapter 13 explains how to research whether copyright protection exists, and, if so, who owns the copyright.
- **Acquiring ownership.** Chapter 15 provides information on acquiring ownership of copyrighted material, not merely getting permission to use it.

2. What Type of Work You Want to Use

This book deals with getting permission to use a variety of materials—text, photographs, artwork, music, trademarks, characters, and images of real people. The type of material you wish to use affects the type of permission you need, the fee you must pay, and your permissions process. For example, the rules for efforts to locate copyright owners vary for photographers, musicians, and writers, and the permission agreement required for using trademarked material is different from that for using copyrighted material. If you know what type of material you wish to use, you can proceed directly to the relevant chapter.

- **Text.** Chapter 2 discusses use of most text, such as quoting from books, magazines, or other written material.
- **Photographs.** Chapter 3 details photographic permissions and the world of stock photography.

- **Artwork.** Chapter 4 provides background on using fine art, graphic art, stock art, and cartoons.
- **Music.** Chapter 5 is devoted to using music and song lyrics.
- **Trademarks and characters.** Chapter 10 explains the rules regarding the use of trademarks and trademarked characters (for example, Mickey Mouse).
- **Images of people.** Chapter 12 deals with using an image of a real person, whether for a news article or advertisement.

Icons Used in This Book

 This alerts you to a practical tip or good idea.

 This is a caution to slow down and consider potential problems.

 This refers you to other sources of information about a particular topic.

 This tells you where in the text you can read more about a particular topic.

 This tells you a digital copy of a form or agreement is included on the CD-ROM that accompanies this book.

3. How You Plan to Use the Work

Creative materials can be used in books, journals, movies, recordings, video, websites, software programs, artwork, and merchandise. The medium in which you use the material and the rights that you need for that use affect the permissions process. The rights you obtain may include certain limitations: how long you may use the material, where you may distribute your project, and whether you have exclusive use of the material. The following chapters discuss the rules for specific uses.

- **Website uses.** Chapter 6 includes some special rules for use of materials on websites.
- **Academic uses.** Chapter 7 explains the unique rules for academic permissions.
- **Merchandise.** Chapter 11 discusses rules for using copyrighted works on merchandise.

 For information about any changes that have occurred since publication of this edition, visit Nolo's website (www.nolo.com).

■

Getting Permission to Use Text

This chapter covers how to get permission to use text—whether from a book, magazine, newspaper, newsletter, website, or journal. This chapter will help you identify the company or person who owns the rights to the text (the "rights holder") and offers suggestions for how to make your permissions request. It also discusses special situations that occur when using text from interviews, speeches, or print publications. At the end of the chapter, you'll find two sample text permission agreements: a short-form agreement and a longer, more detailed agreement.

This chapter does not cover permission to use song lyrics or literary characters, or to create academic coursepacks. For information on these materials, see the following list of cross-references:

- for song lyrics, refer to Chapter 5
- for literary characters, refer to Chapter 10, and
- for academic coursepacks, refer to Chapter 7.

A. Who Owns the Text?

The first step to obtain permission is to make sure you're asking the correct entity for permission. The owner of the text may be the company who published it, the author of the text, or no one at all. Who owns the text depends on how the rights were negotiated between publisher and author and on law and industry traditions. With the advent of online permission services, your search for the rights owner may only require a few clicks of a mouse (as discussed in Section B). If these services don't offer what you need, you will need to contact either the publisher (as discussed in Section C), the author (as discussed in Section D), or both.

Two major industry changes may be relevant to your search: the shift in ownership of articles from author to publisher in the 1980s (discussed in Section A1) and the Supreme Court's 2001 decision that freelancers must be compensated for reprints of their works in electronic databases (discussed in Section A2). Also, special rules apply to certain situations, such as interviews and syndicated columns (as discussed in Section E).

Before seeking out the copyright owner, confirm whether permission is necessary. No permission is required if the text you want to use is in what's known as the "public domain." And, many uses of text are permitted without permission under a principle of copyright law known as "fair use." The public domain is discussed in Chapter 8, and fair use is discussed in Chapter 9.

1. Shifting Ownership of Articles

Before the 1980s, the author of an article was usually the primary rights holder. At that time, periodicals traditionally only asked for first "North American serial rights"—the right to publish the article once in the United States and Canada. However, in the past two decades, magazines, journals, and other periodicals have increasingly obtained reprint, syndication, and other primary rights from authors. Therefore, where multiple publishers have published an article in the last 20 years, your starting point for permission will be the original publisher of the article (see Section C, below). For older articles, your best bet is to start by contacting the author (see Section D, below).

2. Shifting Ownership of Electronic Database Reprints

The rules for ownership of electronic rights to written works changed dramatically in June 2001. The U.S. Supreme Court decided that freelance writers must be compensated when their works are placed on Internet or CD-ROM databases such as LexisNexis. The Court, in the case of *The New York Times v. Tasini*, 533 U.S. 483 (2001), found that *The Times* and other publishers committed copyright infringement when they resold freelance newspaper and magazine articles through electronic databases without asking permission or making additional payments to the freelancers. The ruling applies to any freelancer who sold an article without expressly transferring the electronic rights to the publisher.

If you are seeking electronic rights to an article written by a freelancer written before 1995, chances are good that the freelancer has retained the electronic rights, and you should start by contacting the freelancer (see Section D, below). After 1995, publishers routinely obtained electronic rights from freelance authors, and you're best off contacting the publisher first (see Section C, below).

B. Start With Online Permission Services

Two Internet services, RSiCopyright (www.icopyright .com) and the Copyright Clearance Center (CCC) (www.copyright.com) have drastically simplified the process of obtaining text permissions. Start your quest for permission with one of them. By using such services, you may avoid having to search for or contact the copyright owner directly. Instead, you need only identify the book, journal, or magazine article and complete an online form. If the work is part of the service's online database, you can usually obtain permission within one or two days (sometimes immediately) and pay for the rights you need by credit card. Acting as the agent and broker for publishers and authors, these permission services allow you to pick and click your way through millions of works, including books and journal and magazine articles.

Publishers set the fees with these permission brokers—for example, a national newspaper, via CCC, charges $400 to reprint an article in a book and $600 to reprint an article in a national magazine. These prices are similar to those for permissions granted without the use of an online service—but if you wish to comparison shop, you can contact the copyright owner directly following the suggestions in Sections C and D, below.

The online procedure is often far easier than the traditional system of locating and calling a publisher, negotiating permission, and signing a written agreement. If a service does not represent a publisher—that is, the publisher's works are not designated in the database—you may still use the service to inquire about the use of works on your behalf.

1. Copyright Clearance Center

The CCC is considered the behemoth of text permissions, as it represents over 10,000 print publishers, including *The New York Times* and *The Wall Street Journal*. This makes their website a good place to start your permissions search. Through the CCC, you can obtain permission for:

- **republication**—reproducing text in books, journals, and newsletters
- **electronic use**—reproducing text on websites, in email, in PDF format, or on CD-ROMs, and
- **photocopying**—making multiple photocopies for distribution at events or businesses.

To use the CCC's service, visit the website, complete the free registration, and you will be directed to the "Permissions Online: Services" page. (If not, click the "Services" tab.) After you choose the type of permission, a page opens allowing you to either create an order, get a quick price, or view any existing orders. (You may become frustrated using the "quick price" feature; many rights holders don't permit price quotes. In these cases, the CCC contacts the rights holder and provides you with a quote within several days.)

If you're having trouble at any point in the CCC's process, FAQs and a useful demo on the site can help you.

2. RSiCopyright

RSiCopyright is the innovator of online permissions, but it has a smaller database of available works than the CCC. It offers two ways of licensing reprint rights: directly through its website or by clicking on the RSiCopyright logo (see below) if it appears at the bottom of an article on the Internet.

 RSiCopyright logo

If you see and click on the RSiCopyright logo, you are asked to choose whether you want to create a link to the article (see Chapter 6), reprint the article in email or on a website, or "Do Something Else." When you make the last choice, you must then complete a form that asks for your intended use—for example, to provide reprints at trade shows—and whether your use is commercial, academic, nonprofit, or governmental. Then, like the CCC, the service makes the inquiry to the copyright owner on your behalf.

Looking for Academic Articles?

Ingenta (www.ingenta.com) acts as an online intermediary for users seeking to access articles from over 28,000 academic and professional journals. If you are seeking information, content, permission to link, or online permission for academic or professional articles, check this site.

C. Locate the Publisher

If you cannot obtain permission through an online permission service or if you think you will get a better rate for permission by negotiating directly with the copyright owner, you'll need to search the old-fashioned way. The first step is to locate the publisher—the company that produced and distributed the work. For example, Nolo is the publisher of the book you're reading now. In the case of a quote from a magazine or journal article, the publisher is the company that produces and distributes the magazine or journal. For example, Time-Life Inc. is the publisher of *Time* magazine.

1. Permissions Departments

Many publishers have permissions departments or a person who handles reprints, permissions, and clearances. Information about the permissions department is usually found on or near the copyright page of a book, or in a magazine or journal's masthead page. Online magazines and book publishers' websites generally include copyright and permissions information on the introductory Web page (the index or home page).

If the book, magazine, or journal contains no specific information about permissions, direct your inquiries to the "Permissions Department" at the publisher's main business address, usually listed in the first or last few pages of a publication.

Are You Under Contract to Write a Book?

Have you signed a contract to write an article or book? Publishing contracts usually indicate who has responsibility for obtaining permission for anything you use in your article or book, either the author (you) or the publisher. Your publishing contract may also specify the language to be used in any permission agreement you obtain. Inquire whether your publisher has its own permission form you can use.

---

2. Locating Publishers

Contact information for book publishers can be located through publications such as *Books in Print, Literary Market Place,* and *International Literary Market Place,* all published by R.R. Bowker (www .bowker.com). *Books in Print* includes information about books currently available for sale and can be searched online for a fee. *Writer's Market* (Writer's Digest Books, www.writersdigest.com) provides a list of U.S book publishers as well as publishers of magazines, journals, and greeting cards.

For information on locating periodical publishers, consult *The National Directory of Magazines* and *The Standard Periodical Directory,* both published by Oxbridge Communications (www.mediafinder.com), or review *Ulrich's International Periodicals Directory* (R.R. Bowker) or *The Directory of Small Press and Magazine Editors and Publishers,* published by Dustbooks (www.dustbooks.com). For information on academic publishers, check out *The Association of American University Presses Directory,* published by the University of Chicago Press (www.press.uchicago.edu). Additional publisher resources are provided in Chapter 16, "Help Beyond This Book."

Distributing Photocopies at Work May Be an Infringement

Many businesses save money by photocopying an article from a journal, periodical, or book for employees or outside clients. For example, an insurance company that subscribes to a legal newsletter might make 200 photocopies and distribute photocopied newsletters to employees and customers. Though common, such photocopying is a violation of copyright law if done without permission. This rule was established in 1995, when an oil company was found liable for unauthorized photocopying of academic and scientific journals. *(American Geophysical Union v. Texaco, Inc.,* 60 F. 3d 913 (2d Cir. 1995).)

If a company gets caught, illegal photocopying can turn out to be no savings at all. In 1999, a national law firm paid out over $100,000 when confronted with a charge of illegal photocopying. How do publishers learn about this type of infringement? Often from disgruntled employees or from informants paid by publications that offer payments (sometimes as high as $10,000) for tipoffs.

Permission to photocopy and distribute materials can be acquired directly from the publisher or from the Copyright Clearance Center (www.copyright.com) or RSiCopyright (www.icopyright.com). The CCC provides individual-permission services (as well as "repertory" or "blanket" licensing services), including its basic Transactional Reporting Service. In some cases, a business can obtain an annual blanket license that permits unlimited photocopying from the CCC's collection of 1.75 million works. These blanket licenses are based on the type of industry and the number of employees for whom photocopies will be made. For example, law firms might pay a blanket license fee of $150 per year for each professional employee.

Certain types of photocopying for educational purposes do not require permission. However, this does not extend to the wholesale copying of articles for classroom use in coursepacks. The CCC has a special program that assists educators in obtaining permission for coursepacks. For details, see Chapter 7.

3. When There Is More Than One Publisher

Different publishers may print the same book in different versions. For example, one book may be published first in hardcover, later published in paperback by a different publisher, and then published outside the United States in a foreign language by yet a third publisher. Articles may be printed in magazines and then reprinted in digests or books by different publishers.

In cases of multiple publishers, you must find out who controls the right to reprint the work in another publication (known as "reprint rights"). The person or company who controls a work's reprint rights is known as the "primary rights holder." Often, the first publisher is the primary rights holder. In the case of a book, this is usually the hardcover publisher. You can find the name of the hardcover publisher by searching an online bookstore such as Amazon (www.amazon.com) or Barnes & Noble (www.barnesandnoble.com) using the title and/or author of the book.

If the hardcover publisher tells you that it does not have the right to reprint the work, ask if the publisher knows whom you should contact. If the publisher doesn't know, contact the author. (Contacting and negotiating with authors is discussed in Section D.)

Also, keep in mind that the primary rights holder may only control rights in one country. If you intend to reproduce a work outside that country, you may need to seek additional permission. For example, one rights holder may have the right to publish a work in the U.S., another in Great Britain, and yet another in Canada. If the work for which you're seeking permission will be distributed in the U.S., Britain, and Canada, you will need permission from all three rights holders. The primary rights holder can often lead you to foreign rights holders. If not, information about foreign publishers can be located in the publication *International Literary Market Place* (see Section C2).

Regional Rights Versus Foreign Language Rights

The territory in which a publication is distributed and the language in which it is published involve two separate rights. In other words, reprint rights are sold language by language and territory by territory. When dealing with U.S. publishers, unless you specifically ask for reprint rights in a foreign language, you will only be given the right to reprint the work in English in the territory specified. This means, for example, that acquiring "world" rights is not the same as acquiring rights in all languages. Rather, it means you have the right to publish the work in English throughout the world.

Be specific in your requests and permission agreements and keep the fees you must pay low by asking for only the rights you need. If your work will only be published in English, don't ask for foreign language rights. For example, if your magazine is distributed primarily in the U.S. and Canada, you probably only need one-time North American rights—the right to publish the work one time in the U.S. and Canada in English. However, if you print a French language edition for Canadian readers, you would need one-time North American rights and French language rights.

Check the Copyright Notice

Information about the publisher or other rights holders is often located in the publication's copyright notice. The notice has three elements: the word "Copyright," or a "C" in a circle (©), the name of the copyright owner, and the year of first publication of that version of the work.

EXAMPLE: © 2004 by the Bathroom Reader's Institute

While the name in the copyright notice will indicate the rights holder as of the date of publication, remember that ownership may have been transferred since the notice was published. For example, the original publisher may have been acquired by another, or the copyright owner may have designated someone else to handle permissions. In either case, the name in the notice provides a starting point.

Text first published before March 1, 1989 without a copyright notice may be in the public domain. For more information see Chapter 8.

D. Contact the Author

If the publisher doesn't own the rights you need, it may be able to put you in contact with the author by forwarding your request to the author or, if the author is deceased, to the author's estate. For privacy purposes, it's unlikely that the publisher will give you the author's address or phone number.

You may be able to locate an author using public sources, such as the Author's Registry (www .authorsregistry.org), which maintains a directory of authors and will search for one or two names, usually free of charge. Information about over 1,000 nonfiction writers may be found through the American Society of Journalists and Authors (www.asja.org).

Also, the University of Texas (http://tyler.hrc .utexas.edu) maintains a searchable database entitled WATCH (Writers, Artists, and Their Copyright Holders). This database contains the names and addresses of copyright holders or contact persons for authors and artists whose works are housed in libraries and archives in North America and the United Kingdom. The WATCH database also contains limited information on whether an author's or artist's copyrighted work has entered the public domain.

If the rights for the text are owned by two or more authors, you will need to obtain permission from only one of them—provided that your use is nonexclusive and for U.S. or North American rights. "Nonexclusive" means that other people can use the text for the same purpose as you. If you obtain permission from one of several coauthors, your permission agreement should include a statement that the rights holder has the authority to grant the rights in the agreement. For example, include a statement like "Licensor warrants that it has the right to grant permission." (This language is included in the sample licenses at the end of this chapter; see Section H4.) This provision places you in a better legal position if a dispute arises over your right to use the material.

You will need permission from all of the co-authors if:

- you want to use the text on an exclusive basis—meaning you are the only person who can use the text for a specific purpose
- you want to use the text on a worldwide, nonexclusive basis—because some countries require consent of all co-owners even for nonexclusive uses, or
- you want to use the text for a commercial purpose, to sell a service or product—for example, you want to include a quotation from a book in an advertisement (but simply using the text in a book or article you're writing for money is not considered to be a commercial purpose).

Educational Copying and Coursepacks

Some types of photocopying for educational purposes are allowed without requiring permission. However, this does not extend to the wholesale copying of articles for classroom use in coursepacks. The Copyright Clearance Center (CCC) (www.copyright.com) has a special program that assists educators in obtaining permission to include works in coursepacks. The rules for using copyrighted material in academic coursepacks are discussed in detail in Chapter 7.

E. Special Situations: Ann Landers and Beyond

Finding rights holders for certain types of text, such as syndicated columns, speeches, interviews, and letters, may prove a little tricky. Below are suggestions for getting permission to use these types of works, as well as unpublished and out-of-print texts.

1. Syndicated Text

Rights for works by newspaper columnists such as Dave Barry and Ann Landers are usually controlled by national syndicates. Chapter 4 includes a list of contact information for syndicates for comic strips. Many of these same syndicates also handle text.

For example, to acquire permission to reprint a "Dear Abby" column in a book with an initial printing of 5,000 copies, you would first look at the column in a daily newspaper to find the syndicate's name—Universal Press Syndicate. Then, you would contact the syndicate and request permission to reprint the column. At this book's first printing, the syndicate fees for using "Dear Abby" in this book were $175 for North American rights and $100 more for world rights. In addition, use of the column required a specific credit line supplied by Universal.

2. Interviews

If you want to use an interview from a magazine or book, contact the publisher of the book or magazine. To use a written transcript of an interview from a radio or television show, contact the network or station that originally aired the show. For interviews first published on a website, contact the owner of the site, usually indicated on the bottom of the home or index page.

If you seek permission to use a transcript of a television or radio interview, most stations have permissions departments that will furnish you a printed version. Sometimes you can download interview transcripts from the station's website. If you want to use the actual audio or audiovisual recording of an interview, you will need to obtain the consent of the person or company who recorded the material, often the radio or television station that initially broadcast it. (If you are interviewing someone yourself and want to make sure you have the necessary rights to publish the content of the interview, see Chapter 12, "Releases.")

If the publisher, website owner, or television or radio station is not the rights holder and cannot lead you to the rights holder, try to locate the interviewer through one of the author resources listed in Section D.

On occasion, determining the rights holder of an interview can get messy. In some cases, such as celebrity interviews, the interview subject may have placed restrictions on the use of interview material. In other situations, the interview subject may seek to prevent republication of the interview, claiming copyright ownership of his or her responses. A publication may write to you stating the following: "We are unable to grant your request because our publication holds no rights to the reuse of this material. Quotations that appear within the text remain proprietary to the speaker."

Unfortunately, sometimes a publication will provide you the interview text even if they don't own the rights to it. If you reprint the text, the interview subject could sue you for unauthorized reproduction of his or her remarks. To deal with this possibility, when seeking permission to reprint an interview, ask if there is a written consent by the interview subject on file and, if so, ask for a copy. If there is no release, ask if the rights holder is willing to sign a written assurance that it has the authority to grant the rights you need. Such a document should state: "Licensor warrants that it has the right to grant permission." This will not shield you from liability as effectively as a signed release from the interview subject, but it does provide you with some legal protection. If the interview subject later files a lawsuit, you will have a stronger case against the licensor (the rights holder) for breach of the written assurance it gave you. If you are still worried about whether you have the right to reproduce the interview, your only option is to seek a release from the interview subject. A sample interview release is provided in Chapter 12.

3. Letters

The writer of a letter is usually the owner of the copyright in the letter. However, there are two exceptions to this rule: Letters written by employees within the course of employment are owned by the employer; and letters written by federal employees within the course of employment are in the public domain.

Don't assume that the recipient of the letter owns the rights you need. The recipient owns only the physical letter itself. For example, the owner of a letter written by Elvis Presley could sell the physical letter itself, but only the Estate of Elvis Presley could grant rights to reproduce the text of the letter. And don't assume you can use an unpublished letter, no matter how old, without permission. Review Section E6, on unpublished works, first.

4. Speeches

Not all speeches are protected by copyright. Copyright law only protects a speech if it is written down or recorded ("fixed") and if the writing or recording was done with the speechwriter's permission. If a speaker improvises a speech and his or her words are not written down or recorded with his or her authority, the speech has no copyright protection. Both criteria, fixation (recording) and authorization, are necessary. If the text of a speech is not fixed with the authorization of the speaker, you are free to use it without violating copyright law.

The Right to Use Monica's Words

Monica Lewinsky's infamous telephone conversations with confidante Linda Tripp about President Clinton are not protected under copyright law because they were recorded by Tripp without Lewinsky's authorization. On that basis, Lewinsky has no claim against Tripp or any of the companies who have published the conversations. It's possible that her statements may be protected under principles known as "state common law" copyright, but, as a practical matter, it's difficult to enforce such claims.

This does not mean that you can lure an interview subject into a phone interview, tape it, and use it without the subject's authorization. Some states, including California, have laws prohibiting the recording of telephone conversations without the consent of both parties. In addition, publication of such conversations may trigger claims of invasion of privacy.

a. Determining Whether a Speech Has Been Published

If a speech is protected by copyright, it is important to determine whether the text of the speech has been published, because works that have not been published enjoy longer periods of copyright protection (see Section E6). Giving a speech or lecture in public does not amount to "publication." Legally, publication only occurs when copies of the speech or lecture are distributed to the public.

This rule was fortified in a case involving Martin Luther King Jr.'s "I Have A Dream" speech. A federal court of appeals ruled that Reverend King's 1963 performance of the speech to 200,000 people (and simultaneous broadcast over radio and television) did *not* amount to publication of the speech. *Estate of King v. CBS, Inc.*, 194 F.3d 1211 (11 Cir. 1999).

b. Who Owns the Copyright?

If a speech is written down before it's given, the author usually owns the copyright (assuming the author also delivered the speech—see below for rules on ghostwriters). However, if the speech was written as part of an employment obligation—for example, a speech written by the president of General Motors for a shareholders' meeting—the author's employer owns the speech. If the speech was written by a federal government employee as part of his employment—for example, a speech by the Secretary of the Treasury to Wall Street investors—it is in the public domain. If the speech was ghostwritten—written by someone other than the speaker—the ghostwriter owns the rights, unless the ghostwriter was the speaker's employee or transferred the rights to the speaker (or someone else) under a written agreement.

If the speech was given extemporaneously (improvised, not written down in advance) but recorded with the speaker's permission, the author/speaker usually owns the copyright in the speech itself, the same way as if it was written down (as described above). But, the recording of the speech belongs to the people who recorded it—for example, a TV station news crew or a newspaper reporter. A video, film, or sound recording of a speech is a copyrighted work in its own right, owned by the person who made the work. However, a verbatim written transcription of the speech—made, for example, by a newspaper reporter at the scene—is not separately copyrightable since the author/speaker owns the speech (but not the recording of it).

If the speech was recorded, to use the recorded copy of the speech, you'll need to obtain permission from both the author/speaker and the recorder of the speech. The same rule holds true whenever you want to use a sound recording, film, or video of a speech, instead of the written text.

If you cannot locate the speaker, contact the organization that sponsored the event. Often you can find the full text of a speech reprinted on the Internet, so a search engine may help you locate the rights holder.

Titles and Short Phrases May Be Protected Under Trademark Law

In Chapter 8 we explain that titles and short phrases are not protected under copyright law. However, despite their public domain status, names, titles, and short phrases may be protected under trademark laws. Take, for example, the slogan "Just Do It." Because the phrase does not qualify for copyright protection, you can use it in a song lyric, movie, or book. However, because Nike has a trademark for the phrase, you cannot use it in a manner that is likely to confuse consumers into thinking that you are associated with Nike or that tarnishes Nike's reputation. For more information on using something that is trademarked, see Chapter 10.

5. Out-of-Print Works

Just because a book or magazine is out of print does not mean that its copyright has run out. Your use, without permission, may still amount to an infringement. Therefore, if you intend to use text from an out-of-print publication, start by contacting the publisher as described in Section C. A good way to find the name of the publisher is through online bookstores such as Amazon and Barnes & Noble, who have extensive listings of out-of-print books and publishers.

Locating the copyright owner of out-of-print works becomes more complicated if the publisher no longer exists. Authors often own the rights to their out-of-print works because publishing contracts often return rights to the author if the publisher stops selling the book. You should research the author's whereabouts using the resources described in Section D, above. If your search for the publisher and author lead to dead ends, you will have to perform more extensive copyright research or hire a copyright search firm to determine the current owner. (See Chapter 13 for more on copyright research.)

If you're not sure whether a book is out of print, try consulting *Books Out of Print,* published by R.R. Bowker, which contains a listing of out-of-print books dating back to 1979. *Books Out of Print* is searchable (for a hefty subscription fee) at the R.R. Bowker website (www.bowker.com). Alternatively, it may be easier to check if the book is not listed as being "in print," in which case it's probably out of print. One way to find out if a book is in print is to search online bookstores. The ISBN number (see "ISBNs and ISSNs" below) located on or near the title page may help locate the book.

6. Unpublished Text

As with an out-of-print work, do not assume that an unpublished work is free to use. The rules regarding copyright protection for unpublished works depend on if and when the author died, and, in the event the work was ultimately published, the date of publication. Below are some general rules regarding unpublished works such as letters, diaries, and manuscripts.

Unpublished works created after January 1, 1978 are protected for the life of the author plus 70 years. Unpublished works created after January 1, 1978 that were made for hire or written under a pseudonym or anonymously are protected for 120 years from their creation or, in the event the work was ultimately published, 95 years from first publication, whichever comes first.

ISBNs and ISSNs

ISBNs (International Standard Book Numbers) and ISSNs (International Standard Serial Numbers) identify books and magazines and are sometimes required when seeking permission. ISBNs are used for books; ISSNs are used for magazines, journals, newsletters, and other serial publications. These numbers can be found on or near the title or copyright page or near the publication's UPC bar code. Since several numbers may be printed on the bar code, look for the number preceded by either "ISSN" or "ISBN."

If an unpublished work was created before January 1, 1978:

- Copyright expires 70 years after the death of the author, unless the author died more than 70 years ago. In that case, protection expired on January 1, 2003.
- Regardless of when the author died, the copyright in an unpublished work created before 1978 but published before January 1, 2003 will not expire before December 31, 2047.

EXAMPLE: Jane Austen died in 1817, but someone discovered an unpublished Austen manuscript in the 1990s. If the book remained unpublished, it would be in the public domain. However, the book was published in the 1990s, so it will be protected in the United States through December 31, 2047—230 years after Austen's death.

For more information on copyright protection for unpublished works, see Chapter 13.

As you can imagine, it can be quite difficult to locate copyright owners for unpublished works because there is no publisher to contact. Copyright Office records may help, if the unpublished work was registered. Determining ownership for unpublished works is especially difficult if the author is deceased and the author's estate or heirs are hard to track down. The WATCH database (described previously in Section D) may help you track down the author of an unpublished work. Review the research techniques suggested in Chapter 13.

What Does "Publication" Mean?

"Publication" occurs for copyright purposes when the copyright owner, or someone acting with the copyright owner's authority, distributes one or more copies of the work to the general public or offers the work for distribution, public display, or public performance. Copies do not need to be sold for publication to occur—they can be leased, rented, loaned, or even given away, so long as the work has been made available to the general public.

Publication does *not* occur when:
- copies of the work are made but not distributed
- the text of the work is performed publicly (for example, a speech is presented), or
- the text of the work is displayed (for example, in a slide presentation or on television).

A "limited publication" is also not considered a publication. A limited publication occurs if copies are distributed only to:
1. a selected group of people
2. for a limited purpose, and
3. without the right of further reproduction, distribution, or sale.

For example, it is not a publication when an author sends copies of a manuscript to several publishers seeking publication.

---

7. Using Text From Advertisements

Text in advertisements is usually owned by the corporate sponsor of the ad. However, in some cases it may be owned by the advertising agency or publi-

cation that prepared the ad. To locate an ad agency or corporate advertiser, try using an online search engine, a Web "Yellow Pages" directory, or *The Standard Directory of Advertising Agencies* (Reed Reference Publishing).

Using advertising text will trigger many of the same issues raised by using a corporate trademark. For detailed guidance on trade related permissions, see Chapter 10, "Getting Permission to Use Trademarks."

If the Text Contains a Trademark

A trademark is any word, photograph, or symbol that is used to identify specific products or services. Permission is not required to use a trademark if:
- your use is for informational or editorial purposes—for instance, you use the trademark as part of an article or story, or
- your use is part of accurate comparative product statements.

You do need to obtain permission if:
- your use is commercial and likely to create confusion among consumers of the trademarked product or service
- your use is commercial and reflects poorly on or "tarnishes" the trademark, or
- you modify the trademark.

See Chapter 10, "Getting Permission to Use Trademarks," for an explanation of trademark rights and rules.

F. When You Can't Find the Rights Holder

If you've used the techniques discussed in this chapter and cannot find the person or business whose permission you need, you have a few options. You could try to delve deeper into copyright records at the Copyright Office. These records may help you determine who owns the work currently because many copyright transfers are recorded with the Copyright Office. Copyright Office renewal records will reveal if the publisher has failed to renew the copyright in the work—which puts the work in the public domain if it was published between 1923 and 1964. Chapter 13 offers guidance on the three most common methods of searching Copyright Office records: hiring a search firm, paying the Copyright Office to do the search for you, or searching the Copyright Office records using the Internet.

If you still cannot locate the rights holder, it may be time to consider using the material without permission. As you might imagine, this poses risks. If the rights holder finds out about your use, you (or your publisher) may receive a letter from the rights holder or an attorney demanding that you stop using the material (known as a "cease and desist letter").

Before you use any material without permission, you should answer two questions:

1. How likely is it that the rights holder will see your work?
2. What is your potential legal liability if you are subject to a claim of copyright infringement?

1. Likelihood of Discovery

The likelihood that the author or rights holder will discover your unauthorized use depends on the extent of the distribution of your work and the popularity of the rights holder's work. For example, if you use an excerpt from an obscure writer's work in a book that sells under 2,000 copies, the odds are in your favor that the writer will not learn of your use. On the other hand, if you use a well-known quote from a famous play in an article for a major magazine that sells millions of copies, your use has a much greater chance of being discovered. The more likely it is that the rights holder will see your use of the copyrighted work, the more caution you should take in proceeding without the owner's permission.

2. Potential Liability

When using material without authorization, there is always a risk and potential liability—meaning responsibility under the law for which you may have to pay money damages. The amount of risk depends on several factors, described below. Generally, if you can show that you made a good-faith effort to search for the copyright owner, you will probably only have to pay the rights holder the standard fee within the trade for a similar use. However, there are exceptions to this general rule. A disgruntled copyright owner may refuse to grant permission and insist that you halt distribution of your work. Alternatively, a copyright owner may demand an exorbitant payment and drag you into court.

Consider the following risk factors when proceeding without permission:

- **The investment in the project using the copyrighted work.** The more money spent on your project, the greater the risk in the event that you must halt publication. It may not be worth risking a $100,000 project for the sake of using one unauthorized illustration.
- **The diligence of your copyright search.** The more diligently you searched, the less risk. A thorough search demonstrates that you acted in good faith and may demonstrate that it's not possible to locate the copyright owner.
- **The nature of your work and how easy it would be to remove the offending portion.** There is less risk involved if it is easy for you to remove the unauthorized material from your work. For example, a photo posted on a website can be easily removed, while one printed in a book cannot without wasting any remaining inventory and reprinting the whole thing.
- **The nature of the copyrighted portion and how easy it is to replace.** Although not as important as the other factors, your risk analysis should incorporate how hard it will be to replace the material in the event that you must remove it.

EXAMPLE: Jim publishes a newsletter for seafood restaurants and wants to use material from a cookbook entitled *Steamed Eels,* published in 1977. Jim was unable to locate the publisher; his letters to the publisher were returned with a notice that the company had moved with no forwarding address. Jim later learned from a distributor that the publisher had gone bankrupt in 1983. Jim paid the Copyright Office to perform a search, which turned up only an address for the author who died in 1986. Jim wrote to the author's last known address, but his letter was returned as undeliverable. Jim searched on the Internet for people with the same last name as the author and posted requests for information at several cooking websites. Jim documented this search and then researched the standard fee for a similar text license. Based on this, Jim proceeded to use the material without permission, citing *Steamed Eels* and its author in his work. In the event that the copyright owner turns up, Jim is prepared to pay a reasonable fee for using the work. Jim's risk is relatively low because his search was very diligent and, given the obscurity and relatively low value of the work he's copying, the financial risk for infringement is low.

When weighing risk factors, consider the expense and aggravation of the two worst-case scenarios—litigation and halting distribution of your work.

- **Litigation.** Any "wronged" party can file a lawsuit regardless of the merits of their claim. A frivolous lawsuit can drag on for months, and the attorney fees can amount to several thousand dollars. Even worse, a lawsuit based on a nonfrivolous claim (one in which there is a reasonable basis for the claim) may proceed for years, and your attorney fees can soar into the tens of thousands of dollars.
- **Halting distribution.** If a copyright owner forces you to halt distribution, you face losing the money spent on the printing or distribution of the work, as well as the additional expenses to reprint and redistribute it. In addition, your costs may include recovery of unsold copies from distributors, notification to purchasers, and loss of revenue from advertisers.

G. Paraphrasing, Omissions, and Facts

If you use someone's copyrighted work but don't copy it exactly, do you need permission? This can be a tricky question. When you paraphrase a work, omit text, or use facts taken from a text, there are no fixed rules regarding whether permission is necessary. Instead, you'll have to look to general guidelines fashioned from language in the Copyright Act and court decisions.

For more detailed information on paraphrasing and other issues covered in this section, refer to *The Copyright Handbook,* by Stephen Fishman (Nolo).

1. Paraphrasing

Paraphrasing means using different wording to summarize or restate existing text. There are two general rules about permission when paraphrasing that you should understand:

- paraphrasing will not always prevent a claim of copyright infringement, and
- paraphrasing may be prohibited by a permission agreement.

a. Paraphrasing May Not Avoid Infringement

Some writers believe they can avoid a claim of copyright infringement if they alter a text's wording instead of copying the words verbatim. This can work if the wording is changed so much that it is not recognizable as having been copied from the prior work. In the words of one court, "Copying so disguised as to be unrecognizable is not copying." (*See v. Durang,* 711 F.2d 141 (9th Cir. 1983).)

However, don't assume that paraphrasing is always a cure-all for infringement. There is no bright-line test that clearly tells you when paraphrasing is or is not an infringement. In one case, the author of a biography of novelist J.D. Salinger paraphrased many copyrighted letters. The biographer identified Salinger as the author, but, in an attempt to skirt copyright law, paraphrased the original letters. In one letter, Salinger had written, "She's a beautiful girl, except for her face." The author paraphrased this as: "How would a girl feel if you told her she was stunning to look at but that facially there was something not quite right about her?" The court held that the author's paraphrase infringed upon Salinger's original letter—and the court took offense at how inadequately the paraphrasing had been performed. The court further determined that many readers would have had the impression they had read Salinger's words. (*Salinger v. Random House*, 811 F.2d 90 (2d Cir. 1987).) In other words, even though the paraphrasing was dissimilar, it was considered infringement by the court because it was so poorly accomplished that it reflected negatively on the original author.

b. Permission Agreements May Prohibit Paraphrasing

Many publishers prohibit paraphrasing. A permission agreement may include a statement—such as "You may not alter or adapt this material"—to preserve the author's work as written and guarantee that the text will not be misconstrued.

Why would you paraphrase a work if you had permission to use it? Sometimes an editor wants to shorten the text because of space limitations. It is possible that some paraphrasing may be excused as a fair use. However, if you paraphrase in violation of a permission agreement, you may be subject to a claim of breach of contract. If possible, always clear any major paraphrasing with the rights holder.

2. Omitting Text

As with paraphrasing, consult your permission agreement to determine your right to omit part of the text that you have licensed. For example, one permission agreement reviewed for this book included the following statement: "You may not alter the material. You may omit up to 5% of a story by marking the omission with ellipses." A simple solution is to ask permission for only the material you

want to use. Otherwise, your omissions may violate the permission agreement and subject you to a breach of contract claim.

3. Using Facts

If you wish to use text that is primarily factual, you may or may not have to obtain permission, depending on your use. In general, you don't need to ask for permission if you are using facts or fact-based theories themselves.

> EXAMPLE: The author of a book on the gangster John Dillinger uncovered certain facts and concluded that Dillinger did not die in 1934, but was alive in California as of 1979. A television series incorporated this theory and the supporting facts into one of its episodes. When the author sued, a federal court ruled that the television show was free to use the author's facts and theories. (*Nash v. CBS, Inc.*, 691 F. Supp. 140 (N.D. Ill. 1988).)

a. Copying Facts Versus Expression

Although you can copy facts themselves, you cannot copy the unique words by which a writer expresses those facts. For example, anyone is free to use facts about the life of Abraham Lincoln. However, you cannot copy the exact language Carl Sandburg used to express those facts in his biography of Lincoln.

> EXAMPLE: A company translated and summarized financial business and news articles from a Japanese newspaper. These summaries were offered to the public as abstracts. The Japanese newspaper sued the abstract company, and the court ruled that the creation of the abstracts was an infringement. The court found that 20 of the abstracts were literal translations of portions of the articles. The abstract company had copied more than the facts—they had copied the newspaper's protectible expression of them as

well. *(Nihon Keizai Shimbun, Inc. v. Comline Business Data, Inc.,* 166 F.3d 65 (2d Cir. 1999).)

A major exception to this rule occurs when there are a limited number of ways to express the facts. For example, you are probably permitted to copy the expression, "The U.S.S. *Spiritualized* sank on June 12, 1944 as a result of an explosion in the galley" because there are only so many ways of expressing these facts. This is referred to as the "merger doctrine" because the fact and the expression are merged or inseparable.

b. Copying Compilations of Facts

Although individual facts are not protectible, a creatively organized collection of facts such as the "Harper's Index" is: The editors of the "Harper's Index" organize their facts in a unique manner that creates connections in the reader's mind. You may be infringing copyright if you copy a collection of facts from such a compilation.

There is no clear line as to how many facts you can use from a fact compilation without permission. In some cases, courts have held that people were free to copy an entire factual database such as a phone book or a compilation of codes used on dental bills. In other cases, courts have prevented copying any facts from compilations. For example, a compilation of used car values was held protectible by a court because the values were arranged by locales, equipment, and mileage, making the information sufficiently original to be protected by copyright. *(CCC Info. Servs. v MacLean Hunter Mkt. Reports,* 44 F.3d 61 (2d Cir. 1994).)

c. Copying "Fictional" Facts

You cannot freely copy "fictional facts" such as the plot elements and characters of a television show. If, for example, you are writing a book that summarizes the plots and characters of the 1970s show *Charlie's Angels,* you will need to acquire permission from the production company that owns the copyright in the show.

For example, in 1997, a publisher was sued after releasing a book of trivia questions about the events and characters on the television series *Seinfeld.* The book included questions about 84 *Seinfeld* episodes, and actual dialogue from the show was quoted in 41 of the book's questions. The defendant argued that all that was taken were facts; however, the court ruled that the events and characters on the television show were fiction, not fact, so copying was an infringement. *(Castle Rock Entertainment v. Carol Publishing Group Inc.,* 955 F. Supp. 260 (S.D. N.Y. 1997).)

Unfortunately, the *Seinfeld* case is indicative of a trend among the owners of television and motion pictures to sue the creators of works that summarize or celebrate popular shows. This can be an intimidating tactic, especially when the rights holder is a well-funded motion picture studio. It is possible that a trivia book may be permitted if a court judges it to be a fair use (see Chapter 9 for an explanation of fair use principles), but as a general rule, if a book or website is primarily trading off the popularity of a movie or television show, the copyright owner is likely to send a "cease and desist" letter requesting the publisher to stop making references to the show.

H. Negotiating Text Permission and Fees

Obtaining permission to use text involves a four-step process:

1. First, you must clearly and specifically identify what material you want to use and how you want to use it (see Section H1).
2. Next, you must send a permission request letter to the publisher or rights holder (see Section H2).
3. Then you and the publisher or rights holder must negotiate a permission fee, if any (see Section H3).
4. Finally, you must get a signed permission agreement—your permission request letter may do, or you may need to draft a separate permission agreement (see Sections H2 and H4).

1. Identify the Material and Rights You Need

Your first task is to identify the material you want to use and the rights you will need. You can do this by completing the following worksheet. This information will then be summarized in your permission request letter, described in Section H2.

A tear-out copy of this worksheet is provided in the Appendix. A digital copy is included on the forms CD that comes with this book.

What Is an "Edition"?

An edition is a new version of a book, distinguished from a reprinting, which is simply a new press run to produce more copies of the book. A new edition signifies a publication in which substantial changes have been made to the text.

---

2. Make a Request to the Rights Holder

After you identify the material and rights you need, you should send a letter to the rights holder requesting permission to use the material. Your permission request letter should provide all of the details about the text you want to use, how you expect to use it, and the permission you seek.

There are two different types of request letters you can use:

1. One type of request letter simply informs the rights holder of your needs and anticipates that you and the rights holder will later complete and sign a separate permission agreement.
2. The other type of request letter serves as both a request and a simple permission agreement for your use of the material. The copyright owner reviews the request and gives you permission by signing and returning the letter. This approach is recommended for simple requests to reproduce text.

The second type of letter—that serves as both a request and an agreement—is discussed later in this chapter. This section looks at a basic permission request letter that contemplates that the parties will negotiate and sign a separate permission agreement letter.

Whichever type of request letter you use, include a copy of the text that you wish to reproduce with your letter.

The View From the Permissions Desk: Be Specific

From the point of view of people who grant permissions, the biggest problem with permission inquiries is vagueness. "The biggest tip [for obtaining permission] is simply that people should provide as much specific information as possible," says Richard Vittenson, Director of *Copyrights & Contracts* (American Bar Association Publishing). "It's surprising how often people request permission without giving their name, an address or fax number to which we can respond, the organization that will be publishing our information, or the title or issue number of the publication from which they wish to reprint."

Bill Hammons, manager of rights and permissions for *Newsweek* magazine, agrees. "Definitely, one suggestion I would give is to provide concrete details. A lot of times we get people who don't have issue dates or page numbers. We also need to know how many copies there will be or how many uses." If requesting permission for use on a website, be prepared to provide information about the site and its use. "We may ask for a report on the number of hits per month or the commercial uses of the site," says Hammons. "It's not just the number of hits [we're interested in] but how the site is being used."

Text Permission Worksheet

MATERIAL YOU WANT TO USE: THE "SELECTION"	
Title of text you want to use:	
Name of author:	
Source publication or product from which it came:	
If from a periodical, indicate the ISSN, volume, issue, and date:	
If from a book, indicate the ISBN:	
If from the Internet, indicate the entire URL address (the website address that starts with "http") as it appears when viewing the document:	
Number of pages or segments to be used (actual page numbers are helpful). If you can, provide a word count, since some permission fees are based on word use:	

YOUR INTENDED USE: THE "WORK"	
Title of your publication, program, product, or website:	
Name of publisher or sponsor:	
Type of publication in which the selection will appear (book, periodical, handout, diskette, electronic program, or website):	
If a website, the average number of visitors to the site per month:	
Estimated number of copies to be printed or produced. If a book, include the estimated first print run:	
If copies are to be sold, indicate the price. If copies are free to attendees of an event, indicate the cost of event:	
The date the material will be distributed (for example, the estimated publication date of your book):	
Rights needed (for example, right to reproduce a work, translate a work, or modify the agreement):	

Keep Your Rights Request Simple

Most text permission requests are for the right to reproduce all or part of a work. For example, say you want to reproduce text in your magazine or on your website. If that's all you need, keep your rights request short and simple.

EXAMPLE: Chris wants to reprint a newspaper column on his website. The request he sends is basically as follows: "I am creating a website for the Association of Barking Dog Observers (ABDO) and would like to post the Jan. 20, 1999 Dave Barry column at our site for one month. I would like to know how much it would cost to post this column. Also, I would appreciate it if you could fax or email me a sample permission agreement."

3. Negotiate Permission Fees

Next you'll need to work out how much you'll have to pay for the rights you've requested. The publishing industry does not have standard rates for using text. Some magazine and newspaper publishers use fixed rates for common permission situations and can furnish you with what is known as a "rate card" listing such fees. In other instances, the owner won't be able to assess the fee until after reviewing your request. Below, we've summarized some fee information.

a. Using Text in a Book

The fees for using text in a book are commonly affected by:

- The number of copies to be printed. Pricing is often calculated at print runs of 5,000, 10,000, and 100,000 copies.
- The price of the book.
- Territorial and language rights. World rights may cost double or triple the cost of U.S. rights alone. A rights holder may charge 25% more for permission to reprint in a second language.

- Whether the use is for a nonprofit purpose.
- Placement of the text within the book. For example, a half-column quote placed at the beginning of a chapter or book may result in a higher fee.

Generally you should expect to pay anywhere from $100 to $400 for use of text in a book, depending on the size of the print run and your rights request. By way of example, one national magazine charges $100 per column of text (there are three full columns to a standard page) for use in a book with a print run over 5,000 copies, and $125 for print runs over 100,000. Sometimes, the fees may seem high. For example, a professor who sought to use four lines from a poem by Emily Dickinson was quoted a fee of $200 by a university press. (Note, because of copyright rules regarding unpublished works, not all of Dickinson's work is in the public domain.)

b. Using Text on Your Website

The fees for website uses are evolving—meaning nobody is quite sure how much to charge. The fees are affected by:

- The extent of advertising on the website.
- Whether the site is intended primarily to provide information to the public (sometimes referred to as an "editorial" purpose). The rights holder may want to know whether the purpose of the site is to provide information or sell products or services.
- Whether the organization sponsoring the site is a nonprofit.
- The number of visitors to the site per day.
- Whether the text will be used in a print publication as well as the website. For example, will you use the text in a magazine and on the magazine's website?

A national magazine may charge between $100 and $500 to allow you to post an article on a website, with higher fees being charged for popular commercial sites—for example, posting a review of a movie at a high-traffic Hollywood studio website. Many publishers limit the length of time for these permissions to one year or less.

Permission Request Letter

Dear Ms. Hitchcock:

I am writing to you about your article, "Why I Hate Surround Sound." *New Audio Magazine* informed me that you were the owner of rights in the article. I'm writing a book entitled *DDA: Death to Digital Audio,* and I'd like to use an abridged version of your article in the book. The details are as follows:

Title of Your Article (the "Selection"): "Why I Hate Surround Sound"

Author: Michelle Hitchcock

Source of Article: *New Audio Magazine*

Volume, Issue, ISSN: Vol 23, No. 6, ISSN 1099-8722

Number of Pages: 4

My intended use of the Selection is as follows:

Title (the "Work"): *DDA: Death to Digital Audio*

Publisher: Cumberland Books

Type of Publication: Book (trade paperback)

Rights Needed: 1) the right to shorten or modify the Selection (I'll send you a copy of the abridged version for your approval); and 2) the nonexclusive right to reproduce the Selection in all editions of the trade paperback book, *DDA: Death to Digital Audio.*

Estimated First Print Run: 6,000

Expected Price $12.95

Projected Published Date: January 2004

I'm seeking these rights for myself and my publisher, Cumberland Books, and for any company who might acquire my rights to the book in the future. Please review this request and let me know the terms for licensing rights as well as the required credit. Once you let me know, I can prepare a permission agreement. Thank you very much.

Sincerely,

Roberta Weston

c. Minimizing Fees

It's possible to get fees lowered or avoid them entirely by doing any combination of the following:

- Seeking a one-time nonexclusive use, as long you are not planning to write future editions or different versions of your work.
- Narrowing your permission request. The narrower your request, the less you may have to pay. For example, don't ask for "worldwide rights, all languages" if you only need "United States rights, English."
- Acquiring multiple items from one publisher. Often, you can reduce your per-item fee by licensing more than one work from the same publisher.
- Paying up front. You may be able to lower the fee by offering to pay up front instead of waiting 30 or 60 days.

Giving Credit Where It Is Due

Your permission agreement will detail your obligation to include a written credit for the author or publisher. Make sure the credit is correct as required in your permission agreement. This is a serious subject between you and the rights holder. Unless otherwise required under your permission agreement, you can group credits together on the copyright page. For example:

"Elvis's Toothbrush" originally appeared in *Meet the Stars* © 1985, by Missy Laws. Reprinted by permission of Ross Books.

"You Can Collect Toilet Paper" originally appeared in *Antique and Collecting Magazine* © 1990, by Harriet L. Rinker. Reprinted by permission of the author.

4. Execute a Permission Agreement

Once the rights holder has agreed to grant permission and you've agreed on a fee, you need to complete and sign a written text permission agreement. There are two ways you can go about this:

- you can convert your permission request letter into a permission agreement (a "permission letter agreement"), or
- you can draft and execute a detailed permission agreement that should suffice for most text-licensing situations (a "permissions agreement").

This section provides samples of each.

Does the Agreement Have to Be in Writing?

Unless you have an "exclusive" agreement, (see Chapter 1, Section B3), your license or permission agreement does not have to be in writing to be valid. A nonexclusive oral permission may be enforceable as long as it qualifies as a contract under general contract law principles. However, there are limits on oral agreements. For example, in most states, an oral agreement is only valid for one year. Also, it can be very difficult to prove that an oral agreement exists, not to mention to prove its terms. Because of these limitations, do not rely on an oral licensing or permission agreement—get it in writing.

a. Sample Permission Letter Agreement

This short-form agreement is similar to those used by many magazines. A variation on the permission request letter in Section H2 above, it is intended for authors and publishers who only want to reprint text, whether in printed form or on a website. This approach—turning the request letter into an agreement—is recommended if your request is simple and you have agreed upon the terms. For example, if you want to include several paragraphs from an essay on your website, newsletter, or book, this form should be sufficient.

 A tear-out copy of this agreement is provided in the Appendix. A digital copy is included on the forms CD.

What If the Copyright Owner Furnishes the Permission Agreement?

Many publishers' permissions departments and other copyright owners will provide their own permission agreements. If the permission agreement provided is short, you can probably comprehend its terms. If not, review Chapter 11, Section C, which explains how to review an agreement.

Text Permission Letter Agreement

To _____ ("Licensor"):

I am writing to you to request permission to use the following material.

Licensor Information

Title of Text (the "Selection"): _____

Author: _____

Source publication (or product from which it came): _____

If from a periodical, the ISSN, volume, issue, and date. If from a book, the ISBN:_____

If from the Internet, the entire URL: _____

Number of pages (or actual page numbers) to be used:_____

If you are not the copyright holder or if worldwide rights must be obtained elsewhere, please indicate

that information: _____

Licensee Publication Information

The Selection will appear in the following publication(s) (the "Work"): _____

Title: _____

Name of publisher or sponsor ("Licensee"): _____

Author(s): _____

Type of publication: _____

If print publication, estimated print run: _____

If print publication, projected publishing date: _____

If print publication, expected price: $ _____

If website, the URL: _____

If website, estimated monthly hits: _____

If website, the posting date: _____

Rights needed: _____

Fee

Licensee shall pay a fee of $_____ to Licensor at the following address:

_____ upon publication of the Work or within 6 months of executing this agreement, whichever is earlier.

Credit

A standard credit line including your company name will appear where the Selection is used. If you have a special credit line you would prefer, indicate it below:

_____

Samples

Upon publication, Licensee shall furnish _____ copies of the Work to Licensor.

Signed by Licensee: _____

Name: _____

Title: _____

Address: _____

Date: _____

Licensor's Approval of Request

I warrant that I am the owner of rights for the Selection and have the right to grant the permission to republish the materials as specified above. I grant to Licensee and Licensee's successors, licensees, and assigns the nonexclusive worldwide right to republish the Selection in all editions of the Work.

Permission Granted By: _____

Signed by Licensor: _____

Name: _____

Title: _____

Address: _____

Date: _____

b. Instructions for Permission Letter Agreement

If you use this form, you don't need a separate request letter (as discussed in the previous section). This permission letter agreement is similar to the worksheet in Section H1. Complete the agreement as if you were preparing the worksheet or a request letter. Below are some additional explanations for various sections:

- At the end of the **Licensor Information** section is a section the licensor—the person from whom you are requesting permission—should fill in if he or she does not own the rights you need. If this section is filled in, the licensor cannot grant you the necessary permission, so you will need to obtain permission from whomever the licensor indicates in the blank.
- The **Licensor's Approval of Request** section is a combination of the warranty and grant of rights, both discussed in Chapter 11, Section C11.
- It is possible that the licensor will only want to grant rights for a specific print run or for a specific period of time. Or, the licensor may not want to grant you permission to transfer the rights to someone else. In this event, modify the grant to reflect these requests—for example, strike the language regarding "successors, licensees, and assigns."
- It's possible that you will want more rights than are granted in this letter agreement. For example, you may need rights for all foreign translations and derivative rights and you may want these rights in all media. If you want a broader grant of rights, you can use the **Licensor's Approval of Request** language below to replace the language in the agreement above. Be aware that the licensor may object to such a broad grant, causing a delay in the permissions process.

Licensor's Approval of Request. I warrant that I am the owner of rights for the Selection and have the right to grant permission to republish the materials as specified above. I grant to Licensee and Licensee's successors, licensees, and assigns the nonexclusive worldwide right to adapt and republish the Selection in all languages, in all editions of the Work, and in all versions derived from the Work in all media now known or hereafter devised.

Make the process convenient for the copyright owner. When sending your permission letter agreement, always enclose a stamped self-addressed envelope for the licensor's convenience.

c. Sample Permission Agreement

The permission agreement below is intended for authors and publishers who are negotiating for more than basic reproduction rights—for example, assembling an anthology of short stories, assembling contributions for a CD-ROM encyclopedia, or acquiring multiple or foreign rights to reproduce a work.

A tear-out copy of this agreement is provided in the Appendix. A digital copy is included on the forms CD.

Text Permission Agreement

_____ ("Licensor") is the owner of rights for certain textual material defined below (the "Selection"). _____ ("Licensee") wants to acquire the right to use the Selection as specified in this agreement (the "Agreement").

Licensor Information

Title of Text (the "Selection"): _____

Author: _____

Source publication (or product from which it came): _____

If from a periodical, the ISSN, volume, issue, and date. If from a book, the ISBN: _____

If from the Internet, the entire URL: _____

Number of pages or actual page numbers to be used: _____

Licensee Publication Information

The Selection will appear in the following publication(s) (the "Work"): _____

(check if applicable and fill in blanks)

- [ ] book—title: _____
- [ ] periodical—title: _____
- [ ] event handout—title of event: _____
- [ ] website—URL: _____
- [ ] diskette—title: _____

Name of publisher or sponsor: _____

Author(s): _____

Estimated date(s) of publication or posting: _____

Estimated number of copies to be printed or produced (if a book, the estimated first print run): _____

If for sale, the price: $ _____

If copies are free to attendees of a program, the cost of program: _____

If a website, the average number of visitors per month: _____

Grant of Rights

Licensor grants to Licensee and Licensee's successors and assigns, the:

(select one)

☐   nonexclusive

☐   exclusive

right to reproduce and distribute the Selection in:

(select all that apply)

☐   the current edition of the Work.

☐   all editions of the Work.

☐   all foreign language versions of the Work.

☐   all derivative versions of the Work.

☐   all media now known or later devised.

☐   promotional materials published and distributed in conjunction with the Work.

☐   other rights _____

Territory

The rights granted under this Agreement shall be for _____ (the "Territory").

Fees

Licensee shall pay Licensor as follows:

(select one and fill in appropriate blanks)

☐   **Flat Fee.** Licensee shall pay Licensor a flat fee of $_____ as full payment for all rights granted. Payment shall be made:

☐   upon execution of this Agreement

☐   upon publication

☐   **Royalties and Advance.** Licensee agrees to pay Licensor a royalty of _____ % of Net Sales. Net Sales are defined as gross sales (the gross invoice amount billed customers) less quantity discounts and returns actually credited. Licensee agrees to pay Licensor an advance against royalties of $_____ upon execution of this Agreement. Licensee shall pay Licensor within 30 days after the end of each quarter. Licensee shall furnish an accurate statement of sales during that quarter. Licensor shall have the right to inspect Licensee's books upon reasonable notice.

Credit & Samples

(check if applicable and fill in blanks)

[ ]   **Credit.** All versions of the Work that include the Selection shall contain the following statement: _____

[ ]   **Samples.** Upon publication, Licensee shall furnish _____ copies of the Work to Licensor.

Warranty

Licensor warrants that it has the right to grant permission for the uses of the Selection as specified above and that the Selection does not infringe the rights of any third parties.

Miscellaneous

This Agreement may not be amended except in a written document signed by both parties. If a court finds any provision of this Agreement invalid or unenforceable, the remainder of this Agreement shall be interpreted so as best to effect the intent of the parties. This Agreement shall be governed by and interpreted in accordance with the laws of the State of _____.This Agreement expresses the complete understanding of the parties with respect to the subject matter and supersedes all prior representations and understandings.

Licensor	Licensee
By: _____	By: _____
Name: _____	Name: _____
Title: _____	Title: _____
Address: _____	Address: _____
Date: _____	Date: _____
	Tax ID # _____

d. Instructions for Permission Agreement

- In the introductory paragraph, insert the names of the licensor (the party who owns the material) and the licensee (you or the person who is seeking permission).
- In the **Licensor Information** and **Licensee Publication Information** sections, complete the blank spaces as if you were filling out the worksheet in Section H1.
- In the **Grant of Rights** section, complete the grant to reflect the rights that you have negotiated. More information on the rights associated with grants is provided in Chapter 11, "Art and Merchandise Licenses."
- Complete the **Territory** section to reflect the regions in which you have acquired rights— the World, the United States, Canada, or whatever region you have agreed upon. For more help, review Chapter 11, Section C7.
- In the **Fees** section, indicate what type of fee has been negotiated, check the appropriate boxes and complete the information. For more information on fees, particularly regarding the nuances of royalty payments, review Chapter 11, Section C9.
- Complete the **Credit and Samples** section per your agreement with the licensor. For more information, review Chapter 11, Section C16.

- As explained in Chapter 11, Section C11, a warranty is a contractual promise made by the licensor. Some licensors do not want to make promises, particularly promises that the work does not infringe any third parties' copyright or other rights. You may have to modify the **Warranty** section or strike it entirely if the licensor objects.
- If you believe you have the bargaining power to get the licensor to agree, you may want to include an indemnity provision in the agreement. Indemnity is a financial punishment if the licensor breaks its promises. Indemnity provisions are not included here. If you wish to add such a provision, samples and explanations are provided in Chapter 11, Section C11.
- Explanations for the **Miscellaneous** section (also called "boilerplate" provisions) are provided in Chapter 11, Section C22. If you believe you have the bargaining power to get the licensor to agree, you may want to include a provision that covers attorney fees or arbitration.

Commercial uses are more complex. If you are seeking permission to use text on behalf of an advertising agency or a company selling a product or service (for example, Nike or American Airlines), your use is more likely to be categorized as a commercial endorsement, which will trigger additional legal issues. Review Chapter 12 regarding releases you may be required to obtain.

Getting Permission to Use Photographs

f you're planning on using a photograph in your book, film, website, or other work, you have essentially two options:

- you can take your own photo or hire a photographer to prepare a photograph for your specific purpose, or
- you can obtain the rights to an existing photograph.

The first option—hiring a photographer to create a specific photograph—is known as "assignment photography." Assignment photography is typically used when a unique photo is needed—for example, a photo of a particular automobile for a magazine advertisement. It's common for a photographer to sell all rights in an assignment photograph so that the person who pays the photographer is free to use the photograph for any purpose. Chapter 15 provides sample agreements you can use to acquire ownership of a photograph.

This chapter explains the second option: how to obtain permission to use existing photographs. Existing photographs include those in magazines or on the Web, as well as photos available through image banks (described below).

Using an existing photo—often called a stock photo—is generally cheaper and easier than hiring a photographer for your specific job. A common way to obtain rights to an existing image is to go through a company known as an image bank. Millions of existing photographs are available for license from image banks, which generally specialize in different subjects, such as images of nature, food, or historical eras. The agreement (license) you'll enter into with an image bank depends on the type of image you want to use—whether the image is rights-protected or royalty-free (explained in Sections A1 and E below).

Or, rather than seeking out an image bank to provide the photo you need, you may already have found a specific photograph—say, one you've clipped from a magazine—that you want to use. In this case, you'll need to find the owner of the photograph to obtain permission to use it.

This chapter explains how image banks work, how to find the photos you need, how to find photo owners and negotiate rights with them, and how to work with photo researchers (people who hunt down photographs and obtaining permission to use them). At the end of the chapter you'll find pricing information and a sample photograph permission agreement to use when licensing stock photographs.

Merchandising involves different rules. If you want to use a photo on a poster, cup, T-shirt, or other merchandise, refer to Chapter 11, "Art and Merchandise Licenses."

Review public domain rules. Any photograph first published in the U.S. before 1923 is in the public domain, so you can use it without asking for permission. Photos published after 1923 and before March 1, 1989 are in the public domain only if: 1) the owner failed to renew the copyright or 2) the owner forgot to include the copyright notice.

Don't assume that photographs published without copyright notices are in the public domain. And don't assume that you can use public domain works for free. You may have to pay a fee to obtain a copy of the photograph as explained in Section E.

For more information on public domain issues, refer to Chapter 8.

What's in the photo may trigger other rights. If the photo you want to use contains trademarks, copyrighted artwork, or people, you may need to obtain additional permissions or releases. Review Section G below.

A. The World of Stock Photos

A stock photograph is any photo available to the public for license. Stock photos encompass every conceivable subject—celebrities, science, entertainment, sports, travel, and history—and conjure up every imaginable occasion and emotion. Stock photos are typically handled by agencies known as image banks (also known as stock photo agencies), that control the right to license the stock photos contained in their databases. Image banks typically specialize in certain types or themes of photos, such as nature, vintage Hollywood, or race car images. Later, this chapter explains how to find the right image bank and provides a list of image bank resources.

In addition to the general selection of stock photographs, the entertainment industry has a vast selection of promotional photos and movie stills. If you're looking for an image of a celebrity figure, chances are that there's a promotional photo available for license. Celebrity photos are discussed in Section C.

1. Royalty-Free vs. Rights-Protected Photos

In addition to the different subject matter categories of available photos, there are different ways that you can obtain rights to a photo. There are two basic categories of stock photos: rights-protected and royalty-free.

A rights-protected photo can only be used once you've negotiated for the rights to use that particular image. Generally, you'll be restricted to using it according to specific guidelines outlined in your license agreement. With royalty-free photos, on the other hand, you'll typically be allowed to reproduce the images in a much broader range of uses. You'll usually have to buy a CD-ROM or pay for access to a website that contains a certain number of royalty-free photos. Once you've paid for the CD-ROM or subscribed to the website, you'll be able to use all of the royalty-free photos included. There may be some restrictions as to how you may use the images—for example, you cannot use the images on merchandise—but you'll have much more leeway than with a rights-protected photo. Sometimes, the term "copyright-free" is used instead of "royalty-free," though the term is a misnomer because such photos are not in the public domain.

Which type of photo is better for you depends on your photo needs. As a general rule, the quality and variety of choice is better with rights-protected photos. Most historic, news, celebrity, and entertain-

ment photos are only available as rights-protected. On the other hand, royalty-free stock is generally much less expensive and works well for certain standard corporate and advertising imagery. For example, there are a wide variety of lifestyle, business, and scenic travel photos available in royalty-free format.

There are other significant drawbacks to using royalty-free images that may make them unacceptable for some projects. For example, with many royalty-free CD-ROMs, the photographs come in low resolution formats (72 DPI)—only suitable for websites or limited graphic uses. In addition, you cannot obtain exclusive rights to use royalty-free photos. This means that if, for example, you use a royalty-free photo in a national ad campaign, your competitors are free to use the same image by buying the same CD-ROM. This problem can be avoided by choosing a rights-protected photo instead. With a rights-protected photo, the image bank can tell you whether the photo has been used in advertisements and may be able to grant you exclusive rights, thus preventing competitors from using the same image.

Listings of rights-protected and royalty-free image banks are provided at the end of this chapter.

Thumbmail Reproductions Are Fair Use

In a 2003 case, a court ruled that permission was not needed to reproduce thumbnail copies of photographs on a website. (A "thumbnail" is a small reproduction of an image, normally linked to a larger version.) Arriba Soft Corporation operated an Internet search engine that displayed thumbnails copied from other websites. Kelly, a photographer, discovered that his photographs were part of Arriba's database and filed suit for copyright infringement. The Court of Appeal held that using thumbnail reproductions of copyrighted photographs on a website was a fair use because the use was "transformative" and did not interfere with the photographer's economic expectations. (*Kelly v. Arriba Soft Corporation*, 336 F.3d. 811 (9th Cir. 2003).) For more on fair use, see Chapter 9.

2. Not All Image Banks Are Alike

Not all image banks are created equal. Large corporations run some image banks while individual photographers manage others. Some license rights-protected photos, some sell royalty-free photos, and some offer both. Many image banks specialize in particular genres (for example, travel photos or American history) while others provide a more general, broad range of imagery. To give you an idea of how image banks work, two of the largest—Corbis and Time Life Pictures—are highlighted below.

a. Corbis

Corbis (www.corbis.com) has a reputation for a wide photo selection, fast service, and reasonable professional rates. Corbis has acquired several stock agencies, including the Bettmann Archive of 16 million images documenting 20th century civilization.

EXAMPLE: I wanted to find a photo of 1960s jazz musician Rahsaan Roland Kirk. I posed a request to several image banks, and within hours, a photo researcher at Corbis informed me they had three images of Mr. Kirk. The cost, if I wanted to use a black-and-white image in this book, was reasonably priced at $100. I was unable to locate any images of Kirk at any other image banks.

b. Time Life Pictures

In 1999, Time, Inc. (www.timelifepictures.com), made hundreds of thousands of images available online. These photos came from its stable of magazines (*Time, Life, People,* and *Sports Illustrated*), as well as from its acquisition of the Mansell Collection of over a million historical illustrations, prints, and photographs. Like Corbis, the Time Life Pictures collection is available for license to a broad range of publishers and consumers. At the Time Life Pictures site you can conduct a free search (based on key-words) or pay a Time Life Pictures researcher to locate an image for you.

Looking for Historic Photos?

In addition to Time Life Pictures and Corbis, Hulton/Archive Photos has 20 million photographs, engravings, and drawings spanning over 3,000 years of world history. You can find Hulton/Archive Photos online at www.hultonarchive.com.

---

3. Finding and Working With Image Banks

Finding the right photo is often a matter of finding the right image bank. Each image bank's subject matter, pricing, ease of use, and quality of image can affect your choice of photo. The main difficulty is that with so many photographs available and such varied quality and pricing, searching for the right image bank may feel daunting.

Fortunately, there are many search tools, including the Web and print resources. Most image banks are listed in the New York, Los Angeles, or Washington, DC, phone books. In most cases, a researcher at the image bank will be able to tell you by phone if the image you want is available and what it will cost.

The Web contains a number of helpful resources for sorting through image banks. For example, AG Editions' website (www.agpix.com) provides listings for image banks and photographers. Email your request to this directory (you'll find the email address on the website) and it will direct you to the proper agency or photographer to contact for permission. Paula Berinstein's site (www.berinsteinresearch.com), an online extension of her book, *Finding Images Online,* provides a category directory with links to various online photo resources. Click "Picture Links."

You can also locate image banks by using an Internet search engine. If you want to find a particular image bank, enter its name and the search engine will find the company's website (if it has one). If you aren't looking for a particular company, try using keywords like "stock photo" or "image bank" to find photo-related websites.

In addition, a new type of image bank search has developed in recent years—specialized search engines that scan various image banks. For example, 1StopStock (www.1stopstock.com) searches four massive image banks to identify and display royalty-free and rights-protected images. Another image search engine, Ditto (www.ditto.com), searches for images throughout the Web, not simply at professional image banks. Yahoo! also has its own image search engine (http://gallery.yahoo.com).

Below are some suggestions for researching image banks.

- **Categorize your needs.** To determine which image bank to use, define a general category you wish to search—for example, current events, American history, landscapes, celebrities, or motion pictures. There are no established standard keywords to use when you search. One agency might categorize a bald eagle under "wildlife" while another categorizes it under "birds," so be prepared to try alternative categories. For example, search for John Travolta under both "celebrity" and "movie actor."

- **Locate appropriate image banks and search them.** Find image banks that contain your categories. Call or fax the image bank to describe your needs or search the image bank website. Website searches are based on keywords, photo titles, or categories. For example, you might search an American history database for photos of bank robbers Bonnie and Clyde by typing in keywords like "Clyde Barrow," "Bonnie Parker," "bank robbers," or "criminals."

EXAMPLE: I wanted to find an image bank that had a stock photo of a pelican. I started with Comstock Images, where a photo researcher allowed me to see the pelican photos by establishing a website for my private viewing. The cost to reproduce a black-and-white image of a pelican on a quarter of a page in this book was $230.

Next I searched the AG Editions' website in the "animals" category and located numerous banks that offered pelicans, including Arthur "Birds As Art" Morris, who has over 70,000 high-quality stock photos of birds. Mr. Morris's fee for a quarter-page use of his pelican pictures was reasonably priced at $100. Then, I searched using 1StopStock.com, which led me to various image banks with a variety of inexpensive, royalty-free choices (for example, pelican in flight, pelicans in a tree, pelican close-up).

Finally, I searched using the Ditto image search engine and located pelican images at photo.net. I contacted the photographer, Philip Greenspun, who permitted reproduction of his image in this book at no charge. (Contact information for all resources used is at the end of this chapter.)

Photo credit: © Philip Greenspun (http://philip.greenspun.com). Reprinted with permission of the photographer.

If searching the Web on your own proves unsuccessful, most image banks will research your photo requirements for you and provide alternatives when the particular photo you want is unavailable. An image bank may charge a research fee to determine if a photo is available. Often, this fee is waived if you end up licensing the photo from the image bank.

For a list of resources for locating image banks, see the end of this chapter.

 Always ask whether the image bank possesses all rights for the stock photo. It may seem odd, but there are occasions when an image bank possess a stock photo but not its licensing rights. This is sometimes the case for rare photos or movie stills. In such cases, you need to contact the rights holder to obtain permission to reproduce the photo. (See Section B.)

If You Can't Budge the Budget

Your choice of image bank probably depends on your budget if you—as opposed to your publisher—are paying the fees for acquiring photo rights. Review stock photo prices and prepare a budget before beginning your photo search. See Section H6 for resources on stock photo pricing.

Digital Watermarks

Some image banks allow you to view stock photos online, but attempt to prevent piracy by encoding the photos with a digital watermark. This may take two forms: a visible watermark (usually the name of the stock agency imprinted across a portion of the photo) or an invisible digital watermark that is buried in the software code of your digital photo. Sometimes, the watermark appears only when you print the photo. In 1998, Congress passed legislation making it a violation of copyright law to remove digital watermarks.

Public and Private Institutions

You can also obtain photographs of historical interest (people or events) and of works of art from museums, foundations, art galleries, libraries, and historical societies. These institutions function much like image banks when licensing works in their collection and may have unusual, very old, or obscure photos not obtainable from image banks. Locating these institutions requires the same phone and Internet research techniques used to locate image banks. You can also obtain information on obtaining photos of artworks at many art museums from the *Image Buyers' Guide*, available from the Visual Resources Association (www.vraweb.org).

B. Obtaining Rights to a Photo You've Found

Instead of searching for an image at a stock photo company, you may have already found an image you want to use. If, for example, you've come across a photo in a magazine or on a website that you want to use, your task is to find out who owns copyright in the photo and obtain permission from that owner.

This procedure is usually simple. First, find the photo credit—the phrase that lists who owns the copyright in the photo. If the photo appeared in a book or magazine, the credit is usually on the same page as the photograph, although in some cases photo credits are listed on one page near the beginning or end of the publication. If the photo credit is for a publication, contact the publisher's rights and permissions department. If the photo credit refers to a company or image bank (for example "Photo: Reuters"), locate the image bank using the information and resources described in this chapter. If there is no photo credit, contact the publication in which the photograph was reproduced. See Chapter 2 for detailed guidance on locating a publisher.

If the credit is for a photographer, contact the photographer, his estate (if the photographer is deceased), or the photographer's representative. You can locate a photographer three ways:

- contact the publication in which the photograph appeared
- search the Internet using the photographer's name as a keyword, or
- contact photographer trade organizations.

You'll find a list of photographer trade organizations at the end of this chapter.

EXAMPLE: I sought to locate photographer Bobby Neel Adams, whose work has been featured on the cover of *Life* magazine, to obtain permission to print one of his photographs in this book. I first contacted *Life* magazine by calling the editorial phone number listed in the magazine's masthead. I learned that *Life* doesn't handle the rights for Adams's photos; they suggested I contact Time-Life Syndication services. I did, and they suggested I contact the Time Picture Collection (now Time Life Pictures). After several unreturned phone calls, I switched to the Internet. I used a search engine to search for the keywords "Bobby Neel Adams" and found an agency called Focal Point F8 (www.f8.com) that represents Adams. This company was able to provide contact information for him.

Photo credit: Self-Portrait (Age-Map Series) © 1989, Bobby Neel Adams (www .bobbyneeladams.com). Reprinted with permission of the photographer.

C. Celebrity Photos and Movie Stills

In addition to the vast libraries of photos at image banks, the entertainment industry is a rich source of photos, with thousands of promotional photographs and stills from motion pictures and television programs. Whether you are looking for a photo of Bob Dylan, Jakob Dylan, or Dylan McDermott, you can bet there's a promotional photo available.

There are two basic types of celebrity or entertainment photographs available. One type is created by freelance photographers (paparazzi) and sold to the media, such as a photo of Jack Nicholson walking into the Cannes film festival. Stock photo houses and magazines usually own these photos. The other type is prepared by the entertainment industry as a promotion for a specific project (a film, music recording, or television show), such as a picture from the film *Groundhog Day* or a portrait of the Rolling Stones. Entertainment production companies usually own these photos.

There are a few unique twists to locating and using these entertainment photos. The process of finding the copyright owner and obtaining permission varies depending on whether you already have a copy of the photo you want to use. If so, examine it for a legend or copyright warning such as:

"Permission to reproduce this photograph is limited to editorial uses in regular issues of newspapers and other regularly published periodicals and television news programming."

If your use is not permitted or if there is no legend on the photograph, you will need to contact the rights holder—the photographer, stock house, or entertainment production company that owns the rights to the photo. If the photo includes a photographer credit—particularly if it indicates that the photographer retained the copyright (for example, "Copyright 1982, Roberta Bayley")—contact the photographer using the methods described in Section B.

If there's no credit on the photo, you may still be able to track down either an image bank or a production company that owns the copyright or can direct you to who does. Certain image banks specialize in entertainment-related stock photos. You could try contacting them to ask if they represent the photo you want to use. You'll find a list of image banks, including those that specialize in entertainment photos, at the end of this chapter. In some cases, particularly for rare motion picture and television stills, image banks may not control the copyright but can direct you to the production company or photographer for permission.

If the photo is from a television show or movie, you can locate the name of the production company by using the Internet Movie Database (www.imdb.com), a searchable database of thousands of films and television shows. You can also find entertainment production companies in the New York, Nashville, or Los Angeles telephone listings, through Internet search engines, and in directories such as Yahoo!, Google, and switchboard.com. When you contact the production company, ask for the publicity, media relations, or public relations department.

If you don't have a copy of the photo you want to use but you know that you need a photo of say, Bette Midler in *The Rose,* you must either contact an image bank that has the photo you need or find the production company that owns the rights to such a photo. Search image banks that specialize in the proper type of entertainment (here, movies) or use the resources described in this chapter (such as the Internet Movie Database) to find the company that produced the movie or show in question.

EXAMPLE: I sought to locate stills from the 1974 film *The Conversation.* I started my search by contacting movie still sites such as Star File Photo and the Motion Picture & Television Photo and Archive, but none had stills for this film.

Next, I tried the Internet Movie Database (www.imdb.com) and located the production company for the film—Paramount Pictures. I located phone and fax numbers for Paramount from the Internet Yellow Pages. Paramount directed me to the Paramount Pictures Stock Footage & Stills Library, which licenses stills and footage from Paramount movies, including *The Conversation.*

⚠ **Commercial uses can get tricky.** The permissions situation may become more complex if you are using the photograph as part of an advertisement or to sell a product. Chapter 12 discusses these uses.

D. Using Photo Researchers

Think of a photo researcher as an art detective who can track down an elusive image. If you perform photo licensing regularly—for example, if you are a website designer or a photo acquisitions editor—you may want to consider using a photo researcher as a matter of course. Many photo researchers have specialties—for example, Chicago-based photo researcher Mary Goljenboom has expertise in science, business, and historical images, particularly women's history. New York-based researcher Joan Menschefreund specializes in images of fine arts, current events, and personalities.

Photo researchers are usually paid per day (approximately $250), although some charge by the hour. A researcher will prepare a budget for your needs and may also be able to arrange photo shoots for materials located in archives. The American Society of Picture Professionals (www.aspp.com) publishes a directory of members with their specialties and can help you find the proper researcher for your purposes. Additional resources for locating photo researchers are listed at the end of this chapter.

E. Photo Fees

A picture may be worth a thousand words, but is it worth a thousand dollars? How about $450 or $225? As soon as you start pricing photographs, you'll discover that stock photo prices vary widely. The minimum fee for using a stock photo from a high-end agency is usually $150 and may rise to several thousand dollars, especially if the agency charges reuse fees (additional payments you must make when you reprint the book or article in which the photo first appeared). Some mid-priced image banks, such as Muse, charge lower rates ($10–$100) and may not seek reuse fees. At the low end of the pricing tier are sources that often advertise as being royalty-free or copyright-free.

Some of the factors that affect pricing are described below. If you perform photo clearances on a regular basis, you may want to consult one of several books listed at the end of this chapter that focus exclusively on photo pricing guidelines.

As explained in Section A, above, there are two categories of stock photos: rights-protected and royalty-free. Each type has its own rules regarding fees.

1. Fees for Rights-Protected Photos

Fees for rights-protected photos vary widely and are closely tied to your intended use of the photo, which must be clearly disclosed to the licensor up front. As a general rule, the more intended uses you have for the photo, the more you'll have to pay. For example, you may be charged according to the length of time you use a photo on your website or the size of a print run for a book in which a licensed photo appears. If you want to use the photo for a different purpose in the future, you will likely have to pay an additional reuse fee.

For the most part, the image bank or photographer is concerned with how many people will be see the image. The larger the viewing audience, the higher the fee for your use. The worksheet below lists the information an image bank will typically require from you to calculate its fee and grant you permission.

A tear-out copy of this worksheet is provided in the Appendix. A digital copy is included on the forms CD.

Photo Permission Worksheet

PHOTOGRAPHIC USE	
Title of publication, program, product, or website in which the photograph will appear:	
Name of publisher or sponsor:	
Type of publication (book, periodical, annual report, handout, diskette, or electronic program):	
Estimated number of copies to be printed or produced. If a book, include the estimated first print run:	
If copies are to be sold, indicate the price. If copies are free to attendees of an event, indicate the cost of event:	
The date the material will be distributed (for example, the estimated publication date of a book or the posting date of a website):	
Will the publication be in any language other than English?	yes no
If yes, identify which language:	
Website uses:	
Does the site include advertising?	yes no
Is the site commercial or editorial?	commercial editorial
Will the photo be used on a home page or an internal page?	home page internal page
The number of visitors or hits per day:	
Will the photograph be used in both a print publication and a related website (for example, in a magazine and in the magazine's website)?	
If using in a presentation, the sponsor of the presentation, the number of attendees, and the cost of attendance:	
Rights needed: (1) reproduction of the photograph (2) display of the photograph (3) modification of the photograph	

PHOTOGRAPHIC USE (cont.)	
Territory (for example, North American or world rights):	
The format in which you will need the photograph: scan, print, transparency, or digital (if digital, what DPI and file format):	
The date you need the photo:	
If for a film or TV show, the context of the use (supply a synopsis of the plot):	

Fee Multipliers

Some image banks use a multiplier system to determine the fee. Here's how it works: The image bank starts with a minimum fee, usually the lowest amount that the image bank accepts for a use. For most image banks, the minimum fee is between $150 and $200 (the amount charged for reproducing the photo on a quarter of a page in a 5,000-edition book). Every other use has a multiplier that determines the fee. For example, the multiplier for using a photo on a magazine cover is 4. If the minimum fee is $150, the cover use fee would be $600. The highest multipliers are for national advertising uses. For example, the multiplier for a full-page photo used on the back cover of a national magazine could be 20, raising the $150 minimum fee to $3,000.

a.   Advertising Fees

If you intend to use a rights-protected photo in an advertisement, the fee an image bank will charge you will be based on the circulation and placement of your advertisement. Expect to pay $1,000 to $3,000 to use a photo in a full-page ad in a national magazine and at least $500 for a quarter-page ad inside. Rates may be based on the number of insertions—meaning when an ad is placed in each edition of a magazine. An image bank may charge reuse fees for subsequent insertions (see Section E). Rates may be lower for advertising for nonprofit organizations or for "advertorials"—advertisements dressed up to look like news articles.

Color versus Black-and-White Fees

Don't expect to pay less for black-and-white photos. Some image banks claim it costs as much, or more, to reproduce quality black-and-white prints.

b.   Corporate Use Fees

Image banks charge more for corporate uses—using photos in corporate brochures, annual reports, and in-house publications—than for editorial uses. For example, an image bank may charge $500 for a quarter-page photo in a corporation's annual report with a distribution of 50,000, versus $250 for a similar use in a magazine with a similar circulation.

c. Digital Photograph Quality

Fees may be also affected by the resolution of the photo—meaning the number of dots per inch (DPI) that make up the photo. The denser the dots, the higher the DPI, the better the resolution, and the more expensive the photo. A low-resolution photo (72 DPI) is usually suitable only for use on websites or for nonprofessional uses. Graphics professionals prefer high-resolution photos (300 to 600 DPI). Some stock houses will furnish bundles of low-resolution images as royalty-free or copyright-free. (See Section A.) Other image banks may charge on a sliding scale—for example, $50 for low resolution (72 DPI) to $250 for high resolution (300 DPI or higher).

As you may be aware, resolution also affects the size of the file on your computer. A 72 DPI photo may take up only 500K in disk space, small enough to fit on a floppy disk. The same photo at 300 DPI may take up 10-20 MB of space, requiring a hard drive or large storage device such as a Zip or Jaz drive.

Drum Scans Versus Flatbed Scans

Scanned photograph quality can vary widely. If you need high-quality scans, say for reproduction in a coffee-table book, you should ask for drum scanning—a higher quality scanning process than used by flatbed scanners. If the image bank doesn't indicate the type of scan, ask.

Know your computer. Before downloading a digital image, make sure that your computer and graphics software can accommodate or convert that type of image file (for example, JPG or GIF).

d. Website Use Fees

Fees for using an image on your website can vary widely. Jim and Cheryl Pickerell, authors of *Selling Stock Online,* report that the fee for using a 4x4-inch stock photo on one major corporate home page was $1,000 for six months. Time, Inc. (www.timelifepictures.com), on the other hand, charges $200 for use of one of its photos for the same time period. At the low end of the cost spectrum, imagestate.com offers website images for as low as $30. Chances are you'll be able to find a photo for your website that will fit your budget.

Most image banks base fees for website uses on the following factors:

- the sponsor of the site (who is paying for it)
- whether the photo will reside on the home page or a secondary page
- the prominence or size of the photo
- how long the photo will be displayed, and
- whether the photo will be used on any additional sites.

Image banks may want to know how long the image will be stored on the site, even if it is a relatively short period of time. Some image banks determine fees based on the number of visitors to the site (also known as "hits"). Sometimes, website use fees may be waived if the website use is ancillary to use in a printed work. For example, a website use fee may be waived if a magazine has licensed the photograph for a print publication and also wants to use the photo in its online edition.

e. Additional Fee Factors

In addition to standard fees, the following factors may increase the fees you're required to pay to use a rights-protected photo:

- **Exclusive or nonexclusive rights.** Obtaining an exclusive right to use a photo means that no one else can use that photo in the same manner as you're using it. Exclusive rights are always more expensive than nonexclusive rights. An exclusive rights arrangement often means getting exclusive rights for a specific use—for example, the exclusive right to reproduce the photo in Canada or the exclusive right to use the photo in automobile advertising.

- **Reuse fees.** An image bank may only grant you rights for a specific print run or for a specific time period. If you are planning subsequent uses, you may be charged a reuse fee, usually a reduced version of your original fee. Some image banks charge reuse fees for new editions, not reprintings. (A new edition is a significant revision of a book, as opposed to a simple reprint when inventory runs out.) There may be an additional fee (similar to a reuse fee) when a work is converted to a new medium—for example, when a documentary film is reproduced for sale in video format. Find out the cost for a one-time fee for all potential uses and compare that to the cost of a series of reuse fees.

- **North American or world rights.** Worldwide rights are more expensive than U.S. rights. For example, if you had to pay $100 for North American rights for a quarter-page photograph inside a textbook with a print run of 5,000 copies, you might have to pay $150–$200 for world rights. Note, there is a difference between world rights in all languages and world rights in only one language (see Chapter 2, Section C3, "Regional Rights Versus Foreign Language Rights").

2. Fees for Royalty-Free Photos

In contrast to rights-protected fees, fees for royalty-free photos are not based on use and are less expensive. You generally pay a flat fee of between $25 and $300 for a CD-ROM or website subscription that gives you a wide range of rights to use all the photos on the CD-ROM or website. While the rights granted are broad for royalty-free photos, there are usually some limitations, such as you cannot use the images on merchandise. (Merchandise uses are discussed in Chapter 11.) As long as your use falls within the rights granted, you do not have to pay anything extra for your use of the photo. This means, for example, that you may use the photo several different times in various ways for the one-time fee.

Since the scope of royalty-free rights may vary, you must review the written documentation that accompanies your purchase of the images. If you purchased a CD-ROM product, the limitations on use should be listed in the shrink-wrap agreement (typically a written agreement printed on the envelope containing the software) or in a "Read Me" file on the disk. If you obtain the images from a website, the legal limitations on your use may be presented in a click-wrap agreement, which is a screen that appears when you prepare to download the images. For more information on the enforceability of shrink-wrap and click-wrap agreements, see Chapter 4, Section E. Some suppliers of royalty-free CD-ROM products are listed at the end of this chapter.

F. Photo Permission Agreements

Permission agreements to use photographs vary quite a bit depending on whether you're using a rights-protected or royalty-free image. Agreements to use royalty-free photos are generally much less specific than agreements to use rights-protected photos. Typically, once you purchase a CD-ROM or pay an access fee for a website containing royalty-free photos, you can use the images within the general limitations outlined on the CD or at the website.

If you're using a rights-protected photo, however, you'll generally need to enter into a more specific agreement that outlines the terms of your use. This section outlines the terms commonly found in licenses for rights-protected photos and offers a sample photo permission agreement with explanations of its terms. While using royalty-free photos doesn't require the specific type of agreement discussed in this section, you may want to read Section 2, which explains some of the general terms that may apply to all agreements, including those for royalty-free photos.

⚠ **Check the print or slide for more conditions.** When an image bank furnishes you with photos, always review the back of the photos or the mounts of the slides for additional limitations on the license—for example, a requirement to provide a specific photographer credit. These limitations become a condition of your photo license agreement.

1. Agreement Terms

After agreeing upon a fee for a rights-protected photo, the image bank will usually furnish you with the images (transparencies, prints, scans, or digital images) along with a permission agreement outlining the terms of your license. Alternatively, you may receive an invoice that functions as a permission agreement. The invoice or agreement will list the terms of your license, and should include the following:

- the photograph (identified by title or catalogue number)
- the nature and length of use (for example, the name of the publication or website in which the photo will be used)
- your name or the name of your publisher or sponsor (the company paying for the publication or website)
- the photographer's name or other photo credit requirements
- the fee and to whom and when it should be paid, and
- whether you are required to furnish samples of your work when the photo is published.

2. The Small Print

The bottom or the back of the invoice will ordinarily contain additional terms and conditions for your use of the photos. These conditions often include the following:

- **Additional fees.** Image banks that furnish prints (not digital copies) request that you return the print. Usually, you can retain the originals for a period of 30 to 90 days, sometimes referred to as the "approval period." After you have copied the image for your use, you must return the images to the image bank before the end of the approval period. In some cases, a late fee may be charged ($1 or more per day). If you lose or damage the photo you might be stuck with a fee of $50 to $1,500, depending on your agreement.
- **Late fees.** You may also have to pay late fees if your payment doesn't arrive on time. If your agreement states that "time is of the essence," you will have a harder time getting out of these late fee obligations. Despite the fact that you have a signed agreement, your failure to pay the fee on time may terminate your right to use the photo.
- **Model releases.** A model release is an agreement between the model and the photographer allowing use of the model's image without violating the model's rights of privacy or publicity. (Model releases are discussed in detail in Chapter 12.) If the photo you're licensing has a model in it, make sure the image bank has a model release on file. If the image bank says it has such a release, include this statement somewhere in the permission agreement. Since many photo permission agreements are invoices (with contract language on the back), ask that the model release claim be stated on the invoice. For example, add language such as:

"Image Bank warrants that a model release is on file for the licensed photograph."

In addition, if possible, have the image bank provide you with a copy of the release so that you can compare it to the model release in Chapter 12 on how to analyze a release. These rules should apply regardless of whether the photo is rights-protected or royalty-free.

- **Warranties and representations.** The image bank may want to protect itself from any legal claims resulting from unlicensed use of the photos or uses that are not included in the model release. To do so, your agreement may include language such as "hold harmless" or "indemnify." For more information on these provisions, see Chapter 11. Review royalty-free shrink-wrap and click-wrap agreements for indemnity provisions as well.

- **Dispute resolution, attorney fees, and jurisdiction.** The agreement may provide for methods of dealing with disputes, including arbitration or payment of attorney fees. In addition, the agreement may establish in what state you may have to bring or defend a lawsuit. For more information on these dispute provisions, review Chapter 11. These provisions usually are not included in royalty-free agreements.

Respect Photo Credits

Your agreement may require that you include certain credit information along with the photo. Recent court cases have held that a failure to provide proper credit may justify a lawsuit. Make sure that your credits conform to the requirements of your agreement.

Modifying a Photograph

Unless your agreement prohibits it, you can make minor modifications to the photograph, such as changing its size or resolution. However, major modifications—for example, colorizing a black-and-white image or digitally removing elements of a photo—require permission under copyright law. If the image bank or photographer discovers that you have made a major change without permission, it may decide to sue you for copyright infringement. In this event, it's possible that you could defend yourself under fair use principles, arguing that you had a right to make changes to the image. However, this is an unpredictable defense. In addition, if you are distributing the work of a European photographer in Europe, you may violate certain moral rights (special European copyright rights) if you tinker with the photographer's aesthetic judgment.

To avoid a lawsuit, notify the rights holder of your intent to modify the photo when you seek permission.

3. Basic Photo Permission Agreement

Below is a simple all-purpose photo permission agreement for rights-protected photos. Note that the included agreement lacks some provisions (such as dispute resolution and alternative payment systems) that may be included in more complete artwork agreements, omitted here because it is often easier to negotiate and obtain permission using short agreements. An explanation of the various provisions follows.

A tear-out copy of this agreement is provided in the Appendix. A digital copy is included on the forms CD. Most likely, the image bank will provide you with its own agreement. In that case, you can still use the sample agreement below to help you understand the image bank's version. Or, the image bank may not furnish its own agreement, in which case you can use this version.

Photo Permission Agreement

_____ ("Licensor") is the owner of rights for the photograph described below (the "Selection"). _____ ("Licensee") wants to acquire the right to use the Selection as specified in this agreement (the "Agreement").

Licensor Information

Title of work (the "Selection"): _____

Catalogue number (if applicable): _____

Photographer: _____

Licensee Publication Information

The Selection will appear in the following publication(s) (the "Work"):

(check if applicable and fill in blanks)

| | book—title: _____

| | periodical—title: _____

| | event handout—title of event: _____

| | diskette–title: _____

| | website—URL: _____

If to be used on a website, the Selection will appear on:

(check if applicable)

| | home page

| | internal page

Name of publisher or sponsor (if different from Licensee): _____

Estimated date(s) of publication or posting: _____

If applicable, the estimated number of copies to be printed or produced (if a book, the estimated first print run): _____

If for sale, the price: $ _____

If copies are free to attendees of a program, the cost of program: _____

If a website, the average number of visitors per month: _____

Grant of Rights

Licensor grants to Licensee and Licensee's successors and assigns, the:

(select one)

☐ nonexclusive

☐ exclusive

right to reproduce and distribute the Selection in:

(select all that apply)

☐ the current edition of the Work.

☐ all editions of the Work.

☐ all foreign language versions of the Work.

☐ all derivative versions of the Work.

☐ all media now known or later devised.

☐ promotional materials published and distributed in conjunction with the Work.

☐ other rights _____

Territory

The rights granted under this Agreement shall be for _____ (the "Territory").

Fees

Licensee shall pay Licensor as follows:

(select payment option and fill in blanks)

☐ **Flat Fee.** As full payment for all rights granted, Licensee shall pay Licensor a flat fee of:

$ _____ . Payment shall be made:

☐ upon execution of this Agreement.

☐ upon publication.

☐ **Royalties and Advance.** Licensee agrees to pay Licensor a royalty of____% of Net Sales. Net Sales are defined as gross sales (the gross invoice amount billed to customers) less quantity discounts and returns actually credited. Licensee agrees to pay Licensor an advance against royalties of $_____ upon execution of this Agreement. Licensee shall pay Licensor within thirty

(30) days of the end of each quarter. Licensee shall furnish an accurate statement of sales during that quarter. Licensor shall have the right to inspect Licensee's books upon reasonable notice.

Credit & Samples

(check if applicable and fill in blanks)

☐ **Credit.** All versions of the Work that include the Selection shall contain the following statement: _____

☐ **Samples.** Upon publication, Licensee shall furnish _____ copies of the Work to Licensor.

Warranty

Licensor warrants that it has the right to grant permission for the uses of the Selection as specified above and that the Selection does not infringe the rights of any third parties.

(check if applicable)

☐ Licensor warrants that a model release is on file for the Selection.

Miscellaneous

This Agreement may not be amended except in a written document signed by both parties. If a court finds any provision of this Agreement invalid or unenforceable, the remainder of this Agreement shall be interpreted so as best to effect the intent of the parties. This Agreement shall be governed by and interpreted in accordance with the laws of the State of _____. This Agreement expresses the complete understanding of the parties with respect to the subject matter and supersedes all prior representations and understandings.

Licensor	Licensee
By: _____	By: _____
Name: _____	Name: _____
Title: _____	Title: _____
Address: _____	Address: _____
Date: _____	Date: _____
	Tax ID # _____

4. Explanation for Photo Permission Agreement

- In the **introductory paragraph,** insert the names of the licensor (the party who owns the material) and the licensee (you or the person who is seeking permission).
- In the **Licensor Information** and **Licensee Publication Information** sections, complete the blank spaces.
- In the **Grant of Rights** section, complete the grant to reflect the rights you have negotiated. More information on the rights associated with grants is provided in Chapter 11, "Art and Merchandise Licenses."
- Complete the **Territory** section to reflect the regions in which you have acquired rights. For more information about territory, review Chapter 11, Section C7.
- In the **Fees** section, indicate what type of fee has been negotiated by checking the appropriate box(es) and completing the information.
- Complete the **Credit and Samples** section to reflect your agreement with the licensor.
- As explained in Chapter 11, Section C11, a warranty is a contractual promise made by the licensor. Some licensors do not want to make promises, particularly promises that the work does not infringe any third parties' copyright or other rights. You may have to modify the Warranty section or strike it entirely if the licensor objects.
- If you believe you have the bargaining power to get the licensor to agree, you may want to include an indemnity provision in the agreement. Indemnity is a financial punishment if the licensor breaks its promises. Indemnity provisions are not included here. If you wish to add such a provision, samples and explanations are provided in Chapter 11, Section C11.
- Explanations for the **Miscellaneous** (also known as "boilerplate") provisions are pro-

vided in Chapter 11, Section C22. If you believe you have the bargaining power to get the licensor to agree, you may want to include a provision that covers attorney fees or arbitration.

⚠ Commercial uses are more complex. If you are seeking permission to use a photograph on behalf of an advertising agency or a company selling a product or service (for example, Nike or American Airlines), your use is more likely to be categorized as a commercial endorsement, which will trigger additional legal issues. Review Chapter 12 regarding releases you may be required to obtain.

G. When the Photograph Contains Art, Trademarks, or People

What if the photograph you intend to use contains copyrighted artwork, a trademark, or a person? In that case you may need to obtain more than one permission, because commercial uses of people and trademarks may trigger additional legal rights and claims. In addition to copyright permission from the photographer, you may need permission from the copyright owner or trademark owner of the subject of the photograph or from the person appearing in it. This section offers a brief explanation of these issues. You also may want to refer to Chapter 10, "Getting Permission to Use Trademarks," and Chapter 12, "Releases."

1. When a Photograph Contains Copyrighted Art

You may need two permissions if you want to reproduce a photograph that contains a copyrighted work of art. For example, if you want to use a photo that includes a mural by Diego Rivera in the background, you may need permission from the copyright owner of the Rivera mural as well as from the owner of the photograph. Whether permission is in fact required from the owner of the artwork depends on whether your use of the artwork within the photo would be considered a fair use under copyright law. Fair use principles are discussed in more detail in Chapter 9.

Generally speaking, you might not need permission if the artwork is incidental to your photo, such as artwork that appears in the far background of a street fair. A minimal use such as this may be deemed a fair use not requiring permission. For example, a court has ruled that the momentary appearance of an artist's work in a motion picture did not require permission. In another case, however, the appearance of a copyrighted poster in a television show did require permission. As explained in Chapter 9, relying on fair use principles can be risky as the final word can only come from a judge.

Chapter 4, "Getting Permission to Use Artwork," provides information on the relationship of photos and artwork and discusses how to locate the copyright owners of artwork.

2. When a Photograph Contains Trademarks

A trademark is any word, photograph, or symbol that is used to identify a specific product or service for sale. Familiar trademarks include Chevrolet, McDonald's, and Apple Computer. Under trademark law, you do not need permission to reproduce a trademark if your use is "editorial"—or informational. An example of an editorial use is using the trademark to illustrate a newspaper article, magazine feature, or other literary statement. You do not need permission to use a trademark when making accurate, comparative product statements.

On the other hand, you are much more likely to need permission to use a trademark in a commer-

cial context. You will probably need to get permission under any of the following circumstances:

- **Your use is likely to create confusion among consumers.** For example, your use of a photo of a jogger wearing a Nike shirt in an ad for your sports equipment website may confuse viewers as to whether Nike is associated with or endorses your site. You would need permission from Nike to use its logo or name (which appears in the photo).

- **Your use tarnishes or diminishes the strength of the trademark.** A rule known as the "dilution doctrine" prohibits the use of a trademark that weakens another famous mark by chipping away at its distinctiveness. In other words, the more just anyone is allowed to use the term "Nike," the less customers will make an automatic association between the term and actual Nike products. In addition, you may not be allowed to use a trademark if your use reflects poorly upon the trademark (also known as "tarnishing"). For example, if you use a photo of a woman wearing a Nike shirt on an X-rated website, the Nike company could stop the use.

- **You have modified the trademark.** Comparative advertising uses of trademarks are legal, but it is not permissible to modify the trademark when making comparisons. For example, a tractor company was found liable for animating the trademark of the John Deere Company in a television commercial.

It can be quite tricky to figure out whether or not permission may be required in a given situation. Even if you are legally entitled to use a trademark, some trademark owners—particularly owners of famous marks—will sue first and review the legal rules later.

For more information on trademark rules, review Chapter 10, "Getting Permission to Use Trademarks."

3. When Your Photograph Contains People

In general, you don't need permission to use a photograph of a person if your use is editorial and does not defame or invade the person's privacy (see below). An editorial use is an informational use, in which the photo is used to elaborate or illustrate an article or story. For example, no permission is necessary to use a photo of a paratrooper in an article about the Vietnam War. However, you do need permission (known as a "release" or "consent" in the context of people), for the uses described below. (Releases are discussed in Chapter 12.)

- **Your use is for commercial purposes—to advertise or sell a product or service.** Under "right of publicity" laws, you cannot use a person's name or image for commercial purposes without obtaining a release. For example, if you sell sweaters from your website, you would need permission to use a photo of a model wearing one of your sweaters. This right of publicity can survive a person's death, sometimes for as long as 50 years depending on state law. There are some exceptions to these rules. If your use is editorial—for example, a photo of a fashion model in a book about the fashion industry—you can use the photo to advertise the book without obtaining a release.

- **Your use invades a person's privacy.** Every person has the right to be left alone. If you are using a photograph that was taken surreptitiously (for instance, using a hidden camera on private property) or if your photo depicts very personal or potentially embarrassing activities (for example, treatment at a mental institution), you should obtain a release. Without a release, your use might violate state "right of privacy" laws. Keep in mind that a person's right to privacy only exists while they are alive. This is not true of the right of publicity that survives death in some states.

- **Your use is defamatory.** If your use of a photograph creates a false impression injuring

someone's reputation, you could be liable for defamation, sometimes known as libel. For example, say you use a stock photo of two doctors to illustrate an article on mercy killing. If you did not obtain a release for that specific use, you may be subject to liability if the doctors sue you for damaging their reputations. There are some exceptions to defamation rules for public figures such as politicians and celebrities who have voluntarily thrown themselves into the public eye and, to a limited extent, for people who have become subject of a public controversy. For these people, you will only be liable if the public figure can prove that you acted with actual malice or reckless disregard for the truth—for example, you knowingly printed a damaging lie about someone. For nonpublic figures, if what you said is true, you are protected from liability—truth is an absolute defense. Keep in mind, however, that dredging up old (but truthful) facts may invade a person's right to privacy. A more in-depth explanation of these principles is provided in Chapter 12.

H. Stock Photo Resources

This section lists the many companies, directories, organizations, and other entities that may be able to help you obtain photographs and the rights to use them.

1. Image Banks

The image banks listed below are all accessible online. While they are categorized by whether they provide rights-protected or royalty-free images, some offer both. Selection may vary from company to company, so check out a few to find the company that suits your needs. As with any online services, some of these sites may change their website addresses.

a. Rights-Protected Image Banks

- AP/Wide World Photos: www.apwideworld.com
- Comstock: www.comstock.com
- Corbis: www.corbis.com
- Getty Images: www.gettyimages.com.
- Hulton/Archive Photos: www.hultonarchive.com
- Imagestate: www.imagestate.com
- Pickerell Photo Services: www.pickphoto.com
- Stock Solution: www.tssphoto.com
- Stock, Boston, Inc.: www.stockboston.com
- Time Life Pictures: www.timelifepictures.com
- Tony Stone Images: www.gettyimages.com/stone, and
- Vivid Details: www.vividdetails.com.

b. Royalty-Free Image Banks

- Comstock: www.comstock.com
- Corbis: www.corbis.com
- Corel: www.corel.com
- Cyberphoto: www.cyberphoto.com
- Photodisc: www.gettyimages.com/photodisc
- PhotoEssentials: www.photoessentials.com
- PhotoSource: www.photosource.com, and
- PictureQuest: www.picturequest.com.

2. Celebrity and Entertainment Image Banks

The image banks listed below have extensive collections of promotional photos, including images of celebrities, events, and movie stills.
- Culver (212-645-1672)
- The Everett Collection (212-255-8610)
- Photofest (212-633-6330)
- Shooting Star (323-469-2020)
- Star File (212-929-2525)
- Motion Picture & Television Photo Archive (818-997-8292), and
- Liaison (800-488-0484).

3. Resources for Locating Image Banks

The following websites are useful in finding image banks appropriate for your needs.
- AG Editions: www.agpix.com
- Finding Images Online (Paula Berinstein's site): www.berinsteinresearch.com
- 1StopStock.com: www.1stopstock.com
- Ditto: www.ditto.com
- Yahoo: http://gallery.yahoo.com, and
- AltaVista: http://image.altavista.com.

Two print resources are also available for locating image banks:
- *The Stock Photo Deskbook*, (Exeter, 1998), and
- *Finding Images Online*, by Paula Berinstein (Independent Publishers, 1996).

4. Resources for Locating Photographers

- The American Society of Media Photographers (www.asmp.org)
- Professional Photographers of America (www.ppa.com)
- National Press Photographers Association (www.nnpa.org), and
- Advertising Photographers of America (www.apanational.org).

5. Resources for Locating Picture Researchers

- American Society of Picture Professionals (www.aspp.com).

You may also benefit by using the following texts:

- *Finding Images Online*, by Paula Berinstein (Independent Publishers, 1996), and
- *Practical Picture Research*, by Hilary Evans (Routledge-Blueprint, 1994).

6. Photo Pricing Resources

- *Negotiating Stock Photo Prices and Selling Stock Online*, by Jim and Cheryl Pickerell (Pickerell). You can order it at www.pickphoto.com.
- *Pricing Photography: The Complete Guide to Assignment and Stock Prices*, by Michael Heron and David MacTavish (Amphoto, 1997).

■

Getting Permission to Use Artwork

This chapter explains how to obtain permission to reproduce artwork—meaning fine art or graphic art. Fine art includes one-of-a-kind or limited edition works, such as a limited edition silk-screen print by Andy Warhol, a mobile by Alexander Calder, or a painting by Georgia O'Keeffe. Graphic artwork is any art intended for commercial reproduction, such as an illustration, design, icon, clip art, cartoon, or comic. This chapter addresses these types of works together because the process of obtaining permission to use them and the ways in which they are used are similar, and the rights to use them are sometimes controlled by one company.

This chapter also offer tips for finding clip art (existing images available for license) and sample agreements. At the end of the chapter you'll find two model agreements: a basic license for acquiring permission to use artwork in a publication or website, and an agreement for using artwork in films and videos.

A. Acquiring Rights to Artwork

The way you approach the permissions process for any type of artwork will depend on what you want to use and for what purpose. Your budget will also likely affect how you go about the permissions process.

Generally speaking, if you need to reproduce a specific item of artwork that's not in the public domain—for example, a painting by Pablo Picasso—you will need to negotiate with whoever owns copyright in the artwork (in this case, Picasso's estate) for the right to reproduce it. If, on the other hand, you want to use a fine art painting that is in the public domain—the *Mona Lisa*, for example—you won't have to acquire the rights to reproduce the work, because public domain works are free to copy. Remember, however, that unless you photograph the work yourself, you may have to obtain the rights to use the reproduction (photograph) of the work, from a photographer you hire or from the gallery or artist rights organization that provides you with a photograph.

If you do not need a specific artwork and have a suitable budget, you may want to specially commission artwork and acquire rights to use it. For example, if you need illustrations for a book, you can hire a graphic artist and acquire exclusive and unlimited rights to the artwork. Ownership can be acquired under an employment arrangement, by an assignment, or by using a work-for-hire agreement (acquiring ownership is explained in Chapter 15). Many artists prefer not to convey all rights and instead convey limited rights by granting a license. A sample license agreement is provided at the end of this chapter. When graphic artwork is used on merchandise such as T-shirts or ceramic cups, a special artwork merchandise license agreement is used (see Chapter 11) that provides for ongoing royalty payments to the artist.

If your budget is small, you may prefer to use clip art. The term "clip art" simply refers to existing graphic art images that are available either for a fixed fee or for free. Clip art can often be used for unlimited purposes, so a permission agreement is not required. However, some clip art collections have limitations on use, so you should examine the shrink-wrap or click-wrap agreement accompanying the artwork. For information about clip art, see Section E.

B. Fine Art: Paintings, Sculptures, and Limited Editions

The main thing to remember when seeking permission to use fine art is that one permission may not be enough. As with other forms of creative work, fine art is protected by a number of rights that may be held by different owners. To use just one work, you may need to obtain permission from two or more people or businesses, including:

- **The copyright owner of the artwork.** If the artwork is copyright protected, you need permission from the copyright owner—usually the artist or the artist's estate (if the artist is deceased). Copyright protection for foreign works may last longer than works protected under U.S. law. If you are unsure whether a work is protected under copyright, review Chapter 8.

- **The copyright owner of a photograph of the artwork.** If you are using photographs of artwork, you may need permission from the copyright owner of the photographs as well as from the copyright owner of the artwork itself (see Section B3).
- **The people who appear in or the owners of trademarks or copyrighted art included in the fine art.** Depending on your use, you may need a release for any people, trademarks, or copyrightable art included in the artwork. (Review Chapters 10 and 12.)
- **The owner of the artwork.** If you want to photograph a work of fine art, you may have to get permission from its owner, usually a museum or a private owner. Many museums won't allow you to photograph their art; instead they hire a photographer and charge you for the photograph.

When seeking permission to use fine art, always ask what rights you are obtaining from the person granting you permission. Never assume the person who "rents" you a fine art image controls the copyright in the underlying artwork, as it is often not the case.

1. Obtaining Photos of Fine Art

Photographs of fine art may be obtained from the museum or gallery exhibiting the work or through museums affiliated with the Smithsonian Institution (see "Millions of Images: The Smithsonian," in Section F2). Gallery resources are provided at the end of this chapter. Image banks (companies that license photos and artwork) also supply high-quality copies of copyrighted and public domain fine art. Corbis (www.corbis.com), Hulton/Archive Photo (www.hultonarchive.com), and Time Life Pictures (www.timelifepictures.com) each have an extensive collection of fine art images.

In addition to these sources, the Visual Artists and Galleries Association (VAGA) and the Artists Rights Society (ARS) can, for a fee, help you locate high-quality photographs of public domain works. These organizations are discussed in more detail just below.

2. Getting Permission to Use Copyrighted Fine Art

Two useful organizations that manage permissions for copyrighted fine art are the Visual Artists and Galleries Association (VAGA) and the Artists Rights Society (ARS), which is affiliated with Art Resource. These organizations represent many well-known American and European artists and galleries. They can grant permission for reproduction of copyrighted works for most common uses such as publications, websites, advertisements, and merchandise. Contact information for VAGA and ARS is provided at the end of this chapter.

To locate the rights holder of copyrighted fine art, start by contacting VAGA or ARS. In the case of a fine artist who is not well-known, the best starting point is the institution or gallery in which the artist's work is exhibited. Often, the gallery can refer you to the rights holder.

EXAMPLE: I sought to reproduce a black-and-white copy of *Monogram*, a fine artwork by Robert Rauschenberg. I wanted to use the artwork in a book with an initial pressing of 5,000 copies. I contacted VAGA and ARS and learned that VAGA controls the rights. A VAGA representative explained that the fee for my use would be $75. (That fee was subsequently waived by VAGA for my use.)

Monogram © Robert Rauschenberg, Licensed by VAGA, New York, N.Y.

3. Photographs of Fine Art

Sometimes you must get (and pay for) two permissions to reproduce a photograph of copyrighted artwork: one to use the artwork and a second to use the photograph of the artwork. This practice is derived from the principle that a photograph of an artwork and the artwork itself are two separate copyrighted works. Unfortunately, it's not always easy to figure out if a photograph is protected by copyright and whether a separate permission is necessary.

One factor used to make this determination is whether the subject of the photograph is itself protected by copyright. Another factor, which can be very subtle and difficult to measure, is the way in which the subject was photographed, including aspects such as lighting and camera angle.

In cases involving public domain works, the federal courts have ruled that "slavish" (nearly identical) copies of public domain works don't merit copyright protection. *(Hearn v. Meyer,* 664 F. Supp. 832 (S.D. N.Y. 1987).)* In other words, a photographer cannot acquire protection for a perfect photographic reproduction of the *Mona Lisa. (Bridgeman Art Library Ltd. v. Corel Corp.,* 25 F.Supp.2d 412 (S.D. N.Y. 1997).

Unfortunately, there have not been enough cases to allow photographers, artists, and academics to determine conclusively when a photograph of a painting acquires separate protection. In general, the more the photo is an exact reproduction of the original, the less likely it is protected by copyright (meaning you don't need permission to use the photograph). On the other hand, if the photograph has original elements in it such as unusual colored lighting, special effects, or other additions to the piece of art itself, the more likely it is that the photographer owns copyright in the photo and that you'd need permission to use it.

Regardless of the copyright rules (and regardless of whether the work is in the public domain), you may have to pay to use a photo owned by a museum, gallery, or image bank. In some cases, you may have to sign an agreement promising that you won't reproduce the photographic image other than for the agreed purposes. Such an agreement may not be legally enforceable—for example, if you use an exact photographic reproduction of a public domain work without anything added by the photographer to create a separately copyrightable work. However, as a practical matter, you probably want to avoid the expense and aggravation of a lawsuit on the issue. For that reason, paying for photo reproductions of artwork is often a practical necessity.

Reproductions of Architecture

Under a copyright amendment passed in 1990, some works of architecture were granted copyright protection. You cannot reproduce the architectural plans or the architect's renderings (illustrations of the building) or mock-ups (the miniature constructions of the building). However, you can photograph a copyrighted building if it is visible from a public place and you can reproduce your photograph without infringing copyright.

> EXAMPLE: Donald has acquired copyright protection for the architectural design of his new casino, Plump Towers. The building is visible from the public beach in Atlantic City. Shirley photographs the building and sells her photographs in postcard reproductions. Shirley is not infringing Donald's architectural copyright.

It is also possible that a unique building design may serve as a trademark—for example, the novel shape and appearance of a Fotomat kiosk. In this event, the commercial reproduction of the trademarked appearance of the building may trigger a lawsuit for trademark infringement. This is precisely what happened when a photographer shot and reproduced pictures of the Rock and Roll Hall of Fame—which the owners claimed was protected by trademark. A federal appeals court ultimately ruled that the use was not a trademark infringement. For more information on this case and trademark laws, review Chapter 10, "Getting Permission to Use Trademarks."

C. Graphic Art

Graphic art is any illustration intended for commercial reproduction, whether in magazines, books, advertisements, or on websites. As with other types of artwork, how you obtain the right to use graphic art depends on whether you have the art created specifically for your use or use existing artwork.

1. Obtaining Rights to Works Created for You

If an artist creates a work for you, your right to use the work will be based on an assignment, a work-for-hire agreement, or a license.

- An assignment is a transfer of copyright ownership. In return for a payment (or ongoing payments) you acquire copyright ownership in the artwork. Acquiring ownership is explained in Chapter 15.
- A work made for hire is owned by the hiring party, not the artist. Works made for hire are created in a number of ways. If the artist is your employee and creates the work within the course of employment, the work will be a work for hire. A work for hire can also be created if: 1) you commissioned the work, 2) the work falls into certain categories, or 3) you entered into a written work-for-hire agreement. Assignments and works made for hire are discussed in Chapter 15.
- A license is the right to use the artwork for a specific purpose. A license does not transfer copyright ownership.

2. Obtaining Rights to Existing Artwork

If you want to use graphic art that already exists and was not created for your use, you can usually acquire the rights you need by license. Start by contacting the publisher (magazine, newspaper, or website, for example) in which the graphic art appeared. Since publishers generally try to acquire all rights from graphic artists, it's possible that the publisher may own the rights you need. If the publisher doesn't own the rights or is unable to help, you'll have to search for the graphic artist. Searching the Internet may do the trick, or you could try contacting the Graphic Artists Guild (GAG) (www.gag.org). The GAG has an artist locator service and publishes the *Graphic Artists Guild Handbook.*

Children's Book Illustrators

If you're looking for a graphic artist who has illustrated a children's book, contact the Society of Children's Book Writers and Illustrators, who can put you in touch with any member illustrator. Contact information for this organization appears in the resource section at the end of this chapter.

Reproducing U.S. Postage Stamps

The United States Postal Service (USPS) owns the copyright to all stamps issued after 1977. In other words, you are free to reproduce U.S. Postage stamps issued before 1978. However, if you reproduce pre-1978 public domain postage stamps in color, the reproduction must be at least 50% larger or 25% smaller than the original stamp. Black and white reproductions can be any size.

For stamps issued after 1977, nonprofit reproduction uses are granted regularly and can be accomplished by completing a form at the USPS website (www.usps.com/communications/organization/noncommlicensing.htm). Written permission is required to use stamp images for noncommercial use. Permission is granted at the discretion of the USPS licensing group. Send an email to licensing@usps.gov.

D. Comics and Cartoons

Comics and cartoons include a variety of graphic artwork. Comics may be in strip or book form, both of which involve a series of drawings telling a story. Single-panel drawings telling a joke or gag are often called cartoons. Animated cartoons include TV shows like *The Simpsons*, movies like *Toy Story* or *The Lion King*, and old series like *Bugs Bunny* or *Daffy Duck*. Below we explain the process of obtaining rights to use various types of print or animated comics.

1. Comic Books

To obtain rights to reproduce images from comic books, start with the publisher, who typically owns the rights to the comic books it publishes. Rights for underground, experimental, or other types of comics may be owned by either the publisher or the individual artists. Sometimes, the name located in the copyright notice indicates ownership. If the artist's name is in the notice, for example, "Copyright 1985 Steve Purcell," then the artist has probably retained reprint rights.

Determining the rights for comic books published before 1965 may prove complex, as many comic publishers have folded, sold rights to other companies, or failed to renew their copyright. Comicon (www.comicon.com) is a good source of comic book information and links. A number of major comic book publishers are listed at the end of this chapter.

2. Comic Strips, Editorial Cartoons, and Single-Panel Cartoons

Reprint rights for most newspaper comic strips and for many editorial cartoons (also known as political cartoons) are controlled by syndicates. Editorial cartoons or comic strips not owned by a syndicate are probably owned by the individual newspaper or magazine employing the cartoonist. Contact the syndicate or publication for information regarding permission. You'll usually find the name of the cartoonist and the syndicate printed vertically between the panels of the strip.

Besides the syndicates and publications, other resources exist to help you find cartoonists. For example, a site called Politcalcartoons.com provides email addresses for many editorial cartoonists. For your reference, a list of syndicates as well as other resources for finding editorial cartoonists appears at the end of this chapter.

Single-panel cartoons (not comic strips or editorial cartoons) are often owned by the publications in which they appear. If you're seeking to use a single-panel cartoon from a magazine, start by contacting the publication. For example, if the cartoon first appeared in *Playboy*, contact that magazine's permission department. If calling the publication does not provide leads, you may be able to get contact information for the cartoonist through the National Cartoonists Society. If you're interested in *New Yorker* cartoons, Cartoonbank.com (www .cartoonbank.com) is a great one-stop source for licensing rights.

In the past few years, syndicates have streamlined the licensing process and can accommodate a broad range of licensing requests. Fees for a comic strip or single panel cartoon range from $35 to several hundred dollars depending on the type of use.

3. Animated Cartoons

Rights to an animated cartoon series such as *The Simpsons* or *The Flintstones* are usually owned by an entertainment production company. If the cartoon series is in syndication, you can find the production company by reviewing the credits at the end of any episode. Quite often, this is the last or next to last credit. The production company can also be determined online at the Internet Movie Database (www.imdb.com), a searchable database of thousands of films and television shows.

Most entertainment production companies can be found in the New York, Nashville, or Los Angeles telephone listings and through Internet directories such as Yahoo! Yellow Pages or search engines such as Google. When you contact the company, ask for the publicity, media relations, or public relations department.

⚠ **Reproducing cartoon characters may raise additional issues.** If you want to obtain permission to use a particular cartoon character such as Superman or Andrea Anaconda, review Chapter 10, "Getting Permission to Use Trademarks."

Medical Illustrations

Do you need medical or anatomical imagery? Medical illustrators specialize in anatomical and health-related illustrations. Rights for illustrations are often controlled by publishers. If the publisher is unable to help, you can find a specific medical illustrator by contacting the Association of Medical Illustrators. You can also find medical clip art on the Web. One of the largest sites is provided by the medical publisher Williams & Wilkins Mediclip (www.lifeart.com), which offers medical clip art images at a cost of approximately $10 per image. Other websites offering medical images can be located using the search term "medical clip art."

E. Royalty-Free and Public Domain Clip Art

An alternative to paying licensing fees to use artwork is to use public domain artwork or artwork offered on a royalty-free basis. This type of artwork is sometimes referred to as clip art, or royalty-free or copyright-free artwork, and is sold in books, CD-ROM bundles, or distributed free through websites.

1. The Terms

The terms clip art, public domain, royalty-free, and copyright-free are often used interchangeably (and confusingly).

- **Clip art** is a general term used to refer to any artwork that is available in a collection, either in a book or on a computer disk. Clip art may be in the public domain or royalty-free.

- **Public domain** art is not protected by copyright. Many publishers, such as Dover Books, specialize in offering collections of public domain art. The image of the man and dog above is from a Dover publication entitled *Humorous Victorian Spot Illustrations*. You are free to copy and use the individual artwork in a public domain collection without permission. However, you are not free to copy and sell the collection.

- Unlike public domain art, **royalty-free** art is protected under copyright law and cannot be used for free. However, once you buy the CD-ROM or pay for access to a website that contains royalty-free artwork, your license to use the images is largely unlimited, so you can usually use the works numerous times for a broad range of uses. Use for merchandising or commercial endorsements, however, is usually not allowed—the major exception to the rule that you can use royalty-free images any way you like. See Chapter 11 for special rules surrounding merchandising and commercial uses.

- Because it is used to mean several things, the term **copyright-free** can be confusing. Some people use it to refer to public domain artwork; others use it to refer to royalty-free artwork. Often, it's used to describe artwork that websites offer for free to the public—whether the works are public domain works or royalty-free works. This book does not use the term "copyright-free" but instead sticks with the terms "royalty-free," for artwork that can be licensed for a wide range of uses, and the term "public domain work," for artwork that can be used for free.

2. Finding and Using Clip Art

Clip art is often available on CD-ROM or downloadable from the Web. To find websites that offer clip art, use the keywords "clip art," "royalty free," or "copyright free" in any Internet search engine. If you use America Online, type in the keywords "Image" or "Image Exchange" and you will be directed to stock art sources. Many of the royalty-free photo resources provided in Chapter 3 also provide royalty-free clip art.

Clip art—which generally includes royalty-free and public domain artwork—is fine for most standard business and personal uses. The only significant drawbacks to using this type of artwork are that the quality is often not very good and that competitors are free to use the same image by accessing the same website or CD-ROM. If you are seeking exclusive rights to artwork, you should either hire an artist (see Chapter 15) or enter into an exclusive license to use a graphic work.

Sometimes clip art is sold for a flat fee or a subscription fee. Use is limited only by the terms of the shrink-wrap or click-wrap agreement (discussed below). Inexpensive clip art bundles are available on CD-ROM for $20 to $300.

⚠ **Know your computer and what you're downloading.** The three-letter extension on a graphic file, for example, "JPG," "TIF," or "GIF," tells you what type of file it is. Before downloading a digital image, make sure that your computer and graphics programs can accommodate or convert that type of image file. For example, some TIF files are suitable for PCs and some are not. In addition, be aware that scanned artwork quality can vary widely. If you are seeking the highest quality scans, you should ask for drum-scanned artwork—a higher quality scanning process than used by flatbed scanners. If the image bank doesn't indicate the type of scan, ask.

3. Shrink-Wrap and Click-Wrap Agreements

Always read the shrink-wrap or click-wrap agreement accompanying a clip art collection. These agreements come in two forms: with software packages, such as on the printed sticker under the plastic shrink-wrap; or on the website, such as a page that requires you to click on an "Okay" or "I Agree" button. These agreements contain a list of do's and don'ts—sometimes a more restrictive list than required under copyright law.

For example, the following is a list of conditions you might see in a shrink-wrap agreement for clip art:

This software contains original clip art that is fully protected by copyrights. The original purchaser of the software is authorized to use individual items to produce copyright-free art for the printing of newsletters and the like. However, this software collection may not be reproduced in whole or in part as a collection or individually as stock engravings, prints, negatives, positives, stock printing, and the like.

In other words, you are free to use the clip art as a book illustration or in an ad, but you cannot reprint it the collection in its entirety or sell individual images.

EXAMPLE: A company downloaded several volumes of fire-fighting clip art and then offered clip art packages at its website. The company was found liable for copyright infringement for copying the three volumes of software clip art and placing it on a website for downloading without authorization of the clip art owner. (*Marobie-Fl, Inc. v. National Association of Fire Equipment Distributors,* 983 F. Supp. 1167 (E.D. Ill. 1997).)

Although only a few courts have reviewed the legality of click-wrap and shrink-wrap agreements, the majority of these courts have enforced them. In other words, if you do business with artwork owners who insist on these types of agreements, they'll probably be able to enforce them against you in court if you violate the terms.

F. Researching Art

The methods for searching for artwork are similar to the techniques for searching for photo imagery discussed in Chapter 3, Section A. You can search online by using image search engines or exploring image bank websites. You can also hire an image researcher to help you locate the artwork you seek.

1. Online Searching

If you seek a particular work or a specific artist, you can simply type the artist's name or the name of the work into a search engine. Some image search engines, such as the Clip Art Searcher (http://webplaces.com/search), allow you to use numerous image search engines such as HotBot, Lycos, and Yahoo!, and to search thousands of FTP files on the Web. ("FTP" stands for "file transfer protocol," and refers to files that are specifically for downloading from the Web.)

However, if you don't need a specific image but need a certain type of graphic image—such as a drawing of a horse—locating the right graphic image may be a little trickier. The problem is that search engines cannot distinguish between photographic images and graphic or "art" images, so you'll almost always have to sort through numerous photographic images to find the graphic image you want. As a general rule, you will do better to go directly to image banks that specifically provide artwork and search there. You can get a lengthy listing of websites that provide clip art by simply typing the words "clip art" into a search engine.

EXAMPLE: I wanted to find a classic image of an angel. I began my search using an image search engine, Clip Art Searcher, and typed in the word "angel." The search engine returned dozens of sites (including numerous photos from the TV show *Touched by an Angel*), only one of which had graphic images of angels. Unfortunately, these were cartoon angels.

I abandoned the search engines and went to specific image sites to search there. On AOL, I clicked on KEYWORD and typed in "Image Exchange." I located a folder entitled "Angels From the Vatican" where I found several graphic images in the public domain, including an angel by Raphael Sanzio.

I then used my Internet search engine, typed in "clip art," and found many free image clip art sites. At one of these sites, All Advantage, I downloaded another graphic image of an angel.

2. Using Picture Researchers

If you are having difficulty locating a particular artwork item, consider using the services of a professional picture researcher. Picture researchers are skilled at digging into a variety of resources such as the Library of Congress, the Smithsonian Institution, or online image banks. These researchers are usually paid per day (approximately $250), although some charge by the hour. As explained in Chapter 3, many picture researchers have specialties, so you may want to contact the American Society of Picture Professionals (listed in the resource section at the end of this chapter) to find someone appropriate for your needs.

Millions of Images: The Smithsonian

The Smithsonian Institution in Washington, DC, is more than a single institution—it's an umbrella organization for national museums, libraries, and archives. It provides an invaluable link to millions of photographic, fine art, and historical images from sources such as the Archives of American Art, Freer Gallery of Art, Gem & Mineral Collection, Harvard-Smithsonian Center for Astrophysics, National Air & Space Museum, National Museum of African Art, National Museum of American Art, National Museum of American History, National Museum of Natural History, National Museum of the American Indian, National Portrait Gallery, and the National Postal Museum.

Unfortunately, there is no comprehensive Smithsonian guide that explains how to locate various materials. You may need to make several telephone calls until your request arrives at the correct curatorial or collecting unit. (The collecting unit is the museum or gallery that controls the rights to the work.) Permission to publish a photograph of an item can only be granted by the Smithsonian collecting unit that holds the original object or image. That unit also provides you with the Smithsonian negative number, a necessary element if you need a copy of a photograph. To locate the right collecting unit, use the Public Inquiry Mail Service, the Smithsonian telephone book, or one of the various Smithsonian websites that explain where collecting units are located. These resources are listed at the end of this chapter.

The Smithsonian and its affiliated institutions are not considered to be U.S. government agencies for copyright purposes. This means they are allowed to claim copyright in images they make of works in their collections.

G. Artwork Fees and Agreements

Fees and agreements for using artwork are similar to those for using stock photography—photos and artwork are often licensed from the same source. As with licensing photos, fees and agreements for licensing artwork vary depending on the work and your use, increasing for exclusivity, higher resolution, and advertising and corporate uses. The fee for using a cartoon in a company newsletter may cost as little as $25, while the fee for reproducing fine art within a book may be several hundred dollars. The detailed discussion in Chapter 3, Section E, of fee information for rights-protected photos also applies to artwork. Please refer to that section for in-depth fee information.

Below are two sample agreements: a simple all-purpose artwork license agreement and an agreement for using artwork in a film or video. If you want to reproduce artwork on posters, postcards, mugs, or other merchandise, see Chapter 11, "Art and Merchandise Licenses."

Modifying Artwork

Modifications to artwork—for example, colorizing a black-and-white image or digitally removing elements of a picture—require permission under U.S. copyright law. In addition, under European and U.S. laws, artists possess special rights known as moral rights. You may violate these moral rights if you tinker with the artist's aesthetic judgment. When seeking permission, notify the rights holder of your intent to modify the work or seek a release that grants you permission to make your intended alterations. A statement like: "Licensor grants to Licensee the right to modify the artwork as follows: [describe the modification]" should suffice.

1. Sample Artwork Permission Agreement

Below is a basic all-purpose artwork permission agreement. Note that this agreement lacks some of the provisions (such as dispute resolution and alternative payment systems) that may be included in more complete artwork agreements—omitted here because it is easier to negotiate and obtain permission using short agreements. An explanation of the various provisions follows.

 A tear-out copy of this agreement is provided in the Appendix. A digital copy is included on the forms CD.

Artwork Permission Agreement

_____ ("Licensor") is the owner of rights for the artwork described below (the "Selection"). _____ ("Licensee") wants to acquire the right to use the Selection as specified in this agreement (the "Agreement").

Licensor Information

Title of work (the "Selection"): _____

Catalogue number (if applicable): _____

Artist: _____

Licensee Publication Information

The Selection will appear in the following publication(s) (the "Work"):

(check if applicable and fill in blanks)

☐ book—title: _____

☐ periodical—title: _____

☐ event handout—title of event: _____

☐ diskette–title: _____

☐ website—URL: _____

If to be used on a website, the Selection will appear on:

(check if applicable)

☐ home page

☐ internal page

Name of publisher or sponsor (if different from Licensee): _____

Estimated date(s) of publication or posting: _____

If applicable, the estimated number of copies to be printed or produced (if a book, the estimated first print run): _____

If for sale, the price: $ _____

If copies are free to attendees of a program, the cost of program: _____

If a website, the average number of visitors per month: _____

Grant of Rights

Licensor grants to Licensee and Licensee's successors and assigns, the:

(select one)

☐ nonexclusive

☐ exclusive

right to reproduce and distribute the Selection in:

(select all that apply)

☐ the current edition of the Work.

☐ all editions of the Work.

☐ all foreign language versions of the Work.

☐ all derivative versions of the Work.

☐ all media now known or later devised.

☐ promotional materials published and distributed in conjunction with the Work.

☐ other rights _____

Territory

The rights granted under this Agreement shall be for _____ (the "Territory").

Fees

Licensee shall pay Licensor as follows:

(select payment option and fill in blanks)

☐ **Flat Fee.** As full payment for all rights granted, Licensee shall pay Licensor a flat fee of:

$ _____ . Payment shall be made:

☐ upon execution of this Agreement.

☐ upon publication.

☐ **Royalties and Advance.** Licensee agrees to pay Licensor a royalty of____% of Net Sales. Net Sales are defined as gross sales (the gross invoice amount billed to customers) less quantity discounts and returns actually credited. Licensee agrees to pay Licensor an advance against royalties of $_____ upon execution of this Agreement. Licensee shall pay Licensor within thirty

(30) days of the end of each quarter. Licensee shall furnish an accurate statement of sales during that quarter. Licensor shall have the right to inspect Licensee's books upon reasonable notice.

Credit & Samples

(check if applicable and fill in blanks)

☐   **Credit.** All versions of the Work that include the Selection shall contain the following statement: _____

☐   **Samples.** Upon publication, Licensee shall furnish _____ copies of the Work to Licensor.

Warranty

Licensor warrants that it has the right to grant permission for the uses of the Selection as specified above and that the Selection does not infringe the rights of any third parties.

(check if applicable)

☐   Licensor warrants that a model release is on file for the Selection.

Miscellaneous

This Agreement may not be amended except in a written document signed by both parties. If a court finds any provision of this Agreement invalid or unenforceable, the remainder of this Agreement shall be interpreted so as best to effect the intent of the parties. This Agreement shall be governed by and interpreted in accordance with the laws of the State of _____. This Agreement expresses the complete understanding of the parties with respect to the subject matter and supersedes all prior representations and understandings.

Licensor	Licensee
By: _____	By: _____
Name: _____	Name: _____
Title: _____	Title: _____
Address: _____	Address: _____
Date: _____	Date: _____
	Tax ID # _____

2. Explanation for Artwork Permission Agreement

- In the **introductory paragraph,** insert the names of the licensor (the party who owns the material) and the licensee (you or the person who is seeking permission).
- In the **Licensor Information** and **Licensee Publication Information** sections, complete the blank spaces to describe the artwork you want to use and the work in which you plan to use it.
- In the **Grant of Rights** section, complete the grant to reflect the rights you have negotiated. More information on the rights associated with grants is provided in Chapter 11, "Art and Merchandise Licenses."
- Complete the **Territory** section to reflect the regions in which you are acquiring rights. For more help, review Chapter 11, Section C7.
- In the **Fees** section, indicate what type of fee has been negotiated by checking the appropriate box(es) and complete the information.
- Complete the **Credit and Samples** section to reflect your agreement with the licensor.
- As explained in Chapter 11, Section C11, a warranty is a contractual promise made by the licensor. Some licensors do not want to make promises, particularly promises that the work does not infringe any third parties' copyright or other rights. You may have to modify the Warranty section or strike it entirely if the licensor objects.
- If you believe you have the bargaining power to get the licensor to agree, you may want to include an indemnity provision in the agreement. Indemnity is a financial punishment if the licensor breaks its promises. Indemnity provisions are not included here. If you wish to add such a provision, samples and explanations are provided in Chapter 11, Section C11.
- Explanations for the **Miscellaneous** or "boilerplate" provisions are provided in Chapter 11, Section C22. If you believe you have the bargaining power to get the licensor to

agree, you may want to include a provision that covers attorney fees or arbitration.

⚠ Commercial uses are more complex. If you are seeking permission to use artwork on behalf of an advertising agency or a company selling a product or service (for example, Nike or American Airlines), your use is more likely to be categorized as a commercial endorsement, which will trigger additional legal issues. Review Chapter 12, Section B, regarding releases you may be required to obtain.

3. Using Artwork in Film and Video

Motion pictures, television programs, and videos often include artwork—for example, a painting, poster, photograph, or sculpture. As a general rule, you should obtain permission if the artwork is recognizable with sufficient detail so that the average viewer can clearly see the work.

For example, in one case, a court ruled that the appearance of a copyrighted poster in a television show for a total of 27 seconds required permission from the copyright owner. (*Ringgold v. Black Entertainment Television,* 126 F.3d 70 (2d Cir. 1997).) On the other hand, in a different case, a court ruled that if the artwork appears fleetingly, or is obscured, out of focus, or virtually unidentifiable, permission is not required because the use is too small (or "de minimus"). (*Sandoval v. New Line Cinema Corp.,* 147 F.3d 215 (2d Cir. 1998).) For more on this subject, see Chapter 9, "Fair Use."

If you perform clearance on a regular basis for motion pictures, television, or video, review *Clearance and Copyright: Everything the Independent Filmmaker Needs to Know,* by Michael C. Donaldson (Silman-James Press).

Below is a basic permission agreement for using art within a motion picture.

 A tear-out copy of this agreement is provided in the Appendix. A digital copy is included on the forms CD.

Agreement to Use Artwork in Motion Picture

_____ ("Licensor") is the owner of rights for the artwork described below (the "Selection"). _____ ("Licensee") wants to acquire the right to use the Artwork as specified in this agreement (the "Agreement").

Use of the Artwork

The Artwork will appear in:

(choose one)

- [ ] motion picture
- [ ] television program
- [ ] music video
- [ ] other:
- [ ] entitled _____ (the "Picture").

Grant of Rights

Licensor grants to Licensee and Licensee's successors and assigns the nonexclusive worldwide right (but not the obligation) to include the Artwork in the Picture for the unlimited distribution, advertising, and promotion of the Picture in all languages and in all forms or devices now known or later devised. This use includes, but is not limited to, use of the Artwork in foreign language versions of the Picture, advertising, publicity or trailers of the Picture, and music videos derived from the Picture.

Limitations on Use

Licensee will use the Artwork in a manner that is consistent with the general practices of the television and motion picture industry. Licensee will not materially alter the Artwork or depict it in any manner that conflicts with the restrictions below, without the consent of Licensor.

Restrictions: _____

Fees

As full payment for all rights granted, Licensee shall pay Licensor a flat fee of $_____. Payment shall be made upon execution of this agreement.

Credit

The Picture shall include the following credit for the Artwork: _____

Warranty & Release

Licensor warrants that it has the right to grant permission for use of the Artwork as specified above and that the Artwork does not infringe upon the rights of any third parties. Licensor waives any claims, known or unknown, arising out of Licensee's use of the Artwork. In the event that Licensee breaches this agreement, Licensor's relief shall be limited to damages and Licensor shall not be entitled to injunctive or equitable relief.

Miscellaneous

This Agreement may not be amended except in a written document signed by both parties. If a court finds any provision of this Agreement invalid or unenforceable, the remainder of this Agreement shall be interpreted so as best to effect the intent of the parties. This Agreement shall be governed by and interpreted in accordance with the laws of the State of _____ . This Agreement expresses the complete understanding of the parties with respect to the subject matter and supersedes all prior representations and understandings.

Licensor	Licensee
By: _____	By: _____
Name: _____	Name: _____
Title: _____	Title: _____
Address: _____	Address: _____
Date: _____	Date: _____
	Tax ID # _____

4. Explanation for Film and Video License Agreement

- In the **introductory paragraph,** insert the names of the licensor (the person or company who owns the copyright in the artwork) and the licensee (the person producing the motion picture or the authorized representative of the production company).
- In the **Use of the Artwork** section, indicate the type of program in which the artwork will appear and the title of the program.
- The first sentence of the **Grant of Rights** section is intended to prevent any problems in the event that the scene with the artwork ends up on the cutting room floor. The agreement grants the filmmaker broad rights—for example, to use the artwork in advertising and promotion. This means that additional permissions will not be required from the copyright owner of the artwork. More information on license grants is provided in Chapter 11, Section C4.
- If the copyright owner wants to place some limitations on use, they belong in the **Limitations on Use** section. The owner may write in a restriction such as "Artwork shall not be used in any scene depicting nudity or sexual activity."
- In the **Fees** section, indicate the fee amount, if any, that has been negotiated.
- Complete the **Credit** section if it applies.
- As explained in Section C11 of Chapter 11, a warranty is a contractual promise made by the licensor. The **Warranty Release** section promises that the the licensor does, in fact, have the right to license the artwork and that the licensee won't be liable to a third party (for example, another artist) who claims that the artwork was ripped off. The waiver of claims is intended to prevent the licensor from subsequently claiming that the use violated some undisclosed right—for example, the use violated the artist's moral rights. This

section also includes a limitation on the licensor's potential relief. If the filmmaker breaches the agreement—for example, fails to pay for the use—the licensor can sue for payment. However, the licensor cannot seek to prevent the release of the film.
- Explanations for the **Miscellaneous** or "boilerplate" provisions are provided in Chapter 11. Note that you may want to add a provision on attorney fees or arbitration (see Chapter 11, Section C22), not included here.

H. Artwork Resources

The following resources can help you with various aspects of the permissions process for fine art and graphic art.

1. Fine Art Resources

- Visual Artists and Galleries Association (VAGA): 350 Fifth Avenue, Ste. 2820, New York, NY 10118; 212-736-6666, fax 212-736-6767. Email: rpanzer@vagarights.com.
- Artists Rights Society (ARS): www.arsny.com.

2. Online Fine Art Image Resources

The following websites provide access to a variety of fine art images:

- Corbis: www.corbis.com
- Hulton/Archive Photo: www.hultonarchive.com
- Jacques-Edouard Berger Foundation: www.bergerfoundation.ch
- Time Life Pictures: www.timelifepictures.com, and
- Yahoo!: http://dir.yahoo.com/Arts/ Museums__Galleries__and__Centers.

3. Graphic Arts Resources

- Graphic Artists Guild (www.gag.org), and
- Society of Children's Book Writers and Illustrators (SCBWI) (www.scbwi.org).

4. Cartoon Resources

- Cartoonbank.com (www.cartoonbank.com)
- The National Cartoonists Society (www.reuben.org)
- The Association of American Editorial Cartoonists (www.detnews.com/aaec)
- Politicalcartoons.com (www.politcalcartoons.com), and
- The Professional Cartoonist's Index (www.cagle.com).

5. Comic Book Resources

- Marvel Comics (www.marvel.com)
- DC Comics and Mad Magazine (www.dccomics.com), and
- Harvey Comics (www.harvey.com).

6. Comic Syndicates

- King Features Syndicate (www.kingfeatures.com)
- United Media (www.comiczone.com)
- Universal Press Syndicate (www.uexpress.com)
- Tribune Media Services Inc. (www.tms.tribune.com)
- Creators Syndicate, Inc. (www.creators.com)
- Los Angeles Times Syndicate (www.newscom.com) (Note: There is a fee to view this site.), and
- The Washington Post Writers Group (www.postwritersgroup.com).

7. Medical Image Resources

- Association of Medical Illustrators (www.ami.org)
- Williams & Wilkins Mediclip (www.lifeart.com), and
- Custom Medical Stock Photo (www.cmsp.com).

8. Picture Researchers

- American Society of Picture Professionals (www.aspp.com).

9. Print Resources for Finding Artwork

- *Finding Images Online*, by Paula Berinstein (Independent Publishers, 1996), and
- *Practical Picture Research*, by Hilary Evans (Routledge-Blueprint, 1994).

10. Smithsonian Institution

The resources below can help you locate images affiliated with the Smithsonian Institution.

- Smithsonian Archives: www.si.edu/archives
- Graphic Services: The Office of Imaging offers a cross-section of the Smithsonian's photos in a Web database at http://photo2.si.edu.
- Smithsonian Institution Research Information System (SIRIS): www.siris.si.edu. At this site you can search the holdings of the Smithsonian Institution Libraries, several Smithsonian archival repositories, and other special collections areas.
- Yahoo! Smithsonian Internet directory: http://dir.yahoo.com/Government/U_S__Government/Agencies/Independent/Smithsonian_Institution.

Getting Permission to Use Music

This chapter discusses common music permission situations, describes the options and fees for acquiring music rights, and offers suggestions for locating and dealing with music copyright owners. Acquiring rights for music is often easier than for text or artwork because there are standardized fees and license agreements for most music uses. For example, in some cases, a music owner must permit a use if a fee is paid. It is also easier to track down the copyright owner of music and get permission to use it because clearance services and organizations are available to assist.

Despite the ease with which music can be licensed, the fees are not always predictable. Fees can escalate beyond what they'd be for similar text or artwork uses. In some cases, owners of music copyright are less receptive to permissions and refuse to negotiate.

Also, with music, there's an additional copyright twist. Every musical recording includes two copyrights: one for the song itself and another for the particular recording of the song. Acquiring permission for music often requires obtaining the permission of both of these copyright owners.

A. Acquiring Rights to Music

Music rights are generally acquired in one of the following ways:

- **Assignment or work-for-hire agreement.** If a musician or composer is hired to create music for a specific purpose—for example, a computer game—the music rights are transferred to the hiring party by an assignment or work-for-hire agreement. An assignment is a transfer of ownership of the copyright in the music. A work-for-hire arrangement occurs when the hiring party acquires ownership of the music through an employer-employee relationship or an independent contractor agreement. A sample assignment and an explanation regarding works made for hire are provided in Chapter 15. Under an assignment or work-for-hire agreement, the company

paying for the work becomes the owner of all music rights.

- **License.** If music already exists and is not created for a specific purpose—for example, a Beatles song—the music rights are acquired by a license. This chapter explains how to license music and lyrics. It provides tips on determining the fees and finding the owner of a song or recording, as well as typical license agreements for the use of music or lyrics in books, magazines, movies, videos, commercials, software, live performances, at businesses, and on websites.
- **Production music.** Stock or generic music is available from production music libraries (known as "PMLs"), that provide prerecorded compositions for fixed fees, blanket fees (for multiple uses), or per-use fees. Companies that cannot afford to hire musicians or license popular music commonly use PML music as background or theme music. PMLs are discussed in Section B5.

 If you seek permission to use music in conjunction with merchandise, review Chapter 11, "Art and Merchandise Licenses."

 If you perform music clearance on a regular basis, consult *Kohn on Music Licensing,* by Al Kohn and Bob Kohn (Aspen Law & Business), which provides a complete collection of music licensing agreements.

B. Song and Sound Recording Copyrights

When a song is recorded, two copyrights are created—a song copyright, usually owned by a music publisher, and a sound recording copyright, usually owned by a record company. The song copyright protects the words and music of the song. The sound recording copyright protects the musical performance and audio sound of the recording of the song. As explained below, if you want to use a recorded song, you must get permission from both the song and sound recording copyright owners.

1. Song Copyrights and Music Publishers

The songwriter is the initial owner of a song's copyright. The only exception is if the songwriter writes songs as part of a job, in which case the employer owns the songs. Songwriters usually transfer their copyrights to music publishers who own and manage collections of songs. A music publisher may be a large multinational company or a one-person operation run by the songwriter.

What Do Music Publishers Do?

A music publisher acts like a business agent for the songwriter—promoting songs, administering income from song licensing, and paying the songwriter a royalty. The title "music publisher" refers to the early days of the music business when the primary source of income for songwriters was the publication of sheet music. The concept of using music publishers has become so ingrained in the music business that in order to earn money from his or her songs, a songwriter must either sell or license his or her rights to an established music publisher or create his or her own music publishing business.

---

2. When Permission Is Required From a Music Publisher

There are several common situations in which permission is required from a music publisher, including:
- when sheet music is reproduced
- when song lyrics are reproduced, and
- when a song is released on a recording, played publicly, used in an audiovisual work (such as a movie), or used in a digital format (such as an MP3 music file).

Fortunately, for some of these activities, such as releasing a recording or playing a song publicly, there are streamlined processes and fixed fees for getting permission. For other activities, such as using music in a movie, there are no fixed fees and the costs can be quite high.

a. Reproducing Sheet Music or Lyrics

Permission is required from the music publisher when you reproduce sheet music or song lyrics. The only exceptions to this rule are if the song is in the public domain (see Chapter 8) or if your use qualifies as a fair use (see Chapter 9). Section C describes the procedure for reprinting sheet music and lyrics.

b. Songs Released on Recordings

Permission is required from the music publisher when you sell a song on an audio-only recording, such as a compact disc or cassette. You must also pay a fee to the music publisher for recording and selling a song it owns. This payment is referred to as a "mechanical royalty" (the principles of mechanical royalty payments are discussed further in Section E). Music publishers either collect this money directly or delegate the responsibility to the Harry Fox Agency, an organization that negotiates and collects mechanical royalties. Information about contacting the Harry Fox Agency is provided at the end of this chapter.

c. Songs Played Publicly

Permission is also required from the music publisher when you play songs in public, such as on the radio, on television, at businesses, in concerts, or at clubs. For example, radio stations must pay the music publisher that owns a particular song in order to play it on the air. The fees for these uses are referred to as "performance royalties." Generally, radio stations, clubs, and other places that play music regularly obtain blanket licenses instead of getting permission and paying the fee each time they play a song. The licenses are granted by performing rights societies such as BMI and ASCAP, that execute the agreements, collect the fees, and monitor performances on behalf of music publishers. Section D discusses this process in greater detail.

What Is a Public Performance?

Public performances of music require permission from the music publisher; private performances do not. To perform a work publicly means that music is played at a place open to the public or where a substantial number of people outside the normal circle of a family and social acquaintances are gathered. The fact that a performance is not for profit does not affect this determination.

Transmission of music by a radio or television station is also a public performance. It does not matter if the public receives the music at the same time or place as when it was transmitted. For example, if one station transmits a work and another station receives the broadcast and retransmits it later, the retransmission would be a performance. Webcasting or audio streaming, the process of transmitting music over the Internet in real time, is also considered a public performance (see Section J2).

Examples of public performance include:

- a disc jockey playing a record in a nightclub
- a band playing music during half-time at a football game
- a singer performing a song in a nightclub
- a business playing music through the office loudspeaker system
- a radio station playing music over the air
- a website webcasting music
- a television station broadcasting a television show containing music, and
- a cable company receiving a television station broadcast containing music and rebroadcasting it via cable transmission.

See Section D for more information on obtaining permission to play songs publicly.

d.   Songs Used in Audiovisual Works

Permission is required from the music publisher when you use music in a movie, television show, commercial, or video. This is referred to as a "synchronization license" or a "videogram license." Depending on the use, this license is negotiated either through the Harry Fox Agency or directly by the music publisher. More information about synchronization licenses is provided in Section G.

e.   Songs Used in Digital Formats

Permission is required from the music publisher when you upload, download, and broadcast songs over the Internet (sometimes referred to as webcasting or audio streaming). Depending on the use, permission agreements for digital uses are negotiated by the Harry Fox Agency, performing rights societies, or directly by the music publisher. Section J provides information about the rules regarding digital copies of songs.

3.   Sound Recording Copyrights and Record Companies

Besides the copyright in the song composition itself, each recorded version of a song (often referred to as a "master") is protected by a sound recording copyright. In other words, a sound recording is a separate and distinct work from the musical composition that is being performed. Since a song can be recorded in many different styles and arrangements, each recording is a record of the performance of the composition that is entitled to its own copyright protection. For example, the hundreds of different recorded versions of "White Christmas" are each protected by a separate sound recording copyright, while the song itself is protected by a single song copyright.

Generally speaking, the first owners of a sound recording are the individuals who created it, including the musicians, arrangers, and producer of the recording session. More commonly, however, a musician or band signs a recording agreement, giving the record company that releases its sound recordings the rights to those sound recordings. Even without an official recording agreement, if a company hires the musicians and recording engineers to record the songs, that company as the employer would be the initial owner of the sound recordings.

4.   When Permission Is Required From a Record Company

When using a sound recording, permission is required from the record company in the following situations:

- **Duplicating or sampling a sound recording.** Examples of sound recording duplication include copying a compact disc or portion of it to cassette, using a sample in another recording, using a pop song in a video or motion picture soundtrack, or converting a sound recording into a digital format such as an MP3 file.
- **Digital broadcasting.** Digital broadcasting includes making a sound recording available over the Internet or over a cable music service. Section J provides more information on digital broadcasting.

Permission is not required from the record company—but may be required from the music publisher (see Section A above)—to reprint music or lyrics, to make a different recording of the same song, or to play or broadcast a recording. (Note, this applies only to performances in the U.S. In some countries, permission is required from the record company to broadcast sound recordings.)

When contacting a record company for permission to use its recording, ask for the licensing or special markets department. Most record companies are prepared to issue the licenses described in this chapter and will furnish license agreements, usually known as "master use" licenses. More detailed information on getting permission to use copyrighted recordings is included in Sections M and O. Information on how to locate record companies is included in the resources section at the end of this chapter.

5. Using Production Music Libraries

Production music libraries (PMLs) provide an inexpensive method of obtaining rights for original music and sound effects on a nonexclusive basis. PML music, which is primarily instrumental, is used for films, websites, slide shows, radio and television programming, commercials, software and multimedia, training videos, in-flight services, and similar applications.

Like stock photography, PML music is categorized by genre or mood (for example, old-time rock and roll or outer space music) and is sold on compact disc collections on a royalty-free, blanket fee, or per-use fee basis. A typical PML compact disc may contain ten to 15 original compositions, including a full-length version of each composition as well as shorter "tag" or "cue" version. Larger PMLs have hundreds of compact discs in their collections. Using the Internet, you can search through many of these collections and listen to music samples.

Because the PML owns both the music publishing and sound recording rights, obtaining permission to use PML recordings is simple. A typical PML license permits use for most synchronization purposes, such as using the music in a film or software program. However, the PML license does not permit you to use the music in audio recordings sold to the public. For example, while PML music may be used in a film, it cannot be included on a commercial soundtrack album sold to consumers without special permission from the PML. PMLs generally prohibit the use of the music unless it is used in conjunction with other audio or visual elements. These limitations are usually expressed in the PML license as follows:

> The music may be used only in synchronization or mechanical reproduction with other audio and/or visual elements. The licensee must obtain prior written permission and negotiate a separate license if licensee intends to repackage or alter the music and make it available as commercial soundtracks or videos.

There are three methods of acquiring rights for PML music:

- **Blanket agreements** in which the user obtains unlimited use of all PML music on a compact disc or disc library for a specified period of time, such as two years. If continued use is required, the license must be renewed. Blanket licenses may range from several hundred dollars to four or five thousand dollars per year.
- **Per-use agreements** in which the user makes payments when he or she uses compositions in a production. This method of payment is sometimes referred to as a "needle drop," in reference to the days of vinyl recordings when a radio or film producer paid each time the needle was dropped onto a piece of music. Per-use fees depend on the length and type of use and can range from $50 for a five-minute use in a local television show to $500 for the same music in a feature film.
- **Buyout agreements** in which the user acquires unlimited rights by purchasing the PML's compact disc. Fees for buyout rights range from $50 to several thousand dollars.

PMLs offer a variety of fees and payment plans, making it possible to negotiate discounts based on use. Fees are often based on an estimate of per-unit sales. A list of PMLs is provided in the resources section at the end of this chapter.

Bypassing Sound Recording Rights

It's often more difficult to get permission from a record company than from a music publisher because record companies are obligated to many people—including recording artists and union musicians who receive a reuse fee for certain licensed uses of a sound recording master. Some record companies don't want to bother with master licensing unless there is a return of at least several thousand dollars.

For this reason, many production companies pay for songs to be rerecorded instead of getting permission from a record company to use an existing recording. To do this requires permission from the music publisher only, not from the record company. Rerecorded sound recording masters may also be available from production music libraries on a one-time flat fee buyout basis (see Section 5, above).

It is not an infringement of the sound recording copyright to rerecord a song so that it sounds exactly like the original recording. However, there may be other legal limitations. A performer's style cannot be imitated when the recording is used to sell a product or service or to sell recordings that confuse the public into believing they are buying the original recording. (See "Performer Rights" below.)

Researching Song and Sound Recordings in the Copyright Office

Song copyrights are registered in the Copyright Office using Form PA (performing arts). Sound recording copyrights are registered in the Copyright Office using Form SR (sound recording). Sound recording copyrights exist only for recordings created after 1971, prior to which sound recordings were protected by state laws. (See Chapter 13, "Copyright Research.")

Performer Rights

Under a legal principle known as the "right of publicity," a performer's permission is required if his or her image, name, or style is used to sell a product or service. Permission is also needed to imitate a performer's style if the imitation is likely to cause the public to believe that the performer is affiliated with or endorses a product. For example, an auto company was found liable for infringing the right of publicity when it imitated, without permission, the singing style of Bette Midler. A snack food company was similarly found liable for using an imitation of Tom Waits. If the performer is deceased, you're not off the hook—in many states, permission is required from the performer's estate. For more information on rights of publicity and performer releases, see Chapter 12, "Releases."

Permission from a performer is also required to make an audio or video recording of a live performance or to distribute recordings of the performance. If the performer has signed an exclusive recording agreement with a record company, permission is required from the record company.

C. Reprinting Music or Lyrics

You may need permission to reprint music notation or lyrics,—for example, to quote lyrics on a website or to reprint music and lyrics in an instructional text. In these cases, you are not actually reproducing the sound of the music, only the words or musical notation. Because of this, you only need permission from the music publisher that owns copyright in the composition, not from any record company that may own a sound recording copyright for the song.

Generally, you need permission from the music publisher to reprint all or part of a song's sheet music or lyrics. The fees for such uses are not fixed, so a music publisher can charge whatever the market will bear. In most cases, the fees are reasonable, such as $50 to reprint lyrics in a book. You'll find information about locating music publishers in Section L.

1. Music and Lyric Reproduction

Music and lyrics are commonly sold as unbound sheet music, featuring piano notation, guitar chords, and lyrics printed below the corresponding music. Sheet music is also sold or licensed in folios (collections of sheet music bound into a volume), fakebooks (folios with hundreds of songs), or educational editions (sheet music for use in school instruction arranged for school performances). You'll also often find sheet music reproduced in specialty magazines, instructional booklets for musicians, and on websites. Lyrics are often reproduced separately (without musical notation) for use on websites or in books, greeting cards, advertisements, and magazines.

Occasionally, music publishers permit the use of a few lyric lines for free, but more often they will charge a fee, as described below. To reproduce music and lyrics, contact the music publisher using the methods described in Section L. The reproduction of lyrics for a karaoke recording may require a synchronization license. This type of license is explained in Section G.

Also keep in mind that if a music publisher grants permission to record a song as explained in Section E, it may not include the right to reprint the lyrics, such as in the liner notes to the compact disc booklet. Permission to print the lyrics must be acquired separately.

⚠️ **Don't assume that because sheet music is out of print it is free to use.** Unless it is in the public domain, sheet music is still protected under copyright law. (See Chapter 8 for an explanation of public domain rules.) If you want to reproduce out-of-print sheet music, contact the Music Publisher Association (www.mpa.org/crc.html), which has a procedure for locating and using out-of-print copyrighted music.

EXAMPLE: I wanted to reproduce four lines from the song "Sneakers on a Rooster," performed by Bo Diddley. By searching online, I determined that BMI is the performing rights society that represents the song. BMI provided contact information for the publisher, including an email address. I emailed the publisher, who okayed the request without requiring a fee. The publisher did provide a credit line for me to include with the use.

> The clothes I buy for you is what I thought you always wanted
> But the ones you buy for me, they feel like they're haunted
> Girl I hope your love changes in the future
> Cause lovin' you is like putting sneakers on a rooster.

"Sneakers on a Rooster," written by Sam Dees & David Camon. Lyrics reproduced courtesy of Ginn Music Group, Atlanta, Georgia.

2. Fees

Fees to reproduce music notation or lyrics vary quite widely depending on the use. Below are some general guidelines on what various uses may cost.

- Expect to pay $25 or more for the use of a song's lyrics (or a portion of the lyrics) in a book or magazine.
- Fees for use of lyrics on a website may range from $50 to $1,000, depending on the site and how much traffic it gets. Fees for using lyrics in advertising depend on the type of advertisement, length of use, and territory in which the ad will appear. Fees range from several hundred to several thousand dollars per year.
- For use of lyrics in a greeting card or other merchandise, music publishers seek a royalty of 2% to 5% of the retail price of the merchandise.
- If music and lyrics are reprinted as part of a folio or educational publication, music publishers usually seek a royalty of 10% to 15%

of the wholesale price. If the song is one of several within a publication, the royalty is often pro-rated. Under a pro-rata arrangement, a music publisher would, for example, receive 1/10 of the royalty if it provided one of ten songs.

- Music publishers commonly charge 2 cents per copy to reproduce lyrics on liner notes—for example, the cost to print lyrics on the liner notes of 1,000 copies would be $20.

- Fees for miscellaneous uses typically depend on the length of use, the popularity of the song, and often the publisher's whim.

Under limited conditions, music instructors are permitted to copy portions of sheet music and recordings without permission. For example, under fair use guidelines, a music instructor can copy excerpts of sheet music, provided that the excerpts do not constitute a "performable unit" such as a whole song, section, movement, or aria. In no case can more than 10% of the whole work be copied and the number of copies may not exceed one copy per pupil. See Chapter 7, Section B, for more information on educational uses.

3. Lyric Permission Letter Agreement

Most publishers furnish a short license agreement or letter for use of lyrics. Some may okay the use on the telephone. If an oral "okay" is granted, follow it up with a letter confirming the arrangement or use the Lyric Permission Letter Agreement below. If you're seeking to use lyrics on merchandise, such as a greeting card or poster, use the agreement provided in Chapter 11, "Art and Merchandise Licenses."

 A tear-out copy of this agreement is provided in the Appendix. A digital version is included on the forms CD.

Lyric Permission Letter Agreement

To _____ ("Music Publisher"):

I am writing to you to obtain permission to reprint portions of the lyrics (the "Lyrics") from the song _____ , written by _____ on behalf of _____("Licensee").

The lyrics will appear in the following publication(s) (the "Work"):

(check if applicable and fill in blanks)

☐   Book Use

Book title: _____

Name of publisher or sponsor: _____

Author(s): _____

ISBN: _____

Estimated date(s) of publication: _____

Estimated number of copies to be printed or produced (if a book, the estimated first print run): _____

Language editions: _____

Territory of publication: _____

Estimated price: $ _____

☐   Magazine

Magazine title: _____

Volume, issue, ISSN: _____

Estimated date of publication: _____

Circulation: _____

☐   Website

URL: _____

Name of publisher or sponsor: _____

Estimated dates of use: _____

Estimated visitors per day: _____

☐   Other (describe): _____

_____

Fee

Licensee shall pay a fee of $ _____ to Music Publisher at the following address: _____ upon publication of the Work or within 6 months of executing this Agreement, whichever is earlier.

Samples

Upon publication, Licensee shall furnish _____ copies of the Work to Music Publisher.

Credit

The following credit shall be included with the Work: _____

Signed by Licensee _____

Name: _____

Title: _____

Address: _____

Date: _____

Music Publisher's Approval of Request

Music Publisher warrants that it is the owner of rights for the lyrics and has the right to grant the permission to republish the lyrics as specified above. This license is for the nonexclusive worldwide right to republish the lyrics in all editions of the Work.

Signed by Music Publisher _____

Name: _____

Title: _____

Address: _____

Date: _____

4. Explanation for Lyric Permission Letter Agreement

Use this letter agreement after you have contacted the music publisher and discussed the conditions of the use, number of samples, credit, and fee, if any. Once these details have been agreed upon, you should include them in the agreement, as follows:

- Insert the names of the music publisher (generally, a company name), the song, the songwriter, and the person who has responsibility for acquiring permission ("Licensee"). The licensee may be you; or, if you're acquiring permission on behalf of someone else, such as a publisher or employer, list that person or entity.
- In the next paragraphs, indicate where the reproduced lyrics will appear (book, magazine, website, or other) and provide information about the fee, number of samples, and any required credit (for example, "Lyrics by Kevin Teare, reprinted courtesy of Electric Ladybug Music, Copyright 1999.").
- Provide your address and sign the agreement.
- The **Music Publisher's Approval of Request** is an assurance that the music publisher has the legal ability to grant the rights in the agreement. A representative of the music publisher should sign and date this provision and provide his or her name and title.
- It is possible that the music publisher will want to modify this agreement. For example, the music publisher may want to limit your use to a specific print run of a book or a specific period of time on a website. If necessary, modify what the license grants to reflect your agreement with the music publisher.
- You may need more rights than provided by the standard language of this agreement—for example, rights for foreign translations, derivative rights, or rights in all media. Either specify the additional rights needed or strike the last sentence of **Music Publisher's Approval of Request** and replace it with the

broader grant of rights provided below. Be aware that a music publisher may object to the terms of a broad request, causing a delay in the permissions process.

I grant Licensee's successors, licensees, and assigns the nonexclusive worldwide right to republish the lyrics in all editions of the Work and in all versions derived from the Work in all media now known or hereafter devised.

Arranging a Copyrighted Musical Composition

Musical arrangements or orchestrations of copyrighted musical compositions are considered to be derivative works and cannot be used without permission. For example, if you intend to write and reproduce an arrangement of the Elvis song "Heartbreak Hotel," you will need permission from the music publisher. An "arrangement" means substantial modifications in the song, such as adding intricate harmonies or reworking rhythm and chord structures. For a sample request form and more information on licensing for unique musical arrangements, see the "Request for Permission to Arrange" section of the Music Publisher's Association website (www.mpa.org/crc.html).

5. Using Lyrics Without Permission

If the music publisher cannot be located or permission is denied, the use of small portions of lyrics without permission may qualify as a fair use. Fair use rules for copyrighted materials are based on free speech principles. Permission is not required to use portions of a work if the use is for purposes of education, parody, or disseminating a critical point of view. Unfortunately, there are no quantitative rules as to how many song lyrics can be used as a fair use. However, if the following factors are present, your reproduction is more likely to be allowed without permission:

- the use is limited—for example, four lines or less
- the use is to comment upon or parody the song
- the music publisher is not deprived of income by the use, and
- a reasonable effort was made to locate the music publisher and secure permission.

The last factor, seeking permission, is not a necessity to qualify for fair use, but some courts have suggested that it demonstrates good faith. Fair use factors, along with real life examples, are discussed in greater detail in Chapter 9, "Fair Use."

D. Playing Music at a Business or Event

As a general rule, when you perform music publicly at a business or event, you must obtain permission from the music publisher only. Remember, public performance encompasses more than a musician playing a song live; it also means the playing of recorded music (see "What Is a Public Performance?" in Section B2). This means that permission is required for a disc jockey to play recordings at a club or on the radio. Usually, such permission is not granted directly by the music publisher, but by performing rights societies who handle the process on behalf of the music publishers. This process is described in more detail below.

EXAMPLE: The Emeryville Hotel wants to play tape recordings of popular music in its lobby. The hotel needs to get blanket licenses from the performing rights societies for the public performance of the songs.

1. Performance Rights Blanket Licenses

The two major performance rights organizations that represent music publishers are BMI and ASCAP. There is also a third company, SESAC, that accounts for a smaller share of the performance rights business. These nonprofit organizations collect fees from establishments where music is played (for example, nightclubs, radio and TV stations, concert halls, restaurants, and taverns), and distribute the money to the songwriters and music publishers who own the songs. All three performing rights societies—BMI, ASCAP, and SESAC—issue licenses known as blanket licenses that permit the licensee to play all songs represented by that society. With a blanket license, separate permissions are not required for each play of each song.

Examples of some business uses for which blanket licenses are provided include:

- athletic clubs
- dance classes
- hotels or motels
- restaurants and bars, and
- retail establishments, such as clothing stores.

Blanket licenses for uses other than on radio and TV are sought from BMI and ASCAP. Because of its smaller repertoire, SESAC's blanket licenses are geared more toward gospel and country music users. It's possible that a business could obtain a blanket license from only one performing rights society, but that may prove inefficient because the business would have to make sure that it only played music from that society.

The annual fee for a blanket license is based on the manner in which music is performed and the potential audience for the music. For example, ASCAP computes blanket licenses as follows:

- Restaurant, bar, and nightclub rates are based on whether the music is live or recorded, audio only or audiovisual, the club's seating capacity, the number of nights of music per week, the number of musicians involved, and whether admission is charged.
- Concert event rates are based on the venue's seating capacity and ticket price.

- Corporate rates for playing music at businesses are based on the number of employees.
- Retail store rates depend on the number of speakers in the store and the store's square footage.
- Hotel rates are based on a percentage of entertainment expenses for live music and an additional charge for recorded music.

To obtain a blanket license, contact BMI, ASCAP, or SESAC (contact information is included at the end of this chapter). Ask for the licensing department and explain your business use. The society's representatives will inquire as to the size and type of use and quote you a fee for an annual blanket license.

Permission for Music in Seminars and Training Programs

As explained in Chapter 7, permission is not required if music is played as part of a face-to-face teaching activity at a nonprofit educational institution. Permission is required from BMI and ASCAP when music is used as part of instructional seminars, conventions, or other commercial presentations.

How Is Harry Fox Different from BMI, ASCAP, and SESAC?

The performing rights societies, BMI, ASCAP, and SESAC, grant licenses to play songs on the radio and television, at concerts and public events, over the Internet, and in movie theaters. These organizations are concerned with the public performance of the song only—that is, when the public hears the songs. The Harry Fox Agency, a subsidiary of the National Music Publishers Association (NMPA), collects royalties for music publishers whenever a song is copied or reproduced (referred to as "mechanical royalties"), regardless of whether the public hears the song. Harry Fox provides licenses for reproducing songs in movies, videos, TV commercials, Internet commercials, corporate in-house presentations, trade shows, school shows, concerts, cabaret TV programs, products (such as music boxes or other devices that incorporate songs), jukeboxes, and karaoke systems.

There is some overlap between the territory covered by Harry Fox and performing rights societies. Both organizations grant licenses for songs used in film, radio, Internet, and TV use. However, the purposes of the licenses are different. For example, when granting television rights, the performing rights license permits the user to play the song over a television broadcast. The Harry Fox license grants the user the right to copy the song (or synchronize it) onto the television program's soundtrack.

2. Additional Permissions

Additional permissions are required in the following situations:

- If the business is not just playing the music, but also making a copy of it—for example, compiling songs on a tape or making a new recording—the business should obtain a mechanical license from the Harry Fox Agency. Forms for these licenses are downloadable at the Harry Fox website, as explained in Section O3, below.

- If the music is transmitted in a digital format such as over the Internet or via a digital cable music service, the user must obtain permission from the sound recording copyright owner. Digital rights are discussed in Section J, below.
- If the music is used at a corporate event to promote a product or service, the user must obtain permission from the performer in addition to permission from the music publisher and the record company. For example, if Microsoft debuts a new software product at a convention and plays a song recorded by the Rolling Stones, it must get permission from the music publisher, the record company, and from the Rolling Stones. (See Section F, below.)

Playing the Radio or Television at a Business

Before 1999, businesses using anything larger than a home stereo system had to pay performing rights societies for the right to play the radio or television for customers. However, under new rules, restaurants and bars of less than 3,750 square feet and retail establishments with less than 2,000 square feet don't have to pay any fees to play the radio or television in their establishments. (Note, establishments that play prerecorded music, such as compact discs, are still subject to license requirements.)

In addition, regardless of size, all restaurants, bars, and stores are exempt from paying fees if they have no more than six external speakers (but not more than four per room) or four televisions measuring 55 inches or less (but not more than one per room). These rules only apply to establishments that play radio and television. The National Restaurant Association has a complete explanation of these and related rules about playing music in a business. See its Music Licensing Guide at www.restaurant.org/pdfs/legal/musiclicensing.pdf.

Press 1 for More Music

Music provided for a caller on hold constitutes a public performance because music is being transmitted to the public. The company providing on-hold music must obtain permission from the performing right societies, ASCAP and BMI (and in some cases, SESAC).

3. Nonprofit and Charitable Business Exemptions

Some nonprofit and charitable uses of music don't require permission. Below is a summary of some of the rules, which are located at 17 U.S.C. § 110 of the federal copyright laws. Other educational permission rules are discussed in Chapter 7, "Academic and Educational Permissions."

- **Free shows.** No permission is needed if music is performed before a live audience for which no admission is charged and the performers are not paid.
- **Shows with admission fees.** No permission is needed if music is performed before a live paying audience, so long as the performers are not paid, the net proceeds are used exclusively for education, religious, or charitable purposes, and the music publisher is notified with more than ten days to object. If the publisher objects, the person seeking permission will have to pay for the use and acquire a license from the appropriate performing rights society.
- **Religious services.** No permission is needed to perform music in the course of religious services at a house of worship. However, permission is required to broadcast music performed at a religious service and to copy sheet music for religious services.
- **Agricultural fairs.** Permission is not required for the performance of live music at an an-

nual nonprofit agricultural or horticultural fair. However, see the point below on concessions and for-profit exhibits at fairs.

- **Fraternal and veterans events.** Permission is not required when nonprofit veterans' organizations or fraternal groups perform music provided that the general public is not invited and the net profits are used exclusively for charitable purposes.
- **Fraternity and sorority events.** Permission is not required to perform music at college fraternity and sorority social functions provided that the purpose is solely to raise funds for a charitable cause.
- **Concession stands.** Permission *is* required to play music at concession stands and for-profit exhibits regardless of whether the event at which the stand or exhibit is operating is exempt. For example, permission would be required to play music at a concession stand at a nonprofit agricultural fair.

E. Releasing Music for Sale

This section explains how to obtain permission to record and release a song as an audio recording—for example, if a singer wants to record and release a version of the Lou Reed song "Walk on the Wild Side" on compact disc. Thanks to federal laws, the process of acquiring permission to record a song is relatively simple and inexpensive (approximately 7 cents for each copy you distribute). In addition, the song owner must consent to your use if you follow the procedures described in this section.

This section is only about using songs on audio recordings distributed to the public. Recording a song for use within a film or video is discussed in Section G. Recording and distributing a song over the Internet is described in Section J. Recording of a song for use in a software program is discussed in Section I.

To record a song for release to the public, a performer must obtain permission from the music publisher of the song and pay a fee, called a mechanical royalty. A performer must pay a mechanical royalty to reproduce songs on cassettes, compact discs, and records.

There are two ways to get permission and pay the mechanical royalty:

- use a compulsory license and pay the preset statutory mechanical royalty rate directly to the music publisher, or
- negotiate permission and the mechanical royalty directly with the music publisher or the Harry Fox Agency.

Beware when proceeding without permission. Some musicians producing self-released recordings don't obtain compulsory licenses or pay mechanical royalties. For small pressings, this illegal activity usually goes undetected. But if the copyright owner learns of the unauthorized use, the musician may be forced to pay past due mechanical royalties, plus interest, or to stop distributing the recording entirely. If the music publisher brings a lawsuit, the musician may be subject to additional penalties, including attorney fees.

1. Compulsory Licenses

One way to legally rerecord a song is to use what's known as a "compulsory license." Under this procedure, the user doesn't actually ask for the music publisher's permission to make the recording or negotiate a license fee. Instead, the user merely informs the publisher of the recording (using the compulsory license procedure) and pays a license fee set by law. The music publisher can't prevent the recording of the song so long as the following requirements are satisfied:

- the song was previously released on a recording
- the performer making the new recording does not change the basic melody or fundamental character of the song

• the performer or record company making the new recording provides a Notice of Intention to Obtain Compulsory License (as described below) at least 30 days prior to distributing the recordings, and

• the performer or record company making the new recording pays the statutory mechanical royalty fee.

It's important to note that a compulsory license cannot be used the first time the song is distributed to the public—for example, if the songwriter never released a version of it and your version is the first. Nor can a compulsory license be used if the song was used on television or in a movie, but never released on an audio recording. In these cases, authorization must be acquired directly from the music publisher or songwriter. Since the song has never been recorded, it's possible that the songwriter is still the owner and has not transferred copyright to a music publisher.

Compulsory licenses are usable only when reproducing songs on records, compact discs, or cassettes—that is, sound recordings. They do not apply if making copies for use on a website or in a music video. In addition, compulsory licenses are not available for use of a song in video or digital movies or in conjunction with any other media.

a. Mechanical Royalty Rate

When using the compulsory license procedure, the music publisher must be paid a mechanical royalty rate set by the government (sometimes known as the "statutory rate"). This rate increases every few years.

Table of Statutory Mechanical Royalty Rates 2004-2006

2004-2005	8.5 cents per copy
2006	9.1 cents per copy

For information on the current mechanical rate, call the Copyright Office Licensing Division at 202-707-8150 or check its website at www.copyright.gov/carp.

EXAMPLE: In 2004, Andrea records Lou Reed's "Walk on the Wild Side." She makes and releases 1,000 compact discs of the recording. Andrea must pay $85 to the music publisher of the song (8.5 cents times 1,000 copies).

b. Notice of Intention to Obtain Compulsory License

For uses that meet the criteria described in this section, a Notice of Intention to Obtain Compulsory License should be sent to the copyright owner of the song. An explanation for completing this form is provided below.

Note: A compulsory license to record a song does not grant the right to reprint lyrics on the album artwork. Permission must be acquired separately from the publisher.

 A tear-out copy of this notice is provided in the Appendix. A digital version is included on the forms CD.

Notice of Intention to Obtain Compulsory License for Making and Distributing Sound Recordings

To _____ , the copyright owner of _____ , written by _____ :

Pursuant to the compulsory license provisions of the U.S. Copyright Act (17 U.S.C. § 1115), we apply

for a license to make and distribute phonorecords of _____ and provide the following

information:

Legal name or entity seeking the compulsory license:	
Fictitious or assumed names used for making and distributing phonorecords:	
Address:	
Business organization:	☐ corporation ☐ LLC ☐ partnership ☐ sole proprietor
Name of individuals who own a beneficial interest of 25% or more in the entity:	
If a corporation, names of the officers and directors:	
Configuration(s) to be made under the compulsory license (check all that apply):	☐ 7- or 12-inch vinyl single ☐ 12-inch long-playing vinyl record ☐ cassette ☐ compact disc ☐ minidisc ☐ digital cassette recording
Catalogue number(s):	
Label name(s):	
Principal recording artists:	
Anticipated date of initial release:	

We agree to pay the copyright owner royalties at the statutory rate provided by the Copyright Act.

Date: _____ By: _____

Name/Title: _____

c. Explanation for Notice to Obtain Compulsory License

- In the first blank of the first paragraph, insert the name of the song owner (usually the music publisher of the song). In the next blank insert the name of the song and then the songwriters. In the second paragraph, again insert the name of the song.
- In the first row of the table, insert the legal name of the company that owns your recording. If you or your company owns the recording, insert that name.
- Under **Fictitious or assumed names** insert the fictitious business name, if any, that you or your company uses.
- Insert your company's mailing address.
- Indicate the legal business structure of your company (corporation, LLC, partnership, or sole proprietor).
- In the category **Names of individuals who own a beneficial interest,** insert the names of anyone who has a 25% or more interest in the company. For example, if you and your partner own the recording equally (50%–50%), list both your names. If no one owns at least 25% of the company, leave this blank.
- If your company is a corporation, list the officers and directors in the next row.
- Under **Configuration(s),** check all the types of recordings you expect to release.
- List any catalogue number you may have created for the recording.
- Insert the name of your record label. If your company is putting out the record, the label name is probably the same as your company name.
- Insert the name of the recording artist.
- Insert the expected release date.
- The final paragraph establishes that the statutory rate will be paid. A company seeking a compulsory license (in this case, you or your company) is supposed to issue an accounting statement and pay statutory royalties every month. You can, however, contact the music publisher and ask if it is okay to make payments on a quarterly basis, rather than monthly.
- The compulsory license is signed by the licensee (you or your company, if you have one). The music publisher does not sign the license because consent from the music publisher is not required. All that is required is that the publisher is notified and paid according to the rules. If you have a partnership, a partner should sign in the space next to the word "By" and indicate his or her partner status below that—for example, "Peggi Fournier, a general partner in the Grosse Point Partnership."

2. Negotiating a License Directly With the Music Publisher

Most major labels and established independent record companies do not use compulsory licenses or pay the statutory rate as described above. Instead, they obtain permission to make the recording directly from the music publisher and negotiate a rate lower than the compulsory license rate, usually three-quarters of the statutory rate. It is not a violation of the law to negotiate a rate lower than that provided in the Copyright Act if both parties consent.

As with performance royalties, many music publishers do not negotiate mechanical licenses directly; instead they delegate that authority to the Harry Fox Agency, an organization that negotiates and collects mechanical royalties on behalf of approximately 80% of the music publishers. Sample mechanical licenses can be downloaded from the Harry Fox website (see Section O3).

However, negotiating with the music publisher, either directly or through Harry Fox, may not work for you. Many music publishers won't negotiate a lower rate unless a substantial number of copies of the recording will be distributed or you agree to pay them an advance. If you can't do this, you'll have to use a compulsory license as outlined above.

Creating a Theatrical Musical: Grand Rights

Grand rights are the rights you need to create theatrical presentations, such as Broadway-style musicals. For example, to create a musical drama using the songs of Bob Dylan, you must secure grand rights from Bob Dylan's publisher or the entity he has designated to handle grand rights. Performance rights organizations such as ASCAP and BMI do not control grand rights. To find the company that controls grand rights for a song, start by contacting the music publisher of the song or the Harry Fox Agency.

Although performing rights societies do not control grand rights, these societies do grant performance permissions for songs from Broadway musicals, provided that the songs are not performed in a dramatic context. For example, playing a song from the musical *Rent* over the radio requires permission from a performing rights society but does not require grand rights clearance.

F. Using Music in a Commercial, Radio Show, or as Background Music

Pop music has become a common component of advertising, used extensively in radio and television commercials. Using music in commercials, for syndicated radio shows, or for background music services (such as Muzak) requires permission from the music publisher and record company. The process for obtaining permission for these uses is similar.

If an advertising agency creates a new version of a song, it may only be required to obtain permission from the music publisher. If, however, the agency uses an already-recorded version of the song, it must get permission from both the music publisher and the record company. Using music in a radio or television commercial may also require

permission from the artist performing on the recording as described in Section D2. The same rule applies if the artist's style is imitated by another performer in a commercial.

1. Music Publisher Permissions and Fees

Music publishers grant "electrical transcription licenses" for the use of songs in radio commercials or syndicated radio programs. The music publisher may either furnish the electrical transcription license directly to the licensee or use the Harry Fox Agency to manage the licensing process. Electrical transcription licenses permit the radio program to copy the songs for its particular use. When songs are played on the radio, performing rights societies also collect fees from the radio stations for the performance of the songs. In this case, the radio ad or program does not need to get permission from BMI or ASCAP because the radio station that broadcasts the ad or program arranges for performing rights permission.

Fees for using songs in radio ads often start at $1,000 per week for local radio uses and may go as high as $100,000 per year for national radio uses. If a song is used in a syndicated radio show, the fees are often based on the number of copies of the program broadcast by syndicated stations (for example, $100 per station).

2. Record Company Permissions and Fees

To use an existing recording in a radio commercial or syndicated radio program, sound recording rights should be negotiated with the sound recording owner directly (generally a record company). To use a sound recording this way generally requires a one-time fee for the right to make copies of the sound recording. The amount the sound recording owner will charge varies widely depending on the length and type of use. As noted earlier in this chapter, record companies can be difficult to negotiate with and may charge exorbitant fees for authorizing the use of their recordings. As a result, it's often easier to record a new version of the song—which will only require the music publisher's permission—rather than use the recording itself.

In some countries—but not the U.S.—you must pay the owner of the sound recording when it is played on the radio. In these countries, two performance payments are required each time a radio station plays a song: one payment to the music publisher and another to the record company.

G. Using Music in a Film, Television Show, or Video

Music is an essential component of films, television shows, and videos. The businesses that produce these audiovisual works (known as production companies) generally acquire music rights either by hiring musicians to record music or by obtaining the rights to use an existing recording. If the production company hires musicians to record existing songs—for instance, hires musicians to play Beatles songs—the company needs permission from only the music publisher. If a film or video production company wants to use an existing recording—for example, a Tom Petty recording—it must acquire permission from both the music publisher and the owner of the sound recording (the record company).

 You can also get music for a film, TV show, or other type of program from production music libraries. PMLs, as they're typically called, have broad selections of music to which they own all rights. Licensing music from a PML is generally simple and inexpensive. See Section B5 for a more detailed description of PMLs. A list of PMLs appears at the end of this chapter.

In general, when you use a song in a movie—but not a particular recording of that song—you'll need to obtain a synchronization license from the music publisher. The term "synchronization" means simply that the song is being synchronized with the video track of the program. If you're using a record-

ing of the song that you had created for your movie, you'll also need to obtain the rights to the rerecording from the musicians you hired.

EXAMPLE: Dave is making a movie about Los Angeles and wants to use the song "I Love L.A." by Randy Newman. Dave cannot afford to pay for the Randy Newman master use rights (for the sound recording) so he hires a musician to rerecord the song. He uses a work-for-hire agreement to acquire ownership of the master recording from the musician. To use the song in his movie, Dave needs to obtain permission from only the music publisher of the song.

On the other hand, when you use a specific recording in a movie, you'll also need what's called a master use license from the record company. The term "master use" means you're obtaining permission from the record company to use the master recording of the song.

It's important to understand that to use a particular recording of a song in a movie, television program, or video, you'll generally need both a synchronization license (because you're using a song owned by the music publisher) and a master use license (because you're using the recording owned by the record company). An exception to this is if the song is in the public domain. In that case, you'd only need the master use license from the owner of the sound recording you're using—the protected specific version of the underlying song that is now in the public domain.

This section explains the types of permissions that are required to use music in film, television, or video, and the process for obtaining that permission.

 Acquiring permission for the use of music in motion pictures and videos can be complex. Older songs may be subject to copyright rules that resulted in a transfer of rights back to the original songwriter. If clearance is performed improperly, the costs of correcting permission errors can be substantial. For this reason, and to save time and money, many film and video production companies use music clearance services. These services are described in Section N, and a list of companies that perform these services is included at the end of this chapter.

Two helpful resources for clearing music for films are *Clearance & Copyright: Everything the Independent Filmmaker Needs to Know,* by Michael C. Donaldson (Silman-James Press), and *Kohn on Music Licensing,* by Al Kohn and Bob Kohn (Aspen Law & Business).

1. Synchronization Licenses

As mentioned above, you must obtain permission from the music publisher to use a song in a movie, television show, or video, whether you use an existing recording or create a new recording. The general term for an agreement to use a song in conjunction with a series of visual images—for example, in a television show or movie—is a "synchronization license." There are more specific names for this agreement depending on the type of program that will include the music. For a movie, the specific type of license is a "theatrical motion picture synchronization license." If a song is used in a television commercial, the license is called a "television commercial synchronization license."

In addition, if you plan to release the program on videos, DVDs, or the like for sale to the public, you must also obtain a "videogram license" from the music publisher. In other words, the music publisher's permission to use the song in a movie or other program does not authorize the use of the song on subsequent video or DVD releases of the same program. See Section G1c below for more information on videogram licenses.

The essential terms of the various types of synchronization agreements are very similar. Synchronization licenses for films can also be tailored to specific purposes—for example, for student films or film festival uses.

Granting of synchronization must be made by the music publisher. You can find contact information for the publisher of a particular song by searching for the song title on the websites of performing rights societies BMI, ASCAP, or SESAC. For information on locating music publishers, see Section L.

a. Videogram Licenses

If you use a song in a video or DVD you plan to sell to the public, you will need an additional permission from the music publisher called a "videogram license." Videogram licenses are required for any programs—such as theatrical films, television shows, exercise videos—that are made available for sale to the public on video, DVD, and the like. This is true whether the program was originally made for video or for cinema or TV and later released on video. The key here is that the video is available for sale to the public. If a music video were made, for instance, only to be shown on MTV and not to be sold to the public, a videogram license would not be necessary.

Fees for song rights for a video release of a theatrical motion picture may be several thousand dollars or, on occasion, may be tied to sales of the video. For example, under certain arrangements, an additional payment must be made if video sales pass a certain number. Corporate video uses may be charged a flat fee ($500 to $2,000) or may be tied to the number of units manufactured or distributed.

b. Synchronization Fees

Fees for using a song in a film depend on the nature of the film (documentary or theatrical; independent or major studio release) and the use in the film—whether the song is used in the background, foreground, or in some special manner (such as when a character sings the song). The fee for use of a song in the background of an independent documentary may start at $500. Fees for nontheatrical corporate video synchronization licenses may range from $500 to $1,500. Fees for using a song in an independent theatrical release may range from $5,000 to $15,000. Fees for use in a major motion picture are generally between $10,000 and $25,000. These synchronization fees do not include separate fees and royalties for videogram licenses, described above.

If you plan to make your program available for sale on video, DVD, or the like, you'll have to pay videogram fees as well. For more information on videogram licenses, see Section G1a, above.

c. Music Synchronization and Videogram License

Below is an agreement that provides for both synchronization and videogram rights from a music publisher. It can be used for any film or video that will be released in theaters or on video. This agreement can be used for purposes of comparison, since a music publisher will likely provide its own license agreement.

If the work will only be released on video and not theatrically, you can remove the synchronization language, as described in the explanation following the agreement. Although this agreement is for films and videos, much of the language and principles apply to other audiovisual uses as well.

A tear-out copy of this agreement is provided in the Appendix. A digital version is included on the forms CD.

Music Synchronization and Videogram License Agreement

Music Synchronization and Videogram License Agreement (the "Agreement") is made between:

_____ ("Publisher") and _____ ("Producer").

Publisher is the owner of rights for the compositions listed below:

_____

_____

(the "Compositions").

Producer is the owner of rights for the Motion Picture tentatively entitled _____

(the "Motion Picture"). Producer desires to license the Compositions for use in the Motion Picture and in audiovisual devices for home use such as videotapes and DVDs ("Videograms"). The parties agree as follows:

Grant

(select one or more Grant provisions)

☐ **Grant of Audiovisual License.** Publisher grants to Producer and Producer's successors and assigns the nonexclusive right to record the Compositions solely in synchronization with the Motion Picture (in any medium, now known or later created) within the Territory. Publisher grants to Producer the right to publicly perform the Compositions solely in synchronization to the Motion Picture within the Territory. These public performance rights include public exhibitions of the Motion Picture in theaters and other public places where motion pictures are customarily exhibited, provided that performances outside the United States are cleared by performing rights societies in accordance with customary practice and customary fees. The public performance rights also include television exhibition of the Motion Picture within the Territory, including all methods of television reproduction and transmissions, provided that the entities broadcasting those performances have licenses from the appropriate performing rights societies. Any television performance not licensed by performing rights societies must be cleared directly by the Publisher.

☐ **Grant of Videogram License.** Publisher grants to Producer and his successors and assigns the nonexclusive right to record, copy, and synchronize the Composition, solely as part of the Motion Picture, on audiovisual devices including, but not limited to, video cassettes, DVDs, and similar compact audiovisual devices that reproduce the entire Motion Picture in substantially its original form ("Videogram"). This Videogram license is solely for the distribution of Videograms intended primarily for home use in the Territory.

[ ] **Use in Trailers.** Publisher grants to Producer and his successors and assigns the nonexclusive right to record, copy, synchronize, and perform the Composition in connection with trailers used for the advertising and exploitation of the Motion Picture.

Reservation of Rights

Publisher reserves all rights not granted in this Agreement.

Modifications to Composition

Producer shall not make any change in the original lyrics, if any, or in the fundamental character of the music of the Composition or use the title or any portion of the lyrics of the Composition as the title or subtitle of the Motion Picture without written prior authorization from Publisher.

Territory

The rights granted in this Agreement are for the following: _____ (the "Territory").

Audiovisual License Payments

As payment for the rights granted for the Audiovisual License, Producer shall pay Publisher as follows:

(select payment option and fill in blanks)

[ ] **One-Time Payment.** Producer shall pay Publisher a one-time payment of $ _____ upon first public performance of the Motion Picture or within nine (9) months of signing this agreement, whichever is earlier.

[ ] **Advance and Royalties.** Producer shall pay Publisher a nonrefundable advance ("Motion Picture Advance") in the sum of $ _____ recoupable against royalties derived from the Audiovisual License ("Audiovisual Royalties"). Producer shall pay Publisher Audiovisual Royalties of ___% of net profits from the public exhibition and public performance of the Motion Picture.

[ ] **Royalties.** Producer shall pay Publisher _____ % of the net profits from the public exhibition and public performance of the Motion Picture.

Videogram License Payments

As payment for the rights granted for the Videogram License, Producer shall pay Publisher as follows: (select payment option and fill in blanks)

☐ **One-Time Payment.** Producer shall pay Publisher a one-time payment of $ _____ within nine (9) months of signing this agreement.

☐ **Advance and Royalties.** Producer shall pay Publisher a nonrefundable advance ("Videogram Advance") in the sum of $ _____ recoupable against royalties derived from the Videogram License ("Videogram Royalties"). Videogram Royalties for Videogram copies of the Motion Picture shall be paid as follows:

> ☐ **Net Profits.** Producer shall pay Publisher _____ % of the Producer's net profits for all Videogram revenues including all sales, licenses, or other sources of revenue for Videogram distribution (not including shipping charges or taxes).

> ☐ **Pro Rata Option.** Producer shall pay Publisher _____% ("Publisher's Pro-Rata Portion") of _____ % of the net revenue for all Videogram income including all sales, licenses, or other sources of revenue for Videogram distribution. Publisher's Pro-Rata Portion represents the proportion the Composition bears to the total number of Royalty-bearing compositions contained in the Motion Picture.

Payments & Statements

Within forty-five (45) days after the end of each calendar quarter (the "Royalty Period"), Producer shall furnish an accurate statement of net revenues derived from the licenses granted in this agreement along with any royalty payments. Producer may withhold a reasonable reserve for anticipated returns, refunds, and exchanges of Videograms, and this reserve shall be liquidated no later than twelve (12) months after the respective accounting statement.

Favorable Rates

If a higher royalty rate than set forth in this Agreement becomes payable by operation of law with respect to Videograms sold in a particular country within the Territory, Producer shall either pay the higher royalty to Publisher with respect to that country or delete the Compositions from the Motion Picture with respect to this country. In the event that a musical composition is licensed for a substantially similar use in connection with the Videogram exploitation of the Motion Picture on a more favorable rate, Producer agrees that such favorable rate shall also be granted to Publisher for the licensing of the Composition.

Audit

Producer shall keep accurate books of account and records covering all transactions relating to the licenses granted in this Agreement, and Publisher or its duly authorized representatives shall have the right upon five (5) days prior written notice, and during normal business hours, to inspect and audit these accounts and records.

Warranty

Publisher warrants that it has the power and authority to grant the rights in this Agreement and that the Compositions do not infringe any third-party rights. In no event shall Publisher's liability for a breach of this Warranty exceed the amount of payments received under this Agreement.

Credits

Publisher shall receive credit in the following form: _____ .

This credit shall be provided as follows:

(select all that apply)

☐ similar to all other musical compositions used in the Motion Picture.

☐ a single card in the main titles on all prints of the Motion Picture and Videograms.

☐ in all paid advertising similar to all other musical compositions used in the Motion Picture.

Samples

Producer shall promptly furnish Publisher with _____ copies of each format of Videogram release.

Cue Sheets

Producer agrees to furnish Publisher a cue sheet of the Motion Picture within thirty (30) days after the first public exhibition of the Motion Picture.

Term

The term of this Agreement is for the term of United States copyright in the Composition including renewal terms, if any.

Termination & Breach

In the event that Producer (or Producer's assigns or licensees) breach this Agreement and fails to cure such breach within thirty (30) days after notice by Publisher to Producer, this license will automatically terminate and all rights granted under this Agreement shall revert to Publisher. Failure to make timely payments or to provide credit as provided in this Agreement shall be considered a material breach of this Agreement.

Miscellaneous

This Agreement may not be amended except in a writing signed by both parties. If a court finds any provision of this Agreement invalid or unenforceable, the remainder of this Agreement shall be interpreted so as best to effect the intent of the parties. This Agreement shall be governed by and interpreted in accordance with the laws of the State of _____ . This Agreement expresses the complete understanding of the parties with respect to the subject matter and supersedes all prior representations and understandings. Any controversy or claim arising out of or relating to this Agreement shall be settled by binding arbitration in accordance with the rules of the American Arbitration Association, and judgment upon the award rendered by the arbitrator(s) may be entered in any court having jurisdiction. All notices provided for under this Agreement must be in writing and mailed to the addresses provided in the signature portion of this Agreement.

_____

PUBLISHER

_____

PRODUCER

d. Explanation for Music Synchronization and Videogram License

- The **introductory paragraph** identifies the companies entering into the agreement (the "parties"). Insert the name of music publisher ("Publisher") and producer ("Producer") of the film or video. Sometimes, a synchronization license may substitute the terms "Licensee" for Producer and "Licensor" for Publisher. The terms "Television Show" or "Audiovisual Work," if applicable, can be substituted for the term "Motion Picture." In this event, change all references throughout the agreement.

- The **Grant** provisions establish the rights under copyright law (the licenses) that the music publisher is granting to the film producer. The **Grant of Audiovisual License** establishes the right to synchronize—or use—the music in conjunction with public presentations of the film or video—for example, in theaters or on a television broadcast. The **Grant of Videogram License** establishes the right to synchronize—or use the music with the video version of the motion picture—as well as to make copies for sale for home use. If the licensee is going "direct to video" and the film will not be shown in theaters, he or she does not need the Grant of Videogram License, so do not check the box. If no video rights are sought and the film will only be shown in theaters, the licensee does not need the Grant of Videogram License, so do not check the box. The **Use in Trailers** section permits the use of the Composition in trailers advertising the film.

- The **Reservation of Rights** section establishes that any rights not covered in this agreement are held by the music publisher.

- The **Modifications to Composition** section provides that the producer must acquire written permission from the music publisher to make modifications to the song. Failure to obtain permission may endanger the rights to use the music.

- As for the **Territory,** worldwide rights are preferred if the producer intends to show or distribute the film outside the U.S. If the publisher cannot grant worldwide rights, permission will be required from the holder of rights (usually a foreign music publisher) in each country in which the film will be distributed.

- There are separate payment sections for the audiovisual and the videogram licenses. For each one, choose the payment method that reflects the agreement with the publisher. For the **Audiovisual License Payments,** you can choose either a one-time payment, an advance against royalties, or royalties with no advance. For the **Videogram License Payments,** you can choose a one-time payment or an advance against royalties. You also can choose which type of royalties you will pay—royalties based on net profits or prorated royalties. The pro rata choice provides that you pay a portion of income to the publisher based on the total number of songs being used in the video. For example if ten songs are used on a video, each publisher would receive 1/10 of the music royalty. If you choose this option, enter the composition's proportional share of the whole video in the first blank and the overall royalty rate in the second blank. If there is no videogram license, do not check any options in the Videogram License Payments section.

- The provision entitled **Favorable Rates** is sometimes referred to as a "Most Favored Nation" clause. It provides that if a country establishes a higher rate of payment for any of the uses described in this agreement, the producer must pay the higher rate. Some film producers may not want to include this provision.

- The **Warranty** is a contractual promise that the publisher is legally capable to grant the rights in this agreement. The last sentence in the Warranty section limits the amount of damages the publisher must pay if it breaches the warranty.

- In the **Credits** section, the publisher will establish the type and size of credit the producer should use. A failure to properly credit the composition may result in a loss of licensing rights. The term "single card" refers to a separate credit on a screen with no other credits.
- If the publisher wants the producer to provide samples, indicate the number agreed upon in the **Samples** section.
- A **Cue Sheet** lists each separate musical use on a film or video. This provision simply provides that you will furnish one to the publisher within 30 days of the program's public premiere.
- For an explanation of the **Term, Termination,** and **Miscellaneous** sections, see Chapter 11, "Art and Merchandise Licenses."
- The agreement must be signed by individuals with the authority to represent the music publisher and the film production company. For information about determining who has authority to sign (also known as "signing capacity"), see the explanation in Chapter 11, Section C22.

2. Master Use Licenses

To use a particular recording on a motion picture sound track, the record company that owns the recording must grant a master use license. For instance, if a filmmaker wants to use a recording—not a remake—of Johnny Cash's "Ring of Fire" in a film, the filmmaker will need to obtain a master use license from the record company that owns the recording. The license permits the filmmaker to duplicate the recording on the film sound track. The cost of the master use license depends on the size and type of production and the prominence of the song use within the film (for example, in the foreground or in the background). The cost may range from a few hundred dollars for a student film to thousands of dollars for a feature film.

If a sound track album is released, the record company that owns the original recording will seek a percentage, or "royalty," based upon the sound track album's sales. In some cases, a record company may seek an advance payment plus a "rollover"—a payment made when a certain number of video or soundtrack copies have been sold. Costs are also affected by extra payments (known as "reuse fees") that the record company must make to union and guild members who worked on the recording.

a. Videogram Licenses

If the program will be released on video, DVD, and the like, you must also obtain a videogram license from the record company. In other words, the record company's permission to use the recording in a movie or other program does not authorize the use of the recording on video or DVD releases of the same program. If your program will be available for sale to the public on video (as opposed to shown on MTV but not sold), you'll need a videogram license regardless of the original format of the program. For more on videogram licenses, see Section G1a, above.

b. Master Use and Videogram License

Below is an agreement that provides for both master use and videogram rights from the owner of a sound recording (a record company). It can be used for any film or video that will be released in theaters or on video. Although this agreement is for films and videos, much of the language and principles apply to other audiovisual uses as well.

 A tear-out copy of this agreement is provided in the Appendix. A digital version is included on the forms CD.

If you're obtaining a master use license, you probably need a synchronization license as well. For example, if a producer is obtaining master use rights from a record company to use a specific recording of the song "Stand By Me" in a film, he or she must also obtain synchronization rights from the music publisher of "Stand By Me." However, you won't need synchronization rights from the music publisher if the recorded song you want to use is in the public domain. In that case, you'd only need a master use license from the owner of the specific recording you want to use.

Master Use and Videogram License

This Master Use and Videogram License Agreement (the "Agreement") is made between:

_____ ("Owner") and _____ ("Producer").

Owner is the owner of rights for the master recordings: _____

_____

_____

(the "Masters").

Producer is the owner of rights for the Motion Picture tentatively entitled _____
 (the "Motion Picture").

Producer desires to license the Masters for use in the Motion Picture and in audiovisual devices for home use such as videotapes and DVDs ("Videograms"). The parties agree as follows:

Grant

(select one or more Grant provisions if applicable)

☐   **Grant of Audiovisual License.** Owner grants to Producer and Producer's successors and assigns the nonexclusive right to use and reproduce the Masters solely in synchronization with the Motion Picture in any medium, now known or later created within the Territory. Owner grants to Producer the right to publicly perform the Masters solely in synchronization to the Motion Picture within the Territory. These public performance rights include the public exhibitions of the Motion Picture in theaters and other public places where motion pictures are customarily exhibited and for television exhibition of the Motion Picture including all methods of television reproduction and transmissions within the Territory.

☐   **Grant of Videogram License.** Owner grants to Producer and Producer's successors and assigns the nonexclusive right to record, copy, and synchronize the Masters, solely as part of the Motion Picture, on audiovisual devices including, but not limited to video cassettes, DVDs, and similar compact audiovisual devices that reproduce the entire motion picture in substantially its original form ("Videogram"). This Videogram license is solely for the distribution of Videograms intended primarily for home use in the Territory.

☐   **Use in Trailers.** Owner grants to Producer and Producer's successors and assigns, the nonexclusive right to record, copy, synchronize, and perform the Masters in connection with trailers used for the advertising and exploitation of the Motion Picture.

Reservation of Rights

Owner reserves all rights not granted in this Agreement.

Modifications to Masters

Producer shall not make any change in the Masters without written prior authorization from Owner.

Territory

The rights granted in this Agreement are for the following: _____
(the "Territory").

Union Re-use Fees

Owner agrees to provide Producer with all information regarding any reuse fees required by unions or guilds as a result of this license. Producer agrees to pay all such reuse payments including related pension or welfare payments and to indemnify Owner from claims arising from such payments.

Musical Works Synchronization Rights

Producer agrees to obtain all appropriate synchronization, performance, and reproduction rights for the musical compositions embodied on the Masters and to indemnify Owner for any claims arising from such rights.

Audiovisual License Payments

As payment for the rights granted for the Audiovisual License, Producer shall pay Owner as follows: (select payment option and fill in blanks)

☐ **One-Time Payment.** Producer shall pay Owner a one-time payment of $_____ upon first public performance of the Motion Picture or within nine (9) months of signing this agreement, whichever is earlier.

☐ **Advance and Royalties.** Producer shall pay Owner a nonrefundable advance ("Motion Picture Advance") in the sum of $_____ recoupable against royalties derived from the Audiovisual License ("Audiovisual Royalties"). Producer shall pay Owner Audiovisual Royalties of __% of net profits from the public exhibition and public performance of the Motion Picture.

[ ] **Royalties.** Producer shall pay Owner _____ % of the net profits from the public exhibition and public performance of the Motion Picture.

Videogram License Payments

As payment for the rights granted for the Videogram License, Producer shall pay Owner as follows: (select payment option and fill in blanks)

[ ] **One-Time Payment.** Producer shall pay Owner a one-time payment of $ _____ within nine (9) months of signing this agreement.

[ ] **Advance and Royalties.** Producer shall pay Owner a nonrefundable advance ("Videogram Advance") in the sum of $ _____ recoupable against royalties derived from the Videogram License ("Videogram Royalties"). Videogram Royalties for Videogram copies of the Motion Picture shall be paid as follows:

    [ ] **Net Profits.** Producer shall pay Owner _____ % of the Producer's net profits for all Videogram revenues including all sales, licenses, or other sources of revenue for Videogram distribution (not including shipping charges or taxes).

    [ ] **Pro Rata Option.** Producer shall pay Owner _____ % ("Owner's Pro-Rata Portion") of _____ % of the net revenue for all Videogram income including all sales, licenses, or other sources of revenue for Videogram distribution. Owner's Pro-Rata Portion represents the proportion the Composition bears to the total number of Royalty-bearing compositions contained in the Motion Picture.

Payments & Statements

Within forty-five (45) days after the end of each calendar quarter (the "Royalty Period"), Producer shall furnish an accurate statement of net revenues derived from the licenses granted in this agreement along with any royalty payments. Producer may withhold a reasonable reserve for anticipated returns, refunds, and exchanges of Videograms, and this reserve shall be liquidated no later than twelve (12) months after the respective accounting statement.

Audit

Producer shall keep accurate books of account and records covering all transactions relating to the licenses granted in this Agreement, and Owner or its duly authorized representatives shall have the right upon five (5) days prior written notice, and during normal business hours, to inspect and audit these accounts and records.

Warranty

Owner warrants that it has the power and authority to grant the rights in this Agreement and that the Masters do not infringe any third-party rights. In no event shall Owner's liability for a breach of this warranty exceed the amount of payments received under this Agreement.

Credits

Owner shall receive credit in the following form: _____

This credit shall be provided as follows:

(select one or more if appropriate)

☐ similar to all other Masters used in the Motion Picture.

☐ in all paid advertising similar to all other musical Masters used in the Motion Picture.

Samples

Producer shall promptly furnish Owner with ___ copies of each format of Videogram release.

Cue Sheets

Producer agrees to furnish Owner a cue sheet of the Motion Picture within thirty (30) days after the first public exhibition of the Motion Picture.

Term

The term of this Agreement is for the term of United States copyright in the Masters including renewal terms, if any.

Termination & Breach

In the event that Producer (or Producer's assigns or licensees) breach this Agreement and fails to cure such breach within thirty (30) days after notice by Owner to Producer, this license will automatically terminate and all rights granted under this Agreement shall revert to Owner. Failure to make timely payments or to provide credit as provided in this Agreement shall be considered a material breach of this Agreement.

Miscellaneous

This Agreement may not be amended except in a writing signed by both parties. If a court finds any provision of this Agreement invalid or unenforceable, the remainder of this Agreement shall be interpreted so as best to effect the intent of the parties. This Agreement shall be governed by and interpreted in accordance with the laws of the State of _____ . This Agreement expresses the complete understanding of the parties with respect to the subject matter and supersedes all prior representations and understandings. Any controversy or claim arising out of or relating to this Agreement shall be settled by binding arbitration in accordance with the rules of the American Arbitration Association, and judgment upon the award rendered by the arbitrator(s) may be entered in any court having jurisdiction. All notices provided for under this Agreement must be in writing and mailed to the addresses provided in the signature portion of this Agreement.

_____

OWNER

_____

PRODUCER

c. Explanation for Master Use License and Videogram License

- The **introductory paragraph** identifies the companies entering into the agreement (the "parties"). In the Owner blank, insert the name of the owner of the masters (usually the record company), and in the Producer blank enter the name of the producer of the film or video. Sometimes, a synchronization license may substitute the terms "Licensee" for Producer and "Licensor" for Owner. The terms "Television Show" or "Audiovisual Work," if applicable, can be substituted for the term "Motion Picture." In this event, change all references throughout the agreement.

- For explanations of the sections regarding the **Grant, Reservation of Rights, Modifications to Masters, Territory, License Payments, Payments & Statements, Audit, Warranty, Credits, Samples,** and **Cue Sheet** provisions, see the explanation provided to the Music Synchronization and Videogram License Agreement in Section G1d above. For an explanation of the **Term, Termination,** and **Miscellaneous** sections, see Chapter 11, "Art and Merchandise Licenses."

- The **Union Reuse Fees** and **Musical Works Synchronization Rights** sections refer to obligations of the producer. Reuse fees are payments that must be made to the union musicians and engineers who created the masters whenever the masters are used for additional purposes. Musical works synchronization rights are rights that must be obtained from the music publisher to use the song composition. You can acquire synchronization rights from the music publisher by using the Music Synchronization and Videogram License in Section G1.

H. Performing a Musical or Play

Let's put on a show! If you and some friends decide to rebuild your community playhouse for a production of *Rent* or *Cats*, you'll need to first obtain permission from the rights holder of the musical. The procedure is fairly straightforward: identify the work, identify the rights holder, and secure permission. (If you intend to produce a dramatic nonmusical such as *Waiting for Godot*, the rules are the same.)

Before printing posters and buying ad space for your show, check to see if your choice is available for production. Some musicals and dramatic plays are not available (referred to as "restricted"). In this case, you'll have to move on to your second choice. Assuming your choice is available, here are the ground rules for putting on a live show.

1. Payments

Your payment for rights to perform a musical or play is a "royalty" and does not include the cost of acquiring copies of the piano/conductor score, chorus books, or scripts. There are separate fees for permission to make and distribute these copies. In addition, some musicals require payment of a security deposit.

Royalties are charged for all live performances, whether or not admission is charged. Sometimes, a rights holder will provide two royalty quotes, one for the first performance and the second for succeeding performances.

Usually, you can easily and inexpensively get approval online or by phone for live stage productions by amateur groups with maximum seating capacities of 400 or less. The approval process may involve more negotiation and detail if you're a professional group or amateur group with large seating capacity. Most of the time, you'll pay royalties before performing the work.

2. Rights

Rights owners of musicals and dramatic works commonly put restrictions on performances. They require special permission for performances that include television and radio broadcasting (if you intend to videotape, you'll probably need prior approval). Some rights holders require special clearance for performances in certain cities, for example New York City and Los Angeles. Owners typically insist that authorship credit appear on all on all programs, printing, and advertising for the play.

Other restrictions may include the requirement that the production not deviate from its "published form." One musical publishing house explains it this way:

"The author's intent will be respected in production. No changes, interpolations, or deletions in the text, lyrics, music, title, or gender of the characters shall be made for the purpose of production. This includes changes or updating the time and place/setting of the play. In reference to changing the gender of characters, men will play male roles and women will play female roles."

3. Acquiring Permission

The easiest way to determine who owns the performance rights to a musical or play is to examine a copy of the script. If a copy is not available, check the well-known musical and play publishing houses—for example, the Samuel French Company or Tams-Witmark Musical Library. (Contact information is provided at the end of this chapter.)

Once you've located the rights holder, contact them. They will want to know some basic information, such as the work, location of the performance, seating capacity, ticket prices, whether it's a non-profit performance, the dates for the production, and whether it is a union (Actors' Equity) or non-union show.

Normally, the rights holder will respond shortly with a price quote. Once you accept the quote and pay any required security deposit (usually refundable), it's show time!

I. Using Music in Software, Videogames, or Multimedia Programs

As the sound quality available on computers and videogames has improved, so has the quality of music used in conjunction with software programs. Preparing or acquiring music for popular software products has become a major enterprise, sometimes involving specially scored works by Hollywood film composers.

Software companies commonly acquire music rights by hiring musicians or purchasing music from production music libraries. When a software company hires musicians, it acquires ownership rights to the music they create by assignment or under work-for-hire agreements, as explained in Chapter 15.

On some occasions, however, software companies may use preexisting songs or recordings for video games, educational software, multimedia presentations, or MIDI software (a format used for transmitting musical data). This section deals with situations in which a software company wants to use preexisting music in its products.

1. Music Publisher Permission and Fees

If the software company is rerecording a song, permission is required from the music publisher (usually through the Harry Fox Agency).

EXAMPLE: Softco creates a software program for guitar students and records a new version of the song "Layla." Softco must obtain permission from the music publisher of the song.

Licenses to incorporate music in software or multimedia programs are usually negotiated directly with the Harry Fox Agency, a company that represents music publishers for certain reproduction rights. A sample copy of the Harry Fox multimedia license (the "MMERL License") can be downloaded from their website (listed in Section O3.)

If music is to be used in connection with audio-visual images, such as in an interactive video game, a multimedia synchronization license, similar to the agreement in Section G1, is required. If the music is intended for use in a karaoke program, the content of the license depends upon whether the device will display the lyrics, whether film or video imagery will be synchronized with the music, and whether the program is intended for private or public karaoke uses. Some publishers will charge an additional "fixing fee" for the right to synchronize the music with the visual imagery.

Most music publishers will demand an advance payment from you that you can deduct from any ongoing royalties you owe for use of the music. Advance payments may be several hundred to several thousand dollars depending on the song and use. Royalty rates for multimedia uses also depend on the use. Use of a song in a videogame may range from 0.5% to 1% of the retail price, while royalties for use of a song in MIDI software may start at 5% of the retail price. Fees are often prorated based on the total number of songs included on the software. For typical multimedia CD-ROM uses, the royalty is between 5 and 15 cents per unit, and advances starting at $250 are often required. Few publishers will allow multimedia use of a song for a flat fee. (Flat fee payments are common when using music from production music libraries however. See Section B5.)

2. Record Company Permission and Fees

If a software company is duplicating a previously released recording, permission is required from the record company that owns the recording in addition to the music publisher that owns the song.

EXAMPLE: Softco creates a software program for guitar students and incorporates a specific Eric Clapton recording of the song "Layla." Softco must obtain permission from the record company that owns the recording and from the music publisher of the song.

The form you use to obtain permission from the record company is referred to as a multimedia or software master use license and is usually supplied by the record company. This license is similar to the master use license in Section G2.

A software company should expect to pay a minimum of $500 to $1,000 as an advance fee for use of the master sound recording, plus a continuing royalty. This royalty is separate from the royalty the company must pay the music publisher for use of the song itself (described in Section I1, above). Because of this, software companies often seek to avoid paying two royalties by rerecording songs instead of using existing recordings.

J. Using Music on a Website

Using the Internet, it is possible to preview music before buying a record, download a song by a pop artist, or copy and send a song from one destination to the other—all with perfect sound clarity. With these capabilities have come a new set of rules for Internet users. There are two common ways that music is transmitted over the Internet:

- The song is made available for **digital downloading**—that is, a copy is delivered from a website to users' computers. When downloading, the user obtains a copy. As of the writing of this book, the most popular downloading format is known as MP3.
- The song is broadcast in real time (known as **"webcasting"** or **"audio streaming"**). The listener hears the song as it is played by an Internet website and may or may not have the opportunity to make a digital copy.

Below we discuss both methods of transmitting music and the permissions required for each use.

1. MP3s and Downloading Music

The process of downloading music files, such as MP3 files, is called "digital phonorecord delivery." MP3 is a computer standard that enables a recording to be compressed so that it can be transmitted faster than uncompressed recordings. Other downloadable formats are being developed by the music industry.

EXAMPLE: Kinksology is a website that features music of the rock group The Kinks. Don visits the site, clicks on the song title "You Really Got Me," and an MP3 file with The Kinks' song is downloaded onto Don's computer. Don can play this MP3 file on his computer or on a portable MP3 player. Kinksology is providing digital phonorecord delivery.

Any website providing digital phonorecord delivery must obtain permission from the owner of the song (music publisher) and the owner of the sound recording (record company). The recording industry and music publishers have made it clear—with lawsuits against MP3.com and the file-sharing site, Napster—that they will pursue illegal distribution of recorded music in MP3 format.

a. Music Publisher Permission

To provide digital phonorecord delivery, you must get permission from the music publisher. The rules for how to pay the music publisher are evolving. Music publishers currently seek to get paid in two ways (referred to as "double-dipping"): once for the reproduction of the MP3 file and again for the transmission of the file over the Internet. Each of the payments and permission are discussed below.

- **Payment to the music publisher for reproduction.** If a song was previously recorded and released in the U.S., you can obtain permission to reproduce it using a compulsory license (as described in Section E1) or by ne-

gotiating a digital delivery license directly with the Harry Fox Agency (as described in Section E2).

- **Payment to the music publisher for transmission.** Currently, you must also negotiate a performance license and fee with the appropriate performing rights societies (see Section J2a, below) for the right to transmit a digital recording such as an MP3. Contact the performing rights society and request a license for digital phonorecord delivery.

Both BMI and ASCAP grant blanket licenses for website uses. The minimum fees for these licenses range from $250 to $500, but total annual fees may be higher depending on the website's revenue. Both BMI and ASCAP offer formulas based on a percentage (ranging between 1.6% and 2.5%) of the net revenue of the website. To determine the amount, visit each performing rights society's website and download its website license. Rate calculations are located on the last page of each agreement. For information on determining whether BMI or ASCAP represents a music publisher, review Section L.

b. MP3 Sound Recording Permission

In addition, digital phonorecord delivery, such as providing MP3 files for downloading, requires permission from the sound recording owner, usually a record company. This can prove to be an expensive and time-consuming procedure because most record companies are wary of licensing rights for making digital copies of their sound recordings. For information about locating record companies, see Section M.

2. Webcasting and Audio Streaming

Webcasting and audio streaming are processes by which digital music is broadcast over the Internet, much like a radio station broadcasts music. The computer user hears the music simultaneously as it is being played by the website. Both webcasting and audio streaming are referred to as "digital audio transmissions." The music industry characterizes digital audio transmissions as either being interactive or noninteractive.

a. Interactive Digital Audio Transmissions

An interactive digital audio transmission is one in which a user requests a performance of a particular recording, usually by clicking on a song title. This type of transmission is popular for purposes of promoting recordings.

> EXAMPLE: Kinksology is a website that features music of the rock group The Kinks. Don visits the site, clicks on the song title, "You Really Got Me," and hears The Kinks' song. Don does not receive a copy of the song on his computer. He can only hear it by clicking on the button. Kinksology is providing interactive digital audio transmissions.

The rules for interactive digital audio transmission are the same as for MP3. The website must obtain two permissions from the music publisher: a blanket license from the appropriate performing rights society (such as BMI or ASCAP) for the performance (transmission) of the song and a mechanical license for the reproduction of the song, usually from the Harry Fox Agency. The website must also obtain permission from the sound recording owner, usually a record company, to transmit a particular recording of the song. This permission must be negotiated directly with the record company.

The 30-Second Exception

Music publishers and record companies have reached an agreement between themselves to permit the interactive broadcast of a maximum of 30 seconds of a recording for promotional purposes. This agreement is solely between music publishers and record companies and can be used only to promote their own music and recordings. A website owner that does not own rights in either the sound recording or song cannot participate in this 30-second exception. However, as a practical matter, permission is routinely granted for 30-second digital audio segments of recordings used to promote the sale of those recordings.

b. Noninteractive Digital Audio Transmissions

A noninteractive digital audio transmission is one in which a website broadcasts various recordings over the Internet, much like a radio station, typically referred to as webcasting. Listeners can tune in or out at any time to listen to what is being broadcast. Unlike downloading MP3s, a listener does not receive a copy of any music he or she hears on his or her own computer. A listener can request to hear a particular song via email and, like a radio station, all listeners to the webcast will hear that requested song.

> EXAMPLE: 60s.com is a website that broadcasts music of the 1960s. Don visits the site and hears various songs. Don does not receive a copy of the songs on his computer. He emails a request and, when it is broadcast, all listeners to 60s.com hear the song on their computers. 60s.com is providing noninteractive digital audio transmissions.

A website offering noninteractive digital audio transmission (a "webcaster") must obtain permission from the music publisher in the form of a blanket performance license granted by the performing rights societies. Information about blanket performance licenses is provided in Section D1.

A webcaster must also follow certain rules and pay a fee, fixed by law, to the record company. This permits webcasters to make single copies of recordings necessary in webcasting (known as "ephemeral recordings"). The rules to qualify are lengthy and include requirements such as:

- the digital broadcast cannot be interactive
- the broadcast cannot activate remote recording devices, and
- during a three-hour broadcast period, a site cannot program more than three songs from a single album, nor play two songs in a row from a single album.

More information on these rules can be obtained from the U.S. Copyright Office website (www .copyright.gov).

c. Simulcasting

Local radio stations sometimes send their broadcast signal through the Internet, a practice known as "simulcasting." Simulcasting radio stations are required to pay a licensing fee but follow a simpler set of rules than for noninteractive digital audio transmissions. However, national radio broadcasting companies have announced their opposition to these rules and a court battle is expected to resolve the dispute. To learn more about the rules, visit the U.S. Copyright Office website (www.copyright.gov).

K. Using Music Samples

Sampling is the process of copying a piece of recorded music (usually on a device known as a sampler) and then reproducing it within another recording. Sometimes the sample is used repeatedly, such as a drumbeat or a vocal chorus. Sometimes a sample is used once or twice to accent a composition. Although there are some exceptions for trivial or unrecognizable samples, as a general rule, sampling is illegal without the authorization of the owner of the recording (the record company) and the owner of the song (the music publisher) being sampled.

There are no standardized fees or procedures for obtaining sampling permission, which can prove to be an expensive and time-consuming process. Some artists have had to give up one-third to one-half of their income from a song in order to acquire sampling permissions for the samples it includes.

There are several factors that make getting permission to use a sample a murky subject.

- As discussed throughout this chapter, there are two overlapping copyrights on a record: the song composition copyright and the sound recording copyright. When you take an excerpt of a song recording, you may be infringing both the songwriter's copyright and the copyright for the recording. It may seem that the songwriter's permission wouldn't be necessary—for example, when you want to sample only a few drum beats—but it's not always clear (see "Vocalizing is Not Composing: The Beastie Boys Case," below). Because of this, most record companies producing a song that contains samples play it safe and obtain permission from both the owner of the song (the music publisher) and the owner of the recorded music (the record company) being sampled.
- To make matters more confusing, a music publisher may not be entitled to a payment for some samples, such as the use of James Brown's voice saying "Get Down," because copyright law does not protect short phrases. However, James Brown may have a separate claim under a legal right known as the right of publicity, which protects a celebrity's right to control the use of his image, voice, or persona.
- Also, some samples may be used without permission under "fair use" principles that allow

you to use a short sample for purposes of commentary or criticism. Unfortunately, it's not always clear what constitutes fair use, and most users of samples cannot afford the legal costs to find out. For example, in one case, a judge ruled that the use of a sample was so inconsequential that it did not violate copyright law. But by the time the judge made the decision, both sides in the case had spent thousands in legal fees. For more on fair use, see Chapter 9.

- Despite these considerations, a sample may go unnoticed entirely. Because of this, you need to decide whether to bother with obtaining permission for your sample. See Section K3, below.

For an hourly fee, clearance experts often negotiate these issues or review recordings to determine if a sampling problem exists. You can find clearance experts online by typing "Sample Clearance" or "Music Clearance" into your Internet search engine. Some resources are also listed at the end of this chapter. The following section explains the basic rules and provides a model agreement for obtaining permission to use a music sample.

Sampling the Majors

Major publishers and labels are finally waking up to the sample clearance business. In 1999, when the first edition of this book appeared, only entertainment lawyers could get through the phone lines at the big music companies. Now, many companies are offering online sample clearance. Universal Music (www.universalmusicpublishing .com) and BMG Music (www.bmgmusicsearch .com) are among the major players now offering clearance request forms online.

Vocalizing Is Not Composing: The Beastie Boys Case

When the Beastie Boys recorded the song "Pass the Mic," they repeated a six-second sample from a song entitled "Choir," off an album by award-winning flautist James Newton, Jr. The sample consisted of a three-note pattern (C, D-flat, C), which Newton simultaneously sang and played in a method known as "vocalization." The Beastie Boys obtained permission to use the sample from ECM, the label that owned the sound recording copyright, but failed to get permission from Newton, the owner of the musical composition copyright. Newton sued and, in 2002, a federal judge ruled that the three-note pattern from "Choir" was not, by itself, a protectible composition, so permission from Newton was not necessary. In other words, the three-note pattern, even though it included Newton's rare vocalization skills, was not original enough to merit a payment—it was "de minimis" (too small to matter). *Newton v. Diamond*, 204 F. Supp. 2d 1244, (N.D. Cal. 2002).

If this case is an indication of judicial trends, you may need only one permission—the sound recording owner's—for short samples consisting of generic musical notes or patterns. Unfortunately, there's no sure-fire method of predicting whether your situation mirrors that of the Beastie Boys and only a federal court can determine who is right. You, unlike the Beastie Boys, may not be able to afford a lengthy legal battle if a music publisher chases you. When in doubt as how to proceed, seek advice from a sample clearance expert or a music business attorney.

1. Licenses and Fees for Sampling

While there are no standardized fees for sampling, the music publisher will usually want an advance payment (between $250 and $5,000) plus a percentage of the income derived from the new recording (usually between 15% and 50%). In addition, the owner of the master recording may want an upfront payment (usually at least $1,000) plus a "rollover"—a payment that must be made when a certain number of copies have been sold. Sometimes, instead of a rollover, the owner of the master may want a portion of future record royalties (although sampling consultants advise against this practice).

Record companies and music publishers typically provide sample clearance agreements. You'll also find copies of model sampling agreements in *Music Law: How to Run Your Band's Business* (Nolo), or available to download from the Nolo website (www.nolo.com) for a fee.

2. Reducing Sample Fees

Part of the sampling clearance fees can be avoided by rerecording the sampled section. Instead of sampling the original recording, a company can hire musicians to play the parts, creating a new recording that sounds very similar to the original. In that case, permission is required from the music publisher only. However, this imitation may require additional permissions if it is used to sell a service or product (see Section F).

Likewise, you can avoid paying fees to a music publisher by using a sample of a song that is in the public domain. Do not assume, however, that sampling fees will be avoided entirely by sampling public domain songs. The sound recording may be protected even though the song is in the public domain, requiring permission from (and payment to) the record company that released the recording you wish to sample.

EXAMPLE: In 2004, the singer P.J. Harvey records and releases the public domain song, "I Dream of Jeannie With the Light Brown Hair." George samples the recording and includes the sample on his new album. Although the song is in the public domain, the P.J. Harvey sound recording is not. George must obtain permission from P.J. Harvey's record company.

Of course, all sampling fees can be avoided by rerecording public domain songs. Companies also save money by using sample discs available from production music libraries and other sources. These recordings contain short musical parts that are "pre-cleared." Sample discs grant the user an "unlimited nonexclusive license" to use the samples once the disc is purchased. Always read the accompanying shrink-wrap or license agreement to verify this right before purchasing such a disc. Sample discs are not the same as PML music (see Section B5) and can be purchased through music stores and music supply catalogues. Advertisements for sample discs appear regularly in various music magazines such as *Keyboard* and *Electronic Musician*.

3. Operating Without Sample Clearance

Not every use of a sample constitutes an infringement. If an average listener comparing both works (the new composition and the source) can't hear any substantial similarities, there's no violation of the law. It is also possible that the use of a sample may qualify as fair use. The rap group 2 Live Crew's use of the musical tag and opening line lyric from the song "Oh Pretty Woman" was considered to be a fair use because it was limited (the sampled section was used once) and for purposes of parody. *(Campbell v. Acuff-Rose Music,* 510 U.S. 569 (1994).) For more information on fair use, see Chapter 9.

4. Using Samples to Sell a Product or Service

If a sample is used to sell or endorse a product (for example, using James Brown's voice in a Nike ad), and the sampled performer is identifiable, the sampler must obtain the performer's consent. Without consent, the source artist could sue for violation of the right of publicity (see Chapter 12, "Releases"). The same rule would apply if the performer's voice is imitated by another singer.

L. Finding Music Publishers

The easiest method to locate the music publisher of a song is to search the online song databases at the three performing rights societies, BMI (www.bmi.com), ASCAP (www.ascap.com), and SESAC (www.sesac .com). Alternatively, you can search all three societies at the website of the Music Publishers' Association (www.mpa.org/copyright/searchenter.html). These three societies represent all types of music, although SESAC's catalogue is primarily gospel and country music.

Performing rights societies do not own songs; they represent music publishers for purposes of negotiating certain types of permissions. A song is usually listed with only one of the performing rights societies, although occasionally, songs written by more than one person may be listed in the catalogues for both societies. Online song databases can be searched by title, writer, performer, or publisher. If you don't have access to the Internet, call the performing rights society and ask for writer/publisher information.

If you cannot locate a song through BMI, ASCAP, or SESAC, check the song database at the Harry Fox Agency (www.harryfox.com) which represents approximately 80% of U.S. music publishers (see "How Is Harry Fox Different from BMI, ASCAP, and SESAC," in Section D1). Harry Fox differs from the performing rights societies in that it deals with permission for copying a song onto a CD or tape (referred to as "mechanical rights") rather than performing a song publicly. Mechanical rights permissions are discussed in more detail throughout this chapter.

> **EXAMPLE:** I wanted to find the music publisher of "Ring of Fire." I started by searching the BMI and ASCAP databases online. The BMI database provided three different songs entitled "Ring of Fire." Johnny Cash recorded the version I wanted. Searching the BMI database by artist, I discovered numerous songs recorded by Johnny Cash including "Ring of Fire," for which BMI included the following information:
> Writers: June Carter & Merle Kilgore
> Publisher: Painted Desert Music Corporation, 640 Fifth Avenue, New York, NY 10019-6102; phone: 212-957-0802, fax: 212-397-4638.

If you're unsure of a song's title, verify it through an online music store such as Amazon.com or CDNow. These sites contain databases searchable by song title, album title, or artist and usually offer 30-second previews of the music to verify the correct version.

If you can't locate a music publisher using the resources listed in this section, further research may be required. Try using some of the suggestions in Chapter 13, "Copyright Research," or use the services of a music clearance expert as described in Section N, below.

M. Finding Record Companies

The record company (the owner of the sound recording) can usually be determined by examining an album's cover artwork or liner notes and reviewing the sound recording copyright notice. The notice consists of the letter P in a circle, followed by the date the recording was published and the name of the recording copyright owner—for example: "℗ 1984, NBT Records."

If the recording was made before 1972, there will be no sound recording copyright notice because recordings were not protected by copyright before that time. However, even in these cases the name of the record company usually appears prominently on the recording or artwork. Keep in mind that it is common for companies to transfer ownership of sound recordings, so your information may be out of date if you're using an old recording.

If you're having trouble locating a sound recording owner try the following:

- Check online record stores or the *Phonolog* directory at a local record shop to determine the record company that is currently releasing the music, and contact that company.
- Find the publisher of a song featured on the recording and ask the publisher for information about the sound recording owner.
- Use the services of a music clearance expert (see Section N, below).

When contacting a record company, ask for licensing, clearance, or the special products department. Most large record companies have departments that handle sound recording clearance. For example, Warner Special Products manages the licensing of sound recordings owned by Warner Bros., Elektra, and Atlantic.

N. Music Clearance Companies

Music clearance companies help you locate song and sound recording owners and acquire permission to use music for a wide range of purposes (including film, TV, multimedia, and Web uses). Many clearance companies also help clear sampling rights. There is a wide variety of services offered and companies often specialize in a particular music clearance niche. A list of music clearance companies is provided in Section O, "Music Resources," directly below.

O. Music Resources

This section lists a variety of resources that may be of help in the process of music licensing.

1. Production Music Libraries (PMLs)

Below is a list of PMLs. More can be located using an Internet search engine:

- Smartsound (www.smartsound.com/music)
- British Audio Designs (www.intentscp.com)
- Chestnut Mills Musicraft (www.chestnutmills.com)
- Flying Hands Music (www.flyinghands.com)
- Lazertrax Production Music (www.lazertrax.com)
- LicenseMusic.com (www.licensemusic.com)
- Music Bakery (www.musicbakery.com)
- Network Music (www.networkmusic.com)
- ProBackground Theme Music (PBTM) (www.pbtm.com)
- Production Music and Sound Effects Libraries (www.promusic-inc.com)
- Valentino Production Music, Inc. (www.tvmusic.com), and
- Video Helper: (www.videohelper.com).

2. Performing Rights Societies

- BMI (www.bmi.com)
- ASCAP (www.ascap.com), and
- SESAC (www.sesac.com).

3. Mechanical Rights Societies

- The Harry Fox Agency (www.harryfox.com).

4. Record Company Resources

The following resources provide contact information for record companies:

- The Recording Industry Sourcebook (Intertec Publishing) (http://isourcebook.com), and
- The Recording Industry Association of America (RIAA) (www.riaa.com) This is a trade organization for record labels that may be able to provide contact information for record labels.

5. Music Clearance Companies

The services marked with an asterisk (*) also perform sampling clearance services.

- Arlene Fishbach Enterprises (310-451-5916)
- BZ Rights and Permissions, Inc. (www.bzrights.com), (212-924-3000)
- Clearance Consultants (310-441-2600)
- Clearance Quest (615-244-9305)
- Copyright Clearinghouse, Inc. (818-558-3480)
- *Diamond Time LTD. (212-274-1006)
- Fricon Entertainment Co., Inc. (323-931-7323)
- Jill Meyers Music Consultants (310-441-2604)
- Longo Music Services (818-368-4018)
- *Music Resources (323-993-9915), and
- Parker Music Group (818-905-9552).

6. Musical and Dramatic Rights Resources

- Baker's Plays (http://bakersplays.com)
- Broadway Play Publishing Co. (www.broadwayplaypubl.com)
- Dramatic Publishing Co. (www.dramaticpublishing.com)
- Dramatists Play Service, Inc. (www.dramatists.com)
- Harmony Manor Musicals (www.harmonymanormusicals.com)
- Music Theatre International (www.mtishows.com)
- Rodgers and Hammerstein Theatre Library (www.rnh.com)
- Samuel French, Inc. (www.samuelfrench.com), and
- Tams-Witmark Music Library (www.tams-witmark.com). ■

6

Website Permissions

The opportunities for inexpensive publishing on the Web have made "publishers" out of everyone who posts material online. While Web technology has made publishing more accessible to everyone, it's also brought potential copyright disputes to the masses. The rules for using text, photos, artwork, and music covered in the previous chapters apply just the same to website uses, so they are not repeated here. Instead, this chapter focuses on two specific problem areas for webmasters: unauthorized transfers of information to and from websites and website linking.

First, copyright infringement occurs whenever copyrighted material is transferred to or from a website without authorization from the copyright owner. Transferring information to and from a website can be done in a few ways. A user can take information from a website by copying or "downloading" it onto the user's computer, or material can be "uploaded" or "posted" from a user's computer onto the website. Any time copyrighted information is transferred to or from a website without authorization from the owner, the owner may have a copyright infringement claim against the copier, the website, or both.

Second, links to and from websites create another potential area of copyright conflict. A link takes a user from one website page to another simply by clicking on a word or image. Although permission is not needed for a simple word link (also known as a "hypertext" link), it is required when the link comprises a trademark from the linked site (for example, using the Amazon logo without permission). Some other types of links known as "deep links" or "framed links" may also create problems.

This chapter discusses these Web-specific permission issues and how to obtain the necessary permissions for website uses. It also provides a sample linking agreement for you to use. Since websites are becoming increasingly common targets for infringement lawsuits, this chapter focuses on how website owners and people who manage websites (webmasters) can minimize their liability.

If you hired a webmaster to maintain your site, the information in this chapter will be of use to both of you. While the webmaster will need to understand copyright rules in order to keep the site out of legal trouble, it's generally the owner of the site who will be liable for any claims of infringement. Both the webmaster and the owner of a website should be aware of and comply with copyright rules on the Web.

Previous chapters cover the underlying principles of various unauthorized uses. Readers who turned directly to this chapter may want to cross-refer to these discussions:

- **Copyrighted material used without authorization.** Review Chapters 2 (text), 3 (photographs), 4 (artwork), 5 (music), and 15 (assignments and works for hire).
- **Trademarks used without authorization.** Review Chapter 10, "Getting Permission to Use Trademarks."
- **A person's image used for commercial purposes without authorization.** Review Chapter 12, "Releases."
- **A person's privacy invaded or character defamed.** Review Chapter 12, "Releases."

A. Websites: Five Ways to Stay Out of Trouble

Because the Web is freely accessible and because of the ease of copying material from one site to another, many myths have developed regarding the right to use copyrighted materials and trademarks on the Web. Without repeating the copyright and trademark rules established in other chapters, this section provides five simple rules for your website.

1. Assume It's Protected

As a general rule, it is wise to operate under the assumption that all works are protected by either copyright or trademark law unless conclusive information indicates otherwise. A work is not in the public domain simply because it has been posted on the Internet (a popular fallacy) or because it lacks a copyright notice (another myth). For information on these and other public domain issues, see Chapter 8, "The Public Domain."

2. Read Click-Wrap Agreements

Do not assume that clip art, shareware, freeware, or materials labeled "royalty-free" or "copyright-free" can be distributed or copied without authorization. Read the terms and conditions in any "Click to Accept" agreements (often called click-wrap agreements) or "Read Me" files ordinarily accompanying such materials to be certain that your intended use is permitted. One company that failed to honor the terms of a click-wrap agreement was found liable for illegally distributing three volumes of software clip art. (*Marobie-Fl, Inc. v. National Association of Fire Equipment Distributors*, 983 F. Supp. 1167 (E.D. Ill. 1997).)

3. Remove Unauthorized Material

If someone complains about an unauthorized use on your website, remove the offending material immediately. In the case of unauthorized uploads, downloads, or links, the webmaster should disable access to the offending material or link. This is not to imply that you should cave in to every complaint. However, you should remove the material for the period during which you investigate the claim and, if necessary, consult with an attorney. Attempts to "contain" the damage will likely help your case should it find its way into court. Continuing to use the offensive material after being notified may aggravate the claim and the chances of your being found liable—and increase the amount of damages you may have to pay.

Removal of infringing material is also an element of the Digital Millennium Copyright Act (DMCA), a 1998 law establishing that an Internet Service Provider (ISP, a company that provides Internet access to individuals and businesses) can avoid liability by following certain rules including speedy removal of infringing material. You can read a summary of the DMCA on the U.S. Copyright Office website, at www.copyright.gov/legislation/dmca.pdf.

4. Investigate Claims Promptly

If someone complains about an unauthorized use, investigate the claim quickly and seek evidence of copyright ownership and validity from the complaining person. The webmaster can verify the facts through copyright research (see Chapter 13, "Copyright Research"). The webmaster must also investigate the transfer of the infringing material, if any, to and from the site. If copies were downloaded, how many and to whom? If copies were uploaded, by whom?

Below is a sample letter that you can adapt and use in response to a claim of infringement by your website.

5. When in Doubt, Seek Permission

Many webmasters manage personal websites or sites for small organizations such as a local tennis team. Do all of the rules on copyright and permissions apply to these intimate or personal uses? For example, is permission needed to reproduce a photo taken by a club member, a friend, or a relative? The short answer is: "Legally, yes, practically, maybe."

Copyright protection extends to any original work regardless of who created it, and permission is required for reproduction, display, or distribution of the work. One of the main reasons for acquiring permission is to avoid a lawsuit. If the webmaster is confident that a friend or family member has consented to the use, the concern over a lawsuit diminishes, as does the need for a formal written permission agreement. Oral consents are valid, although sometimes difficult to prove.

Sample Response to Infringement Claim

Dear Ms. Crancastle:

I received your certified letter of May 1, 2004, in which you state that my website, Chihuahua Planet, contains an unauthorized reproduction of a photo entitled "Jimmy the Flying Chihuahua." According to your letter, you are the copyright owner of the photo.

I have not had an opportunity to investigate your claim. However, pending resolution of the dispute, all copies of "Jimmy the Flying Chihuahua" have been removed from the site and access to the file containing the photo was disabled, thereby preventing downloading.

I would like to resolve this matter quickly and to do so will require some evidence of your copyright ownership. At your earliest convenience, please send me a copyright registration or some other evidence that you are the copyright owner of the photo. Once I have that information, I shall complete my investigation and promptly provide you with a response.

Sincerely,

Don Daly

But, if you are in doubt about a use, always seek a written permission, even if the material comes from a friend or relative. Formal permission agreements are provided at the end of this book. However, in cases of cooperative friends and relatives, an informal release can be used, such as the following sentence:

I am the owner of rights to _____

[title of work] and I authorize its display and

reproduction on the _____

[name of website] website located at _____

[insert URL for site] for a period of _____

[insert length of time].

If you want to include additional items in the agreement, such as a requirement that a credit line for the work appear on the site, you can add them to this brief agreement.

> EXAMPLE: Sally is the webmaster for the Jefferson Elementary School and intends to post student paintings. Sally has the parent of each child sign a one-sentence permission agreement stating, "I authorize the display and reproduction of the artwork entitled _____ , credited to my child, _____ , on the Jefferson Elementary School website for a period of one year."

The Likelihood of Getting Caught

As Web commerce increases, so does the likelihood of being caught for unauthorized uses. Many companies such as McDonald's, MTV, Levi's, Mattel, Walt Disney, and Coca-Cola aggressively patrol the Web for infringement. New technology makes it possible for copyright owners to encode music, artwork, photographs, and text with digital tags or marks that allow rapid tracking. Companies such as Markwatch (www.markwatch .com) function as cyber bounty hunters. In addition, artist and writer organizations, such as the Association for the Protection of Internet Copyright (APIC) (also known as WebPosse, at www .a-w.org), seek out violations. If a website is controversial and angers some visitors, they may report perceived violations to copyright or trademark owners. Disgruntled employees are also common sources of infringement reports.

Besides the fact that the Web abounds with efficient ways of sniffing out copyright violations, the general rule is that the chances of an unauthorized use being discovered will increase as the site becomes more popular. Therefore, if the goal of a site is to increase its Web traffic, it should avoid unauthorized uses from the start as they rarely justify the potential aggravation and financial loss they can cause.

B. Transferring Information to and From a Website

Copyright infringement occurs whenever copyrighted material is copied from or posted to a website without authorization from the copyright owner. This section discusses the various ways that information can be transferred between your site and its users and the copyright conflicts that may arise with each.

1. Posting Information on a Website

Posting involves a user sending information from the user's computer to the website (sometimes referred to as "uploading"). Once posted, others can view or copy the material. If your site does not offer users a chance to post material, you can skip this section.

> EXAMPLE: A member of a discussion group posts a chapter from a John Grisham book to the group's chat room on the Web, making it available for others to copy.

While the person who uploaded the material is the actual infringer, whoever maintains the site can be held liable for allowing the material to be posted on the site. As with any unauthorized material, the wisest approach to dealing with an unauthorized upload is to remove it quickly or disable access to it pending resolution of the dispute. (See Section A3.)

A site that permits uploading of material can post a notice prohibiting any unauthorized activities and require that perpetrators pay for any damages caused by such activities. The notice should be placed prominently so that persons performing uploads will see it. Alternatively, the site may include a "Click to Accept" agreement (often called a click-wrap agreement) setting forth similar terms. A click-wrap agreement is a page or window that appears before the user is allowed to perform a certain function (in this case, an upload) which states the terms of an agreement. The user will not be allowed to proceed until he or she has clicked a box that indicates that the user has read and accepts the agreement.

Below is an example of a "Click to Accept" agreement intended to prohibit unauthorized postings.

UPLOADING RESTRICTIONS

User agrees not to post:

- any materials protected under copyright, trademark, or trade secret laws unless with the express authorization of the owner; or

- any material likely to defame or invade the privacy of any individual.

User agrees to indemnify the owners of the site and their affiliates and employees from any liability (including attorney fees) related to User's violation of this agreement.

CLICK TO ACCEPT

Unfortunately, notices and "Click to Accept" agreements are not enforceable in all states. And, as a practical matter, a notice or agreement requiring a person who commits an illegal activity to pay your attorney fees is worthless if the person has no money. Nevertheless, it's worthwhile to include some form of notice or "Click to Accept" agreement on your website. It may deter some users from making illegal uploads, and it may help to show your diligence in trying to prevent them.

2. Taking Information From a Website

Just as users can sometimes post information onto a website, a user may—in the reverse process—take material from the website and transfer it to the user's own computer. This is typically done either by downloading or by copying and pasting. Many sites are set up for users to download material. Shareware sites, for example, allow users to download software they want by clicking on a downloadable file, which will then be transferred onto the user's computer. Another way of obtaining material from websites is to select text, copy, and paste it into a word processing document on the user's computer. Strictly speaking this is not downloading, but the effect is the same. The user has obtained material from the website and copied it onto his or her own computer.

> **EXAMPLE:** Jenny visits a Nirvana website that posts unauthorized copies of Kurt Cobain's lyrics. She copies them and pastes them into a Microsoft Word document that she saves on her computer.

a. Unauthorized Copying

If you don't offer material to download at your site, your main concern isn't whether you'll infringe someone else's copyright, but whether users will copy your material without your permission. Particularly if your site contains copyrightable works by outside authors—for instance, if you publish a Web magazine—you'll want to do everything you can to prevent users from unauthorized copying of the material. One attempt at deterrence (though not necessarily an effective one) is to display a copyright notice prominently on some or all of your Web pages, clearly stating that the material is protected by copyright.

To deal with the fact that many users may copy information anyway, you can include a prohibition on any commercial use of the material in your copyright notice. In addition, you can require that the copyright notice be included with the material, so that anyone who reads it will know who created it. Many webmasters are willing to accept some limited copying by users for personal use, especially if the copies show who originally generated the material.

> **EXAMPLE:** Nolo, the publisher of this book, maintains a website with extensive self-help legal information. Since Nolo's goal is to empower people to take care of their own legal affairs, it is willing to accept some copying of the material at its site, with some limitations. Its copyright notice, which can be accessed from nearly every page, reads, in part, as follows:

NOLO'S COPYRIGHT POLICY FOR SITE CONTENT

Nolo.com provides the information on this site to be read by anyone, but retains the copyright on all text and graphics. To use this information in any other way, you must strictly follow these guidelines.

Framing of the Nolo.com site by another site is prohibited.

Use by Individuals

As long as it is for your own personal use only, you may print copies of this information, store the files on your computer, and use hypertext links to reference the information. Any other use or redistribution is strictly prohibited.

Licensing and Reprint Rights

[See below] to learn how to license or reprint any of the information on this site (for example, as part of an article, book or pamphlet).

Framing of the Nolo.com site by another site is prohibited.

We reserve the right to change the terms of and/ or withdraw this permission at any time and for any reason.

REPRINT PERMISSIONS Q & A

Thanks for your interest in Nolo's award-winning content. Nolo's licensing and permissions program is designed to make our content available to the broadest possible audience. Please read the frequently asked questions below to help you in obtaining the reprint permission you need:

Why do I need to get permission?

Reproducing copyrighted work or trademarks without the owner's permission is known as infringement, and it leaves you vulnerable to lawsuits from the copyright or trademark owner.

How hard is it to get permission from Nolo?

Not difficult. [See] the Permission Requests and Agreement form and the information Nolo needs in order to grant permission.

Why do I need to fill out a whole form before I talk to someone at Nolo?

We receive hundreds of permissions requests a month and using the form is the quickest, most efficient way to review and respond to them. It also helps us keep our costs down, which translates into savings for everyone.

Why doesn't Nolo have a price list for reprint rights? Or a list of free content?

Nolo publishes hundreds of titles, articles, and digital products. For each, the royalty and financial arrangements vary—and they also vary by the type of permission. For example, reprint rights for an entire book are different from a one-page excerpt. Reprint rights for one-time academic use are different from rights to resell our content. Becaue of the richness of our product line and our author obligations, we can't provide a simple price list. Instead we work with individual partners to come up with a program that best suits your needs.

If you take this more liberal approach, make sure that any contributors to your site who may retain copyright in their work understand and accept your policy. Otherwise, if they later discover that their article was copied, they might sue you for allowing their work to be infringed.

b. Unauthorized Downloading

The concept of unauthorized downloading may seem strange, considering that most sites that offer files for download are obviously consenting to the practice. However, even if downloads are specifically allowed from your site, you may still have concerns over unauthorized uses of the downloaded material. For instance, if you offer free clip art for download at your site, you may want to prohibit users from selling the clip art and limit their use to personal use. If the user violates the restriction, you may be able to sue for breach of contract. This approach has been successful in disputes based upon clip art and stock photos. Even if the agreement is not enforceable, its presence may defeat a claim of innocent infringement by the user.

A sample downloading restriction appears below. You can post it as a notice displayed where a downloader would clearly see it or implement it as a "Click to Accept" agreement, as described in Section B1 above.

DOWNLOADING RESTRICTIONS

User agrees that the material provided for downloading is to be used solely for personal purposes such as on a home computer and may not be reproduced, displayed, or distributed for any commercial purpose.

CLICK TO ACCEPT

C. Connecting to Other Websites

One of the central features of the Web is the ability for each Web page to offer connections to other Web pages in the click of a button. There are a few ways that websites connect with one another, each with different legal implications for getting permission. This section discusses the issues raised when your site connects to other websites, and it provides a sample linking agreement.

1. Linking and Framing

Two common ways websites connect to other sites are linking and framing.

a. Linking

Most often, a website will connect to another in the form of a link (also known as a "hypertext" link). A link is simply a specially coded word or image that when clicked upon, will take a Web user to another webpage. A link can take the user to another page within the same site (an "internal link"), or to another site altogether (an "external link").

> EXAMPLE: At the Nolo.com website, each page offers several links to other areas of the site. For example, from Nolo's Legal Encyclopedia area on Small Business information, you can link to Nolo's bookstore. These are internal links. Nolo.com also includes links to other sites such as Findlaw.com and the Small Business Administration's websites. These are external links.

You do not need permission for a regular word link to another website's home page (however, see the warning about "deep linking" below). Even if your link appears perfectly legal, it is considered good online etiquette ("netiquette") to obtain consent for all links. Most linking issues can be squared away by having the linked site sign a linking agreement that gives permission for your link (provided in Section C2).

⚠️ **Linking to a page other than a website's home page sometimes angers Web owners.**
The reason Web owners dislike this practice, known as "deep linking," is that it allows users to bypass the home page, which often contains information the website owner wants its users to see. Advertisements, for instance, are usually placed on a home page, and the fewer viewers that see it, the less the website can charge for advertising space. In 1997, the Ticketmaster company sued Microsoft over deep links to Ticketmaster's ordering forms, and the case eventually settled. In another case involving Ticketmaster and Tickets.com, a federal court ruled that deep linking by itself did not constitute a violation of law, but that other conduct in connection with the deep linking—for example, an implication that the two sites were associated with each other—could result in a valid claim. *Ticketmaster v. Tickets.com,* 54 U.S.P.Q. 2d 1344 (C.D. Cal. 2000).

Many copyright experts believe that deep linking is not copyright infringement—after all, the author of a novel can't prevent readers from reading the end first if they so desire, so why should a website owner have the right to determine in what order a user can access a website? Some well-known websites such as Amazon.com welcome deep links. However, if a commercial website has no linking policy or says that deep links are not allowed, it's wise to ask for permission before deep linking. Why? Because many websites—even the listener-friendly National Public Radio—have begun to assert rights against deep linkers under both copyright and trademark law principles.

International law is equally murky. For example, in 2002, a Danish court prevented a website from deep linking to a newspaper site. But in 2003, Germany weighed in on the issue when its federal court ruled that deep linking was not a violation of German copyright law. Until the law is settled in the U.S. and abroad, be prudent when creating deep links.

b. Framing

Besides using external links, another way to connect from your website to other websites is by "framing." Framing is a lot like linking in that you code a word or image so that it will connect to another Web page when the user clicks on it. What makes framing different is that instead of taking the user to the linked website, the information from that website is imported into the original page and displayed in a special "frame." Technically, when you're viewing framed information your computer is connected to the site doing the framing—not the site whose page appears in the frame.

EXAMPLE: John starts a site devoted to auto racing news called John's RacingVision. He offers a number of links to racing industry Web magazines like Autosport, whose content he displays within a frame on his site. When users click on "Read Autosport News," for example, the content from the Autosport site is displayed within John's RacingVision website, in a frame. When the user reads Autosport's news, the user's computer is still connected to John's website, not Autosport's.

Framing is generally unpopular with websites whose content is framed on another site (unless they have agreed to it). Websites that frame the content of other sites are often seen as stealing the other site's content. One court found framing to be a copyright infringement because the process resulted in an unauthorized modification of the linked site. (*Futuredontics Inc. v. Applied Anagramic Inc.,* 45 U.S.P.Q. 2d 2005 (C.D. Cal. 1998).) In another case, *The Washington Post,* CNN, and several other news companies sued a website, TotalNews, which framed their news content. Under the terms of a settlement agreement, TotalNews agreed to stop framing and agreed to use text-only links.

While case law hasn't developed definitive rules on the issue, a framer is more likely to be found liable for copyright (or trademark) infringement if copyrighted material is modified without authorization or if customers are confused about the association between the two sites or the source of a product or service. For more information on trademark infringement, see Chapter 10, "Getting Permission to Use Trademarks."

⚠ Beware of "inlining" content. "Inlining" (sometimes referred to as "mirroring") is the process of incorporating a graphic file from one website onto another website. In the first case involving inlining (*Kelly v. Arriba Soft Corp.*, 336 F.3d 811 (9th Cir. 2003)), an image search engine called ditto.com used inline links to reproduce full-size photographic images from a photographer's website. By clicking on the link, the user got a window containing a full-sized image imported from the photographer's website, surrounded by the search engine's advertising. The lower court held that this inlining constituted copyright infringement—it violated the photographer's exclusive right to display his images. But the court of appeals disagreed and sent the case back for review on this issue. As of the second edition of this book (August 2004), the court had not made a final determination.

The court of appeals in the *Kelly* case did, however, uphold the lower court's ruling that the search engine's practice of creating small reproductions ("thumbnails") of the images and placing them on its own website was permitted as a fair use. The thumbnails were much smaller and of much poorer quality than the original photos and served to index the images, thereby helping the public access them.

Keep in mind that some forms of framing are perfectly legal. For instance, many sites use frames as a way of organizing their own content. When framing the content of another site, however, you are entering hazardous territory. Unless you know a site won't object (and preferably have their agreement in writing), you should proceed very carefully if you want to frame its content.

2. Linking Agreements

The purpose of a linking agreement, like all permission agreements, is to avoid a dispute. If a webmaster is confident that a link will not create a dispute, then a linking agreement is probably not necessary.

However, the following types of links may create disputes:

- image links, particularly where the image is a trademark from the linked site
- deep links that bypass the site's home page
- links that result in framing, and
- inlining links that only pull certain elements from a site, such as an image.

The permission may be informal, such as a written statement from the distant site stating, "You have permission to link to our website's home page using the words *[insert the words in the link]."* Or, you can use a longer agreement that covers the terms more specifically.

The agreement provided below can be used to avoid disputes over any of these types of links.

 A tear-out copy of this agreement is provided in the Appendix. A digital version is included on the forms CD.

a. Explanation for Linking Agreement

- In the **introductory** section, insert the name of the company or person that owns the source site. The source site is the site where the link is located—that is, the starting point for the link. Once the link is clicked the user is taken to the destination site. Insert the URL (Web address—for example, http:// or www .address.com) for each site.
- In the section entitled **The Link,** describe the pages that are linked. For example:
    "A link between Source Site's 'Other References' page and Destination Site's internal page entitled 'Copyright Developments.'" Or,

Linking Agreement

This Agreement (the "Agreement") is made between _____ ("Source Site"), with its home page URL of _____ , and _____ ("Destination Site"), with its home page URL of _____ .

The parties agree as follows:

The Link

Source Site will provide a link to the Destination Site as follows: _____ _____ (the "Link")

The Link includes Destination Site's URL and:

(select if appropriate)

☐   Hypertext link—the words: _____ .

☐   Image link: _____ .

☐   Framed link: _____ .

Grant

Destination Site grants the right to display the Link at Source Site and the nonexclusive right to display publicly the trademarks or images in the Link. Source Site obtains no trademark rights under this Agreement other than the right to display the marks. Any goodwill associated with Source Site's trademarks automatically vests in Destination Site.

Standards and Notifications

(select if appropriate)

☐   Source Site shall maintain its site in accordance with industry standards and, upon notice from Destination Site, shall promptly remove the Link if required. Source Site shall promptly notify Destination Site of any change to the Link or to Source Site that affects the Link.

By: _____   By: _____

Date: _____   Date: _____

Source Site Title: _____   Destination Site Title: _____

Source Site Mailing Address: _____   Destination Site Mailing Address: _____

email: _____   email: _____

"A link between Source Site's home page and Destination Site's image entitled 'Two Chihuahuas' encapsulated as 2Chihua.JPG." Or,

"A link between Source Site's home page and Destination Site's internal page entitled 'Today's News,' resulting in a framed page with the frame incorporating Source site's trademarks and advertisements."

Sometimes, the best way to describe a frame or inlined link is to provide a screen snapshot and attach it to the agreement. In that case, write in: "As attached and incorporated into this agreement" and attach the image to the agreement.

- In the next section, choose a hypertext link or image link (or both if necessary). A hypertext link is a word link (usually viewed as color highlighted text). An image link should be described. If it is a trademark of the destination site, ask the destination site to supply the image (usually in a GIF or JPG format).

- The **Grant** section permits the use of the link and related trademarks or images. The statement, "Any goodwill associated with Source Site's trademarks automatically vests in Destination Site" is a requirement of trademark law. It guarantees that the destination site preserves its trademark rights.

- The optional section **Standards and Notification** is a further assurance sometimes required by a destination site that the source site won't operate in an unlawful manner or change the link dramatically. It offers the option of instant termination. Even if this section is not included, the destination site can probably force the removal of the link if it desires.

- Both parties should sign the agreement. For information regarding signing authority, see Chapter 11, "Art and Merchandise Licenses." Many of the miscellaneous provisions included in legal agreements, such as dispute resolution, are not included here for brevity and ease. Include any that you wish to apply to your agreement.

b. Linking Disclaimers

To minimize liability for any activities that occur when a visitor is taken to a linked website, a webmaster may want to include a disclaimer on the home page. A disclaimer is a statement denying an endorsement or waiving liability for a potentially unauthorized activity. A sample disclaimer appears below.

Linking Disclaimer

By providing links to other sites, *[name of site]* does not guarantee, approve, or endorse the information or products available on these sites.

A disclaimer is not a cure-all for infringement, but if a disclaimer is prominently displayed and clearly written a court may take it into consideration as a factor limiting damages (see Chapter 12, "Releases"). For example, in a case involving a dispute between websites for two restaurants, both named Blue Note, one factor that helped the lesser-known restaurant avoid liability was a prominently displayed disclaimer stating that it was not affiliated with the more famous restaurant. (*Benusan Restaurant v. King*, 937 F. Supp. 295 (S.D. N.Y. 1996).)

Academic and Educational Permissions

This chapter focuses on getting permission to use copyrighted works for academic purposes. It provides information on assembling academic coursepacks and using copyrighted material in the classroom. The chapter also includes form agreements you can use to obtain clearances for coursepacks and information on educational fair use guidelines. This information has its own chapter because there are special legal rules that apply to academic uses, as well as special services that can help educators obtain academic permissions.

The first half of this chapter focuses on the most common need for academic permission—permission to compile a collection of copyrighted materials used for teaching into a "coursepack" or "reader." The second half of the chapter is devoted to an analysis of academic fair use guidelines, under which permission is not required for educational use of copyrighted materials.

A. Academic Coursepacks

An academic coursepack is a (usually photocopied) collection of materials used in the classroom, distributed either in book format or as class handouts. Coursepacks are commonly offered for sale in campus bookstores, although professors may arrange to sell them in class. Most publishers grant "clearances" for coursepacks—that is, for a fee, publishers give permission for their books or articles to be copied and distributed in educational contexts. Such clearances normally last for one semester or school term. After that, the instructor must seek clearance again. In addition to these paper coursepacks, some companies now help assemble electronic coursepacks used in distance learning and electronic teaching programs.

1. Coursepacks and Copyright

Until 1991, many instructors and photocopy shops assembled and sold coursepacks without permission and without compensating the authors or publishers. This was based on the assumption that educational copying qualified as a "fair use" under copyright law, which, legally speaking, is a use that is exempt from permissions requirements that normally apply to copyrighted materials. (For a full explanation of fair use principles, see Chapter 9.)

However, in 1991, a federal court ruled that a publisher's copyright was infringed when a Kinko's copy shop reprinted portions of a book in an academic coursepack. (*Basic Books Inc. v. Kinko's Graphics Corp.*, 758 F. Supp. 1522 (S.D. N.Y. 1991).) The court said that reprinting copyrighted materials in academic coursepacks was not a fair use and that permission was required.

The owner of a copy shop in Ann Arbor, Michigan, began a personal crusade to prove that the Kinko's case was wrongly decided by advertising that he would copy course materials for students and professors. As a result, he was sued by several book publishers. A federal Court of Appeals decided against the copy shop owner, ruling that the copying did not qualify as a fair use. This ruling was based on the amount and substantiality of the portions taken and because academic publishers were financially harmed—they lost licensing revenues—while the copy shop was making money on the coursepacks. (*Princeton Univ. v. Michigan Document Servs.*, 99 F.3d 1381 (6th Cir. 1996).)

This and similar court rulings establish the rule that you need to obtain permission before reproducing copyrighted materials for an academic coursepack. Many campus copy shops still perform coursepack assembly. However, these copy shops have either affiliated with established clearance services or are prepared to obtain clearance on behalf of instructors.

2. Obtaining Clearance for Coursepacks

It's the instructor's obligation to obtain clearance for materials used in class. Instructors typically delegate this task to one of the following:

- **Clearance services.** These services are the easiest method of clearance and assembly. More information about them is provided in Section A3, below.
- **University bookstores or copy shops.** University policies may require that the instructor delegate the task to the campus bookstore, copy shop or to a special division of the university that specializes in clearances.
- **Department administration (generally, the instructor's secretary).** In Section A4, we offer some suggestions for these kinds of administrators on how to assemble a courespack without a clearance service.

3. Using a Clearance Service

It can be time-consuming to seek and obtain permission for the 20, 30, or more articles you want to use in a coursepack. Fortunately, private clearance services will, for a fee, acquire permission and assemble coursepacks on your behalf. After the coursepacks are created and sold, the clearance service collects royalties and distributes the payments to the rights holders. Educational institutions may require that the instructor use a specific clearance service. As noted earlier in this chapter, some clearance companies also provide clearance for nonpaper electronic coursepacks used in distance learning.

The largest copyright clearing service is the Copyright Clearance Center (CCC), which clears millions of works from thousands of publishers and authors. Among the CCC's services are the Academic Permissions Service (APS), which obtains permission for paper coursepacks, and the Electronic Course Content Service (ECCS), which

obtains permissions for electronic coursepacks, electronic reserves, and other new uses of copyrighted material in electronic academic environments.

In 2001, XanEdu (www.xanedu.com), a division of Bell & Howell, acquired the coursepack service formerly known as Campus Custom Publishing. In addition to providing traditional coursepack assembly, XanEdu offers an electronic online service that provides supplemental college course materials directly to the instructor's desktop via the Internet.

Contact information for several clearance companies is provided in Section E.

a. Clearance Company Fees

The total fees that clearance companies charge for assembling a coursepack are based on the cost of copyright permission for the material copied, plus copying, binding, the clearance service's processing fee, and, if sold in a campus bookstore, the store's markup (usually 20%, sometimes 25%). Permission fees vary, but most publishers charge approximately 8 cents per copied page (for example, $4.80 for a 60-page coursepack). Ultimately, the cost of the permission is absorbed by the student buying the coursepack. One advantage of using a coursepack service is that fees are often based on the number of copies sold, not printed.

The Copyright Clearance Center (CCC) ordinarily charges customers an annual service fee of $120, regardless of the number of services in which a customer participates, although the CCC has been known to clear individual permissions for professors and those who don't have accounts without charging them the annual service fee.

Clearance companies will sometimes work on a "copyright only" basis. This means the company acquires permission to include the material in the coursepack, but does not assemble the coursepacks itself. This task is usually left to the bookstore, copy shop, or academic support staff. Most clearance services provide free estimates for coursepack permissions and assembly.

ISBNs and ISSNs

When filling out a coursepack permission request, you'll need to provide the ISBN or ISSN for the publications you want to copy. ISBNs and ISSNs are part of a standardized numbering system all publishers use. ISBNs (International Standard Book Numbers) are used for books. ISSNs (International Standard Serial Numbers) are used for magazines, journals, newsletters, and other serialized publications. These numbers can be found on or near the title or copyright page or near the publication's UPC bar code. Since several numbers may be printed on the bar code, look for the number preceded by either "ISSN" or "ISBN."

b. Coursepack Application Forms

To begin the clearance process, you must complete and submit a coursepack application form to the clearance service. Each clearance service has its own application form. Most clearance services have websites from which you can download the forms. Generally, you must print the form, complete it, and fax it back. As with all permissions, if you don't make the payment as required under the agreement, the permission may be terminated.

c. Clearance Company Agreements

In addition to filling out and submitting an application, you must enter into a written agreement with a clearance company. The agreement establishes that the company will act as your agent to acquire permissions and assemble the coursepack, and details your obligations regarding payment and copyright law.

As noted above, the Copyright Clearance Center's Academic Permissions Service (APS) provides photocopy permissions for paper and electronic coursepacks. In order to use CCC services, a coursepack producer must sign the appropriate APS agreement (see sample agreement below) that lists the general terms which govern all permissions. The agreement includes various limitations based on the CCC's years of experience in the industry, similar to those you would receive if you asked the author or publisher for permission directly. For example: no more than 25% may be copied from a single book or journal issue; only one institution may sell a coursepack; and no permission takes legal effect until payment is made (although this does not mean that you must make payment in advance).

Reprinted below is a recent version of the CCC's User Agreement for its Academic Permissions Service. Check the CCC's website (www.copyright.com) to be sure that this is the latest version of the document. The website provides additional information about copyright and CCC services, many of which can be conducted over the Internet.

 A tear-out copy of this agreement is provided in the Appendix. A digital version is included on the forms CD.

APS/CCC Coursepack Agreement
(courtesy Copyright Clearance Center)

PERMISSIONS AGREEMENT made this ____ day of _____ , _____ , between the Copyright Clearance Center, Inc. ("CCC") and _____ ("User").

1. Nature and Form of Program. This Agreement provides for participation by User in CCC's Academic Permissions Service ("APS"). The APS grants authorizations to photocopy and to create photocopy anthologies for sale and/or distribution to students and other academic customers. The copies and anthologies may be made and assembled by faculty members individually or at their request by on-campus bookstores or copy centers, or by off-campus copy shops and other similar entities. It does not permit "publishing ventures" where any particular anthology would be systematically marketed at multiple institutions. User acknowledges that the holders of copyright rights have complete discretion under the United States Copyright Act, 17 United States Code, whether to grant any permission, and whether to place any limitations on any grant, and that CCC has no right to supersede or to modify any such discretionary act by a rightsholder.

2. Grant of Permissions. In order to receive a permission to photocopy a portion of a printed publication, User must first submit to CCC a form as prescribed in CCC's published APS Guidelines. CCC shall not accept any form that is not complete. Within CCC's published response time (measured from CCC's receipt of a completed form), CCC shall notify User whether or not a permission has been granted and the royalty fee due, if any. CCC shall notify User of any limitations imposed by a rightsholder on that permission and, unless User notifies CCC of its intention to decline any particular permission, User shall pay the amount due as set forth in the notification and shall be bound by any such limitation. Any act by User that involves copying beyond that set forth in the notification shall be deemed in its entirety to be an unpermitted act of copying. Separate portions of a work, even if they are to be included in the same anthology, shall require a separate permission under the APS.

3. Payment for Permissions. User shall pay to CCC the amount set forth in the permissions notification in full payment for any permission set forth therein (which will include both the amount due to the rightsholder and the service fee payable to CCC), within the time set forth therein. In the event of a failure by User to pay any such amount by the due date, the applicable permission shall be null and void. In the event that User sells fewer copies than the number for which permissions were granted, User shall pay CCC only for the total number of copies sold, and permissions for the unsold copies shall be null and void.

4. General Terms and Conditions of the Program. Subject to any further limitations determined by any particular rightsholder, the copying permitted under the APS is limited as follows:

(i)   no more than 25% of the text of a book or of the items in a published collection of essays, poems, or articles may be copied;

(ii)   no more than the greater of (A) 25% of the text of an issue or of a journal or other periodical, or (B) two articles from such an issue, may be copied;

(iii)   no User may sell or distribute any particular anthology at more than one institution of learning;

(iv)   each copy sold by User must contain a proper copyright notice, identifying the copyright rightsholder in whose name CCC has granted permission and a statement to the effect that such copy was made pursuant to permission; and

(v)   no materials may be entered into electronic memory by User except in order to produce an identical copy of a work before or during the academic term (or analogous period) as to which any particular permission is granted.

In the event that User shall choose to retain the materials in electronic memory for purposes of producing identical copies more than one day after such retention (but still within the scope of any permission granted), User must notify CCC of such fact in the applicable permission request form and such retention shall constitute one copy actually sold for purposes of calculating permissions fees. No permission granted under the APS shall in any way include any right by User to create a non-identical copy of the work or to edit or in any other way modify the work (except by means of deleting material immediately preceding or following the entire portion of the work copied).

5. Term and Termination. This Agreement shall be in force beginning as of the date hereof and shall continue for an initial period of one year. This Agreement is automatically renewable for subsequent one-year periods in the absence of timely notice of termination. Either party may terminate this Agreement for any reason by giving 90 days' prior written notice thereof to the other party. In the event of termination of this Agreement for any reason, any permissions the periods of which have not yet ended shall remain in effect until their respective terminations. Termination of this Agreement shall have no effect on any party's obligation to pay money to the other party.

6. Warranty. Each copyright rightsholder which has granted CCC the right to grant permission under the APS to use any particular Work has warranted that it has all rights necessary to authorize CCC to act on its behalf.

7. Books and Records; Right to Audit. As to each permission granted under the APS, User shall maintain for at least four full calendar years books and records sufficient for CCC to determine the numbers of copies made by user under such permission. CCC and any representatives it may designate shall have the right to audit such books and records at any time during User's ordinary business hours, upon two days' prior notice. If any such audit shall determine that User shall have underpaid for, or underreported, any copies sold by three percent (3%) or more, then User shall bear all the costs of any such audit; otherwise, CCC shall bear the costs of any such audit. Any amount determined by such audit to have been underpaid by User shall immediately be paid to CCC by User, together with interest thereon at the rate of 10% per annum from the date such amount was originally due. The provisions of this paragraph shall survive the termination of this Agreement for any reason.

8. Notices. All notices and communications under this Agreement shall be in writing addressed, in the case of User, to the person designated below, and in the case of CCC, its President, and shall be deemed to have been given on the day of delivery or transmission if delivered by hand or if sent by electronic mail or facsimile transmission (with receipt confirmed), or on the fifth business day following the day of mailing if mailed, postage prepaid:

Person and/or title: _____

Address: _____

(if different from that set forth at end of Agreement)

Telephone Number: _____

Facsimile Number: _____

Email Address: _____

9. No Assignment; Integrated Agreement; Governing Law. Neither party to this Agreement shall have the right to assign or sublicense any of its rights or obligations hereunder without the prior written consent of the other party. This agreement constitutes the entire agreement between the parties with respect to the subject matter hereof and may not be modified or amended except in a writing signed by the parties hereto. This Agreement shall be interpreted, construed, governed and enforced in accordance with and under the laws of the State of New York, without giving effect to the principles thereof of conflicts of law.

User's Name: _____

Address: _____

Signature: _____

Printed Name: _____

Title: _____

Copyright Clearance Center, Inc.

222 Rosewood Drive

Danvers, Massachusetts 01923 USA

Signature: _____

4. Assembling Your Own Coursepack

Instead of hiring a clearance company to obtain clearance and assemble a coursepack for you, you (or your secretary) can do it yourself. Why take on this extra work? First, a clearance company may be unable to obtain permission for certain items that you may be able to obtain yourself. Second, by doing it yourself you can save students' money by minimizing your fees.

It's not unusual for a clearance company to be unable or unwilling to acquire permission for certain works. Clearance companies typically enter into affiliations with academic publishers—that is, they get permission in advance to use all the material in the publisher's catalogue. This allows them to avoid having to ask for permission to use each individual item. If the material you want to use comes from publishers who have affiliated with the coursepack company, this will work for you. But if the material you want is not from one of these precleared publishers, the clearance company may not even try to get permission or if they do try, may be unable to obtain permission.

For example, Nolo, the publisher of this book, has not authorized APS to grant rights for its works. Therefore, APS could not acquire permission for Nolo books in its coursepacks. If you wanted to obtain permission to use Nolo's material, you might want to pursue clearance from Nolo directly on your own. Before paying membership or annual fees, inquire whether the clearance service is affiliated with the publishers of the articles or books you want to include in your coursepack.

The Association of American Publishers (AAP) also provides sample request forms and information on coursepack requests on its website (www .publishers.org).

Here are some suggestions for preparing your own coursepack:

- Start with the publisher (not the author) of the item you want to use; direct your request to the publisher's permissions, licensing, or clearance department. If the publisher doesn't control the rights you need, they can probably direct you to the rights holder. Information about locating publishers is provided in Chapter 2, Section C2.
- Obtain permission for works whether or not they are in still print. Even if a work is out of print, you still need permission to use it unless it is in the public domain.
- Fax or mail your request at least three to nine weeks before your class begins (most publishers will not accept email requests for permission).

What Copyright Notice Should You Use in a Coursepack?

Your coursepack's copyright notice must identify the copyright owners of the materials it includes. A clearance company can help you create the notices. If you are handling clearance on your own, your clearance agreement should require each rightsholder to provide the format for their notice. Below is an example of a notice for a coursepack:

"Dangerous Similarities" by Stan Soocher is excerpted from *They Fought the Law* © Schirmer Books (1998);

"Who Will Own Your Next Good Idea" by Charles C. Mann is excerpted from *Atlantic Monthly* © Atlantic Monthly (Sept. 1998).

a. Sample Coursepack Request Form

Below is a sample coursepack permission request form prepared by the Association of Academic Publishers.

Coursepack Permission Request Form
(Association of Academic Publishers)

To:

Publisher Contact: _____

Publisher: _____

Fax Number: _____

Date of Request: _____

From:

Your Name: _____

Department: _____

School name: _____

Address: _____

City: _____

State: _____

Zip code: _____

Phone #: _____

Fax #: _____

Course name and number: _____

Number of copies needed: _____

Instructor: _____

Semester and year: _____

ISBN/ISSN number: _____

Book or journal title: _____

Author: _____

Translator: _____

Editor: _____

Edition: _____

Volume: _____

Copyright year: _____

Publication year: _____

Chapter/article title: _____

Chapter/article author: _____

Page numbers: _____

Total pages: _____

Is it an out-of-print work? _____

Have you included a copy of the material with this request? _____

Are you the author? _____

Permission is requested for use during one term only. _____

Mail or fax this to the publisher or other rights holder. If you have already discussed rights with the copyright owner and agreed upon the terms, bypass the request form and send the Coursepack Permission Agreement.

 A tear-out version of this form is provided in the Appendix. A digital version is included on the forms CD.

b. Coursepack Permission Agreement

Ordinarily, when you create your own coursepack you will seek permission to photocopy the materials. You should always obtain written permission from the copyright owners for this. Use the agreement below for this purpose. In the section entitled "Number of Copies & Assembly," indicate the number of copies you will produce for the class and check the box that indicates how the coursepack will be assembled. Coursepack agreements are almost always limited to one semester and to one institution. Unlike the non-negotiable coursepack agreements provided by clearance companies, you can modify this agreement if you wish to negotiate a multiterm agreement.

A tear-out copy of this agreement is provided in the Appendix. A digital version is included on the forms CD.

Coursepack Permission Agreement

_____ ("Licensor")

_____ ("User")

Department: _____

School Name: _____

Course name and number: _____ ("the Course").

Date when Course starts: _____ (the "Course date").

Authorization

Licensor authorizes User to photocopy the Selection, as defined below, for purposes of creating a photocopy anthology (the "Coursepack") for sale or distribution to students and academic customers in the Course.

Number of Copies & Assembly

_____ copies of the Coursepack shall be assembled and distributed for the Course:

☐   by User

☐   by on-campus bookstores or copy centers, or

☐   by off-campus copy shops.

Number of pages (or actual page numbers) to be used _____ .

The permission granted in this Agreement is limited to the Course and institution listed above and to be used for one semester only. Any further rights must be negotiated separately.

Material for Which Permission Is Sought

Title of text or artwork: _____ (the "Selection").

Author: _____ .

Source publication (or product from which it came): _____ .

If from a periodical, the ISSN, volume, issue, and date. If from a book, the ISBN:_____ .

If from the Internet, the entire URL address: _____ .

Credit

A standard credit line including Licensor's name will appear where the Selection is used. If you have a special credit line you would prefer, indicate it here: _____ .

Fee

User shall pay a fee of $ _____ to Licensor at the following address: _____

_____ within 30 days of commencement date, listed above.

Warranty

Licensor warrants that it is the owner of rights for the Selection and has the right to grant the permission to republish the materials as specified above.

_____ (User signature)

Name: _____

Title: _____

Address: _____

Date: _____

Permission Granted By:

_____ (Licensor signature)

Name: _____

Title: _____

Address: _____

Date: _____

B. Educational Uses of Noncoursepack Materials

Unlike academic coursepacks, other copyrighted materials can be used without permission in certain educational circumstances under copyright law or as a fair use. "Fair use" is the right to use portions of copyrighted materials without permission for purposes of education, commentary, or parody. While Chapter 9 is devoted entirely to explaining fair use principles, special fair use rules for educational purposes are discussed in this chapter. Fair use rules for educational uses are very specific and, if complied with, can generally prevent lawsuits—which is not the case for general fair use principles.

1. Educational Fair Use Guidelines

Publishers and the academic community have established a set of educational fair use guidelines to provide "greater certainty and protection" for teachers. While the guidelines are not part of the federal Copyright Act, they are recognized by courts and the Copyright Office as minimum standards for fair use in education. A teacher or pupil following the guidelines can feel comfortable that a use falling within these guidelines is a permissible fair use and not an infringement.

The educational use guidelines can be found in Circular 21, provided by the Copyright Office. See the resources in Section E2 for the website address and more information on educational guidelines.

Keep in mind that none of these guidelines permit creation of coursepacks as described in Section A. They only allow uses that involve copying much less material than in a coursepack. This section answers some basic questions about these guidelines. Section C discusses proposed guidelines that have yet to be adopted.

a. What Is the Difference Between the Guidelines and General Fair Use Principles?

The educational guidelines are similar to a treaty that has been adopted by copyright owners and academics. Under this arrangement, copyright owners will permit uses that are outlined in the guidelines. In other fair use situations, the only way to prove that a use is permitted is to submit the matter to court or arbitration. In other words, in order to avoid lawsuits, the various parties have agreed on what is permissible for educational uses, codified in these guidelines.

b. What Is an "Educational Use"?

The educational fair use guidelines apply to material used in educational institutions and for educational purposes. Examples of "educational institutions" include K-12 schools, colleges, and universities. Libraries, museums, hospitals, and other nonprofit institutions also are considered educational institutions under most educational fair use guidelines when they engage in nonprofit instructional, research, or scholarly activities for educational purposes.

"Educational purposes" are:
- noncommercial instruction or curriculum-based teaching by educators to students at nonprofit educational institutions
- planned noncommercial study or investigation directed toward making a contribution to a field of knowledge, or
- presentation of research findings at noncommercial peer conferences, workshops, or seminars.

2. Rules for Reproducing Text Materials for Use in Class

The guidelines permit a teacher to make one copy of any of the following: a chapter from a book; an article from a periodical or newspaper; a short story, short essay, or short poem; a chart, graph, diagram, drawing, cartoon, or picture from a book, periodical, or newspaper.

Teachers may photocopy articles to hand out in class, but the guidelines impose restrictions. Classroom copying cannot be used to replace texts or workbooks used in the classroom. Pupils cannot be charged more than the actual cost of photocopying. The number of copies cannot exceed more than one copy per pupil. And a notice of copyright must be affixed to each copy.

Examples of what can be copied and distributed in class include:

- a complete poem if less than 250 words or an excerpt of not more than 250 words from a longer poem
- a complete article, story, or essay if less than 2,500 words or an excerpt from any prose work of not more than 1,000 words or 10% of the work, whichever is less; or
- one chart, graph, diagram, drawing, cartoon, or picture per book or per periodical issue.

Not more than one short poem, article, story, essay, or two excerpts may be copied from the same author, nor more than three from the same collective work or periodical volume (for example, a magazine or newspaper) during one class term. As a general rule, a teacher has more freedom to copy from newspapers or other periodicals if the copying is related to current events.

The idea to make the copies must come from the teacher, not from school administrators or other higher authority. Only nine instances of such copying for one course during one school term are permitted. In addition, the idea to make copies and their actual classroom use must be so close together in time that it would be unreasonable to expect a timely reply to a permission request. For example, the instructor finds a newsweekly article on capital punishment two days before presenting a lecture on the subject.

Teachers may not photocopy workbooks, texts, standardized tests, or other materials that were created for educational use. The guidelines were not intended to allow teachers to usurp the profits of educational publishers. In other words, educational publishers do not consider it a fair use if the copying provides replacements or substitutes for the purchase of books, reprints, periodicals, tests, workbooks, anthologies, compilations, or collective works.

3. Rules for Reproducing Music

A music instructor can make copies of excerpts of sheet music or other printed works, provided that the excerpts do not constitute a "performable unit," such as a whole song, section, movement, or aria. In no case can more than 10% of the whole work be copied and the number of copies may not exceed one copy per pupil. Printed copies that have been purchased may be edited or simplified provided that the fundamental character of the work is not distorted or the lyrics altered (or added).

A student may make a single recording of a performance of copyrighted music for evaluation or rehearsal purposes, and the educational institution or individual teacher may keep a copy. In addition, a single copy of a sound recording owned by an educational institution or an individual teacher (such as a tape, disc, or cassette) of copyrighted music may be made for the purpose of constructing aural exercises or examinations, and the educational institution or individual teacher can keep a copy.

Instructors may not:

- copy sheet music or recorded music for the purpose of creating anthologies or compilations used in class
- copy from works intended to be "consumable" in the course of study or teaching such as workbooks, exercises, standardized tests and answer sheets, and like material

- copy sheet music or recorded music for the purpose of performance, except for emergency copying to replace purchased copies which are not available for an imminent performance (provided purchased replacement copies are substituted in due course); or
- copy any materials without including the copyright notice which appears on the printed copy.

If copyrighted sheet music is out of print (not available for sale), an educator can request permission to reproduce it from the music publisher. Information about contacting music publishers is provided in Chapter 5. A library that wants to reproduce out-of-print sheet music can use a system established by the Music Publishers' Association by downloading and completing a form called the "Library Requisition for Out-of-Print Copyrighted Music" from the Association's website at www.mps.org/copyright/searchenter/html.

4. Rules for Recording and Showing Television Programs

Nonprofit educational institutions can record television programs transmitted by network television and cable stations. The institution can keep the tape for 45 days, but can only use it for instructional purposes during the first ten of the 45 days. After the first ten days, the video recording can only be used for teacher evaluation purposes, to determine whether or not to include the broadcast program in the teaching curriculum. If the teacher wants to keep it within the curriculum, he or she must obtain permission from the copyright owner. The recording may be played once by each individual teacher in the course of related teaching activities in classrooms and similar places devoted to instruction (including formalized home instruction). The recorded program can be repeated once if necessary, although there are no standards for determining what is and is not necessary. After 45 days, the recording must be erased or destroyed.

A video recording of a broadcast can be made only at the request of and only used by individual teachers. A television show may not be regularly recorded in anticipation of requests—for example, a teacher cannot make a standing request to record each episode of a PBS series. Only enough copies may be reproduced from each recording to meet the needs of teachers, and the recordings may not be combined to create teaching compilations. All copies of a recording must include the copyright notice on the broadcast program as recorded and (as mentioned above) must be erased or destroyed after 45 days.

C. Proposed Educational Guidelines on Fair Use

The guidelines discussed in the previous section have been approved by a consensus of educators, scholars, and publishers (copyright owners). Since these educators and copyright owners have come to an agreement, it is unlikely that a publisher will sue an educator who uses material in a manner that is permitted by the guidelines. Besides these guidelines, there are others that have been discussed and proposed, but not formally approved. These proposed guidelines lack the official consensus of the adopted guidelines described in Section B. However, the parties created some standards which were included in a report and it is hoped that these proposed guidelines will eventually be adopted. This section discusses these proposed educational guidelines.

The proposed guidelines are provided here to give you a ballpark idea of what may be permissible. For example, these standards may help you formulate a fair use analysis, as described in Chapter 9. You can access the full report from which these proposed guidelines originated at the Patent and Trademark Office's Conference on Fair Use (CONFU) site. See the resources section at the end of this chapter for the website address.

1. Proposed Guidelines for Digital Copying

Under proposed guidelines, educators can digitize analog images (nondigital photographic prints or paintings). Digitizing is traditionally accomplished by scanning a printed photo. In this process, an analog image (that is, a three-dimensional printed photograph or slide created by a noncomputer photo processing method) is converted into a digital format known as binary code. This digital format is stored in a computer file. Under the proposed guidelines, educators can digitize a lawfully acquired analog image for educational use unless the image is readily available in usable digital form at a fair price. The proposed guidelines for digital imaging are located at the Patent and Trademark Office's CONFU site. See the resources section at the end of this chapter for the website address.

Under the proposed guidelines, an educational institution may include digital thumbnail images created from analog images in a searchable catalogue used by the institution. A thumbnail is a small scale, typically low resolution, digital reproduction which has no commercial or reproductive value.

An educational institution may display images digitized under the proposed guidelines through its own secure electronic network, provided that it includes a notice stating that the images shall not be downloaded, copied, retained, printed, shared, modified, or otherwise used, except as provided in the educational use guidelines.

2. Proposed Guidelines for Using Digitized Images in Lectures, Scholarly Presentations, or Publications

Under proposed guidelines, an educator may display a digital image prepared from an analog image if the display is for educational purposes, such as face-to-face teaching or scholarly activities at a nonprofit educational institution. An educational institution may compile digital images for display on the institution's secure electronic network to students enrolled in a course for classroom use, after-class review, or directed study. Educators, scholars, and students may use or display digital images in connection with lectures or presentations in their fields, including uses at noncommercial professional development seminars, workshops, and conferences.

The proposed guidelines do not permit reproducing and publishing images in publications, including scholarly publications in print or digital form, for which permission is generally required.

AMICO—A System for Educators to Negotiate Digital Images

In an attempt to provide educational access to copyrighted images, a consortium of art museums and archives created the Art Museum Image Consortium (AMICO) (www.amico.net). AMICO maintains and licenses a collective digital library of images and documentation. AMICO enables its members to negotiate digital rights with artists, artists' estates, and museums in other countries and provides members with access to each others' holdings for their own educational uses.

3. Proposed Guidelines for Students or Instructors Preparing Multimedia Works

There are extensive proposed guidelines for the creation and use of multimedia works. Multimedia works include music, text, graphics, illustrations, photographs, and/or audiovisual images combined into a presentation using equipment. For example, an instructor in copyright law may use a software program such as Microsoft PowerPoint to create a class presentation that includes still and moving images, music, and spoken words. If you are contemplating preparing multimedia works for classroom instruction, you should download and review Appendix J of the CONFU Report (website listed in the resources section at the end of this chapter).

In general, students and instructors may create multimedia works for face-to-face instruction, directed self-study, or remote instruction provided that the multimedia works are used only for educational purposes in systematic learning activities at nonprofit educational institutions. Instructors may use their multimedia works for teaching courses for up to two years after the first use.

There are also certain "portion limitations." An educational multimedia presentation may include:

- Up to 10% or 1,000 words, whichever is less, of a copyrighted text work. For example, you may use an entire poem of less than 250 words but no more than three poems by one poet or five poems by different poets from the same anthology.
- Up to 10%, but not more than 30 seconds, of the music and lyrics from an individual musical work.
- Up to 10% or three minutes, whichever is less, of a copyrighted motion media work—for example, an animation, video, or film image.
- A photograph or illustration in its entirety but no more than five images by the same artist or photographer. When using photographs and illustrations from a published collective work, you may use no more than 10% or 15 images, whichever is less. Or,
- Up to 10% or 2,500 fields or cell entries, whichever is less, from a copyrighted database or data table. A "field entry" is defined as a specific item of information, such as a name or Social Security number in a database file record. A "cell entry" is defined as the intersection at which a row and a column meet on a spreadsheet.

Only two copies of an educational multimedia project may be made, only one of which may be placed on reserve. An additional copy may be made for preservation purposes, but may only be used or copied to replace a copy that has been lost, stolen, or damaged. If an educational multimedia project is created by two or more people, each creator may retain one copy for the educational purposes described in the proposed guidelines. Permission is required for uses that are commercial or go beyond the limitations of the proposed guidelines.

D. Library Photocopying

The Copyright Act at 17 U.S.C. § 108 provides a set of rules regarding library reproductions. In general, a library or archive open to the public (or whose collection is available to specialized researchers other than those affiliated with the institution) will not be liable for copyright infringement based upon a library patron's unsupervised use of reproducing equipment located on its premises, provided that the copying equipment displays a notice that the making of a copy may be subject to the copyright law. The notice must appear in a specific form, as shown below.

NOTICE WARNING CONCERNING COPYRIGHT RESTRICTIONS

The copyright law of the United States (Title 17, United States Code) governs the making of photocopies or other reproductions of copyrighted material. Under certain conditions specified in the law, libraries and archives are authorized to furnish a photocopy or other reproduction. One of these specified conditions is that the photocopy or reproduction is not to be "used for any purpose other than private study, scholarship, or research." If a user makes a request for, or later uses, a photocopy or reproduction for purposes in excess of "fair use," that user may be liable for copyright infringement. This institution reserves the right to refuse to accept a copying order if, in its judgment, fulfillment of the order would involve violation of copyright law.

When patrons ask the library to copy text works, the warning notice must be printed within a box located prominently on the order form, either on the front side of the form or immediately adjacent to the space for the name and signature of the user. The library may make only one copy of such works per patron. Copying a complete work from the library collection is prohibited unless the work is not available at a "fair price." This is generally the case when the work is out of print and used copies are not available at a reasonable price. If a work, located within the library's collection, is available at a reasonable price, the library may reproduce one article or other contribution to a copyrighted collection or periodical issue, or a small part of any other copyrighted work, for example, a chapter from a book. This right to copy does not apply if the library is aware that the copying of a work (available at a fair price) is systematic. For example, if 30 different members of one class are requesting a copy of the same article, the library has reason to believe that the instructor is trying to avoid seeking permission for 30 copies.

The copying, whether performed by the library or whether unsupervised by the library patron, cannot be for a commercial advantage. This means that the library (or a copying service hired by the library) cannot profit from the copying. In addition, the copying for the patron must be done for purposes of private study, scholarship, or research.

If a library or educational institution makes a copy of a work for a patron, it must include the actual copyright notice from the material being copied, for example, "© 1953, Grove Press". Under 17 U.S.C. § 108(a), if the material contains no copyright notice, the material should be stamped with the notice "This material may be protected by copyright law (Title 17 U.S. Code)." In addition to limiting the library's liability, the use of the warning notice will defeat an infringer's defense that the copying was an "innocent infringement" and might even support an argument that the infringement was willful, thereby increasing the damages paid to the copyright owner.

Library Copying After 75 Years

In 1998, the Sonny Bono Copyright Term Extension Act extended the period of copyright protection for an additional 20 years. As part of the Act, Congress provided that during the last 20 years of any term of copyright of a published work, a library or archives may reproduce a copy of the work for purposes of preservation, scholarship, or research provided that: the work was not being distributed commercially; the work cannot be obtained at a reasonable price; or the copyright owner or its agent provides notice that either of the above conditions applies.

E. Academic Permission Resources

The following resources can help you obtain permission to use materials for academic purposes.

1. Coursepack Resources

- The Association of Academic Publishers (www.publishers.org)
- The Copyright Clearance Center (www.copyright.com), and
- XanEdu (www.xanedu.com).

2. Educational Fair Use Guidelines

- The established educational guidelines, as well as other rules regarding libraries, are available in Copyright Office Circular 21, "Reproduction of Copyrighted Works by Educators and Librarians," which can be downloaded from www.copyright.gov/circs/circ21.pdf. See Chapter 13 for more information about Copyright Office circulars and contacting the U.S. Copyright Office.

- Copies of proposed guidelines in the report from the Patent and Trademark Office Conference on Fair Use (CONFU) may be downloaded from www.uspto.gov/web/offices/dcom/olia/confu/confurep.pdf or may be obtained, free of charge, by mailing or faxing a written request to: CONFU Report, Office of Public Affairs, U.S. Patent and Trademark Office, Washington, DC 20231; fax: 703-308-5258.

- Information about established and proposed guidelines can also be found in the extensive list of links regarding educational uses of copyrighted material at Christine Sundt's Art and Copyright website located at http://darkwing.uoregon.edu/~csundt/copyweb. ∎

The Public Domain

ABSOLUTELY FREE! MUSIC, TEXT, AND ART!! COPY ALL YOU WANT!! If you saw an advertisement like this, you might wonder, "What's the catch?" When it comes to the public domain, there is no catch. If a book, song, movie, or artwork is in the public domain, then it is not protected by intellectual property laws (copyright, trademark, or patent laws)—which means it's free for you to use without permission.

As a general rule, most works enter the public domain because of old age. This includes any work published in the United States before 1923 or works published before 1964 for which copyrights were not renewed. (Renewal was a requirement for works published before 1978.) A smaller group of works fell into the public domain because they were published without a copyright notice, which was necessary for works published in the United States before March 1, 1989. Some works are in the public domain because the owner has indicated a desire to give them to the public without copyright protection. As discussed throughout this chapter, the rules establishing the public domain status for each of these types of works are different.

For a detailed analysis of public domain rules and issues, see *The Public Domain: How to Find & Use Copyright-Free Writings, Music, Art & More,* by Stephen Fishman (Nolo).

A. Welcome to the Public Domain

The term "public domain" refers to creative materials that are not protected by intellectual property laws such as copyright, trademark, or patent laws. The public owns these works, not an individual author or artist. Anyone can use a public domain work without obtaining permission, but no one can ever own it.

An important wrinkle to understand about public domain material is that, while each work belongs to the public, collections of public domain works may be protected by copyright. If, for example, someone has collected public domain images in a book or on a website, the collection as a whole may be protectible even though individual images are not. You are free to copy and use individual images but copying and distributing the complete collection may infringe what is known as the "collective works" copyright. Collections of public domain material will be protected if the person who created it has used creativity in the choices and organization of the public domain material. This usually involves some unique selection process, for example, a poetry scholar compiling a book—*The Greatest Poems of e.e. cummings.*

There are four common ways that works arrive in the public domain:

- the copyright has expired
- the copyright owner failed to follow copyright renewal rules
- the copyright owner deliberately places it in the public domain, known as "dedication," or
- copyright law does not protect this type of work.

The following section looks at each of these routes into the public domain more closely.

1. Expired Copyright

Copyright has expired for all works published in the United States before 1923. In other words, if the work was published in the U.S. before January 1, 1923 you are free to use it in the U.S. without permission. As an example, the graphic illustration of the man with mustache (above) was published sometime in the 19th century and is in the public domain, so no permission was required to include it within this book. These rules and dates apply regardless of whether the work was created by an individual author, a group of authors, or an employee (a work made for hire).

Because of legislation passed in 1998, no new works will fall into the public domain until 2019, when works published in 1923 will expire. In 2020, works published in 1924 will expire, and so on. For works published after 1977, if the work was written by a single author, the copyright will not expire until 70 years after the author's death. If a work was written by several authors and published after 1977, it will not expire until 70 years after the last surviving author dies.

Year-End Expiration of Copyright Terms

Copyright protection always expires at the end of the calendar year of the year it's set to expire. In other words, the last day of copyright protection for any work is December 31. For example, if an author of a work died on June 1, 2000, protection of the works would continue through December 31, 2070.

---

2. The Renewal Trapdoor

Thousands of works published in the United States before 1964 fell into the public domain because the copyright was not renewed in time under the law in effect then. If a work was first published before 1964, the owner had to file a renewal with the Copyright Office during the 28th year after publication. No renewal meant a loss of copyright.

If you plan on using a work that was published after 1922, but before 1964, you should research the records of the Copyright Office to determine if a renewal was filed. Chapter 13 describes methods of researching copyright status.

3. Dedicated Works

If, upon viewing a work, you see words such as "This work is dedicated to the public domain," then it is free for you to use. Sometimes an author deliberately chooses not to protect a work and dedicates the work to the public. This type of dedication is rare, and unless there is express authorization placing the work in the public domain, do not assume that the work is free to use. For example, many people mistakenly assume that shareware and freeware are in the public domain (see "Shareware and Freeware," below).

An additional concern is whether the person making the dedication has the right to do so. Only the copyright owner can dedicate a work to the public domain. Sometimes, the creator of the work is not the copyright owner and does not have authority. If in doubt, contact the copyright owner to verify the dedication. Information about locating copyright owners is provided in Chapter 13.

Dedicating Works to the Public Domain Through Creative Commons

Creative Commons, a nonprofit organization designed to foster the public domain, helps copyright owners dedicate their works to the public domain. Copyright owners may dedicate their works immediately or they can choose to use the "Founders' Copyright"—the original copyright term adopted by the first copyright law in 1790. This consists of copyright protection for an initial term of 14 years after publication, renewable for an additional 14 years if the copyright owner so desires. The copyright owner fills out an online application and sells the copyright to Creative Commons for one dollar; in return, the organization gives the copyright owner an exclusive license to the work for 14 or 28 years.

Original authors can also choose to require that users of the works they dedicate attribute the works to the authors. Works dedicated to the public domain are listed on the Creative Commons website so people can easily find them. For detailed information, visit the website at www .creativecommons.org.

O'Reilly & Associates, a major publisher of computer and technical books, uses the Founders Copyright for its publications (if their authors agree). This means that, 14 or 28 years after publication, hundreds of its titles will be released to the public domain. The Creative Commons website lists what will be available at http:// creativecommons.org/projects/founderscopyright/ oreilly.

Shareware and Freeware

Shareware is a system of marketing software. It is distributed at no charge on a trial basis after which, if the recipient likes the software and intends to use it, he or she must pay a fee. Freeware is software that is made available to the public for free. Unlike shareware, there are no fees. Both of these forms of software are protected under copyright law: you cannot reproduce or distribute these programs unless authorized by the copyright owners—even if you got them for free. For example, in one case, a company gathered various shareware programs and offered them in a CD-ROM collection, despite warnings on the shareware prohibiting such use. A court ruled that the shareware, originally placed on the Internet for free distribution, was entitled to copyright protection. Do not assume that because you acquired a work for free, it is in the public domain.

Clip Art Compilations

Generally clip art is sold in books, CD-ROM bundles, or from websites, and is often offered as "copyright-free." The term "copyright-free" is usually a misnomer that actually refers to either royalty-free artwork or work in the public domain. Keep in mind that much of the artwork advertised as copyright-free is actually royalty-free artwork, which *is* protected by copyright. Your rights and limitations to use such artwork are expressed in the artwork packaging or in the shrink-wrap agreement or license that accompanies the artwork. These principles are discussed in more detail in Chapter 3.

If the artwork is in the public domain, you are free to copy items without restriction. However, even if the artwork is in the public domain, the complete collection may not be reproduced and sold as a clip art collection because that may infringe the unique manner in which the art is collected (known as a compilation or collective work copyright).

4. Copyright Does Not Protect Certain Works

There are some things that copyright law does not protect. Copyright law does not protect the titles of books or movies, nor does it protect short phrases such as "Make my day." Copyright protection also doesn't cover facts, ideas, or theories. These things are free for all to use without authorization.

a. Short Phrases

Phrases such as "Show me the money" or "Beam me up" are not protected under copyright law. Short phrases, names, titles, or small groups of words are considered common idioms of the English language and are free for anyone to use. However, a short phrase used as an advertising slogan is protectible under trademark law. In that case, you could not use a similar phrase for the purpose of selling products or services. Subsequent chapters explain how this rule applies to specific types of works. For more information on trademarks, see Chapter 10.

b. Facts and Theories

A fact or a theory—for example, the fact that a comet will pass by the Earth in 2027—is not protected by copyright. If a scientist discovered this fact, anyone would be free to use it without asking for permission from the scientist. Similarly, if someone creates a theory that the comet can be destroyed by a nuclear device, anyone could use that theory to create a book or movie. However, the unique manner in which a fact is expressed may be protected. Therefore, if a filmmaker created a movie about destroying a comet with a nuclear device, the specific way he presented the ideas in the movie would be protected by copyright.

EXAMPLE: Neil Young wrote a song, "Ohio," about the shooting of four college students during the Vietnam War. You are free to use the facts surrounding the shooting but you may not copy Mr. Young's unique expression of these facts without his permission.

In some cases, you are not free to copy a collection of facts because the collection of facts may be protectible as a compilation (see Section B5). For more information on how copyright applies to facts, refer to Chapter 2, Section G3.

Are Local Laws in the Public Domain?

For decades, publishers of model codes—sample laws that a city or state could adopt—have claimed copyright in their creations. State and local laws and ordinances based on such codes often contain copyright notices in the publisher's name or some other indication the publisher claims the copyright. In a significant victory for public domain proponents, a federal appellate court found that model codes enter the public domain when they are enacted into law by local governments.

The case came about when Peter Veeck posted the local building codes of Anna and Savoy, two small towns in north Texas, on his website. Both towns had adopted a model building code published by Southern Building Code Congress International, Inc. (SBCCI). Veeck made a few attempts to inspect several towns' copies of the Building Code, but he was not able to locate them easily.

Eventually, Veeck purchased the model building codes directly from SBCCI; he paid $72 and received a copy of the codes on disk. Although the software licensing agreement and copyright notice indicated that the codes could not be copied and distributed, Veeck cut and pasted their text onto his website. Veeck's website did not specify that the codes were written by SBCCI. Instead, he identified them, correctly, as the building codes of Anna and Savoy, Texas.

SBCCI sued Veeck for copyright infringement. Veeck lost in the trial court, but ultimately won on appeal. The court held that the model codes were in the public domain because:

- The law is always in the public domain, whether it consists of government statutes, ordinances, regulations, or judicial decisions.
- When a model code is enacted into law, it becomes a fact—the law of a particular local government. Indeed, the particular wording of a law is itself a fact, and that wording cannot be expressed in any other way. A fact itself is not copyrightable, nor is the way that the fact is expressed if there is only one way to express it. Since the legal code of a local government cannot be expressed in any way but as it is actually written, the fact and expression merge, and the law is uncopyrightable.

(*Veeck v. Southern Building Code Congress International, Inc.*, 293 F.3d 791 (5th Cir. 2002).)

The *Veeck* decision's reasoning has the effect of placing every model code that has been adopted by a government entity in the public domain. Any person may reproduce such a code, as adopted, for any purpose, including placing it on a website. However, model codes that have not been adopted by any government body are protected by copyright.

c. Ideas

Copyright law does not protect ideas; it only protects the particular way an idea is expressed. What's the difference between an idea and its expression? In the case of a story or movie, the idea is really the plot in its most basic form. For example, the "idea" of the movie *Contact* is that a determined scientist, seeking to improve humankind, communicates with alien life forms. The same idea has been used in many motion pictures, books, and television shows including *The Day the Earth Stood Still*, *The Abyss*, and *Star Trek*. Many paintings, photographs, and songs contain similar ideas. You can always use the underlying idea or theme—such as communicating with aliens for the improvement of the world—but you cannot copy the unique manner in which the author expresses the idea. This unique expression may include literary devices such as dialogue, characters, and subplots.

In a 2003 case, the producers of the television show *Survivor* claimed that their show was a "new genre" of television show with a unique format combining the elements of "voyeur verité, hostile environment in the deserted island sense, building of social alliances, challenges arising from the game show element, and serial elimination." They sued to prevent a similar reality-competition show called *Celebrity*.

The court found that this genre of television show was an unprotectible idea, as is any genre. In other words, anyone could produce a show based on the basic idea of contestants in a "reality" situation eliminating each other. *Celebrity* would infringe on *Survivor* only if it copied a substantial amount of the specific details of *Survivor*, which it did not do. There were many differences between the two shows—for example, the way the contestants were eliminated—and *Celebrity* had an audience participation element and a comedic tone, unlike the serious *Survivor*. (*CBS Broadcasting, Inc. v. ABC, Inc.* 2003 U.S. Dist. LEXIS 20258 (S.D. N.Y. 2003).)

The Merger Doctrine

There is an exception to the principle that you cannot copy the unique expression of a fact or idea. If there are a limited number of ways to express the fact or idea, you are permitted to copy the expression. This is known as the "merger doctrine"—meaning the idea and the expression are merged or inseparable. For example, in the case of a map, there may be very few ways to express the symbol for an airport other than by using a small image of an airplane. In that case, you are free to use the airport symbol. Similarly, there may be a limited way of expressing a rule about the public domain, for example, the statement, "Works published in the U.S. before 1923 are in the public domain." The fact and the expression are inseparable so you are free to copy the expression. As you can imagine, this is a heavily litigated area, and many companies have butted heads to determine the boundaries of the merger doctrine. For example, Microsoft and Apple litigated over the right to use the trash pail icon as a symbol for deleting computer materials. A federal court of appeals ruled that design constraints made the trash can an unprotectible element of the graphic interface and that Apple could not claim infringement solely based on another company's use of a similar icon. (*Apple Computer, Inc. v. Microsoft Corp.*, 35 F.3d 1435 (9th Cir. 1994).)

d. U.S. Government Works

In the U.S., any work created by a federal government employee or officer is in the public domain, provided that the work was created in that person's official capacity. For example, during the 1980s, a songwriter used words from a speech by then-President Ronald Reagan as the basis for song lyrics. The words from the speech were in the public domain so the songwriter did not need permission from Ronald Reagan. Keep in mind that this rule applies only to works created by federal employees and not to works created by state or local government employees. However, state and local laws and court decisions are in the public domain. (See "Are Local Laws in the Public Domain?" above)

Some federal publications (or portions of them) are protected under copyright law, which is usually indicated on the title page or in the copyright notice. For example, the IRS may acquire permission to use a copyrighted chart in a federal tax booklet. The document may indicate that a certain chart is "Copyright Dr. Matt Polazzo." In that case, you could not copy the chart without permission from Dr. Polazzo.

Publishing Legal Cases and Pagination

As noted above, federal, state, and local laws and court decisions are in the public domain. (See "Are Local Laws in the Public Domain?" above.) However, legal publishers have attempted to get around the public domain status by claiming that unique page numbering systems are copyrightable. These publishers argued that you can copy and distribute a court decision, but you cannot copy the page numbering, which is crucial to the official citation system used by the courts. For many years, Lexis and other computerized legal research systems could not cite to the official page numbering system used by West publications. In a 1994 case, West Publishing Company sued when a legal publisher, Matthew Bender, incorporated West's page numbering system on a CD-ROM product. A court of appeals ruled that the use of West's pagination was not protectible and in any case, the page citation copying was permitted as a fair use. As a result of this ruling, you are free to copy a publisher's reproduction of court decisions and page numbering. *(Matthew Bender & Co. v. West Publishing Co.,* 158 F.3d 693 (2d Cir. 1998). But see also *West Publishing Company v. Mead Data,* 799 F.2d 1219 (1986).)

Loss of Copyright From Lack of Copyright Notice

Under copyright laws that were in effect before 1978, a work that was published without copyright notice fell into the public domain. If the work did not include the word "Copyright" or a © (a "c" in a circle) and the name of the copyright owner, the work would enter the public domain. This rule was repealed; copyright notice is not required for works first published after March 1, 1989 (although works first published prior to that date must still include notice). Just because you find a copy of a book without a copyright notice doesn't mean that the work is in the public domain. It's possible that the copy you are viewing is unauthorized or that the notice has only been removed from a very small number of copies, both of which are excusable. It is also possible that the author followed a copyright law procedure for correcting the error. And, if you're using text from a journal, anthology, newsletter, or magazine published before March 1, 1989, check to see if there is a copyright notice either for the individual article or for the whole publication. Either type of notice will prevent the work from falling into the public domain.

The table below may help you determine public domain status.

Table for Determining Public Domain Status	
Works published in the U.S. before 1923	In the public domain
Works published in the U.S. after 1922 but before 1964	Initial term of 28 years. If not renewed during the 28th year, the work falls into the public domain.
Works published in the U.S. after 1922 but before March 1, 1989	Generally, if a work was published without copyright notice under the authorization of the copyright owner and the law does not provide an exception for the omission, the work is in the public domain.

B. Public Domain Trouble Spots

While it's true that no strings are attached to using public domain materials, you should be aware of certain potholes on the public domain highway, as described below.

1. Multilayered Works

Works such as movies or sound recordings may contain many underlying works, such as musical sound tracks, painted illustrations, or other works. There has been a disturbing trend by some copyright owners to assert protection in an element of a public domain work. For example, the film *It's a Wonderful Life* fell into the public domain because of a failure to renew copyright. For years, anyone was free to copy and sell the movie on videotape. However, a production company recently acquired rights to the musical sound track that is used in the movie. That sound track is not in the public do-

main. The copyright owner of the sound track can now prevent anyone from copying the music, thereby effectively stopping anyone from copying the film (unless the sound track is removed). Multi-layered works can create confusion when trying to determine public domain status.

Usually you don't have to be concerned with this type of legal maneuver as it is only used in connection with popular and older multilayered works such as classic films. It would be difficult, if not impossible, to apply this procedure to a public domain book or painting.

EXAMPLE: A movie musical containing songs by Cole Porter is in the public domain because of a failure to renew copyright. However, the Cole Porter songs were renewed in time, so they are still protected by copyright and cannot be reproduced without permission. Therefore, you must obtain permission from the copyright owner of the Cole Porter songs in order to copy the public domain film. If you do not want to obtain permission from the owner, you must delete the songs from the film.

2. Public Domain Works That Are Modified

Modifications to a public domain work may be protected by copyright and cannot be used without permission. A famous example used in many copyright classes is the artist who paints an elaborate hat and mustache on the Mona Lisa. Even though anyone is free to copy the image of the Mona Lisa, the modified image (with mustache and hat) is protected under the artist's copyright.

EXAMPLE: Color has been added to the black-and-white public domain film *God's Little Acre*. This colorization process is copyrightable. Therefore, the colorized version of *God's Little Acre* cannot be copied without permission.

3. Works Protected by Trademark Law

It is possible that a work may not be protected by copyright, but is still protected by trademark laws. Chapter 10 provides more information on trademarks.

> EXAMPLE: The gold-colored top of the New York Life building is in the public domain—anyone can photograph it. However, that image also functions as a trademark for the New York Life Company, and a competing company could not use the image if it would be likely to confuse life insurance consumers.

Plagiarism, Attribution, and the Public Domain

If you copy from a public domain writing, do you have to credit the author? The United States Supreme Court has answered "No," holding that there is no legal requirement to provide any attribution when public domain works are copied and placed into new works. (*Dastar Corp. v. 20th Century Fox Film Corp.*, 123 S.Ct. 2041 (2003).)

However, just because there is no legal requirement to give credit to the creators of public domain works, doesn't mean you don't have to do it. When copying works from the public domain, be careful to avoid plagiarism. Plagiarism occurs when someone poses as the originator of words he did not write, ideas he did not conceive, or facts he did not discover. Although you cannot be sued for plagiarizing a public domain work, doing so can result in serious professional and personal penalties. For example, in the case of college professors and journalists, it may result in termination; for students, it could lead to expulsion; if done by well-known historians, it can result in public humiliation.

4. Works Protected in Other Countries

Before 1978, most countries had different periods of copyright protection than the United States. As a result, many works that are public domain in the United States are still protected by copyright in foreign countries and vice versa. Therefore, you may have to research public domain status in each country in which you plan to publish your work.

5. Compilations

Often an author creates a work by selecting various public domain components and grouping them together. If the selection, coordination, and arrangement of the material is unique, it will be protected as a copyrightable compilation.

> EXAMPLE: The owners of the book *Bartlett's Familiar Quotations* selected and arranged famous quotes. Anyone may copy a few quotes from *Bartlett's Familiar Quotations,* but no one may copy the selection and arrangement of all the quotes.

6. Works First Published Outside the U.S.

The copyrights of some works first published outside the United States have been resurrected, removing them from the public domain. As a result of international treaties signed in the 1990s, public domain works that meet certain qualifications are now protected. (For a detailed discussion, see *The Copyright Handbook*, by Stephen Fishman (Nolo).)

You may be able to do some public domain detective work yourself (see the research tips offered in Chapter 13) or you can hire private companies or individuals to perform public domain searches for you. Information about such companies is included in Chapter 13.

Fair Use

Fair use is a copyright principle based on the belief that the public is entitled to freely use portions of copyrighted materials for purposes of commentary and criticism. For example, if you wish to criticize a novelist, you should have the freedom to quote a portion of the novelist's work without asking permission. Absent this freedom, copyright owners could stifle any negative comments about their work.

Unfortunately, if the copyright owner disagrees with your fair use interpretation, the dispute may have to be resolved by a lawsuit or arbitration. If it's not a fair use, then you are infringing upon the rights of the copyright owner and may be liable for damages.

The only guidance for fair use is provided by a set of factors outlined in copyright law. These factors are weighed in each case to determine whether a use qualifies as a fair use. For example, one important factor is whether your use will deprive the copyright owner of income. Unfortunately, weighing the fair use factors is often quite subjective. For this reason, the fair use road map can be tricky to navigate.

This chapter explains the various rules behind fair use principles. To help you get a feel for which uses courts consider to be fair uses and which ones they don't, several examples of fair use lawsuits are provided at the end of this chapter.

 For educational fair use guidelines, see Chapter 7, which deals with academic permissions.

A. What Is Fair Use?

In its most general sense, a fair use is any copying of copyrighted material done for a limited and "transformative" purpose, such as to comment upon, criticize, or parody a copyrighted work. Such uses can be done without permission from the copyright owner. In other words, fair use is a defense against a claim of copyright infringement. If your use qualifies as a fair use, then it would not be considered an illegal infringement.

So what is a "transformative" use? If this definition seems ambiguous or vague, be aware that millions of dollars in legal fees have been spent attempting to define what qualifies as a fair use. There are no hard-and-fast rules, only general rules and varied court decisions, because the judges and lawmakers who created the fair use exception did not want to limit its definition. Like free speech, they wanted it to have an expansive meaning that could be open to interpretation.

Most fair use analysis falls into two categories: 1) commentary and criticism, or 2) parody.

1. Commentary and Criticism

If you are commenting upon or critiquing a copyrighted work—for instance, writing a book review—fair use principles allow you to reproduce some of the work to achieve your purposes. Some examples of commentary and criticism include:

- quoting a few lines from a Bob Dylan song in a music review
- summarizing and quoting from a medical article on prostate cancer in a news report
- copying a few paragraphs from a news article for use by a teacher or student in a lesson, or
- copying a portion of a *Sports Illustrated* magazine article for use in a related court case.

The underlying rationale of this rule is that the public reaps benefits from your review, which is enhanced by including some of the copyrighted material. Additional examples of commentary or criticism are provided in the examples of fair use cases in Section C.

2. Parody

A parody is a work that ridicules another, usually well-known work, by imitating it in a comic way. Judges understand that, by its nature, parody demands some taking from the original work being parodied. Unlike other forms of fair use, a fairly extensive use of the original work is permitted in a parody in order to "conjure up" the original.

B. Measuring Fair Use: The Four Factors

Unfortunately, the only way to get a definitive answer on whether a particular use is a fair use is to have it resolved in federal court. Judges use four factors to resolve fair use disputes, as discussed in detail below. It's important to understand that these factors are only guidelines that courts are free to adapt to particular situations on a case-by-case basis. In other words, a judge has a great deal of freedom when making a fair use determination, so the outcome in any given case can be hard to predict.

The four factors judges consider are:

- the purpose and character of your use
- the nature of the copyrighted work
- the amount and substantiality of the portion taken, and
- the effect of the use upon the potential market.

Educational Fair Use Guidelines

Since the current copyright law was adopted, various organizations and scholars have established guidelines for educational uses. These guidelines are not part of the Copyright Act. However, the guidelines establish the standards for uses and copying in education. These guidelines, as well as other rules regarding educational uses are summarized in Chapter 7, which deals with academic and educational permissions.

1. The Transformative Factor: The Purpose and Character of Your Use

In a 1997 case, the Supreme Court emphasized this first factor as being a primary indicator of fair use. At issue is whether the material has been used to help create something new or merely copied verba-tim into another work. When taking portions of copyrighted work, ask yourself the following questions:

- Has the material you have taken from the original work been transformed by adding new expression or meaning?
- Was value added to the original by creating new information, new aesthetics, new insights, and understandings?

In a parody, for example, the parodist transforms the original by holding it up to ridicule. Purposes such as scholarship, research, or education may also qualify as transformative uses because the work is the subject of review or commentary.

EXAMPLE: Roger borrows several quotes from the speech given by the CEO of a logging company. Roger prints these quotes under photos of old-growth redwoods in his environmental newsletter. By juxtaposing the quotes with the photos of endangered trees, Roger has transformed the remarks from their original purpose and used them to create a new insight. The copying would probably be permitted as a fair use.

2. The Nature of the Copyrighted Work

Because the dissemination of facts or information benefits the public, you have more leeway to copy from factual works such as biographies than you do from fictional works such as plays or novels.

In addition, you will have a stronger case of fair use if you copy the material from a published work than an unpublished work. The scope of fair use is narrower for unpublished works because an author has the right to control the first public appearance of his or her expression.

3. The Amount and Substantiality of the Portion Taken

The less you take, the more likely that your copying will be excused as a fair use. However, even if you take a small portion of a work, your copying will not be a fair use if the portion taken is the "heart" of the work. In other words, you are more likely to run into problems if you take the most memorable aspect of a work. For example, it would probably not be a fair use to copy the opening guitar riff and the words "I can't get no satisfaction" from the song "Satisfaction."

This rule—less is more—is not necessarily true in parody cases. A parodist is permitted to borrow quite a bit, even the heart of the original work, in order to conjure up the original work. That's because, as the Supreme Court has acknowledged, "the heart is also what most readily conjures up the [original] for parody, and it is the heart at which parody takes aim." (*Campbell v. Acuff-Rose Music*, 510 U.S. 569 (1994).)

4. The Effect of the Use Upon the Potential Market

Another important fair use factor is whether your use deprives the copyright owner of income or undermines a new or potential market for the copyrighted work. Depriving a copyright owner of income is very likely to trigger a lawsuit. This is true even if you are not competing directly with the original work.

For example, in one case an artist used a copyrighted photograph without permission as the basis for wood sculptures, copying all elements of the photo. The artist earned several hundred thousand dollars selling the sculptures. When the photographer sued, the artist claimed his sculptures were a fair use because the photographer would never have considered making sculptures. The court disagreed, stating that it did not matter whether the photographer had considered making sculptures; what mattered was that a potential market for sculptures of the photograph existed. (*Rogers v. Koons*, 960 F.2d 301 (2d Cir. 1992).)

Too Small for Fair Use: The De Minimis Defense

In some cases, the amount of material copied is so small (or "de minimis") that the court permits it without even conducting a fair use analysis. For example, in the motion picture *Seven*, several copyrighted photographs appeared in the film, prompting the copyright owner of the photographs to sue the producer of the movie. The court held that the photos "appear fleetingly and are obscured, severely out of focus, and virtually unidentifiable." The court excused the use of the photographs as "de minimis" and didn't require a fair use analysis. (*Sandoval v. New Line Cinema Corp.*, 147 F.3d 215 (2d Cir. 1998).)

As with fair use, there is no bright line test for determining a de minimis use. For example, in another case, a court determined that the use of a copyrighted poster for a total of 27 seconds in the background of the TV show "Roc" was not de minimis. What distinguished the use of the poster from the use of the photographs in the *Seven* case? The court stated that the poster was clearly visible and recognizable with sufficient observable detail for the "average lay observer" to view the artist's imagery and colorful style. (*Ringgold v. Black Entertainment Television, Inc.*, 126 F.3d 70 (2d Cir. 1997).)

Again, parody is given a slightly different fair use analysis with regard to the impact on the market. It's possible that a parody may diminish or even destroy the market value of the original work. That is, the parody may be so good that the public can never take the original work seriously again. Although this may cause a loss of income, it's not the same type of loss as when an infringer merely appropriates the work. As one judge explained, "The economic effect of a parody with which we are concerned is not its potential to destroy or diminish the market for the original—any bad review can have that effect—but whether it fulfills the demand for the original." (*Fisher v. Dees*, 794 F.2d 432 (9th Cir. 1986).)

5. The "Fifth" Fair Use Factor: Are You Good or Bad?

When you review fair use cases, you may find that they sometimes contradict one another or conflict with the rules expressed in this chapter. Fair use involves subjective judgments and are often affected by factors such as a judge or jury's personal sense of right or wrong. Despite the fact that the Supreme Court has indicated that offensiveness is not a fair use factor, you should be aware that a morally offended judge or jury may rationalize its decision against fair use.

For example, in one case a manufacturer of novelty cards parodied the successful children's dolls the Cabbage Patch Kids. The parody card series was entitled the Garbage Pail Kids and used gruesome and grotesque names and characters to poke fun at the wholesome Cabbage Patch image. Some copyright experts were surprised when a federal court considered the parody an infringement, not a fair use. (*Original Appalachian Artworks, Inc. v. Topps Chewing Gum, Inc.*, 642 F. Supp. 1031 (N.D. Ga. 1986).)

Does It Help to Use a Disclaimer?

A disclaimer is a statement that "disassociates" your work from the work that you have borrowed. For example, if you write an unauthorized biography of Mickey Mouse, you may include a disclaimer such as "This book is not associated with or endorsed by the Walt Disney Company." Will it help your position if you use a disclaimer? In close cases where the court is having a difficult time making a fair use determination, a prominently placed disclaimer may have a positive effect on the way the court perceives your use. However, generally a disclaimer by itself will not help. That is, if the fair use factors weigh against you, the disclaimer won't make any difference. For example, in a case involving a *Seinfeld* trivia book (see Section C, below), the publisher included a disclaimer that the book "has not been approved or licensed by any entity involved in creating or producing *Seinfeld*." Despite the disclaimer, the court held that the use of the *Seinfeld* materials was an infringement, not a fair use.

What If You Acknowledge the Source Material?

Some people mistakenly believe it's permissible to use a work (or portion of it) if an acknowledgment is provided. For example, they believe it's okay to use a photograph in a magazine as long as the name of the photographer is included. This is not true. Acknowledgment of the source material (such as citing the photographer) may be a consideration in a fair use determination, but it will not protect against a claim of infringement. In some cases, such as advertisements, acknowledgments can backfire and create additional legal claims, such as a violation of the right of publicity. When in doubt as to the right to use or acknowledge a source, the most prudent course may be to seek permission of the copyright owner.

C. Summaries of Fair Use Cases

The best way to understand the flexible principle of fair use is to review actual cases decided by the courts. Below are summaries of a variety of fair use cases.

1. Cases Involving Text

- **Fair use.** A biographer of Richard Wright quoted from six unpublished letters and ten unpublished journal entries by Wright. **Important factors:** No more than 1% of Wright's unpublished letters were copied and the purpose was informational. (*Wright v. Warner Books, Inc.*, 953 F.2d 731 (2d Cir. 1991).)

- **Fair use.** Publisher Larry Flynt made disparaging statements about the Reverend Jerry Falwell on one page of *Hustler* magazine. Rev. Falwell made several hundred thousand copies of the page and distributed them as part of a fund-raising effort. **Important factors:** Rev. Falwell's copying did not diminish the sales of the magazine (since it was already off the market) and would not adversely affect the marketability of back issues. (*Hustler Magazine, Inc. v. Moral Majority, Inc.*, 606 F. Supp. 1526 (C.D. Cal. 1985).)

- **Not a fair use.** An author copied more than half of an unpublished manuscript to prove that someone was involved in the overthrow of the Iranian government. **Important factors:** A substantial portion was taken (half of the work) and the work had not been published yet. (*Love v. Kwitny*, 772 F. Supp. 1367 (S.D.N.Y. 1989).)

- **Not a fair use.** A biographer paraphrased large portions of unpublished letters written by the famed author J.D. Salinger. Although people could read these letters at a university library, Salinger had never authorized their reproduction. In other words, the first time that the general public would see these letters was in their paraphrased form in the biography. Salinger successfully sued to prevent publication. **Important factors:** The letters were unpublished and were the "backbone" of the biography—so much so that without the letters the resulting biography was unsuccessful. In other words, the letters may have been taken more as a means of capitalizing on the interest in Salinger than in providing a critical study of the author. (*Salinger v. Random House*, 811 F.2d 90 (2d Cir. 1987).)

- **Not a fair use.** *The Nation* magazine published excerpts from ex-President Gerald Ford's unpublished memoirs. The publication in *The Nation* was made several weeks prior to the date Mr. Ford's book was to be serialized in another magazine. **Important factors:** *The Nation's* copying seriously damaged the marketability of Mr. Ford's serialization rights. (*Harper & Row v. Nation Enters.*, 471 U.S. 539 (1985).)

- **Not a fair use.** A company published a book entitled *Welcome to Twin Peaks: A Complete Guide to Who's Who and What's What*, containing direct quotations and paraphrases from the television show *Twin Peaks,* as well as detailed descriptions of plots, characters, and setting. **Important factors:** The amount of the material taken was substantial and the publication adversely affected the potential market for authorized books about the program. (*Twin Peaks v. Publications Int'l, Ltd.* 996 F.2d 1366 (2d Cir. 1993).)

- **Not a fair use.** A company published a book of trivia questions about the events and characters of the *Seinfeld* television series. The book included questions based upon events and characters in 84 *Seinfeld* episodes and used actual dialogue from the show in 41 of the book's questions. **Important factors:** As in the *Twin Peaks* case, the book affected the owner's right to make derivative *Seinfeld* works such as trivia books. (*Castle Rock Entertainment, Inc. v. Carol Publ. Group*, 150 F.3d 132 (2d Cir. 1998).)

2. Artwork and Audiovisual Cases

- **Fair use.** A search engine's practice of creating small reproductions ("thumbnails") of images and placing them on its own website (known as "inlining") did not undermine the potential market for the sale or licensing of those images. **Important factors:** The thumbnails were much smaller and of much poorer quality than the original photos and served to help the public access the images by indexing them. (*Kelly v. Arriba-Soft*, 336 F.3d. 811 (9th Cir. 2003).)

- **Fair use.** The makers of a movie biography of Muhammad Ali used 41 seconds from a boxing match film in their biography. **Important factors: A small portion of film was taken and the purpose was informational. (*Monster Communications, Inc. v. Turner Broadcasting Sys. Inc.*, 935 F. Supp. 490 (S.D.N.Y. 1996).)

- **Fair use.** In a lawsuit commonly known as the *Betamax* case, the Supreme Court determined that the home videotaping of a television broadcast was a fair use. This was one of the few occasions when copying a complete work (for example, a complete episode of the *Kojak* television show) was accepted as a fair use. Evidence indicated that most viewers were "time-shifting" (taping in order to watch later) and not "library-building" (collecting the videos in order to build a video library). **Important factors:** The Supreme Court reasoned that the "delayed" system of viewing did not deprive the copyright owners of revenue. (*Universal City Studios v. Sony Corp.*, 464 U.S. 417 (1984).)

- **Not a fair use.** A television news program copied one minute and 15 seconds from a 72-minute Charlie Chaplin film and used it in a news report about Chaplin's death. **Important factors:** The court felt that the portions taken were substantial and part of the "heart" of the film. (*Roy Export Co. Estab. of Vaduz v. Columbia Broadcasting Sys., Inc.*, 672 F.2d 1095, 1100 (2d Cir. 1982).)

- **Not a fair use.** A television station's news broadcast used 30 seconds from a four-minute copyrighted videotape of the 1992 Los Angeles beating of Reginald Denny. **Important factors:** The use was commercial, took the heart of the work, and affected the copyright owner's ability to market the video. (*Los Angeles News Service v. KCAL-TV Channel 9*, 108 F.3d 1119 (9th Cir. 1997).)

- **Not a fair use.** A poster of a "church quilt" was used in the background of a television series for 27 seconds. **Important factors:** The court was influenced by the prominence of the poster, its thematic importance for the set decoration of a church, and the fact that it was a conventional practice to license such

works for use in television programs. (*Ringgold v. Black Entertainment Television, Inc.*, 126 F.3d 70 (2d Cir. 1997).)

3. Internet Cases

- **Fair use.** *The Washington Post* used three brief quotations from Church of Scientology texts posted on the Internet. **Important factors:** Only a small portion of the work was excerpted and the purpose was for news commentary. (*Religious Technology Center v. Pagliarina*, 908 F. Supp. 1353 (E.D. Va. 1995).)

- **Not a fair use.** Entire publications of the Church of Scientology were posted on the Internet by several individuals without Church permission. **Important factors:** Fair use is intended to permit the borrowing of portions of a work, not complete works. (*Religious Technology Center v. Lerma*, 40 U.S.P.Q. 2d 1569 (E.D. Va. 1996).)

4. Music Cases

- **Fair use.** A person running for political office used 15 seconds of his opponent's campaign song in a political ad. **Important factors:** A small portion of the song was used and the purpose was for purposes of political debate. (*Keep Thomson Governor Comm. v. Citizens for Gallen Comm.*, 457 F. Supp. 957 (D.N.H. 1978).)

- **Fair use.** A television film crew, covering an Italian festival in Manhattan, recorded a band playing a portion of a copyrighted song "Dove sta Zaza." The music was replayed during a news broadcast. **Important factors:** Only a portion of the song was used, it was incidental to the news event, and it did not result in any actual damage to the composer or to the market for the work. (*Italian Book Corp, v. American Broadcasting Co.*, 458 F. Supp. 65 (S.D.N.Y. 1978).)

5. Parody Cases

- **Fair use.** The rap group 2 Live Crew borrowed the opening musical tag and the words (but not the melody) from the first line of the song "Pretty Woman" ("Oh, pretty woman, walking down the street"). The rest of the lyrics and the music were different. **Important factors:** The group's use was transformative and borrowed only a small portion of the original song. The 2 Live Crew version was essentially a different piece of music; the only similarity was a brief musical opening part and the opening line. (Note: The rap group had initially sought to pay for the right to use portions of the song but were rebuffed by the publisher, who did not want "Pretty Woman" used in a rap song.) (*Campbell v. Acuff-Rose Music*, 510 U.S. 569 (1994).)

- **Fair use.** The composers of the song "When Sunny Gets Blue" claimed that their song was infringed by "When Sonny Sniffs Glue," a 29-second parody that altered the original lyric line and borrowed six bars of the song. A court determined this parody was excused as a fair use. **Important factors:** Only 29 seconds of music were borrowed (not the complete song). (*Fisher v. Dees,* 794 F.2d 432 (9th Cir. 1986).) (Note: As a general rule, parodying more than a few lines of a song lyric is unlikely to be excused as a fair use. Performers such as Weird Al Yankovic, who earn a living by humorously modifying hit songs, seek permission of the songwriters before recording their parodies.)

- **Fair use.** Comedians on the late-night television show *Saturday Night Live* parodied the song "I Love New York" using the words "I Love Sodom." Only the words "I Love" and four musical notes were taken from the original work. **Important factors:** The *Saturday Night Live* version of the jingle did not compete with or detract from the original song. (*Elsmere Music, Inc. v. National Broadcasting Co.*, 482 F. Supp. 741 (S.D.N.Y.), aff'd 632 F.2d 252 (2d Cir. 1980).)

- **Fair use.** A movie company used a photo of a naked pregnant woman onto which it superimposed the head of actor Leslie Nielsen. The photo was a parody using similar lighting and body positioning of a famous photograph taken by Annie Leibovitz of the actress Demi Moore for the cover of *Vanity Fair* magazine. **Important factors:** The movie company's use was transformative because it imitated the pho-tographer's style for comic effect or ridicule. (*Leibovitz v. Paramount Pictures Corp.*, 137 F.3d 109 (2d Cir. N.Y. 1998).)

- **Not a fair use.** An author mimicked the style of a Dr. Seuss book while retelling the facts of the O.J. Simpson murder trial in *The Cat NOT in the Hat! A Parody by Dr. Juice*. The Ninth Circuit Court of Appeals determined that the book was a satire, not a parody, because the book did not poke fun at or ridicule Dr. Seuss. Instead, it merely used the Dr. Seuss characters and style to tell the story of the murder. **Important factors:** The author's work was nontransformative and commercial. (*Dr. Seuss Enterprises, L.P. v. Penguin Books USA, Inc.*, 109 F.3d 1394 (9th Cir. 1997).)

- **Not a fair use.** An artist created a cover for a *New Yorker* magazine that presented a humorous view of geography through the eyes of a New York City resident. A movie company later advertised their film *Moscow on the Hudson* using a similar piece of artwork with similar elements. The artist sued and a court ruled that the movie company's poster was not a fair use. **Important factors:** Why is this case different than the previous case involving the Leslie Nielsen/Annie Leibovitz parody? In the *Leibovitz* case, the use was a true parody, characterized by a juxtaposition of imagery that actually commented on or criticized the original. The *Moscow on the Hudson* movie poster did not create a parody; it simply borrowed the *New Yorker's* parody (the typical New York City resident's geographical viewpoint that New York City is the center of the world). (*Steinberg v. Columbia Pictures Industries, Inc.*, 663 F. Supp. 706 (S.D.N.Y. 1987).)

D. Disagreements Over Fair Use: When Are You Likely to Get Sued?

The difficulty in claiming fair use is that there is no way to guarantee that your use will qualify as fair. You may believe that your use qualifies—but, if the copyright owner disagrees, you may have to resolve the dispute in a courtroom. Even if you ultimately persuade the court that your use was in fact a fair use, the expense and time involved in litigation may well outweigh any benefit of using the material in the first place.

EXAMPLE: Sam quotes from four pages of a biography in his documentary film about poet Allen Ginsberg. He believes that his use qualifies as a fair use and he does not seek permission from Barbi, the author of the biography. Barbi does not think that Sam's copying is a fair use and wants to be paid for having her work used in his film. She sues Sam for copyright infringement, and Sam is forced to hire a lawyer to defend him in the lawsuit. Even though the court ultimately rules that Sam's use was a fair use, Sam's lawyer fees exceed $20,000, which far exceeds any profits he earned from the film.

Because there is a sizable gray area in which fair use may or may not apply, there is never a guarantee that your use will qualify as a fair use. The fair use doctrine has been described as a murky concept in which it is often difficult to separate the lawful from the unlawful. Two types of situations are especially likely to cause legal problems:

- Your work causes the owner of the original work to lose money. For example, you borrow portions of a biology text for use in a competing biology text.
- The copyright owner is offended by your use. For example, you satirize the original work and your satire contains sexually explicit references or other offensive material.

Remember, these criteria do not determine whether you will prevail in a fair use lawsuit—they simply indicate whether you are likely to trigger a lawsuit. When you use someone's work and deprive them of money or offend them, the chances of being sued increase.

Just as there are situations that are more likely to cause lawsuits, there are some situations that may lower the risk:

- You use a very small excerpt of a factual work, for example, one or two lines from a news report, for purposes of commentary, criticism, scholarship, research, or news reporting.
- You diligently tried to locate the copyright owner but were unsuccessful, and after analyzing the fair use factors (see Section B), you became convinced that your use would qualify as a fair use.

If in doubt about your fair use assessment, consult with a copyright attorney. For information on dealing with attorneys, see Chapter 16, "Help Beyond This Book."

■

Getting Permission to Use Trademarks

This chapter is about obtaining permission to use trademarks—words, symbols, or devices that identify specific products and services. It includes an explanation of when trademark permission is necessary, how to find a trademark owner, and how to license a trademark for commercial purposes.

In many ways, the use of a trademark is trickier to manage than use of copyrighted material. Even though certain informational and parody uses of trademarks are permitted without permission, there is no guaranteed shield from trademark disputes. Trademark owners are notoriously protective of their business interests and often use trademark law as a means to bully competitors and critics.

Trademark rights are also complex because there is an overlap with copyright law. For example, a fictional character such as Superman can be protected by both trademark and copyright laws. This chapter provides some guidance in sorting out the differences.

At the end of the chapter, you'll find an agreement for licensing a trademark for merchandise purposes. Although there are a few minor differences, you will notice that this agreement is similar to the merchandise agreement in Chapter 11.

Even if your use is legally permissible, an aggressive trademark owner might file a lawsuit to intimidate you and get you to stop using the mark. Sometimes you may be legally entitled to use a trademark without permission on the grounds of free speech (see Section B1). But defending your right to free speech can be expensive, easily costing tens of thousands of dollars. The chances of a legal confrontation increase when you use a famous trademark without permission. Review the rules in this chapter carefully and weigh the benefits against the potential risks before making unauthorized uses of famous trademarks.

A. Trademark Basics

This section provides an overview of trademark basics. Readers familiar with basic trademark principles may skip it and proceed to Section B.

For more trademark information, consult *Trademark: Legal Care for Your Business & Product Name,* by Stephen Elias (Nolo).

1. What Is a Trademark?

A trademark is any word, symbol, or device that identifies and distinguishes a product or service. For example, the word "McDonalds," the distinctive yellow arches, and the Ronald McDonald character are all trademarks of the McDonald's company.

Trademarks used to identify services are also known as service marks. For example, the service mark "UPS" represents a company that provides package delivery services; the mark "The Eagles" identifies a band that provides music services. Service marks have the same legal rights and follow the same rules as trademarks. For this reason, the term "trademark," or sometimes simply "mark," is often used when discussing either trademarks or service marks.

Most trademarks, such as brand names, slogans, and logos, are easy to spot because the trademark owner displays them in a distinct manner, often using stylized lettering. A trademark may also be explicitly identified with the symbols ®, TM, or SM (see Section A5). While most trademarks are easily identifiable, some are more difficult to discern, particularly trade dress, product configurations, colors, and other nontraditional trademarks. The next section discusses the different kinds of trademarks in more depth.

2. Types of Trademarks

There are many different types of trademarks, including:

- **Brand names.** The most common form of trademark is a brand name—for example, Sweet 'N Low or FedEx. Brand names are usually words, although they can be a combination of words, letters, and numbers such as 7-Up.
- **Slogans.** A combination of words used as a slogan qualifies as a trademark—for example, "Where do you want to go today?" for Microsoft computer products or "Hair Color So Natural Only Your Hairdresser Knows for Sure" for Miss Clairol hair products.
- **Logos.** A graphic image or symbol may serve as a trademark—for example, the open-banded cross used by Chevrolet.
- **Sounds.** A sound can function as a trademark—for example, the foghorn sound used by San Francisco radio station KFOG.
- **Trade dress.** Any distinctive combination of elements may serve as a trademark—for example, the combination of yellow and black colors and distinctive lettering used on the Cliff's Notes books.

Websites and Trade Dress

A website using a distinctive combination of colors, graphic borders, and buttons can stop a competitor from imitating this combination of trade dress elements under trademark law. Although website designers are free to incorporate animations, java applets, and other eye-catching features, the chances of litigation increase if you copy a competitor's distinctive combination of website elements such that consumers confuse the two websites.

- **Product configurations.** Distinctive product packaging that is primarily nonfunctional is protected as a trademark—for example, the shape of the Mrs. Butterworth's syrup bottle (resembling a female cook).
- **Fictional characters.** Trademark law protects a fictional character used to sell a product or service. Rules about acquiring permission to use characters are explained in Section B6.

EXAMPLE: The Pebble Beach Company incorporated a distinctive Cypress tree growing on its golf course into an abstract design. This graphic image became a logo distinguishing the Pebble Beach Company's golf services and products from other golf courses. The public is free to photograph the tree, and other golf courses can grow cypress trees, but only the Pebble Beach Company can use this distinctive tree image to identify its golfing services and goods.

3. Trademark Rights

Trademark protection is granted to the first company to use a particular trademark in the marketplace. Trademark rights are created only when the mark is actually used in commerce—that is, in an effort to sell a product or service. Trademark protection lasts for as long as a business continuously uses a trademark to help sell goods or services. Many trademarks have been protected for over a century.

On rare occasions, however, trademark rights end if the public believes that the trademark is a generic term. For example, the terms "aspirin" and "escalator" were trademarks that lost protection once the public used the term to describe all versions of these products, not one manufacturer's version. Nowadays, companies such as Kimberly-Clarke (manufacturer of Kleenex) and Dow Chemical (manufacturer of Styrofoam) aggressively oppose this loss of trademark rights (known as "genericide") by educating the public. For example, a journalist who mistakenly writes "styrofoam cup" will probably receive a letter from Dow indicating that its trademarked Styrofoam products are not used in drinking cups (they are used primarily in boat and house insulation).

4. Trademark Registration

A trademark owner can register the mark with the federal or state government. Registration is not required to obtain trademark protection, but it strengthens and broadens your rights, which is especially important if someone infringes your trademark.

The United States Patent and Trademark Office (PTO) administers federal registrations. The PTO can be accessed on the Web at www.uspto.gov. State registrations are handled by the Secretary of State offices of the 50 states. For an index of all state and federal trademark law websites, see the All About Trademarks website at www.ggmark.com.

5. Trademark Symbols

Typically, the symbols ®, TM, or SM are used along with trademarks—for example, "NIKE®." The symbol ® indicates that a trademark has been registered at the U.S. Patent and Trademark Office (PTO). It is illegal to use the ® symbol if the trademark in question has not been registered with the PTO. There is no legal requirement that the ® be used, but the failure to use it may limit the amount of damages that the trademark owner can recover in an infringement lawsuit. If the trademark hasn't been registered, the owner can use the TM symbol. Similarly, the owner can use the SM symbol for service marks that have not been registered. The TM and SM have no legal significance other than to indicate that the owner is claiming trademark rights.

6. Violations of Trademark Owners' Rights

Trademark owners' rights can be violated in two ways: by direct infringement and by dilution.

a. Direct Infringement

Infringement occurs when one company uses another company's trademark (or a substantially similar mark) in a manner that is likely to confuse consumers into believing that there is some connection, affiliation, or sponsorship between the two companies. Usually this occurs when a trademark is used on similar goods—for example a counterfeit Rolex watch. The counterfeiter is relying on the unauthorized Rolex trademark to confuse consumers into believing that the watch came from the Rolex company. Subtler forms of consumer confusion occur when companies use similar but nonidentical marks or use similar marks on related but nonidentical products or services.

> **EXAMPLE:** A comic book store uses the name "The Batcave" without authorization. Because "Batcave" is a trademark of DC Comics, consumers may believe that DC Comics endorses or is connected with the store. On this basis, the owners of the "Batcave" trademark can bring a trademark infringement lawsuit against the comic book store to stop the unauthorized use.

b. Trademark Dilution

Trademark dilution occurs when the integrity of a trademark is "muddied" by an unwanted commercial association, either by a vulgar or insulting affiliation (tarnishment) or by a connection with a lesser product (blurring).

- **Tarnishment.** A company may tarnish the image of a famous trademark if it uses the trademark to promote a product or service that may be considered offensive. For example, if an X-rated website named itself "Candyland," its use might tarnish the image of the trademark "Candyland" used on the children's game.

- **Blurring.** Normally, the rules of trademark prohibit someone from using a trademark commercially that's owned by someone else if the use is likely to cause customer confusion. However, sometimes even if there's little likelihood of customer confusion, one company can stop another company that uses its famous trademark commercially in a manner that blurs the two companies in the customers' minds. For example, say a toilet paper maker named its product "Rolls Royce Toilet Paper." Even though most people wouldn't think that Rolls Royce toilet paper was produced by the famous luxury car maker, the Rolls Royce car company might pursue the toilet paper maker for diluting its trademark.

In March 2003, in a case involving Victoria's Secret, the Supreme Court ruled that a trademark owner making a dilution claim under the federal dilution act must prove actual harm—that is, that consumers actually believed the mark was tarnished or blurred by the second use—not the likelihood of harm. (*Moseley v. Secret Catalogue, Inc.*, 537 U.S. 418 (2003).)

Dilution is a vague concept, often used by companies to justify going after an offensive use of a trademark. Dilution does not result from an informational use, such as a critical product review, but can, however, result from a commercial uses, such as a comparative advertisement (see Section B).

Altering a Trademark

In addition to blurring and dilution, altering a trademark in a comparative advertisement has also been found to violate a trademark owner's rights. In a television advertisement, a competitor of the farm equipment company John Deere animated the John Deere "deer" logo and appeared to make it run from the competition. The competitor was found liable for trademark dilution. (*Deere & Company v. MTD Prods. Inc.*, 34 U.S.P.Q. 1706 (S.D. N.Y. 1995).) Based on this ruling, it would be unwise to modify another company's trademark unless it can be justified under free speech or parody rules. See Section B for more information on these rules.

---

7. Disparagement and Defamation

Other practices for which you can be sued by a trademark owner are disparagement and defamation. Disparagement is making false statements that interfere with a company's business relations. Defamation is making false statements that injure a business's reputation. Disparagement affects a company's ability to do business; defamation affects the manner in which the public perceives the company's trademarked products.

Unlike infringement and dilution, defamation and disparagement do not have to occur in a commercial context. For example, using a trademark in a newspaper article, if based on false statements, can result in a claim of disparagement or defamation. Disparagement and defamation are not claims under trademark law; they fall into a broad category of laws known as "business torts." For more information on basic defamation principles, see Chapter 12.

B. When You Need Permission to Use a Trademark

This section describes when permission is required for various types of trademark uses. In certain situations you can use a trademark without obtaining the owner's permission. In others, you'll need to do a bit more analysis before using a trademark without an okay from the owner. Whether a given use is legally okay depends on a number of factual issues that can be tricky to figure out.

Below we discuss the various ways that trademarks are typically used and whether permission is required for each type of use. Keep in mind, however, that even if you're legally entitled to use a trademark, that doesn't mean that the trademark owner will always be agreeable. If you're forced into court to prove that your use is allowed by law, in a sense you've already lost the battle. Make sure your use is, in fact, within the bounds of the law, and be aware of the trademark owner's likely response. You'll need to weigh the benefits of using the trademark carefully if you suspect the owner will fight you with legal action.

Also remember that what might be permitted under trademark law might not be permitted under copyright law. Therefore, if the trademark contains some copyrightable elements, analyze your use under both trademark and copyright rules.

1. Informational Uses

Informational (or "editorial") uses of a trademark do not require permission. These are uses that inform, educate, or express opinions protected under the First Amendment of the United States Constitution—freedom of speech and of the press. For example, permission is not required to use the Chevrolet logo in an article describing Chevrolet trucks, even if the article is critical of the company. Similarly, if you are making a documentary film on the history of American trucks, you do not need permission to include the Chevrolet logo. However, the use of the logo must have some relevance to the work. For

example, it would not be wise to publish an article critical of overseas auto manufacturing practices and include the Chevrolet logo unless Chevrolet were mentioned in the article.

Whether to Use Trademark Symbols

When using a trademark in text for informational purposes, it is not necessary to include the ®, TM, or SM symbols. However, it is good trademark etiquette to distinguish a trademark by capitalizing or italicizing it—for example, "The house was constructed with Styrofoam insulation," or "He used a NordicTrak exercise machine."

---

2. Comparative Advertising

It's permissible to use a trademark when making accurate comparative product statements in advertisements. However, since comparative advertisements tend to provoke trademark owners into legal action, an attorney knowledgeable in trademark or business law should review the advertisement before publication. As noted in Section A, modification of another company's trademark may result in a claim of dilution.

3. Commercial Uses

Commercial uses of a trademark include advertising, promotion, or marketing, and require permission (except for cases of comparative advertising as explained in the previous section). Commercial uses include business-sponsored promotional activities (such as public presentations), informational advertisements (known as "advertorials"), and merchandise.

EXAMPLE: An auto insurance company publishes a booklet on drunk driving. The booklet includes the logo for a beer company. The use of the logo would be considered a commercial use, so the insurance company should obtain permission.

Include Trademark Symbols for Commercial Uses

When using a trademark in a commercial context, such as an advertisement, product manual, or in connection with the sale of a product or service, include the ®, TM, or SM symbols adjacent to the trademark—for example, "Adobe®" or "PageMaker®." Remember—the ® symbol should only be used if the trademark is federally registered. This may be evident from the trademark owner's use, or you can find it out by researching the federal trademark database. Also, include a statement such as "Adobe and PageMaker are registered trademarks of the Adobe Corporation." Place the statement on the index page of a website, the copyright page of a publication, or at the end of a movie.

---

4. Parodies: Laughing All the Way to Court

A trademark parody occurs when someone imitates a trademark in a manner that pokes fun at the mark. A newspaper called *The San Francisco Chomical*, meant to poke fun at *The San Francisco Chronicle*, is an example of a parody. Chapter 9, on dealing with fair use of copyrighted materials, provided some general rules as to when parodies are permissible and when they infringe copyright. Below are some specific rules for trademark parodies.

Keep in mind the general rule that applies to both types of parodies: offensive parodies often trigger lawsuits. Therefore, weigh the legal consequences carefully before proceeding.

Generally speaking, a trademark parody is less likely to run into problems if it:

- **Doesn't compete.** The use of the parody product does not directly compete with the trademark product.
- **Doesn't confuse.** The parody does not confuse consumers; they get the joke and do not believe the parody product comes from the same source as the trademarked goods.
- **Does parody.** Not all humorous uses are parodies. To avoid trouble, the use should specifically poke fun at the trademark.

Below are some court cases that may provide some context:

- **Allowable trademark parody.** A college student sold T-shirts at Myrtle Beach depicting a red, white, and blue beer can with the phrase, "This Beach is for You." Anheuser-Busch, the owners of the Budweiser trademark, filed a lawsuit, seized all of the T-shirts, and raided the college student's home and his mother's business. A jury determined that the T-shirts were a parody, but the lower court judge overturned the jury verdict and ruled for Anheuser-Busch. An appeals court reversed the ruling again and ruled that the use was a parody. Seven years and several lawsuits later, the parties reached a settlement in which Anheuser-Busch granted a license for sales of the T-shirt. (*Anheuser-Busch, Inc. v. L & L Wings, Inc.*, 962 F.2d 316 (4th Cir.), cert. denied, 113 S.Ct. 206 (1992).)
- **Allowable trademark parody.** During a half-time show, the San Diego Chicken mascot initiated a fistfight with Barney, the popular purple dinosaur. A court held the use of the Barney trademark a permissible parody because the aggressive manner in which Barney behaved was not likely to cause consumer confusion. (*Lyons Partnership L.P. v. Giannoulas*, 14 F. Supp. 2d 947 (N.D. Texas).)

- **Not an allowable trademark parody.** A gaudy, '60s style nightclub in Houston used the trademark "The Velvet Elvis" and, after being sued by the owner of the Elvis trademark, claimed that the club's name was an Elvis parody. A court disagreed, pointing out that the intent of the club's name and decor was to parody the Las Vegas lounge scene and the velvet painting craze, not to parody Elvis. (*Elvis Presley Enterprises v. Capece*, 141 F.3d 188 (5th Cir. 1998).)

Conflicting case law and the discretionary power of judges make it difficult to predict the outcome of a lawsuit based on trademark parody. It is also difficult to predict when a company will take action against a parodist. Some companies, like Anheuser-Busch, prefer to fight to the end while others believe that chasing parodists generates negative publicity and prefer to let the parody run its course.

5. Using a Trademark Containing Copyrightable Elements

Use of a trademark containing a copyrightable image such as a character, photograph, or illustration may be prohibited under copyright law even if permitted under trademark law. Examples of copyrightable trademarks include:

- animated logos such as the Microsoft Internet Explorer spinning globe
- logos containing artwork or photos, such as the floral bouquet in the Herbal Essence logo, and
- characters such as Mr. Peanut or Betty Crocker.

Characters are discussed in the next section.

Before proceeding with the unauthorized use of a trademark containing copyrightable elements, compare trademark and copyright rules to minimize potential liability. Certain elements such as fonts, simple geometric shapes, individual words, and short phrases are not protected under copyright law (see Chapter 8, Section A4).

6. Using Characters

As discussed in previous chapters on artwork and photographs, literary and pictorial characters such as Sam Spade and Fred Flintstone are protected under copyright law. In addition, these characters may be protected under trademark law, which protects a wide range of text and images that are used to sell products or services. Trademarked characters can be either graphic (for example, Snoopy or Spider-man) or human (for example, Rambo or Mr. Whipple). Characters may have an association with a specific product or service, such as Mr. Clean and home cleaning products. Or, a character may be used to sell a variety of merchandise—such as the Teenage Mutant Ninja Turtle characters that were used to sell breakfast cereal, T-shirts, and other assorted merchandise.

Because characters often tell stories and sell products simultaneously, the difference between the two forms of legal protection is often indistinct. If this overlap seems confusing, take solace in the fact that it has often confounded attorneys and the courts. In the real world, this overlap is sometimes an academic issue, since the owner of the fictional character usually controls both copyright and trademark rights. Therefore, the company will tailor your license to permit all appropriate uses. If there are a number of owners involved, however, obtaining permission to use the character may become somewhat trickier.

The section below offers guidance on how to deal with using various types of characters, particularly when trademark and copyright rules may overlap.

a. Graphic Character; Informational Use

Trademark permission is not required to reproduce a graphic character, such as Woody Woodpecker, for informational purposes. Copyright authorization, on the other hand, is required. Chapter 4, "Getting Permission to Use Artwork," provides information on getting permission to use cartoon and comic characters. Keep in mind that copyright permission is not required if the character is in the public domain or if the reproduction qualifies as a fair use. For example, the use of Mickey Mouse (a character owned by the Disney Corporation) in a news story qualifies as a fair use, but the use of Mickey Mouse in a trivia book about Disney characters requires permission. See Chapter 9 for detailed information on whether a use of copyrighted material qualifies as fair use.

b. Human Character; Informational Use

Using a photograph of a human character, such as Captain Kirk, for an informational use, such as in a news story, does not require trademark permission. However, it does require copyright authorization from the owner of the photograph (usually an entertainment production company). Chapter 3, "Getting Permission to Use Photographs," explains how to locate production companies. Permission is not required from the actor portraying the character.

c. Graphic Character; Commercial Use

Trademark permission is required for the commercial use of a graphic character in an advertisement or on merchandise. For example, reproducing the Road Runner character in an advertisement for an auto race would require permission from the owners of Road Runner. Follow the rules in this chapter. As we mentioned earlier, the trademark owner almost always controls the copyright as well and will tailor the license to permit both uses.

d. Human Character; Commercial Use

Trademark permission is required to reproduce an image of a human character, such as James Bond, for commercial uses. Permission must also be obtained from the person portraying the character. Chapter 12, "Releases," provides model releases that

you can use to obtain permission from actors who portray fictional characters. Failure to obtain permission from the human who portrays the character may prove expensive. For example, a federal court permitted two actors from the TV show *Cheers* to sue a company that sold robots based on their characters without obtaining their permission. The case eventually settled. (*Wendt v. Host Int'l, Inc.*, 125 F.3d 806 (9th Cir. 1997).) Based on the *Cheers* litigation, a company that uses fictional characters personified by human actors for a commercial purpose should obtain permission from the actors or risk a lawsuit.

7. Using a Trademark in a Title

You should also obtain permission to use a trademark on the cover of a book, in the title of a film or song, or in advertising for an informational work. The following cases illustrate that failure to obtain such permission can easily result in a lawsuit.

- The owner of the Godzilla trademark successfully stopped a book publisher from selling a film-study book entitled *Godzilla*. The court ruled that the use of the name without a prominent disclaimer amounted to a trademark infringement. (*Toho Inc. v. William Morrow and Co.*, 33 F. Supp. 2d 1206 (C.D. Cal. 1998).)
- A film company producing a movie satirizing Minnesota beauty queens was prohibited from using the title *Dairy Queen* even though no Dairy Queens or Dairy Queen trademarks were seen in the film. The court ruled that consumers would be confused as to the source of the film and would believe that the owner of the Dairy Queen trademark had permitted the use. (*American Dairy Queen Corp. v. New Line Productions Inc.*, 35 F. Supp. 2d 727 (Minn. 1998).)
- The makers of Tron fuses sued the makers of the film *Tron,* not over the use of the name in the film, but over use of the name on merchandise related to the film—video games

and telephones, two products that might cause confusion among consumers of Tron fuses. The case was ultimately settled. (*McGraw-Edison Co. v. Walt Disney Productions*, 787 F.2d 1163 (7th Cir. 1985).)

8. Using a Trademark as a Character Name

You don't need permission to name a fictional character in a story or movie after a trademark—for example, naming a character Nerf or Advil. However, this practice is likely to provoke the trademark owner if the character is unsavory or is used to sell merchandise. In one case, Hormel, the makers of Spam, sued the makers of a Muppet movie because a pig character was named Sp'am. The court ruled against Hormel, noting that it did not tarnish Spam's trademark to be associated with a pig, and that Spam had been so maligned in popular culture that the association with the film character, a helpful boar who befriends Muppet characters, could not possibly tarnish the trademark. (*Hormel Foods Corp. v. Jim Henson Productions Inc.*, 73 F.3d 497 (2d Cir. 1996).)

9. Trademark Practices: Books, Movies, Songs, and Websites

How to acquire trademark permissions differs within various media industries. Some of these rules are provided below. Often, permission is not required by law, so a court will permit an unauthorized use. However, since book publishers, software companies, Internet providers, and movie companies do not want to risk a lawsuit, they often seek permission anyway. Some short model permission forms are provided.

a. Book Publishing

Although publishers are not usually required to obtain permission for informational uses of trademarks, many seek authorization anyway. Note that authorization is required to use a trademark in a book published as a means of promoting a product or service. For example, a computer company publishing a manual on desktop publishing should obtain permission to reproduce trademarks from software companies whose products are mentioned in the manual.

An example of a simple permission statement is provided below.

A tear-out copy of this agreement is provided in the Appendix. A digital version is included on the forms CD.

Basic Permission to Use a Trademark in a Book or Magazine

_____ ("Owner") is the owner of rights in the trademark _____ (the "Trademark"). Owner grants permission to reproduce the Trademark in the format indicated below in the publication _____ and in any subsequent editions or derivative versions in any media. Any goodwill associated with the Trademark vests in Owner.

Owner Name:_____

Signature: _____

Date: _____

[Insert Sample of Trademark]

b. The Film Industry

Most film, video, and television production companies obtain permission for the use of trademarks that appear in their movies and videos. This includes trademarks on signs in public locations. Below is a sample permission agreement for use of a trademark in a film, television show, or video.

Companies with trademarks that are eager to see their products in films will enter into special permission agreements known as "product placement agreements." Under these agreements, the companies that own the trademarks may provide free products, services, or cross-promotions. For example, America Online allowed use of its trademarks, including the phrase "You've Got Mail," in the film of the same name. On the other hand, the FCC prohibits the use of product placements in programming made for television. Clearance companies in Los Angeles and New York review scripts and prepare clearance reports. For further information regarding film clearance, see *Clearance and Copyright*, by Michael C. Donaldson (Silman-James Press).

 A tear-out copy of this agreement is provided in the Appendix. A digital version is included on the forms CD.

Basic Permission to Use a Trademark in a Movie

_____ ("Owner") is the owner of rights in the trademark _____ (the Trademark"). Owner grants permission to reproduce the Trademark in the format indicated below in all versions of the film _____ (the "Film") and any derivative versions in any media. Any goodwill associated with the Trademark vests in Owner.

Owner Name: _____

Signature: _____

Date: _____

[Insert Sample of Trademark]

c. Artwork and Photography

Artwork and photographs sometimes include trademarks. Permission from the trademark owner is required if the art or photograph is created and reproduced for commercial purposes, such as in advertising or on merchandise. For example, a company that sold trading cards of collectible cars was prohibited from reproducing Chrysler trademarks and trade dress because Chrysler licensed similar collectible products. (*Chrysler Corp. v. Newfield Publications Inc.*, 880 F. Supp. 504 (E.D. Mich. 1995).)

A photograph that portrays a trademark in a morally offensive manner is liable to trigger a trademark dispute. For example, lawsuits were filed over lewd photos of the Pillsbury Doughboy and of photos showing the Barbie and Ken dolls in compromising positions. Below is a sample permission form for use of a trademark in artwork.

 A tear-out copy of this agreement is provided in the Appendix. A digital version is included on the forms CD.

Basic Permission to Use a Trademark in a Photograph or Artwork

_____ ("Owner") is the owner of rights in trademark _____ (the "Trademark"). Owner grants permission to reproduce the Trademark in the format indicated below in all versions of the artwork _____ (the "Artwork"), and any derivative versions in any media. Any goodwill associated with the Trademark vests in Owner.

Owner Name: _____

Signature: _____

Date: _____

[Insert Sample of Trademark]

d. The Internet

Using a word trademark as a link on a website (known as a hypertext link) is permitted without authorization. For example, no authorization is needed to link to the General Motors website by using the text link "General Motors." However, use of another company's trademark as a graphic or visual link requires authorization. Chapter 6, "Website Permissions," provides a linking agreement and discusses additional website issues. Chapter 12, "Releases," explains how to figure out whether a site is primarily informational or commercial. For information about domain name and related trademark uses, review Chapter 16, "Help Beyond This Book."

e. The Music Industry

The unauthorized use of a trademark in a song title or album title may be permitted under First Amendment principles, provided that the title does not confuse or dilute the mark. Regardless of the law, however, this type of use is likely to provoke a trademark dispute. For example, toymaker Mattel Inc. sued MCA Records over a song entitled "Barbie Girl" by the Danish pop group Aqua. A federal court ruled in favor of the record company based upon First Amendment issues and refused to halt the sale of the song. (*Mattel, Inc. v. MCA Records, Inc.*, 28 F. Supp. 2d 1120 (C.D. Cal. 1998).) The owner of the Dr. Feelgood trademark, used primarily on hospital scrubs, sued The band Mötley Crüe over its song by the same name. In that case, the band prevailed by demonstrating there was no customer confusion. (*Reeves v. Motley Crue Inc.*, 21 U.S.P.Q. 2D (BNA) 1587, (N.D. Ala. 1991).)

10. Using a Trademark in Connection With an Award

A business receiving an award or a favorable review from an organization needs authorization to use the organization's trademark. For example, if a software company received an award from a computer magazine called *MegaSoft*, the software company could state it received an award from *MegaSoft*, but would have to obtain permission in order to use the magazine's graphic awards trademark in an advertisement.

Generally, companies that provide ratings or create awards have guidelines for how their trademarks can be used in advertising. For example, one computer magazine requires that a company using the magazine's trademarks in stating its award include the date it issued the award and the version of the software to which it gave the award. Some consumer companies do not permit the use of their trademarks for other companies' products regardless of the rating, review, or award.

The person at a publication who grants trademark permission is usually in the company's business department. Larger companies have departments for managing trademark rights and permission. For help locating trademark owners, see Section C.

11. Using a Certification Mark

Certain trademarks certify that a product or service meets a certain standard. For example, the "CCOF" logo guarantees that produce is from a California Certified Organic Farm. These certification marks may also establish standards for the materials used in, the accuracy of, source of labor for, or region of origin of a product.

If your company or business wants to be certified to use a certification mark, you must contact the certification mark owner and obtain the standards. For example, if you were a potato farmer in Idaho who wanted to use the "Idaho Potatoes" certification mark, you would contact the mark owner to learn the standards you must meet.

12. Trademark Disclaimers

A disclaimer is a statement intended to minimize confusion in consumer's minds or deflect liability. A disclaimer is only effective if it is placed prominently, affixed permanently, readable and understandable, and really minimizes confusion. A disclaimer, by itself, will not provide a shield against litigation but, when done properly, can minimize confusion and prevent dilution.

> EXAMPLE: An individual publishes a parody of the newspaper *Newsday*, entitled *Snoozeday*. A prominently displayed disclaimer, such as "This newspaper is intended as a parody of *Newsday* and makes no claim to *Newsday*'s trademarks or related proprietary rights," may minimize potential liability.

C. Locating a Trademark Owner

You can usually locate a trademark owner through business directories, by contacting the trademark owner's website, or by searching trademark records to locate the name and address of the trademark owner. Many large companies such as Coca-Cola, General Motors, and FedEx have departments that handle licensing and permission arrangements.

1. Business Directories

There are several general business directories on the Internet that your Internet search engine should be able to find. For example, Big Yellow, the NYNEX business directory (www.bigyellow.com), enables the user to search by business category, name, street address, state, or zip code.

2. Federally Registered Marks

You can research ownership of federally registered trademarks at the PTO website, which provides free access to records of marks that are registered or pending (meaning an application is undergoing examination at the PTO). Searching tips and techniques are provided at the site. The PTO's database can be accessed at www.uspto.gov/tmdb/index .html.

> EXAMPLE: A movie company wants permission to include a Tower Records sign in a film. Accessing the PTO Trademark database and typing in Tower Records uncovers the following information:
>
> Word Mark: TOWER RECORDS
> Owner Name (REGISTRANT): MTS, Incororated
> Owner Address: 2500 Del Monte Street
> West Sacramento CALIFORNIA 95691
> CORPORATION CALIFORNIA
> Attorney of Record: Rochelle D. Alpert

The PTO trademark database has limitations. It may not include applications filed during the last two to four months, nor does it contain information on state, foreign, or common law trademarks or inactive applications and registrations (that is, abandoned applications or canceled or expired registrations). The database may be as much as four months out of sequence with the PTO's internal trademark database, so it may not be possible to locate the owner of a mark for which an application was filed recently. For more up-to-date federal registration trademark information, consider using the Micropatent database described in Section 4, below.

3. Common Law Marks

Trademark owners do not have to register their trademarks to obtain trademark rights. These unregistered trademarks are sometimes referred to as "common law marks." The owners of these marks are harder to locate than registered mark owners because they don't appear in government databases. It may be possible to locate common law marks using Internet search engines (type the mark in as the keyword) or in online business directories.

4. Private Trademark Databases

Private trademark databases such as Micropatent are the most current and comprehensive trademark research sources. They include state trademarks, international marks, and inactive, canceled, and abandoned marks. Micropatent's website is located at www.micropatent.com.

5. Owners of Characters

You can locate the owner of a character by contacting the business owner directly, searching trademark databases (see example below), or searching journals that specialize in character and trademark licensing.

> **EXAMPLE:** A nonprofit children's organization wants permission to use Daffy Duck on fund-raising posters. Accessing the PTO trademark database and typing in Daffy Duck produces the following information:
>
> DAFFY DUCK
> Owner Name (REGISTRANT): Time Warner Entertainment Company, L.P.
> Owner Address: 75 Rockefeller Plaza New York NEW YORK 10019
> LIMITED PARTNERSHIP DELAWARE
> Attorney of Record: Elise A. Tenen

6. Character and Brand Resources

The following resources can help you locate the owners of trademarked characters and brands.

- Apparel Search (www.apparelsearch.com/licensing.htm) provides a comprehensive listing of fictional characters, brands, and real people available for licensing, along with licensing contacts. Click "Licensing By Brand."
- *Licensing Journal* (www.aspenpub.com) is a newsletter that serves as one of the leading sources of legal information for the licensing industry. (A subscription costs $345 per year.)
- *EPM Licensing Letter* and *EPM Licensing Letter Sourcebook* (www.epmcom.com) are written by EPM—a leading source of licensing news and resources for the licensing industry.

7. Trademark Services

For a listing of companies that provide trademark research services, review the resources at the Yahoo! Trademarks directory at http://dir.yahoo.com/Business_and_Economy/Companies/Law/Intellectual_Property/Trademarks/Services.

D. Trademark Licensing

This section deals with trademark licensing, primarily the use of a trademark on merchandise in return for periodic payments known as royalties. The underlying principle of trademark licensing is that consumers are more likely to buy merchandise if it includes a familiar trademark. Trademarks are often licensed in the following situations:

- Characters such as Barney or the Power Rangers are often licensed to merchandise producers, providing lucrative licensing income for the trademark owners.
- Licensing collegiate trademarks to merchandise producers provides an important revenue source for universities. (In 1999, Ohio University and Ohio State settled a bitter dispute over which university could license the word "Ohio.")

- Companies such as Harley-Davidson and Jack Daniels earn income by licensing their corporate trademarks.
- Designers such as Calvin Klein have created billion-dollar enterprises placing their names on a wide array of products.
- Entertainment trademarks such as "MTV" or "Late Night With David Letterman" provide additional earnings for entertainment companies.
- Annual festivals and activities such as the Gilroy Garlic Festival license their trademarks to augment income for the event.
- State and municipal tourism offices license trademarks such as "Ski Colorado."
- Trademark licensing earns revenue for nonprofit causes—for example the Audubon Society licenses its name for a clock that provides birdcalls.
- Licensing of league and sports team trademarks for teams like the Chicago Bulls or the San Francisco Forty-Niners is probably the greatest single generator of trademark licensing revenue.

The rest of this section describes the trademark licensing process in more detail and provides a sample licensing agreement.

1. Overview of the Licensing Process

The trademark licensing process is usually more challenging than the process for licensing copyrighted works. The trademark owner often has a strong interest in controlling the quality and consistency of affiliated merchandise and is concerned about misuse of the mark or that shoddy goods bearing the mark will diminish the trademark's goodwill.

The trademark licensing process is initiated in one of three ways: a licensee locates a trademark owner, the trademark owner contacts a licensee, or a third-party agency facilitates the licensing arrangement. Many famous trademarks such as "Harley-Davidson" are represented by agencies who seek out suitable merchandise partners. After the parties

make contact, they sort out the basic terms of the agreement. Chapter 11 provides a worksheet for organizing the various aspects of a merchandise license agreement.

It is quite common for owners of well-known trademarks to dictate the terms and furnish the agreements for merchandise licensing. Often these terms are on a "take it or leave it" basis—if the licensee does not agree, the trademark owner will go elsewhere. In other cases, a licensee will furnish the trademark license agreement. Usually, prior to furnishing the agreement, the licensee and the licensor have worked out all of the business terms. Even after the terms are agreed upon and the license is furnished, the parties can make additional changes.

2. Royalty Payments

Payment of royalties depends on industry trends. To use a trademark on merchandise such as clothing or ceramic goods, a licensee must pay royalties ranging from 2% to 10% of net sales. A trademark owner may accept a lump-sum payment for a one-time license—for example, the use of the image on 10,000 T-shirts at a sporting event.

 For more information on trademark licensing, review *A Primer on Licensing,* by Jack Revoyr (Kent Press).

3. Sample Trademark License Agreement

Below is a sample trademark license agreement, followed by an explanation of selected provisions. This trademark license is very similar to the merchandise license provided in Chapter 11, "Art and Merchandise Agreements." The primary distinctions are in quality control standards and ownership rights related to the trademarks. These distinctions are explained in Section 4.

 A tear-out copy of this agreement is provided in the Appendix. A digital version is included on the forms CD.

Trademark License Agreement

Introduction

This Trademark License Agreement (the "Agreement") is made between _____ (referred to as "Licensor") and _____ (referred to as "Licensee").

The parties agree as follows:

The Trademarks

The "Trademarks" refer to any trademark, service mark, trade name, logo, or other device and its associated goodwill used to identify and distinguish Licensor's products and services as included in Exhibit A. Licensor is the owner of all rights to the Trademarks, and Licensee shall not claim any right to use the Trademarks except under the terms of this Agreement.

Licensed Products

Licensed Products are defined as Licensee's products incorporating the Trademarks specifically described in Exhibit A (the "Licensed Products").

Grant of Rights

Licensor grants to Licensee:

(select one)

☐   an exclusive license

☐   a nonexclusive license

to reproduce and distribute the Trademarks on the Licensed Products.

Sublicense

(select one)

☐   **Consent required.** Licensee may sublicense the rights granted pursuant to this Agreement provided: Licensee obtains Licensor's prior written consent to such sublicense; and Licensor receives such revenue or royalty payment as provided in the Payment section below. Any sublicense granted in violation of this provision shall be void.

☐ **No sublicensing permitted.** Licensee may not sublicense the rights granted under this Agreement.

Reservation of Rights & Assignment of Goodwill

Licensor reserves all rights other than those being conveyed or granted in this Agreement. Licensee assigns to Licensor any goodwill from the Trademarks that may accrue under this Agreement or from the distribution of the Licensed Products. Licensee's rights to the Trademarks are only in connection with the Licensed Products and Licensee shall not assert any other association with Licensor or the Trademarks. Licensee acknowledges the validity of the Trademarks and agrees not to challenge Licensor's ownership of the Trademarks or their validity.

Territory

The rights granted to Licensee are limited to _____ (the "Territory").

Term

The "Effective Date" of this Agreement is defined as the date when the agreement commences and is established by the latest signature date.

(select one)

☐ **Specified term with renewal rights.** This Agreement shall commence upon the Effective Date and shall extend for a period of _____ years (the "Initial Term"). Following the Initial Term, Licensee may renew this Agreement under the same terms and conditions for___consecutive _____ periods (the "Renewal Terms"), provided that Licensee provides written notice of its intention to renew this Agreement within thirty (30) days before the expiration of the current term.

☐ **Term with renewal based upon sales.** This Agreement shall commence upon the Effective Date and shall extend for a period of _____ years (the "Initial Term") and may be renewed by Licensee under the same terms and conditions for consecutive_____year periods (the "Renewal Terms"), provided that:

(a) Licensee provides written notice of its intention to renew this Agreement within thirty days before the expiration of the current term; and

(b) Licensee has met the sales requirements as established in Exhibit A.

☐ **Indefinite term. This** Agreement shall commence upon the Effective Date and shall continue until terminated pursuant to a provision of this Agreement.

☐ **Fixed term.** This Agreement shall commence upon the Effective Date and shall continue for _____ unless sooner terminated pursuant to a provision of this Agreement.

☐ **Term for as long as Licensee sells Licensed Products. This** Agreement shall commence upon the Effective Date as specified in Exhibit A and shall continue for as long as Licensee continues to offer the Licensed Products in commercially reasonable quantities or unless sooner terminated pursuant to a provision of this Agreement.

Approval of Samples & Quality Control

Preproduction. Licensee shall submit to Licensor a reasonable number of preproduction designs and prototypes at no cost prior to production, as well as production samples of every Licensed Product to assure that the product meets Licensor's quality standards. Licensee agrees not to distribute any Licensed Product until receipt of Licensor's written approval of such Licensed Product.

Production and Promotion. At least once every six (6) months, Licensee shall submit to Licensor two (2) production samples of each Licensed Product for review. Licensee shall pay all costs for delivery of these materials. In the event that any production sample does not meet Licensor's quality standards, Licensee agrees to immediately correct such deficiencies. Licensor shall have the right to inspect Licensee's premises upon reasonable notice for purposes of observing the manufacturing process. Licensee shall submit all advertising and promotional materials to Licensor and shall not distribute such materials until receipt of written approval from Licensor.

Royalties

All royalties ("Royalties") provided for under this Agreement shall accrue when the respective Licensed Products are sold, shipped, distributed, billed, or paid for, whichever occurs first.

Net Sales

"Net Sales" are defined as Licensee's gross sales (the gross invoice amount billed to customers) less quantity discounts or rebates and returns actually credited. A quantity discount or rebate is a discount made at the time of shipment. No deductions shall be made for cash or other discounts, commissions, manufacturing costs, uncollectible accounts, or for fees or expenses of any kind that the Licensee may incur in connection with the Royalty payments.

Fees

(select one or more provisions)

☐   **Advance Against Royalties.** As a nonrefundable advance against royalties (the "Advance"), Licensee agrees to pay to Licensor upon execution of this Agreement the sum of $_____.

☐   **Licensed Product Royalty.** Licensee agrees to pay a Royalty of____% percent of all Net Sales revenue of the Licensed Products ("Licensed Product Royalty").

☐   **Per Unit Royalty.** Licensee agrees to pay a Royalty of $___for each unit of the Licensed Product that is ☐ manufactured ☐ sold [select one].

☐   **Guaranteed Minimum Annual Royalty Payment.** In addition to any other advances or fees, Licensee shall pay an annual guaranteed royalty (the "GMAR") as follows: $_____. The GMAR shall be paid to Licensor annually on_____. The GMAR is an advance against royalties for the twelve-month (12-month) period commencing upon payment. Royalty payments based on Net Sales made during any year of this Agreement shall be credited against the GMAR due for the year in which such Net Sales were made. In the event that annual royalties exceed the GMAR, Licensee shall pay the difference to Licensor. Any annual royalty payments in excess of the GMAR shall not be carried forward from previous years or applied against the GMAR.

☐   **License Fee.** As a nonrefundable, nonrecoupable fee for executing this license, Licensee agrees to pay to Licensor upon execution of this Agreement the sum of $_____.

☐   **Sublicensing Revenues.** In the event of any sublicense of the rights granted pursuant to this Agreement, Licensee shall pay to Licensor _____% percent of all sublicensing revenues.

Payments and Statements to Licensor

Within thirty (30) days after the end of each calendar quarter (the "Royalty Period"), an accurate statement of Net Sales of Licensed Products along with any royalty payments or sublicensing revenues due to Licensor shall be provided to Licensor, regardless of whether any Licensed Products were sold during the Royalty Period. All payments shall be paid in United States currency drawn on a United States bank. The acceptance by Licensor of any of the statements furnished or royalties paid shall not preclude Licensor questioning the correctness at any time of any payments or statements.

Audit

Licensee shall keep accurate books of account and records covering all transactions relating to the license granted in this Agreement, and Licensor or its duly authorized representatives shall have the right upon five days prior written notice, and during normal business hours, to inspect and audit Licensee's records relating to the Licensed Products under this Agreement. Licensor shall bear the cost of such inspection and audit, unless the results indicate an underpayment greater than $ _____ for any six-month (6-month) period. In that case, Licensee shall promptly reimburse Licensor for all costs of the audit along with the amount due with interest on such sums. Interest shall accrue from the date the payment was originally due and the interest rate shall be 1.5% per month, or the maximum rate permitted by law, whichever is less. All books of account and records shall be made available in the United States and kept available for at least two years after the termination of this Agreement.

Late Payment

Time is of the essence with respect to all payments to be made by Licensee under this Agreement. If Licensee is late in any payment provided for in this Agreement, Licensee shall pay interest on the payment from the date due until paid at a rate of 1.5% per month, or the maximum rate permitted by law, whichever is less.

Licensor Warranties

Licensor warrants that it has the power and authority to enter into this Agreement and has no knowledge as to any third-party claims regarding the proprietary rights in the Trademarks that would interfere with the rights granted under this Agreement.

Indemnification by Licensor

(select one if appropriate)

☐　**Licensor indemnification without limitations.** Licensor shall indemnify Licensee and hold Licensee harmless from any damages and liabilities (including reasonable attorney fees and costs) arising from any breach of Licensor's warranties as defined in Licensor's Warranties, above.

☐　**Licensor indemnification limited to amounts paid.** Licensor shall indemnify Licensee and hold Licensee harmless from any damages and liabilities (including reasonable attorney fees and costs) arising from any breach of Licensor's warranties as defined in Licensor's Warranties, above. Licensor's maximum liability under this provision shall in no event exceed the total amount earned by Licensor under this Agreement.

Licensee Warranties

Licensee warrants that it will use its best commercial efforts to market the Licensed Products and that sale and marketing of the Licensed Products shall be in conformance with all applicable laws and regulations, including but not limited to all intellectual property laws.

Indemnification by Licensee

Licensee shall indemnify Licensor and hold Licensor harmless from any damages and liabilities (including reasonable attorney fees and costs) arising from any breach of Licensee's warranties and representation as defined in the Licensee Warranties above or arising out of any alleged defects of the Licensed Products, any product liability claims, or any claims arising out of advertising, distribution, or marketing of the Licensed Products.

Intellectual Property Rights

The license granted in this Agreement is conditioned on Licensee's compliance with the provisions of the intellectual property laws of the United States and any foreign country in the Territory.

Proprietary Notices

Licensee shall identify Licensor as the owner of rights to the Trademarks and shall include the notices provided in Exhibit A on all copies of the Licensed Products.

Infringement Against Third Parties

In the event that either party learns of imitations or infringements of the Trademarks or Licensed Products, that party shall notify the other in writing of the infringements or imitations. Licensor shall have the right to commence lawsuits against third persons arising from infringement of the Trademarks or Licensed Products. In the event that Licensor does not commence a lawsuit against an alleged infringer within sixty (60) days of notification by Licensee, Licensee may commence a lawsuit against the third party. Before filing suit, Licensee shall obtain the written consent of Licensor to do so, and such consent shall not be unreasonably withheld. Licensor will cooperate fully and in good faith with Licensee for the purpose of securing and preserving Licensee's rights to the Trademarks.

Any recovery (including, but not limited to a judgment, settlement, or licensing agreement included as resolution of an infringement dispute) shall be divided equally between the parties after deduction and payment of reasonable attorney fees to the party bringing the lawsuit.

Exploitation Date

Licensee agrees to manufacture, distribute, and sell the Licensed Products in commercially reasonable quantities during the term of this Agreement and to commence such manufacture, distribution, and sale by _____. This is a material provision of this Agreement.

Advertising Budget

(select if appropriate)

☐   Licensee agrees to spend at least ____% of estimated annual gross sales for promotional efforts and advertising of the Licensed Products.

Licensor Copies and Right to Purchase

Licensee shall provide Licensor with _____copies of each Licensed Product. Licensor has the right to purchase from Licensee, at Licensee's manufacturing cost, at least_____copies of any Licensed Product, and such payments shall be deducted from royalties due to Licensor.

Confidentiality

The parties acknowledge that each may have access to confidential information that relates to each other's business (the "Information"). The parties agree to protect the confidentiality of the Information and maintain it with the strictest confidence, and no party shall disclose such information to third parties without the prior written consent of the other.

Insurance

(select if appropriate)

☐   Licensee shall, throughout the Term, obtain and maintain, at its own expense, standard product liability insurance coverage, naming Licensor as an additional named insured. Such policy shall provide protection against any claims, demands, and causes of action arising out of any alleged defects or failure to perform of the Licensed Products or any use of the Licensed Products. The amount of coverage shall be a minimum of $_____,with no deductible amount for each single occurrence for bodily injury or property damage. The policy shall provide for notice to the Licensor from the insurer by Registered or Certified Mail in the event of any modification or termination of insurance. The provisions of this section shall survive termination for three (3) years.

Right to Terminate

Licensor shall have the right to terminate this Agreement in the following situations:

(select one or more provisions)

☐ **Failure to Make Timely Payment.** Licensee fails to pay Royalties when due or fails to accurately report Net Sales, as defined in the Payment Section of this Agreement, and such failure is not cured within thirty days after written notice from the Licensor.

☐ **Failure to Introduce Product.** Licensee fails to introduce the product to market by the date set in the Exploitation section of this Agreement or to offer the Licensed Products in commercially reasonable quantities during any subsequent year.

☐ **Assignment or Sublicensing.** Licensee assigns or sublicenses in violation of the Agreement.

☐ **Failure to Maintain Insurance.** Licensee fails to maintain or obtain product liability insurance as required by the provisions of this Agreement.

☐ **Failure to Meet Quality Standards or Submit Samples.** Licensee fails to provide Licensor with samples for approval or fails to meet the quality standards established by Licensor.

Licensor shall have the right to terminate the grant of license under this Agreement with respect to any country or region included in the Territory in which Licensee fails to offer the Licensed Products for sale or distributions or to secure a sublicensing agreement for the marketing, distribution, and sale of the product within two years of the Effective Date.

Effect of Termination

Upon termination of this Agreement, all Royalty obligations as established in the Payments Section shall immediately become due. After the termination of this license, all rights granted to Licensee under this Agreement shall terminate and revert to Licensor, and Licensee will refrain from further manufacturing, copying, marketing, distribution, or use of any Licensed Product or other product which incorporates the Trademarks. Within thirty (30) days after termination, Licensee shall deliver to Licensor a statement indicating the number and description of the Licensed Products that it had on hand or is in the process of manufacturing as of the termination date.

Sell-Off Period

Licensee may dispose of the Licensed Products covered by this Agreement for a period of ninety (90) days after termination or expiration, except that Licensee shall have no such right in the event this agreement is terminated according to the Licensor's Right to Terminate, above. At the end of the post-termination sale period, Licensee shall furnish a royalty payment and statement as required under the Payment Section. Upon termination, Licensee shall deliver to Licensor all original designs or reproductions of Trademarks used in the manufacture of the Licensed Products. Licensor shall bear the costs of shipping for these materials.

Attorney Fees and Expenses

The prevailing party shall have the right to collect from the other party its reasonable costs and necessary disbursements and attorney fees incurred in enforcing this Agreement.

Dispute Resolution

(select one if appropriate)

☐ **Mediation & Arbitration.** The Parties agree that every dispute or difference between them, arising under this Agreement, shall be settled first by a meeting of the Parties attempting to confer and resolve the dispute in a good faith manner. If the Parties cannot resolve their dispute after conferring, any Party may require the other Parties to submit the matter to nonbinding mediation, utilizing the services of an impartial professional mediator approved by all Parties. If the Parties cannot come to an agreement following mediation, the Parties agree to submit the matter to binding arbitration at a location mutually agreeable to the Parties. The arbitration shall be conducted on a confidential basis pursuant to the Commercial Arbitration Rules of the American Arbitration Association. Any decision or award as a result of any such arbitration proceeding shall include the assessment of costs, expenses, and reasonable attorney's fees and shall include a written record of the proceedings and a written determination of the arbitrators. An arbitrator experienced in trademark and merchandising law shall conduct any such arbitration. An award of arbitration shall be final and binding on the Parties and may be confirmed in a court of competent jurisdiction.

☐ **Arbitration.** If a dispute arises under or relating to this Agreement, the parties agree to submit such dispute to binding arbitration in the State of_____ or another location mutually agreeable to the parties. The arbitration shall be conducted on a confidential basis pursuant to the Commercial Arbitration Rules of the American Arbitration Association. Any decision or award as a result of any such arbitration proceeding shall be in writing and shall provide an explanation for all conclusions of law and fact and shall include the assessment of costs, expenses, and reasonable attorney fees. An arbitrator experienced in trademark and merchandising law shall conduct any such arbitration. An award of arbitration may be confirmed in a court of competent jurisdiction.

Governing Law

This Agreement shall be governed in accordance with the laws of the State of _____ .

Jurisdiction

The parties consent to the exclusive jurisdiction and venue of the federal and state courts located in _____ in any action arising out of or relating to this Agreement. The parties waive any other venue to which either party might be entitled by domicile or otherwise.

Waiver

The failure to exercise any right provided in this Agreement shall not be a waiver of prior or subsequent rights.

Invalidity

If any provision of this Agreement is invalid under applicable statute or rule of law, it is to be considered omitted, and the remaining provisions of this Agreement shall in no way be affected.

Entire Understanding

This Agreement expresses the complete understanding of the parties and supersedes all prior representations, agreements, and understandings, whether written or oral. This Agreement may not be altered except by a written document signed by both parties.

Attachments & Exhibits

The parties agree and acknowledge that all attachments, exhibits, and schedules referred to in this Agreement are incorporated in this Agreement by reference.

No Special Damages

Licensor shall not be liable to Licensee for any incidental, consequential, punitive, or special damages.

Notices

Any notice or communication required or permitted to be given under this Agreement shall be sufficiently given when received by certified mail or sent by facsimile transmission or overnight courier.

No Joint Venture

Nothing contained in this Agreement shall be construed to place one of the parties in the relationship of agent, employee, franchisee, officer, partner, or joint venturer to the other party. Neither party may create or assume any obligation on behalf of the other.

Assignability

(select one)

☐ **Assignment Requires Licensor Consent.** Licensee may not assign or transfer its rights or obligations pursuant to this Agreement without the prior written consent of Licensor. Any assignment or transfer in violation of this section shall be void.

☐ **Licensor Consent Not Required for Assignment to Parent or Acquiring Company.** Licensee may not assign or transfer its rights or obligations pursuant to this Agreement without the prior written consent of Licensor. However, no consent is required for an assignment or transfer that occurs: (a) to an entity in which Licensee owns more than fifty percent of the assets; or (b) as part of a transfer of all or substantially all of the assets of Licensee to any party. Any assignment or transfer in violation of this Section shall be void.

Each party has signed this Agreement through its authorized representative. The parties, having read this Agreement, indicate their consent to the terms and conditions by their signature below.

By: _____   By: _____

Date: _____   Date: _____

Licensor Name: _____   Licensee Name/Title: _____

EXHIBIT A

The Property _____

_____

Licensed Products _____

_____

Sales Requirements

$ _____ in Gross Sales per year.

Proprietary Notices

All licensed products shall bear the following

proprietary notice: _____

_____

4. Explanation for Trademark License Agreement

The Trademark License Agreement is similar to the Merchandise License Agreement provided in Chapter 11. For explanations of most of the terms, see Chapter 11, Section C. Explanations of three items—goodwill, quality control, and proprietary notices—are not covered in Chapter 11, so they are provided below.

a. Reservation of Rights: Assignment of Goodwill

This section of the license provision establishes that the trademark owner is only delivering a narrow group of rights and is retaining everything else. This section also provides that the trademark owner always owns the goodwill associated with the mark. Goodwill is an intangible item—a measurement of the consumer's attitude towards the trademark. The stronger the goodwill, the more momentum the trademark maintains. For example, Coca-Cola trademarks have extraordinary goodwill, demonstrated by the fact that consumers insist on Coca-Cola product over other products that may claim to have similar ingredients.

This license provision guarantees that only the trademark owner earns the goodwill. If the licensee accumulates any goodwill, it is automatically transferred to the trademark owner. In the real world,

this simply means that the licensee can't make any claims to the trademark.

This license provision also provides that the licensee won't attack the licensor's ownership of the trademarks. This is to avoid the possibility of a successful licensee attempting to destroy the trademark owner's rights.

b. Approval of Samples & Quality Control

Failure of a trademark owner to maintain quality standards over the trademark uses can result in the loss of trademark rights (known as "abandonment"). For this reason, every trademark license agreement includes reasonable quality control standards. The important issue for trademark owners is not simply that the agreement provides for quality control, but that the control is actually exercised.

The license provision provides for written approval both prior to production and during production. The termination section of the agreement permits the licensor to terminate the agreement if the licensee does not meet these quality control standards.

c. Proprietary Notices

The Proprietary Notices provision, included in Exhibit A, establishes what notices must be included on the licensed products. For example, if the licensor wants the products to include a registered trademark notice such as "™ Meathead Designs," this should be indicated here.

CHAPTER 11

Art and Merchandise Licenses

This chapter is about merchandising: the business of affixing an image or text to products you plan to sell, such as T-shirts, buttons, caps, and posters. Nowadays, it is difficult to escape the presence of licensed merchandise. Sweatshirts, posters, postcards, shower curtains, tote bags, and even underwear are covered with copyrighted images.

Getting permission for merchandising is similar to establishing other permission arrangements in that a copyright owner must consent to a specific use. The primary difference between merchandising and other permission situations is the payment system. In merchandising, the copyright owner usually negotiates an arrangement for continuing periodic payments known as "royalties."

In this chapter we analyze the principles of merchandise licensing and analyze two merchandise agreements: a long-form merchandise agreement and an abbreviated merchandise agreement.

A. Overview of Merchandise Licensing

Acquiring permission to sell merchandise that incorporates copyrighted material is similar to other permission arrangements—you need to locate the copyright owner, negotiate an agreement, and execute the agreement in writing. However, the agreement used in merchandise licensing is usually more complex than a typical permission agreement and contains additional responsibilities for the parties.

Under the terms of a merchandise license, the owner of the image or text being used (the licensor) is usually paid an advance plus a royalty based on a percentage of income from sales. The company selling the merchandise (the licensee) must meet certain obligations including payments, quality control, and enforcement of rights. If the licensee fails to do so, the license can be terminated. Termination can be very expensive for both parties due to the loss of income for the licensor and the loss of a substantial investment for the licensee.

There are alternatives to licensing rights under a merchandise agreement. One alternative is to purchase the copyright in the artwork (known as an assignment). The other choice is to hire an artist, photographer, or musician to create the material and acquire ownership under a work-for-hire agreement. These options are explained in Chapter 15.

"Copyright-Free" Artwork and Merchandise Agreements

Some artwork is labeled "copyright-free" or "royalty-free" to indicate that it can be used without permission after a one-time payment is made. Can this type of artwork be used freely on merchandise? Not necessarily. Despite the name, copyright-free artworks are often protected under copyright laws, so there are limitations on their use. (This book tries to avoid such confusion by using the term "royalty-free artwork" to refer to a work that does have copyright protection, but can be used in a wide range of ways once a fee is paid.) Only public domain artworks are truly free to use however you want. In order to determine if permission is required, read the shrink-wrap, click-wrap, or other license agreement supplied with the royalty-free artwork. These principles and rules are explained in Chapter 3.

1. What Is Merchandise?

Licensable merchandise is any consumer product on which an image or text can be affixed. In general, merchandise has some utility or function, such as clothing, jewelry, or stationery. However, there are no limitations on what can be merchandise; artwork can be placed on anything that can be reproduced. Products that are commonly the subject of merchandise licenses include: auto sunshades, auto tire covers, backpacks, badges, bank checks, beach mats, bed sheets, belt buckles, belts, blankets, bumper stickers, caps, casual shoes, calendars, ceramic cups, children's wear, clocks, cuff links, decals, desk sets, dress shirts, drink holders, fabric, flags, gift wrap, golf bags, golf club covers, greeting cards, handkerchiefs, hats, heat transfer patches, jackets, jerseys, jewelry, key rings, knit shirts, lamps, letter openers, license plate frames, loose-leaf binders, magnets, mittens, napkins, neckties, notebooks, pennants, pens, pins, polo shirts, postcards, posters, pot holders, rain jackets, rings, running shorts, running shoes, scarves, shower curtains, sleepwear, snack trays, socks, squeeze bottles, stationery, stuffed animals, sunglasses, sweatpants, sweatshirts, sweaters, swimwear, tablecloths, tank tops, tie clips, tote bags, towels, toys, training suits, T-shirts, umbrellas, underwear, wallpaper, and watches.

Information about locating copyright owners of text, photos, art, and music is provided in Chapters 2 through 5.

2. Different Types of Materials Used on Merchandise

Most merchandise licenses are for artwork or photographs. However, text and music are also licensed in connection with merchandise. In general, the rules are the same. But when it comes to licensing music, additional issues arise depending on whether you are licensing an already-recorded composition or whether you will be rerecording a composition for your specific use.

a. Using Art on Merchandise

Using art on merchandise generally consists of using an artistic image such as a drawing or painting on items you plan to sell. Examples include reproducing a Keith Haring painting on a T-shirt or using images from Georgia O'Keeffe paintings on notecards. Of course, if the image is in the public domain, such as the *Mona Lisa*, no permission is required. If the artwork is labeled "royalty-free," you will need to review the license or agreement that accompanies the purchase of the artwork (see

"'Copyright-Free' Artwork and Merchandise Agreements," above) to determine if your merchandise use is permitted.

Agreements for the use of art on merchandise are sometimes called "art licenses" or "design licenses." Whatever such an agreement is called, it is essentially a merchandise license as described in this chapter. You may occasionally find unique provisions in some art licenses for the use of fine artworks—for example, a clause permitting the artist to enter and inspect a poster-making facility to ensure a quality production process. While special provisions such as these are sometimes included to protect the artist, they don't change the basic character of the agreement as a merchandise license.

b. Using Music on Merchandise

The ability to place music onto computer chips has made it possible to include music in merchandise such as greeting cards, watches, toys, musical equipment, music boxes, and even clothing.

Most songs used on merchandise are not copied directly from an existing recording; instead, they are rerecorded in order to be embedded on a computer chip. Since an existing recording of the song isn't being used, permission is required from the music publisher (who owns a song composition) but not from the record company (which owns a specific sound recording). Similarly, if lyrics will be reprinted on merchandise but no recording will be reproduced, permission is required from the music publisher, not the record company. Rules for using music are explained in detail in Chapter 5.

The merchandise license agreements provided in this chapter can be used for licensing music or for reprinting lyrics on merchandise. However, the licensor (the music publisher) may want to incorporate additional requirements—for example, that the music cannot be used in advertisements for the merchandise. The music publisher usually provides the language for such provisions.

An example of a music merchandise license is also available at the Harry Fox Agency website (www.harryfox.com). (Harry Fox is an organization that represents music publishers.) Although the license agreement provided by Harry Fox is intended for use with agency-affiliated publishers, it establishes basic music licensing standards and can be adopted for your purposes. Chapter 5 explains how to locate copyright owners of songs and sound recordings.

c. Using Trademarks, Fictional Characters, or Celebrities on Merchandise

A trademark is any word, photograph, or symbol that is used to identify a business's products or services. Trademarks are commonly licensed for merchandise—for example, the licensing of a university's trademark (the school name or the name of its mascot) on sports equipment or apparel.

Fictional characters include characters from books, television, or movies such as Mickey Mouse, Sabrina the Witch, or Daffy Duck. A fictional character may be animated (Homer Simpson), literary (Willie Loman), or cinematic (James Bond). The rules for licensing characters may change if a real person has portrayed the character (John Goodman as Fred Flintstone), in which case, additional permission may be required, as explained in Chapter 10. (See Chapter 10, Section B6.)

Most of the provisions contained in a merchandise agreement are also used in trademark, character, and celebrity licenses. However, there are some unique aspects to these agreements, some of which require knowledge of trademark law or the right of publicity. For example, character licensing involves overlapping trademark, copyright, and design patent laws. These types of licenses are often handled by special licensing agencies that represent trademark owners, fictional characters, and celebrities. A sample trademark license and additional trademark licensing information is provided in Chapter 10, "Getting Permission to Use Trademarks."

d. Using Short Phrases on Merchandise

Merchandise, by its nature, can generally only accommodate small amounts of text. Since copyright law does not protect short phrases (see Chapter 8, Section A4a), most of the text used on merchandise—for example, "Honk if you like Prune Tacos"—can be used without permission.

However, in the following situations, you should obtain permission to use a short phrase.

- **The phrase is associated with a fictional character.** For example, the unauthorized use of the phrase "E.T., Phone Home." on a ceramic cup was found to be a copyright infringement. (*Universal City Studios, Inc. v. Kamar Indus.*, 217 U.S.P.Q. (BNA) 1162, (S.D. Texas 1982).) In this case, the outcome was directly related to use of "E.T." in the phrase. The use of "Phone Home" without "E.T." would not require authorization.

- **The phrase is a trademark.** You should always obtain permission to use a phrase on merchandise if it is used as a trademark or is taken from an advertising campaign, such as Coke's "It's the Real Thing" or Microsoft's "Where Do You Want to Go Today?" You also need permission to use a phrase that is used to indicate a product or service, such as the "Marlboro Man." (See Chapter 10, "Getting Permission to Use Trademarks.")

- **The phrase is extremely inventive.** An extremely clever phrase such as Ashleigh Brilliant's epigram, "I may not be perfect but parts of me are excellent," or Lewis Caroll's phrase, "Twas brillig and the slithy toves," are protectible. There is no hard and fast rule for how inventive the phrase must be, but it's best to avoid phrases that appear highly inventive to you. Additional rules on the protection of text are provided in Chapter 2, "Getting Permission to Use Text."

3. Royalty Rates for Merchandise Licensing

When you license text, art, graphics, or music for use on merchandise, you are ordinarily required to pay the owner of the licensed material a royalty—that is, a continuing payment based upon a percentage of the income you earn from the sale of the merchandise.

Royalty rates for merchandise licensing vary depending on the merchandise involved. Below are some royalty estimates:

- Greeting cards and gift wrap: 2% to 5%.
- Household (cups, sheets, towels): 3% to 8%.
- Fabrics, apparel (T-shirts, caps, etc.), decals, bumper stickers: 5% to 10%.
- Posters and prints: 10% or more.

4. Additional Information About Merchandise Licensing

Many libraries contain general business directories, such as the multivolume publication *Thomas Register of American Manufacturers* (Thomas Register Publishing) (searchable online at www5.thomasregister.com.) or the *Directory of Corporate Affiliations* (*DCA*) (Reed Reference Publishing Company). The *Thomas Register* lists manufacturers by subject, including profiles and phone numbers. The *DCA* lists companies by name, brand name product or service, geographic location, or SIC code—a four-digit number created by the Department of Commerce to classify a business by service or product types.

A good place to search for information about merchandise licensing, brands, and related news is Apparel Search (www.apparelsearch.com/licensing .htm), which provides a comprehensive contact listing of licensing agents, brands, and licensees.

General business directories on the Internet can also identify merchandise manufacturers; you should be able to find them using a search engine. One website that may be helpful is BigYellow, the NYNEX business directory located at www.bigyellow .com. It enables the user to search by business category, name, street address, state, or zip code. Most online services have general business directories that perform the same functions.

If you're pursuing merchandise licensing on a regular basis, consider a subscription to *The Licensing Journal* (Aspen Law & Business) (www.aspenpub .com). Although pricey at $345 a year, the journal contains thorough information on current trends in art, merchandise, trademark, and toy licensing.

B. Merchandise License Agreement

Occasionally, a seasoned copyright owner who has licensed many copyrighted items may furnish the merchandise license agreement. However, most of the time, the licensee—the company that is manufacturing and selling the merchandise—furnishes the merchandise license agreement. Usually, prior to furnishing the agreement, the licensee and the licensor have worked out all of the business terms. For example, they have already determined the royalty rate, the rights being transferred, the length of time for the agreement, and other financial terms.

To help you prepare this information, a Merchandise License Worksheet is included in Section D. In addition to helping you determine the essential elements of the license agreement, the worksheet is also helpful for monitoring the license agreement after it is signed. Sometimes essential elements from the worksheet are included on an "exhibit" sheet that is attached to the agreement and incorporated into its provisions. Our model agreement includes such an exhibit.

Even after the terms are agreed upon and the license is furnished, the parties can make additional changes. For example, the licensor may want to modify provisions about sublicensing or dispute resolution. Be prepared to make modifications, to cut and paste provisions, or to restructure the agreement so that the sections are in a different order. These types of changes are common.

Below is a long-form merchandise license agreement for licensing artwork, text, or music for use in merchandise.

 A tear-out copy of this form is provided in the Appendix. A digital version is included on the forms CD.

Merchandise License Agreement

Introduction

This License Agreement (the "Agreement") is made between _____ (referred to as "Licensor") and _____ (referred to as "Licensee").

The parties agree as follows:

The Work

The Work refers to the work described in Exhibit A. Licensor is the owner of all rights to the Work and Licensee shall not claim any right to use the Work except under the terms of this Agreement.

Licensed Products

Licensed Products are defined as Licensee's products incorporating the Work specifically described in Exhibit A (the "Licensed Products").

Grant of Rights

Licensor grants to Licensee:

(select one)

☐ an exclusive license

☐ a nonexclusive license

to reproduce and distribute the Work in or on the Licensed Products.

Licensor grants to Licensee:

(select if appropriate)

☐ the right to modify the Work to incorporate it in or on the Licensed Products provided that Licensee agrees to assign to Licensor its rights, if any, in any derivative works resulting from Licensee's modification of the Work. Licensee agrees to execute any documents required to evidence this assignment of copyright and to waive any moral rights and rights of attribution provided in 17 U.S.C. § 106A of the Copyright Act.

☐ the right to publicly display the Work as incorporated in or on the Licensed Products.

☐ the right to publicly perform the Work as incorporated in or on the Licensed Products.

Sublicense

(select one)

☐   **Consent required.** Licensee may sublicense the rights granted pursuant to this agreement provided: Licensee obtains Licensor's prior written consent to such sublicense; and Licensor receives such revenue or royalty payment as provided in the Payment section below. Any sublicense granted in violation of this provision shall be void.

☐   **Consent to sublicense not unreasonably withheld.** Licensee may sublicense the rights granted pursuant to this agreement provided: Licensee obtains Licensor's prior written consent to such sublicense. Licensor's consent to any sublicense shall not be unreasonably withheld, and Licensor receives such revenue or royalty payment as provided in the Payment section below. Any sublicense granted in violation of this provision shall be void.

☐   **No sublicensing permitted.** Licensee may not sublicense the rights granted under this agreement.

Reservation of Rights

Licensor reserves all rights other than those being conveyed or granted in this Agreement.

Territory

The rights granted to Licensee are limited to _____ (the "Territory").

Term

The "Effective Date" of this Agreement is defined as the date when the agreement commences and is established by the latest signature date.

(select one)

☐   **Specified term with renewal rights.** This Agreement shall commence upon the Effective Date and shall extend for a period of__years (the "Initial Term"). Following the Initial Term, Licensee may renew this agreement under the same terms and conditions for ___consecutive _____ periods (the "Renewal Terms"), provided that Licensee provides written notice of its intention to renew this agreement within thirty (30) days before the expiration of the current term. In no event shall the Term extend beyond the period of United States copyright protection for the Work.

☐ **Term with renewal based upon sales.** This Agreement shall commence upon the Effective Date and shall extend for a period of ___ years (the "Initial Term") and may be renewed by Licensee under the same terms and conditions for consecutive _____ year periods (the "Renewal Terms"), provided that:

(a) Licensee provides written notice of its intention to renew this agreement within thirty days before the expiration of the current term; and

(b) Licensee has met the sales requirements as established in Exhibit A.

☐ **Indefinite term.** This Agreement shall commence upon the Effective Date and shall continue until terminated pursuant to a provision of this Agreement.

☐ **Fixed term.** This Agreement shall commence upon the Effective Date and shall continue for _____ unless sooner terminated pursuant to a provision of this Agreement.

☐ **Term for as long as Licensee sells Licensed Products.** This Agreement shall commence upon the Effective Date as specified in Exhibit A and shall continue for as long as Licensee continues to offer the Licensed Products in commercially reasonable quantities or unless sooner terminated pursuant to a provision of this Agreement. In no event shall the Term extend beyond the period of U.S. copyright protection for the Work.

Payments

All royalties ("Royalties") provided for under this Agreement shall accrue when the respective Licensed Products are sold, shipped, distributed, billed, or paid for, whichever occurs first.

Net Sales

Net Sales are defined as Licensee's gross sales (the gross invoice amount billed to customers) less quantity discounts or rebates and returns actually credited. A quantity discount or rebate is a discount made at the time of shipment. No deductions shall be made for cash or other discounts, commissions, manufacturing costs, uncollectible accounts, or for fees or expenses of any kind that the Licensee may incur in connection with the Royalty payments.

Fees

(select one or more provisions)

☐ **Advance Against Royalties.** As a nonrefundable advance against royalties (the "Advance"), Licensee agrees to pay to Licensor upon execution of this Agreement the sum of $_____ .

☐   **Licensed Product Royalty.** Licensee agrees to pay a Royalty of____% percent of all Net Sales revenue of the Licensed Products ("Licensed Product Royalty").

☐   **Per Unit Royalty.** Licensee agrees to pay a Royalty of $__ for each unit of the Licensed Product that is: (select one)

   ☐   manufactured.

   ☐   sold.

☐   **Guaranteed Minimum Annual Royalty Payment.** In addition to any other advances or fees, Licensee shall pay an annual guaranteed royalty (the "GMAR") as follows: $_____ . The GMAR shall be paid to Licensor annually on _____. The GMAR is an advance against royalties for the twelve-month period commencing upon payment. Royalty payments based on Net Sales made during any year of this Agreement shall be credited against the GMAR due for the year in which such Net Sales were made. In the event that annual royalties exceed the GMAR, Licensee shall pay the difference to Licensor. Any annual royalty payments in excess of the GMAR shall not be carried forward from previous years or applied against the GMAR.

☐   **License Fee.** As a nonrefundable, nonrecoupable fee for executing this license, Licensee agrees to pay to Licensor upon execution of this Agreement the sum of $_____.

☐   **Sublicensing Revenues.** In the event of any sublicense of the rights granted pursuant to this Agreement, Licensee shall pay to Licensor_____% percent of all sublicensing revenues.

Payments and Statements to Licensor

Within thirty (30) days after the end of each calendar quarter (the "Royalty Period"), an accurate statement of Net Sales of Licensed Products along with any royalty payments or sublicensing revenues due to Licensor shall be provided to Licensor, regardless of whether any Licensed Products were sold during the Royalty Period. All payments shall be paid in United States currency drawn on a United States bank. The acceptance by Licensor of any of the statements furnished or royalties paid shall not preclude Licensor questioning the correctness at any time of any payments or statements.

Audit

Licensee shall keep accurate books of account and records covering all transactions relating to the license granted in this Agreement, and Licensor or its duly authorized representatives shall have the right upon five days prior written notice, and during normal business hours, to inspect and audit

Licensee's records relating to the Work licensed under this Agreement. Licensor shall bear the cost of such inspection and audit, unless the results indicate an underpayment greater than $_____for any six-month (6-month) period. In that case, Licensee shall promptly reimburse Licensor for all costs of the audit along with the amount due with interest on such sums. Interest shall accrue from the date the payment was originally due and the interest rate shall be 1.5% per month, or the maximum rate permitted by law, whichever is less. All books of account and records shall be made available in the United States and kept available for at least two years after the termination of this Agreement.

Late Payment

Time is of the essence with respect to all payments to be made by Licensee under this Agreement. If Licensee is late in any payment provided for in this Agreement, Licensee shall pay interest on the payment from the date due until paid at a rate of 1.5% per month, or the maximum rate permitted by law, whichever is less.

Licensor Warranties

Licensor warrants that it has the power and authority to enter into this Agreement and has no knowledge as to any third-party claims regarding the proprietary rights in the Work that would interfere with the rights granted under this Agreement.

Indemnification by Licensor

(select one if appropriate)

☐ **Licensor indemnification without limitations.** Licensor shall indemnify Licensee and hold Licensee harmless from any damages and liabilities (including reasonable attorney fees and costs) arising from any breach of Licensor's warranties as defined in Licensor's Warranties, above.

☐ **Licensor indemnification limited to amounts paid.** Licensor shall indemnify Licensee and hold Licensee harmless from any damages and liabilities (including reasonable attorney fees and costs), arising from any breach of Licensor's warranties as defined in Licensor's Warranties, above. Licensor's maximum liability under this provision shall in no event exceed the total amount earned by Licensor under this Agreement.

☐ **Licensor indemnification with limitations.** Licensor shall indemnify Licensee and hold Licensee harmless from any damages and liabilities (including reasonable attorney fees and costs) arising from any breach of Licensor's warranties as defined in Licensor's Warranties, above, provided that:

(a) such claim, if sustained, would prevent Licensee from marketing the Licensed Products or the Work;

(b) such claim arises solely out of the Work as disclosed to the Licensee and not out of any change in the Work made by Licensee or a vendor;

(c) Licensee gives Licensor prompt written notice of any such claim;

(d) such indemnity shall only be applicable in the event of a final decision by a court of competent jurisdiction from which no right to appeal exists; and

(e) the maximum amount due from Licensor to Licensee under this paragraph shall not exceed the amounts due to Licensor under the Payment Section from the date that Licensor notifies Licensee of the existence of such a claim.

Licensee Warranties

Licensee warrants that it will use its best commercial efforts to market the Licensed Products and that sale and marketing of the Licensed Products shall be in conformance with all applicable laws and regulations, including but not limited to all intellectual property laws.

Indemnification by Licensee

Licensee shall indemnify Licensor and hold Licensor harmless from any damages and liabilities (including reasonable attorney fees and costs):

(a) arising from any breach of Licensee's warranties and representation as defined in the Licensee Warranties, above;

(b) arising out of any alleged defects or failures to perform of the Licensed Products or any product liability claims or use of the Licensed Products; and

(c) any claims arising out of advertising, distribution, or marketing of the Licensed Products.

Intellectual Property Registration

Licensor may, but is not obligated to, seek in its own name and at its own expense, appropriate copyright registrations for the Work. Licensor makes no warranty with respect to the validity of any copyright that may be granted. Licensor grants to Licensee the right to apply for registration of the Work or Licensed Products provided that such registrations shall be applied for in the name of

Licensor and licensed to Licensee during the Term and according to the conditions of this Agreement. Licensee shall have the right to deduct its reasonable out-of-pocket expenses for the preparation and filing of any such registrations from future royalties due to Licensor under this Agreement. Licensee shall obtain Licensor's prior written consent before incurring expenses for any foreign copyright applications.

Compliance With Intellectual Property Laws

The license granted in this Agreement is conditioned on Licensee's compliance with the provisions of the intellectual property laws of the United States and any foreign country in the Territory. All copies of the Licensed Product as well as all promotional material shall bear appropriate proprietary notices.

Licensor Credits

Licensee shall identify Licensor as the owner of rights to the Work and shall include the following notice on all copies of the Licensed Products: "_____. All rights reserved."

Licensee may, with Licensor's consent, use Licensor's name, image, or trademark in advertising or promotional materials associated with the sale of the Licensed Products.

Infringement Against Third Parties

In the event that either party learns of imitations or infringements of the Work or Licensed Products, that party shall notify the other in writing of the infringements or imitations. Licensor shall have the right to commence lawsuits against third persons arising from infringement of the Work or Licensed Products. In the event that Licensor does not commence a lawsuit against an alleged infringer within sixty days of notification by Licensee, Licensee may commence a lawsuit against the third party. Before filing suit, Licensee shall obtain the written consent of Licensor to do so, and such consent shall not be unreasonably withheld. Licensor will cooperate fully and in good faith with Licensee for the purpose of securing and preserving Licensee's rights to the Work. Any recovery (including, but not limited to a judgment, settlement, or licensing agreement included as resolution of an infringement dispute) shall be divided equally between the parties after deduction and payment of reasonable attorney fees to the party bringing the lawsuit.

Exploitation Date

Licensee agrees to manufacture, distribute, and sell the Licensed Products in commercially reasonable quantities during the term of this Agreement and to commence such manufacture, distribution, and sale by _____ . This is a material provision of this Agreement.

Advertising Budget

(select if appropriate)

☐   Licensee agrees to spend at least _____% of estimated annual gross sales for promotional efforts and advertising of the Licensed Products.

Approval of Samples & Quality Control

Licensee shall submit a reasonable number of preproduction designs, prototypes, and camera-ready artwork prior to production as well as preproduction samples of the Licensed Product to Licensor to assure that the product meets Licensor's quality standards. In the event that Licensor fails to object in writing within ten (10) business days after the date of receipt of any such materials, such materials shall be deemed to be acceptable. At least once during each calendar year, Licensee shall submit two (2) production samples of each Licensed Product for review. Licensee shall pay all costs for delivery of these approval materials. The quality standards applied by Licensor shall be no more rigorous than the quality standards applied by Licensor to similar products.

Licensor Copies and Right to Purchase

Licensee shall provide Licensor with ____ copies of each Licensed Product. Licensor has the right to purchase from Licensee, at Licensee's manufacturing cost, at least _____copies of any Licensed Product, and such payments shall be deducted from royalties due to Licensor.

Confidentiality

The parties acknowledge that each may have access to confidential information that relates to each other's business (the "Information"). The parties agree to protect the confidentiality of the Information and maintain it with the strictest confidence, and no party shall disclose such information to third parties without the prior written consent of the other.

Insurance

Licensee shall, throughout the Term, obtain and maintain, at its own expense, standard product liability insurance coverage, naming Licensor as an additional named insured. Such policy shall provide protection against any claims, demands, and causes of action arising out of any alleged defects or failure to perform of the Licensed Products or any use of the Licensed Products. The amount of coverage shall be a minimum of $_____, with no deductible amount for each single occurrence for bodily injury or property damage. The policy shall provide for notice to the Licensor from the insurer by Registered or Certified Mail in the event of any modification or termination of insurance. The provisions of this section shall survive termination for three years.

Licensor's Right to Terminate

Licensor shall have the right to terminate this Agreement for the following reasons:

(select one or more provisions)

- [ ] **Failure to Make Timely Payment.** Licensee fails to pay Royalties when due or fails to accurately report Net Sales, as defined in the Payment Section of this Agreement, and such failure is not cured within thirty (30) days after written notice from the Licensor.

- [ ] **Failure to Introduce Product.** Licensee fails to introduce the product to market by the date set in the Exploitation section of this Agreement or to offer the Licensed Products in commercially reasonable quantities during any subsequent year.

- [ ] **Assignment or Sublicensing.** Licensee assigns or sublicenses in violation of this Agreement.

- [ ] **Failure to Maintain Insurance.** Licensee fails to maintain or obtain product liability insurance as required by the provisions of this Agreement.

- [ ] **Failure to Submit Samples.** Licensee fails to provide Licensor with preproduction samples for approval.

- [ ] **Termination as to Unexploited Portion of Territory.** Licensor shall have the right to terminate the grant of license under this Agreement with respect to any country or region included in the Territory in which Licensee fails to offer the Licensed Products for sale or distribution or to secure a sublicensing agreement for the marketing, distribution, and sale of the product within two (2) years of the Effective Date.

Effect of Termination

Upon termination of this Agreement ("Termination"), all Royalty obligations as established in the Payments Section shall immediately become due. After the Termination of this license, all rights granted to Licensee under this Agreement shall terminate and revert to Licensor, and Licensee will refrain from further manufacturing, copying, marketing, distribution, or use of any Licensed Product or other product which incorporates the Work. Within thirty (30) days after Termination, Licensee shall deliver to Licensor a statement indicating the number and description of the Licensed Products that it had on hand or is in the process of manufacturing as of the Termination date.

Sell-Off Period

Licensee may dispose of the Licensed Products covered by this Agreement for a period of 90 days after Termination or expiration except that Licensee shall have no such right in the event this agreement is terminated according to the Licensor's Right to Terminate, above. At the end of the post-Termination sale period, Licensee shall furnish a royalty payment and statement as required under the Payment Section. Upon termination, Licensee shall deliver to Licensor all original artwork and camera-ready reproductions used in the manufacture of the Licensed Products. Licensor shall bear the costs of shipping for the artwork and reproductions.

Attorney Fees and Expenses

The prevailing party shall have the right to collect from the other party its reasonable costs and necessary disbursements and attorney fees incurred in enforcing this Agreement.

Dispute Resolution

(select one if appropriate)

☐ **Mediation & Arbitration.** The Parties agree that every dispute or difference between them, arising under this Agreement, shall be settled first by a meeting of the Parties attempting to confer and resolve the dispute in a good faith manner. If the Parties cannot resolve their dispute after conferring, any Party may require the other Parties to submit the matter to nonbinding mediation, utilizing the services of an impartial professional mediator approved by all Parties. If the Parties cannot come to an agreement following mediation, the Parties agree to submit the matter to binding arbitration at a location mutually agreeable to the Parties. The arbitration shall be conducted on a confidential basis pursuant to the

Commercial Arbitration Rules of the American Arbitration Association. Any decision or award as a result of any such arbitration proceeding shall include the assessment of costs, expenses, and reasonable attorney's fees and shall include a written record of the proceedings and a written determination of the arbitrators. An arbitrator experienced in copyright and merchandising law shall conduct any such arbitration. An award of arbitration shall be final and binding on the Parties and may be confirmed in a court of competent jurisdiction.

☐ **Arbitration.** If a dispute arises under or relating to this Agreement, the parties agree to submit such dispute to binding arbitration in the state of_____or another location mutually agreeable to the parties. The arbitration shall be conducted on a confidential basis pursuant to the Commercial Arbitration Rules of the American Arbitration Association. Any decision or award as a result of any such arbitration proceeding shall be in writing and shall provide an explanation for all conclusions of law and fact and shall include the assessment of costs, expenses, and reasonable attorney fees. An arbitrator experienced in copyright and merchandising law shall conduct any such arbitration. An award of arbitration may be confirmed in a court of competent jurisdiction.

Governing Law

This Agreement shall be governed in accordance with the laws of the State of _____.

Jurisdiction

The parties consent to the exclusive jurisdiction and venue of the federal and state courts located in _____ in any action arising out of or relating to this Agreement. The parties waive any other venue to which either party might be entitled by domicile or otherwise.

Waiver

The failure to exercise any right provided in this Agreement shall not be a waiver of prior or subsequent rights.

Invalidity

If any provision of this Agreement is invalid under applicable statute or rule of law, it is to be considered omitted, and the remaining provisions of this Agreement shall in no way be affected.

Entire Understanding

This Agreement expresses the complete understanding of the parties and supersedes all prior representations, agreements, and understandings, whether written or oral. This Agreement may not be altered except by a written document signed by both parties.

Attachments & Exhibits

The parties agree and acknowledge that all attachments, exhibits, and schedules referred to in this Agreement are incorporated in this Agreement by reference.

No Special Damages

Licensor shall not be liable to Licensee for any incidental, consequential, punitive, or special damages.

Notices

Any notice or communication required or permitted to be given under this Agreement shall be sufficiently given when received by certified mail or sent by facsimile transmission or overnight courier.

No Joint Venture

Nothing contained in this Agreement shall be construed to place one of the parties in the relationship of agent, employee, franchisee, officer, partner, or joint venturer to the other party. Neither party may create or assume any obligation on behalf of the other.

Assignability

(select one)

☐ **Assignment Requires Licensor Consent.** Licensee may not assign or transfer its rights or obligations pursuant to this Agreement without the prior written consent of Licensor. Any assignment or transfer in violation of this section shall be void.

☐ **Licensor Consent Not Unreasonably Withheld.** Licensee may not assign or transfer its rights or obligations pursuant to this Agreement without the prior written consent of Licensor. Such consent shall not be unreasonably withheld. Any assignment or transfer in violation of this section shall be void.

☐ **Licensor Consent Not Required for Assignment to Parent or Acquiring Company.** Licensee may not assign or transfer its rights or obligations pursuant to this Agreement without the prior written consent of Licensor. However, no consent is required for an assignment or transfer that occurs: (a) to an entity in which Licensee owns more than fifty percent of the assets; or (b) as part of a transfer of all or substantially all of the assets of Licensee to any party. Any assignment or transfer in violation of this Section shall be void.

Each party has signed this Agreement through its authorized representative. The parties, having read this Agreement, indicate their consent to the terms and conditions by their signature below.

By: _____   By: _____

Date: _____   Date: _____

Licensor Name: _____   Licensee Name/Title: _____

EXHIBIT A

The Property _____

_____

Licensed Products _____

_____

Sales Requirements

$ _____ in Gross Sales per year.

C. Explanation of Merchandise License Agreement

Every merchandise license agreement contains essential elements including a grant of rights, territory, term, and identification of the parties. Most, like the model merchandise license agreements in this chapter, contain additional provisions such as warranties, indemnity, termination, and miscellaneous clauses.

What If the Licensor Furnishes the Agreement?

If the licensor (the copyright or trademark owner) furnishes the merchandise license agreement, the licensee (merchandise seller) will need to review its provisions. Deciphering a license agreement can be a challenge, even for experienced attorneys. Unfortunately, there are no rules for how to order or arrange provisions in a license agreement. Many agreements seem to be organized haphazardly. In order to analyze a new agreement, use the following strategies:

- Be prepared to spend several hours making an analysis.
- Make a photocopy of the agreement.
- Locate the major provisions (as discussed below) and label them in the margin.
- Compare each provision with the language suggested in this book.
- Underline everything you don't like or don't understand.
- Prepare a chart, listing the number of the provision and your concerns about that section.
- Convert the chart into a response letter detailing your requested changes.

---

1. The Introductory Paragraph: Identifying the Parties

The introductory paragraph identifies the people or companies entering into the agreement, known as the "parties." The licensor (the copyright or trademark owner) grants permission. The licensee is the person or company seeking permission. The introductory paragraph may also include the parties' business form (for example, corporation or sole proprietorship) and business address. Insert that information, if desired, following the name of each party—for example, "Artco Printing, a California corporation located at 434 W. Oakdale Avenue, Los Angeles, California, 90015."

"Whereas" Provisions

In some license agreements, the introductory information is referred to as the "Whereas" provisions, for example: "Whereas DTK publishing (the licensee) desires to acquire rights...." The use of the term "whereas" has no particular legal significance and it is not included in this book's model agreements.

Instead of licensee and licensor, the agreement can be drafted to use the names of the parties throughout the agreement or terms such as "Artist" for the licensor and "Manufacturer" for the licensee, as long as this terminology is used consistently within the agreement.

2. The Work

The licensor's material (the art, text, or music licensed) is referred to as the "Work." Any term can be substituted instead of "Work"—for example, the "Photograph" or the "Book"—as long as this terminology is used consistently within the agreement. If more than one work is being licensed from the licensor, each work can be identified separately, such as "Work #1," "Work # 2," and so on. In Exhibit A, each work should be described or, if possible, a photocopy of the artwork or text should be attached to the agreement and referenced in Exhibit A. (Exhibit A is an attachment to the agreement, described in Section C23, below.)

3. The Licensed Product

A licensed product is any merchandise that incorporates the work. If the definition of the product is too narrow, the licensee may be precluded from certain markets. For example, if the licensed product is described as "T-shirts," the licensee cannot sell other shirts like tank tops. Similarly, the term "ceramic cups" precludes the sale of plastic cups. If you don't want to exclude large categories of items from the merchandise you can sell, be sure to define your licensed product broadly enough. For instance, instead of "T-shirts," you could define your licensed product as "upper body apparel." Any plain-language definition is suitable. Consider some of the examples in Section A1. Insert your definitions in Exhibit A.

4. The Grant of Rights

The grant of rights (also known as simply the "grant") officially permits use of the work, describes the rights under copyright law that the copyright owner is licensing, and establishes whether the rights are exclusive or nonexclusive. In a merchandise license agreement, the grant must include the following rights:

- **The right to reproduce.** This refers to the right to make copies of the art or other work on merchandise. This is similar to the grant of rights for a regular license agreement that gives the right to make copies on various media such as print or film. This right is essential for the merchandise agreement—without it, the material cannot be duplicated. Note that the right to reproduce is not unlimited. The agreement specifically limits it to the use of the material on "Licensed Products." In other words,

the artwork can only be used on specific products as defined in the attached exhibit.
- **The right to distribute copies.** This refers to the right to sell or give away the work as reproduced on the merchandise.

Reproduction and distribution are closely related, and every merchandise license agreement requires both rights.

Other rights, however, are optional. The section below discusses what optional rights may be granted and the difference between exclusive and nonexclusive rights.

a. Optional Rights

The following rights may be included in a merchandise agreement:

- **The right to adapt or create derivatives.** This refers to the right to modify the work— for example, to alter a photograph so that only a portion is used. The result of the modification is referred to as a "derivative work." If you plan to create a derivative work, the grant of rights must include permission to modify the original work. For example, if the licensee plans on creating a series of T-shirts based upon a character, each modification of the character would be a derivative. The language in the model agreement allows the licensor to own any modifications or contributions the licensee makes to the work. This is standard contract language, and you have little choice but to accept it. If this language is not included, the licensee and licensor may become co-authors of any jointly created derivative work.
- **The right to display publicly.** This refers to the right to exhibit or display a licensed product publicly. As a general rule, the licensee should always acquire this right, as it permits activities like displaying the work—for example, selling posters of artwork over the Internet. However, even without this right, the licensee can display the artwork as it appears on the merchandise in connection with

advertisements. The U.S. Copyright Act (17 U.S.C. § 113) permits the reproduction of artwork or photographs on "useful articles" in advertisements. A useful article includes clothing, tote bags, or most other merchandise that has a utilitarian function.

- **The right to perform publicly.** This refers to the right to perform the work publicly—for example, if you license music for use in a toy and the toy is demonstrated in a television or radio commercial. Note that if you are obtaining a license to use music in merchandise, you will always need this right. For more information on public performance of music, see Chapter 5, "Getting Permission to Use Music."

b. Exclusive versus Nonexclusive Rights

Every merchandise license agreement is either exclusive or nonexclusive. Exclusive means that only the licensee will have the rights granted in the agreement—no one else can be given the same rights during the term of the agreement. Nonexclusive means that the licensor (the copyright owner) can give the same rights to someone else. The primary reason for seeking exclusive rights is to prevent a competitor from using the same material in the same way.

An exclusive license is usually more expensive than a nonexclusive license, but not always. For example, the fee for an exclusive license to use an image on auto seat covers may be the same as a nonexclusive license simply because the seat cover market is limited and has few manufacturers. However, an exclusive license for T-shirts or calendars may be two or three times the cost of a nonexclusive license.

Note that if you're seeking exclusive rights, you must obtain the consent of all owners of the work, not just one. Sometimes more than one person or entity owns a copyrighted work. For nonexclusive rights, you need only the consent of one owner. But all owners must agree to grant exclusive rights.

5. Sublicenses

A sublicense allows the licensee to license its rights to another company. Often, a licensee will sublicense rights to foreign companies. Retaining or granting sublicensing rights depends on each situation. For example, if a licensee has experience in foreign markets and can handle the licensing abroad, then the licensee would want to prohibit foreign sublicensing and retain those rights. If the licensor was unsure of whether it could license rights abroad, then the licensor may want a provision requiring written consent. That way, the licensor could review each sublicensing arrangement to determine its relative advantages and disadvantages.

Our model agreement provides that sublicensing is permitted with written consent of licensor, but the consent cannot be withheld unreasonably. This is the preferred option for most licensees because it means that the licensor can only withhold consent for a valid business reason.

6. Reservation of Rights

If a licensor does not grant a specific right, the licensor has retained or "reserved" that right. Although it is not essential to state this fact, most licensors prefer to include this statement.

7. Territory

Geographic limits ("territory") determine where the licensee can exercise rights. The territory can be as small or as large as desired. Worldwide rights are always desirable because they allow the licensee to sell his or her merchandise in every country in the world. If the territory is the world, insert the word "worldwide" into this section. If the territory is a specific region or country, insert that information. Many merchandise licenses are only for the U.S. and Canada. Since the cost of a worldwide license is usually greater than for a license for an individual country, review your sales potential in any country before you include it in the territory.

8. Term

Term refers to the length of the merchandise license. As a general rule, the licensee wants permission for as long as possible while the licensor prefers to give permission for a shorter period of time. The date that an agreement commences is usually referred to as the "effective date." If the agreement has a fixed date of termination, say ten years, the agreement would end ten years from the effective date.

The agreement prohibits a term that is longer than United States copyright protection because after copyright expires, the licensee should not have to pay to use the once copyrighted materials. Even if no time limit is expressed, under some circumstances the law allows the copyright owner to terminate the merchandise license after 35 years. This is true even if the agreement contains a statement that the license is "forever" or "in perpetuity."

9. Payments

Most merchandise licenses are based on a payment system of royalties. A "royalty" is a continuing payment based on a percentage of the income from the licensed product. The advantage of a royalty system is that the licensee only has to pay if the licensed product earns money. The disadvantages are that royalty obligations often include advance or guaranteed annual payments and continuing accounting responsibility. Below are the definitions of some royalty terms.

- "Gross sales" are the total amount billed to customers. "Net sales" are the licensee's gross sales minus certain deductions. In other words, the licensee calculates the total amount billed to customers and then deducts certain items before paying the royalty. It is generally acceptable to deduct from gross sales any amounts paid for shipping, freight, taxes, credits, returns, and discounts made at the time of sale.

- An "advance against royalties" is an up-front payment to the licensor, usually made at the time the license agreement is signed. An advance is almost always credited or "recouped" against future royalties unless the agreement provides otherwise. It's as if the licensee is saying, "I expect you will earn at least $1,000 in royalties so I am going to advance you that sum at the time we sign the agreement." When the licensor starts earning royalties, the licensee keeps the first $1,000 as repayment for the licensor's advance. If the licensor doesn't earn the $1,000 in royalties, the licensee takes a loss. Generally, a licensor does not have to return the advance unless he or she breaches the agreement.

- The "licensed product royalty" is the most common form of royalty payment—a percentage of net sales. Net sales royalty payments are computed by multiplying the royalty rate against net sales. For example, a royalty rate of 5% multiplied by net sales of $1,000 equals a net sales royalty of $50. Estimates of merchandise royalties are provided in Section A3.

- A "per-unit royalty" is tied to the number of units sold or manufactured, not the total money earned by sales. For example, under a per-unit royalty, a licensor might receive 50 cents for each licensed product sold or manufactured. (Note that the licensee cannot choose both per-unit and net sales royalties.) If the licensor is using the merchandise as part of a free distribution, for example, giving out hundreds of the products at a promotion for a restaurant, check the "manufactured" box. If the merchandise will be offered for sale, check the "sold" box. Generally, net sales royalties are used instead of per-unit royalties because revenue may come from sources such as sublicensing, in which case the total net sales will be easier to track.

- The guaranteed minimum annual royalty payment (GMAR) is an annual payment that guarantees that the licensor receives a specific payment, regardless of how well the merchandise sells in any year. At the end of each year, the earned royalties are totaled and, if they are more than the GMAR, the licensor is paid the difference. If the earned royalties are less than the GMAR, the licensee takes a loss. In some cases, a licensee may not want to take the loss and will insist that this difference be carried forward and deducted against the next year's royalties. If a license agreement includes a GMAR, the licensee may want to limit the initial term of the agreement. Otherwise, the licensee risks being locked into paying GMARs when the merchandise no longer sells.

- A license fee is a one-time fee usually paid at the time the agreement is signed. The licensee may arrange to make the payment when the licensed product is first distributed. That way, if the licensed product is not produced, the licensee does not have to pay.
- Include the provision for sublicensing revenue in the agreement if the licensor permits sublicensing. (See Section C5, above.)

10. Audits

The audit provision describes when the licensor (or the licensor's representative) can have access to the licensee's records. If the licensee has failed to pay the licensor properly, the audit will detect that information. The licensee will have to pay for the audit if the audit detects an error of a certain magnitude, usually anywhere from $500 to $2,000 dollars. Insert an amount in the blank space.

11. Warranties and Indemnity

Warranties are contractual promises. If the licensor breaches a warranty, under an indemnity provision, the licensee will have to pay for certain costs that result from the breach. In this way, warranties and indemnity work together. They are each discussed in more detail below.

Keep in mind that the merchandise license can be executed without including warranties or an indemnity provision. They are recommended but not essential for the agreement.

a. Warranties

In some agreements, warranties are labeled "covenants" or "representations." Regardless of the title, they are essentially the same things: promises made between the parties regarding certain aspects of the contract. A common warranty, for instance, is that the licensor owns the rights to the work and has the power to grant them to the licensee. In addition, the licensee should seek a promise that the work doesn't infringe third-party rights (rights of people who are not part of the agreement). Since licensors are often wary of making this type of assurance, the model agreement provides a more palatable warranty that the licensor "has no knowledge as to any third-party claims." This means that a reasonable person in the licensor's position would know whether the work is infringing someone else's rights.

A licensor may ask that the licensee provide a warranty that sales and marketing of the licensed product will conform to applicable laws. A sample provision is included in the model merchandise agreement.

If an agreement includes a warranty but no indemnity provision, the parties can still sue for "breach of warranty." However, a judge or jury will decide whether the breaching party must pay the costs or attorney fees associated with the breach.

b. Indemnity

A licensor who provides indemnity is agreeing to pay for the licensee's damages for certain situations. For example, if the licensor indemnifies the licensee against infringement, the licensor will have to pay damages (and legal fees) if the licensee is sued for infringement for his or her use of the work. Indemnity acts like a shield: the licensee can deflect a lawsuit from him or herself, and the licensor pays for the damages. Indemnity provisions are also sometimes referred to as "hold harmless" provisions because the provision often states that the "Licensor shall hold the Licensee harmless from any losses, etc."

Licensors are often unwilling to provide indemnity because they don't want to be legally obligated to pay legal costs. Since indemnification involves a financial risk, many licensors will avoid it completely or will only agree to it with further limitations. For example, a licensor may agree to pay indemnity but only if the amount is not larger than any amounts they received under the agreement. The licensor may request that the licensee provide indemnification as well. For example, if the licensee promises to market and distribute the licensed product in a legal manner, the licensee may indemnify the licensor from any liability arising out of the licensee's marketing and distribution.

It is also important to remember that indemnity is only worthwhile if the party who agrees to pay has money or insurance to cover the costs. An indemnity provision is useless if the indemnifier (the person who is supposed to indemnify) is broke.

12. Intellectual Property Rights

If the licensor has not filed a copyright registration and does not plan to do so, the licensee may register for protection under this provision. It is common for the licensee to deduct the reasonable costs of registration from future royalties.

13. Credits

The licensor should insert any credit he or she wants to appear on the merchandise. For instance, a photographer who wanted to be credited for a photograph he's licensing could insert the desired credit line: "Tom Bamberger Photo Studios."

If the licensee does not display the credit on the merchandise, it could provide a basis for the licensor to terminate the agreement.

The credit section also provides the licensee with the right to use the licensor's name and trademark in advertising for the merchandised product. This is essential if the licensor is an established artist or writer whose name or image the licensee intends to use in promotional materials.

14. Infringement Against Third Parties

If the licensed product is successful, unethical competitors may create imitations. If the licensor does not have the financial resources to fight the infringer, this provision allows the licensee to deal with infringers. It provides for funding of a lawsuit and for dividing any money that is recovered from the infringer. The provision in the model agreement establishes a 50/50 division of any award money after payment of attorney fees.

15. Exploitation Date

This provision establishes the date by which the licensee must release the licensed product. Without this assurance, a licensor may be worried that the licensee will simply sit on the work and not exploit it. Sometimes the release date coincides with a specific trade show or a seasonal catalogue. If the licensee fails to meet this date, the licensor can claim that there has been a "material breach" which is a basis for termination of the license agreement.

16. Approval of Samples and Quality Control

The licensor needs to guarantee that the work is being reproduced properly and that the licensed product is not inferior to competing products. This provision permits the licensor to review the preproduction artwork and prototypes before providing approval (within a ten-day period).

17. Licensor Copies and Right to Purchase

The licensor will want free copies of the licensed product and the right to purchase more at wholesale cost. If the licensee is concerned that the copies will be sold or transferred to a competitor, he or she can add a statement to this provision that prevents the licensor from selling the copies.

18. Confidentiality

It's possible that the licensee or licensor may be disclosing confidential information in the course of the merchandise license. Confidential information includes any information that gives the business an advantage and is maintained in confidence. This clause requires that each party to the agreement preserve confidential information. For example, if the licensor has a secret marketing plan and the licensee discloses that information in an interview, that would be a breach of the agreement.

19. Insurance

If a consumer is injured using the licensed product and claims it's defective, the licensee and licensor may be sued for product liability. It is for this reason that the sellers of merchandise (licensees) acquire product liability insurance. By naming the licensor in the policy, the licensee shields the licensor from claims of product injuries as well. The minimum amount of coverage inserted for the policy should be $1,000,000. Note that this type of insurance usually does not cover infringement lawsuits. Usually, a separate business policy is required for protection against claims of infringement.

20. Termination

Even without a termination provision, either party can terminate a merchandise license agreement if there is a material breach. A "material breach" is a substantial abuse of the agreement—for example, if the licensee used the work for purposes that were not described in the agreement. Most licensors will insist upon including a termination provision, including some or all of the clauses listed in the sample agreement (for example, the right to terminate as to a specific portion of the territory if the work is not exploited there).

21. Effect of Termination

At the time of termination, the licensee may have boxes of licensed products left in the warehouse. If the agreement has ended amicably, it is reasonable to allow the licensee a period of time to sell off the remaining inventory. Naturally, the licensor is entitled to royalties for these products. A period between three and six months is probably sufficient for sell-off. In addition, the licensor should obtain an accounting of the remaining inventory. If the licensee is not paying royalties or has breached the agreement, the licensee is not permitted to sell off the remaining inventory.

22. Miscellaneous Provisions

Many agreements contain a section of provisions entitled "Miscellaneous" or "General." These provisions actually have little in common except that they don't fit anywhere else in the agreement, so they are grouped together at the end. Lawyers often refer to these provisions as "boilerplate."

Don't be misled by the fact that these provisions are buried in the back of the agreement. They can affect important issues like how disputes are resolved and how a court should enforce the agreement. However, even though they are important, they are not mandatory—they can be removed without affecting the validity of the agreement. Below is a summary of some common boilerplate provisions.

a. Attorney Fees

In the event of a legal dispute between the licensee and licensor, the attorney fees provision establishes that the winner of the dispute will receive payment for legal fees. Without this provision, neither party will be reimbursed for attorney fees unless the lawsuit is for copyright infringement. Even in that case, the award is not mandatory; it is at the judge's discretion.

b. Dispute Resolution

Arbitration is like going to court with less formality and expense. Instead of filing a lawsuit, the parties hire one or more arbitrators to evaluate the dispute and make a determination. Arbitrators are trained to evaluate disputes; many of them are retired judges.

Mediation is similar to arbitration except that instead of making a determination, a neutral evaluator attempts to help the parties settle their dispute themselves. That is, the mediator offers advice so that the parties reach a solution together. Mediation and arbitration are often referred to as "alternative dispute resolution" or "ADR."

The model agreement includes two alternative dispute resolution provisions. The first provides for mediation first, then arbitration if mediation fails. The second provides for arbitration only.

Pros and Cons of Arbitration

Arbitration has both good and not-so-good aspects when compared to litigating a dispute in court. Here is an overview of the pros and cons of arbitration:

- **Pros:** Arbitration is usually less expensive and more efficient than litigation. Also, the parties can select an arbitrator who has knowledge in the merchandising field.
- **Cons:** Unlike in a lawsuit, there is no right to discovery—the process by which parties must disclose documents and information about their cases. However, the licensee can include a requirement for discovery in the arbitration provision. Also, unlike a court ruling, a binding arbitration ruling is not appealable. It can only be set aside if the arbitrator was biased or the ruling violated public policy. Arbitrators must be paid (unlike state and federal judges), and fees can run to $10,000 or more. And, most participants in arbitrations hire attorneys, so the licensee will still have to pay attorney fees (although probably less than in a lawsuit).

Private arbitration is offered by a number of organizations, the best known of which is the American Arbitration Association (AAA). For information on arbitration and the AAA, check its website at www.adr.org.

---

c. Governing Law

In the event of a dispute, this provision (sometimes called "Choice of Law") determines which state's law will govern the lawsuit. Every state has laws regarding contract interpretation. The licensor usually favors the state in which its headquarters are located, often New York or California. Does it matter which state is chosen? Some states have a reputation as being favorable for certain kinds of disputes, but generally, the differences in state law are not great enough to make this a major negotiating issue.

d. Jurisdiction

In the event of a dispute, this provision establishes in which state (and, if you want to specify, which county) the lawsuit or arbitration must be filed. Each party will prefer having jurisdiction in its home location, so this section is sometimes a matter of negotiation.

If the section creates contention, remove it. If there is no reference to jurisdiction, the location is usually determined by whoever files a lawsuit. If you use a jurisdiction clause, it should conform to the governing law section (as discussed above) and designate the same state.

In Some States, Jurisdiction Clauses Are Invalid

In the past, many courts believed that citizens should not be able to bargain for jurisdiction (sometimes referred to as "forum shopping") and refused to enforce jurisdiction provisions. Today, only two states—Idaho and Montana—refuse to honor these provisions. In other states (Florida, for example), courts have required that the parties have some contacts with the state designated by this provision beyond the existence of the contract provision itself. *McRae v. J.D./M.D., Inc.,* 511 So.2d 540 (1987).

e. Waiver

This provision permits the parties to waive (forgo or give up claim to) a portion of the agreement without establishing a precedent—that is, without giving up future claims under the same portion of the agreement.

f. Invalidity

This provision (sometimes referred to as "severability") permits a court to remove an invalid provision and keep the rest of the agreement intact. Otherwise, if one portion of the agreement is invalid, a court may rule that the whole agreement is invalid.

g. Entire Understanding

This provision (sometimes referred to as "integration") establishes that the agreement is the final version and that any further modification of the agreement must be in writing.

h. Attachments

This provision guarantees that any attachments or "exhibits" attached to the agreement will be included as part of the agreement.

i. No Special Damages

If either party breaches the agreement, state laws provide that the nonbreaching party can recover the amount of the loss resulting from the breach. For example, if the licensee fails to pay royalties accurately, the licensor can sue to recover the unpaid amount and attorney fees, if the agreement provides for such fees (see Section 22a). Under some state laws, a party can make claims for additional damages—for example, special or punitive damages that are awarded to punish the breaching party. This provision prevents either party from claiming any damages other than those actually suffered directly from the breach.

j. Notices

If a dispute arises, each party is entitled to be notified of the problem; the purpose of the notice provision is to establish the method of notification. If the notice procedures are not followed, claims against either party may be delayed until proper notification is provided.

k. No Joint Venture

The relationship between the parties is defined by the agreement. But to an outsider, it may appear that a licensee and licensor have a different relationship, such as a partnership or joint venture. It's possible that an unscrupulous licensor will try to capitalize on this appearance and make a third-party deal. That is, a licensor may claim to be a partner of the licensee to obtain a benefit from a distributor or sublicensee. In order to avoid liability for such a situation, most agreements include a provision disclaiming any relationship other than licensee/licensor.

l. Assignability

It is possible that the licensee may, at some point, want to transfer the rights under this agreement to another company. For example, say the licensee has two agreements with a licensor, one for shirts and another for hats. The licensee later decides it only wants to concentrate on shirts, so it wants to assign its rights in the hat agreement to a company that specializes in hat merchandising. Since agreements are only binding between the parties who sign them, the hat company can only acquire the licensee's rights in the contract if the licensee assigns those rights. The licensor may not be happy with the change. For example, the new company may have a bad reputation when it comes to paying royalties. Since assignability can be a sensitive issue, three choices are provided in the model agreement.

The first option requires that the licensor's written consent be given for an assignment. In that case, the licensor can review the deal and decide, for any reason, whether or not it wants to participate with the new licensee.

The second choice also requires written consent, but requires that the licensor cannot withhold consent unreasonably. In that situation, the licensor can review the prospective arrangement and, if there is a valid business reason for refusing to consent, the licensor can refuse. A valid business reason usually relates to some financial quality of the new licensee.

The third provision permits the transfer of rights without the licensor's consent provided that the transfer is made to a company that is purchasing the licensee's company. In this arrangement, another company is acquiring all of the licensee's interests. Some licensees insist on this because they want the freedom to sell their whole company (and its licenses).

m. Signatures

Each party must sign the agreement. The people who sign on each party's behalf must have the authority to do so. Use the following rules to determine how the agreement should be signed:

- **Sole Proprietorship.** If either party is a sole proprietorship, that party signs using his or her own name. If either party is using a fictitious business name (sometimes known as a "d.b.a."), list the name of the business above the signature line.

EXAMPLE: Tom Lennon is a sole proprietor who calls his business "Lennonism." He would sign as follows:

Lennonism

By: _____

Tom Lennon, sole proprietor

- **Partnership.** If either party is a general or limited partnership, the only person authorized to sign the agreement is a general partner or someone who has written authority from a general partner (usually in the form a partnership resolution). The name of the partnership must be mentioned above the signature line or the partnership will not be bound—only the person who signed the agreement.

EXAMPLE: Cindy Peacock is a general partner in Speculative Ventures Partnership. She would sign as follows:

Speculative Ventures Partnership
By: _____
Cindy Peacock, general partner

- **Corporation or LLC.** If either party is a corporation or limited liability company (LLC), only a person authorized by the corporation can sign the agreement. The president or chief operating officer (CEO) usually has such power, but not every officer of a corporation has the authority to bind the corporation. If in doubt, ask for written proof of the authority. This proof is usually in the form of a corporate resolution. The name of the corporation should be mentioned above the signature line or the corporation may not be bound—only the person who signed the agreement.

EXAMPLE: Matthew LaNotta is CEO of Sunday Marketing. He would sign as follows:

Sunday Marketing, Inc., a New York corporation
By: _____
Matthew LaNotta, CEO

If either party has doubts about any person's authority to sign the agreement, don't proceed until satisfied that the person has full authority to represent the company.

May a Signature Be Faxed?

A faxed signature is suitable assuming that both parties accept the authenticity of the signature. If there is a dispute about the signature later—that is, one party claims a forgery—a party may have difficulty proving the signature is authentic from a fax. If executing the agreement by fax, follow the fax up by mailing signed copies.

23. Exhibit A

Agreements often have attachments known as "exhibits" that are separate documents stapled or joined to the agreement. In license agreements, the exhibit summarizes some of the essential business elements. For example, in the model agreement, Exhibit A includes a description of the work, the licensed product, and, if applicable, the sales minimum required to renew the agreement.

Right of First Refusal and Most Favored Nation Provisions

Some merchandise agreements include a provision known as a right of first refusal. The purpose of this provision is to give the licensee the first shot at licensing any new works from the licensor. For example, if the licensor creates new illustrations, the licensee will have the first opportunity to license those new works. If another company makes a better offer than the licensee, the licensee has a period of time to match the offer. A sample right of first refusal provision reads as follows:

> **Right of First Refusal.** Licensor may identify and develop new works suitable to be used as Licensed Products ("New Works"). Licensee shall have the first right to license such New Works, and the parties shall negotiate in good faith to reach agreement as to the terms and conditions for such license. In the event that the parties fail to reach agreement and Licensor receives an offer from a third party for the New Works, Licensee shall have 30 days to notify Licensor whether Licensee desires to execute a license on similar terms and conditions. In the event that Licensee matches any third-party terms and conditions, Licensor shall enter into a License Agreement with Licensee and terminate negotiations with any third parties.

A right of first refusal is occasionally confused with a "most favored nations" provision. A most favored nations provision is common in a nonexclusive arrangement and guarantees that a licensee won't be charged any more for new works than any other licensee. For example, say your film company has a nonexclusive license agreement (that includes a most favored nations clause) to use a song. You pay $10,000 for the rights. The owner/licensor subsequently licenses the same song under a nonexclusive license with another film company for $9,000. Under the most favored nation provision, the licensor must lower your rate to $9,000.

D. Merchandise License Worksheet

The Merchandise License Worksheet below is provided to help you (the licensee, presumably) keep track of the merchandise license agreement elements discussed throughout this chapter. It can function in two ways: as a record of the elements upon which the parties agreed or to help decipher an agreement furnished by the licensor.

 A tear-out copy of this form is provided in the Appendix. A digital version is included on the forms CD.

Merchandise License Worksheet

Licensor	Name of licensor business: _____ Licensor address: _____ Licensor business form: ☐ sole proprietorship ☐ general partnership ☐ limited partnership ☐ corporation ☐ state of incorporation _____ ☐ limited liability company ☐ state of organization _____ Name and position of person signing for licensor: _____
The Work(s)	Source: _____ Description: _____ Page number: _____ Relevant data (e.g., ISBN, copyright notice): _____
Licensed Product(s)	Tentative title: _____ Format: _____
Grant of Rights (check those rights needed)	☐ reproduce ☐ distribute ☐ modify, adapt ☐ display ☐ perform
Market and Format Limitations	☐ specific market: _____ ☐ specific format: _____
Territory	☐ worldwide ☐ countries or states (name which): _____
Exclusivity	☐ exclusive ☐ nonexclusive

Merchandise License Worksheet (cont.)

Term	☐ no time limits
	☐ fixed term (how long: _____)
	☐ unlimited term until one party terminates
	☐ an initial term with renewals (see below)
	☐ other _____
Renewals	If the parties have agreed upon an initial term with renewals: _____
	How many renewal periods? _____
	How long is each renewal period? _____
	What triggers renewal? _____
Fee	☐ one time fee $ _____
	date due: _____
	☐ recurring fee $ _____
	date due/trigger _____
	☐ advance against royalties $ _____
	date due: _____
	☐ royalty rate(s): _____% of
	☐ net sales
	☐ gross sales
	☐ If royalty payments, are there any:
	☐ deductions: _____
	☐ audits (how many per year: _____)
Warranties	☐ licensor warranty conditions: _____
	☐ licensee warranty conditions: _____
Indemnity	☐ licensor indemnity conditions: _____
	☐ licensee indemnity conditions: _____
Credit	☐ licensor credit: _____
Furnished Samples	☐ licensor samples required (how many: _____)
	(when: _____)
Miscellaneous	☐ jurisdiction state: _____
	☐ governing law state: _____
	☐ arbitration
Termination	☐ conditions: _____

E. Short-Form Merchandise License Agreement

Below is a short-form merchandise license agreement. It is intended primarily for licensing an image on merchandise such as a T-shirt. The short-form agreement eliminates many of the choices in the longer agreement and, instead, includes the most commonly used provisions. You should consider using this agreement if your arrangement is limited to one or two years or to a specific number of cop-

ies (for example, 2,000 T-shirts). This agreement is suitable if the relationship and trust between the parties is such that you do not need the increased formality of a full-length agreement.

For an explanation of the various provisions, review Section C.

 A tear-out copy of this form is provided in the Appendix. A digital version is included on the forms CD.

Short-Form Merchandise License Agreement

Introduction

This License Agreement (the "Agreement") is made between _____ (referred to as "Licensor") and _____ (referred to as "Licensee").

The parties agree as follows:

Grant of Rights

The "Work" is defined as follows: _____ .

Licensed Products are Licensee's products incorporating the Work, specifically_____ (the "Licensed Products").

Licensor is the owner of all rights to the Work, and Licensee shall not claim any right to use the Works except under the terms of this Agreement. Licensor grants to Licensee:

(select one)

☐   an exclusive license

☐   a nonexclusive license

to reproduce and distribute the Work in or on the Licensed Products.

Sublicense

Licensee may sublicense the rights granted pursuant to this agreement provided: Licensee obtains Licensor's prior written consent to such sublicense, and Licensor receives such revenue or royalty payment as provided in the Payment section below. Licensor's consent to any sublicense shall not be unreasonably withheld. Any sublicense granted in violation of this provision shall be void. Licensor reserves all rights other than those being conveyed or granted in this Agreement.

Territory

The rights granted to Licensee are limited to _____ (the "Territory").

Term

This Agreement shall commence upon the "Effective Date," established by the latest signature date, and shall extend for a period of____years (the "Initial Term"). Following the Initial Term, Licensee may renew this agreement under the same terms and conditions for_____consecutive _____ periods (the "Renewal Terms") provided that Licensee provides written notice of its intention to renew this agreement within thirty (30) days before the expiration of the current term.

Royalties

All royalties ("Royalties") provided for under this Agreement shall accrue when the respective Licensed Products are sold, shipped, distributed, billed, or paid for, whichever occurs first.

Net Sales

Net Sales are defined as Licensee's gross sales (the gross invoice amount billed to customers) less quantity discounts or rebates and returns actually credited. A quantity discount or rebate is a discount made at the time of shipment. No deductions shall be made for cash or other discounts, commissions, manufacturing costs, uncollectible accounts, or for fees or expenses of any kind which the Licensee may incur in connection with the Royalty payments.

Advance Against Royalties

As a nonrefundable advance against royalties (the "Advance"), Licensee agrees to pay to Licensor upon execution of this Agreement the sum of $ _____ .

Licensed Product Royalty

Licensee agrees to pay a Royalty of_____% percent of all Net Sales revenue of the Licensed Products ("Licensed Product Royalty").

Sublicensing Revenues

In the event of any sublicense of the rights granted pursuant to this Agreement, Licensee shall pay to Licensor _____% percent of all sublicensing revenues.

Payments and Statements

Within thirty (30) days after the end of each calendar quarter (the "Royalty Period"), an accurate statement of Net Sales of Licensed Products along with any royalty payments or sublicensing revenues shall be due to Licensor. The acceptance by Licensor of any of the statements furnished or royalties paid shall not preclude Licensor from questioning the correctness at any time of any payments or statements.

Audit

Licensee shall keep accurate books of account and records covering all transactions relating to the license granted in this Agreement, and Licensor or its duly authorized representatives shall have the right upon five (5) days prior written notice, and during normal business hours, to inspect Licensee's records relating to the Work licensed under this Agreement.

Late Payment

If Licensee is late in any payment provided for in this Agreement, Licensee shall pay interest on the payment from the date due until paid at a rate of 1.5% per month, or the maximum rate permitted by law, whichever is less.

Warranties

Licensor warrants that it has the power and authority to enter into this Agreement and has no knowledge as to any third-party claims regarding the proprietary rights in the Work that would interfere with the rights granted under this Agreement.

Licensee warrants that it will use its best commercial efforts to market the Licensed Products and that sale and marketing of the Licensed Products shall be in conformance with all applicable laws and regulations, including but not limited to all intellectual property laws.

Licensor Credits

Licensee shall identify Licensor as the owner of rights to the Work and shall include the following notice on all copies of the Licensed Products:

"_____ . All rights reserved."

Licensee may, with Licensor's consent, use Licensor's name, image, or trademark in advertising or promotional materials associated with the sale of the Licensed Products.

Exploitation

Licensee agrees to manufacture, distribute, and sell the Licensed Products in commercially reasonable quantities during the term of this Agreement and to commence such manufacture, distribution, and sale by _____ . This is a material provision of this Agreement.

Approval of Samples & Quality Control

Licensee shall submit a reasonable number of preproduction samples of the Licensed Product to Licensor to assure that the product meets Licensor's quality standards. In the event that Licensor fails to object in writing within ten (10) business days after the date of receipt of any such materials, such materials shall be deemed to be acceptable.

Licensor Copies and Right to Purchase

Licensee shall provide Licensor with ___ copies of each Licensed Product. Licensor has the right to purchase from Licensee, at Licensee's manufacturing cost, at least _____copies of any Licensed Product, and such payments shall be deducted from royalties due to Licensor.

Licensor's Right to Terminate

Licensor shall have the right to terminate this Agreement for the following reasons:

(select one or more provisions)

☐ **Failure to Make Timely Payment.** Licensee fails to pay Royalties when due or fails to accurately report Net Sales, as defined in the Payments and Statements section of this Agreement, and such failure is not cured within thirty (30) days after written notice from the Licensor.

☐ **Failure to Introduce Product.** Licensee fails to introduce the product to market by the date set in the Exploitation section of this Agreement or to offer the Licensed Products in commercially reasonable quantities during any subsequent year.

Effect of Termination

After the termination of this license, all rights granted to Licensee under this Agreement shall terminate and revert to Licensor, and Licensee will refrain from further manufacturing, copying, marketing, distribution, or use of any Licensed Product or other product which incorporates the Work. Licensee may dispose of the Licensed Products covered by this Agreement for a period of 90 days after termination or expiration, except that Licensee shall have no such right in the event this agreement is terminated according to the Licensor's Right to Terminate, above.

Miscellaneous

The prevailing party shall have the right to collect from the other party its reasonable costs and attorney fees incurred in enforcing this Agreement. This Agreement expresses the full, complete and exclusive understanding of the parties with respect to the subject matter and supersedes all prior proposals, representations, and understandings. If a dispute arises between the parties arising under or relating to this Agreement, the parties agree to submit such dispute to arbitration conducted under the rules of the American Arbitration Association. An arbitration award may be confirmed in a court of competent jurisdiction. The waiver or failure of any party to exercise in any respect any right provided for in this Agreement shall not be deemed a waiver of any further right under this Agreement. No party shall represent themselves to be the employee, franchisee, franchiser, joint venturer, officer, or partner of the other party, and nothing in this Agreement shall be construed to place the parties in the relationship of partners or joint venturers. If any provision of this Agreement is invalid under any applicable statute or rule of law, it is to that extent to be deemed omitted and the remaining provisions of this Agreement shall in no way be affected or impaired. Licensee may not assign or sublicense the rights granted under this Agreement without the written consent of Licensor. Such consent shall not be unreasonably withheld. Each party has signed this Agreement through its authorized representative. The parties, having read this Agreement, indicate their consent to the terms and conditions by their signature below.

By: _____   By: _____

Date: _____   Date: _____

Licensor Name: _____   Licensee Name/Title: _____

Releases

A "release" is an agreement by which someone waives (gives up) any rights to sue arising from a certain activity. A release is usually needed when a publication (or broadcast) of a person's name or image may trigger legal claims such as defamation, invasion of privacy, or violation of the right of publicity. These types of legal claims are personal and relate to false statements, intrusions into personal affairs, or commercial uses of a personality. The person signing the release usually foregoes any right to sue over these claims.

Traditionally, releases (sometimes known as "model releases") are needed when a person's name or image is used for commercial purposes. However, there may be other instances as described within this chapter in which it may be prudent to obtain a signed release. This chapter provides samples and explanations of two types of personal releases, a release to use interview statements, and a release to use images of property (such as photos of a building) in an advertisement.

A. Legal Risks of Failing to Obtain a Release

Without a written release, if you reproduce photos, video, or other representations of an individual, that person might be able to bring you into court for various violations of personal rights. These include defamation and invasion of the right to privacy or the right of publicity. Each of these legal claims is discussed in more detail below.

Keep releases as short and simple as possible, because people are often asked to sign them with short notice and may balk if they are complex or intimidating.

There are many instances in which releases are not required, discussed in Section B. As a general rule you will not need a release for the use of a person's name or image if your use is not defamatory, does not invade privacy, and is not for a commercial purpose. For example, a celebrity's photo can be used in a news story without a release. Remember, however, that you often will need to obtain copyright permission from the owner of the photograph. See Chapter 3 for more information on obtaining permission from the copyright owners of a photograph.

1. Invasion of Privacy

Every person has a right to be left alone—this is called the right of privacy. You need a release to use a living person's name or image in a manner that constitutes an invasion of the person's right to privacy. Releases are vital because the person whose privacy you invade can sue you for monetary damages. Generally, invasion of privacy isn't an issue if an individual is deceased.

There are several different ways a person's right to privacy can be invaded, including:

- **False Light.** This type of invasion of privacy occurs when an individual is falsely portrayed in a highly offensive manner—for example, posting a photograph of a man who has never committed a crime at the "America's Most Wanted" website.
- **Disclosure of Private Facts.** This invasion of privacy occurs when private or embarrassing facts are disclosed about an individual without relation to a legitimate public concern.
  EXAMPLE: A man who had served time for a robbery 20 years earlier rehabilitated himself and is now a pastor. Publication of the facts of the 20-year-old robbery would be an invasion of privacy unless there was a related public interest—for example, the pastor was again arrested for a crime.
- **Intrusion.** Intruding upon situations in which people have a reasonable expectation of privacy—for example, spying on a person at home, secretly eavesdropping on conversations, or opening mail—can give rise to an invasion of privacy claim. However, it is not an invasion of privacy to photograph someone in a public place or at any event where

the public is invited. Such photos can be used freely for informational purposes, provided that the use does not defame or hold the individual up to a false light.

EXAMPLE: Mary is photographed sleeping on a bench in a public park. The photo appears in the newspaper under the caption, "A Sunny Day in the Park." No release is required. However, if the caption were "Crack Addicts Seek Refuge in Park," Mary would have a claim for invasion of privacy and defamation (provided she was not a crack addict).

2. Right of Publicity

The right of publicity grew out of the general principles of invasion of privacy that prohibit using a person's name or likeness to gain a benefit. Within the past few decades, the right of publicity has emerged as an independent type of claim that a person can make when his or her name or likeness is used for commercial purposes. Although the right of publicity is commonly associated with celebrities, every person, regardless of how famous, has a right to prevent unauthorized use of their name or image to sell products. This right also prohibits any implication that a person endorses a product (without the person's permission).

The right of publicity extends to a performer's identifiable voice. For example, in two separate cases, advertisements that used vocal performances that sounded like singers Tom Waits and Bette Midler were found to violate the singers' rights of publicity. In both of these cases, the advertising agency had sought permission from the performer and, when it was not granted, hired someone to deliberately imitate the singer's voice—a good example of what not to do. As a rule of thumb, if your performer's voice mimics a well-known performer, either accidentally or intentionally, don't use it.

In many states, the right of publicity survives death and can be asserted by a person's estate.

3. Defamation

Defamation occurs when information is published about a person that creates a false impression and injures the person's reputation. Defamation is often divided into two categories: slander, which is an oral comment made to others, and libel, which is a fixed statement printed, broadcast, or published electronically. The rules for both types of defamation are similar. A deceased person cannot be defamed, but a false statement about a deceased person that reflects badly on a living relative can be defamation. In addition to personal defamation, a corporation or partnership can also be defamed if a false statement affects the business's integrity, credit, or solvency.

The key to a defamation claim is determining the injury caused to the victim's reputation in the community. The term "community" can be interpreted as narrowly as a small group of persons acquainted with the injured person. Courts have permitted claims for statements that ridicule, humiliate, or subject the victim to contempt.

If the information that is published is true, there is no defamation. Or, as some courts have stated, the truth is an absolute defense to defamation. Literal truth in every element is not required, provided that the statement is substantially true.

There are exceptions to defamation rules for politicians and celebrities and, to a limited extent, for people who have become the subjects of a public controversy. Because they are in the public eye, already subject to public attention, these people are expected to have tougher skins. They can only be defamed if it is proven that the false statements were made with actual malice and a reckless disregard for the truth—for example, a website owner posting what he knows to be false information about a celebrity's sex life.

B. When to Use a Release

Whether you need to obtain a release depends on why you want to use a person's name or image. If your use is for commercial purposes—for example, using a person's photo in an advertisement—you need to obtain a release. If your use is for informational purposes such as a documentary film or news article, you may not need a release. However, even if a release is not required, you should be careful that your use does not defame or invade the privacy of the individual. If there's any potential that your use might violate these laws, a release will provide legal protection. Sorting out these differences can be confusing; examples are provided below. When in doubt, however, obtain a signed release.

1. Informational Uses

You do not need release to use a person's name or image for informational purposes. An informational (or "editorial") purpose is anything that informs, educates, or expresses opinions protected under the First Amendment of the United States Constitution—freedom of speech and of the press. An informational use would include using a person's name or photograph in a newspaper or magazine article, educational program, film, nonfiction book, or informational website.

If you use a person's name or image in an informational publication, you may also use that name or image in incidental advertising for the publication. For example, in an advertisement for a publication that includes an interview, you may state "Featuring an interview with Johnny Depp." However, to use a person's name in an advertisement posing as an informational publication, you need a release. (See Section 3, below, for examples.)

Even if your use is informational, a release may be required if the person's name or image is used in a defamatory manner (see Section A3) or invades the person's privacy (see Section A1). It may seem odd to seek a release for a use that may defame a person or invade privacy. After all, why would any-one sign a release for a use that would create a false impression? Such releases are usually used in cases where a model or actor is posing to illustrate an article, such as "The Horror of Date Rape."

2. Commercial Uses

You need a release for the commercial use of a person's name or image. A "commercial use" occurs when a name or image appears while a product or service is being sold or endorsed. For example, if your website offers hair products and features photographs of people using the products, you would need a release from the people in the photos. You do not need a release if the person cannot be recognized in the photo: for example, if the photo only includes the person's hands.

Several decades ago, the failure to obtain such a release would have led to an invasion of privacy lawsuit. However, the "right of publicity" has now become the more popular claim for those whose names or images are used for commercial purposes without their permission.

3. Is Your Use Commercial or Informational?

Unfortunately, there is no definitive test that tells you whether your intended use is informational or commercial. Below are summaries of cases that straddle the border between informational and commercial uses. Cases with similar facts may seem to have different results because judges have broad discretion in making these determinations.

- **Informational use.** A photo of football player Joe Namath was featured on the cover of *Sports Illustrated* and later used in advertisements to sell subscriptions to *Sports Illustrated*. No permission was required because the initial use of the photo was editorial and the subscription ads were "merely incidental" to indicate the nature of the magazine contents. (*Namath v. Sports Illustrated,* 371 N.Y.S.2d 10 (1975).)

- **Informational use.** *The National Enquirer* and *USA Today* conducted telephone polls about the musical group New Kids on the Block. Use of the names and images of the members of the group to publicize the newspapers' profit-making telephone numbers did not require permission because it was primarily for purposes of "news gathering and dissemination." (*New Kids on the Block v. News America Publishing Inc.*, 971 F.2d 302 (9th Cir. 1992).)

- **Informational use.** Public domain film clips of Fred Astaire were used as a prologue to an instructional dance video. The use of Mr. Astaire's name was permitted in the prologue based on the informational content of the video. (*Astaire v. Best Film & Video Corp.*, 136 F.3d 1208 (9th Cir. 1998).)

- **Informational use.** A film company that acquired the rights to rerelease two 1950s films featuring actress Betty Page commissioned drawings of Ms. Page to promote the films. Ms. Page sued to prevent the use of her image and name to promote the films. A court permitted the use because the advertising was incidental to the rerelease and was "newsworthy" due to the reemergence of the two 1950s movies. (*Page v. Something Weird Video*, 960 F. Supp. 1438 (C.D. Cal. 1996).)

- **Informational use.** Following a Superbowl victory, a San Jose newspaper sold posters of quarterback Joe Montana. Mr. Montana sued but, in a surprising ruling, a court permitted the use, claiming it was newsworthy because of the "relatively contemporaneous" publication of the posters with the news event. (*Montana v. San Jose Mercury News*, 34 Cal. App. 4th 790 (1995).)

- **Commercial use.** During the NCAA tournament broadcast, an ad for Oldsmobile featured a voice asking who held the record for being voted the most outstanding player of the tournament. The answer printed onscreen "Lew Alcindor, UCLA, '67, '68, '69." (The basketball player Kareem Abdul-Jabbar was pre-

viously known as Lew Alcindor.) The ad stated that Oldsmobile was the winner of a *Consumer's Digest* award three years in a row and ended with the statement "A Definite First Round Pick." Abdul-Jabbar sued, claiming that his name was used without permission. The court decided in his favor, ruling that although the advertisement provided information, the overall effect was commercial and required permission. (*Abdul-Jabbar v. General Motors Corp.*, 85 F.3d 407 (9th Cir. 1996).)

- **Commercial use.** *Los Angeles Magazine* printed a fashion article that featured a digitally modified photograph combining Dustin Hoffman's head with a male model's body in a gown and woman's shoes. The text stated: "Dustin Hoffman isn't a drag in a butter-colored silk gown by Richard Tyler and Ralph Lauren heels." Although the photo was used in an informational article, the overall effect of the use was commercial, promoting the specific designers. (*Hoffman v. Capital Cities/ABC Inc.*, 33 F. Supp. 2d 867 (C.D. Cal. 1999).)

- **Commercial use.** A photo of Cher was featured in *Forum Magazine* and was later used in advertisements for subscriptions to the magazine. Beneath Cher's photo in the advertisements was a caption implying Cher's endorsement of the magazine. The implied endorsement created a commercial use of Cher's name that distinguished it from the *Sports Illustrated* case involving Joe Namath, above. (*Cher v. Forum Inter. Ltd.*, 692 F.2d 634 (9th Cir. 1982).)

4. Are Websites Commercial or Informational?

Can a website be informational if its primary purpose is to promote a business? Websites raise many of the issues highlighted in the cases described in the previous section. Several factors determine whether the use of a name or image on a website is commercial or informational:

- If the use of the name or image at the website relates to a newsworthy event, the use is more likely to be informational.
- The more website space devoted to selling, the less likely the use is informational.
- The longer the person's name or image remains at the site, the less likely the use is informational.
- The more separation between informational content and the sponsorship of the site and related advertisements, the more likely the use is informational.

5. Releases and Free Speech

You can use a person's name or image for commercial purposes without permission if the commercial use qualifies as free speech. Generally, this occurs when the use is categorized as a parody. (For more information on trademark parodies see Chapter 10. For more information on copyright parodies, see Chapter 9).

For example, a company sold trading cards featuring caricatures of major league baseball players. Text on the cards ridiculing player salaries and egos included a statement: "Cardtoons baseball is a parody and is NOT licensed by Major League Baseball Properties or Major League Baseball Players Association." A federal court permitted the use of player's names and caricatured images as free speech. (*Cardtoons v. Major League Baseball Players Assn.*, 838 F. Supp. 1501 (N.D. Okla. 1993).)

However, individuals wary of litigation should weigh the consequences and costs of a lawsuit before claiming a free speech right to use an individual's name or image.

What Good Are Disclaimers?

"Disclaimers" are statements advising readers about potential confusion or danger and disavowing legal responsibility. When using a person's name or image, some businesses attempt to avoid liability for breaching a person's publicity or privacy rights by providing a disclaimer, such as "Woody's One-Liners is not associated with or endorsed by Woody Allen."

A disclaimer by itself will never shield a business from liability. In many cases, disclaimers have been found to create rather than reduce confusion in the minds of customers or readers as to whether or not a celebrity is endorsing a product or service. Moreover, a disclaimer is an acknowledgment that the business admits the potential for confusion, a fact that may be used against the business in a lawsuit.

To have any legal effect, a disclaimer must be in close proximity to the person's image or name and as prominent as the name or image. It must also disclaim any sponsorship, endorsement, or association with the product or service involved. Because of the legally tenuous value of disclaimers, it is not wise to rely on them for protection.

C. Personal Release Agreements

This section provides and discusses personal release agreements that permit the use of a person's name and image. Personal releases are often referred to as "model releases," although the term "model" can be used for anyone, not just professional models. There are two classes of personal releases: blanket releases and limited releases.

- A **blanket release** permits any use of the photographic image of the person signing the release and is suitable if the company or photographer needs an unlimited right to use the image. Stock photographers who sell their photos for unlimited purposes commonly use blanket releases.

- Celebrities and professional models usually sign **limited releases** that specify the particular ways their image and name may be used. If a use exceeds what's permitted under the limited release, the person can sue for breach of the agreement. For example, a model that signed a release limiting use of her image for a museum brochure sued when the photo appeared on a Miami transit card.

Later, Section D introduces two other types of releases: a release for an interview and a release for use of property (a photograph).

1. General Rules for Releases

In addition to the specific legal rules for releases discussed throughout this chapter, some general advice is helpful when dealing with release situations.

a. Get It in Writing

Although oral releases are generally valid, you should always try to get a release in writing. This way, the model can't claim he or she never agreed to the release. In addition, the terms of an oral release can be hard to remember and even harder to prove in court if a dispute arises.

b. Make It Clear

When a release is sought for a specific purpose, do not hide or misrepresent facts to get the signature. A fraudulently obtained release is invalid. For example, a model who was told that his image would be used by an insurance company signed a blanket release based on that statement. However, a company that pays cash for life insurance policies owned by AIDS victims used the photo. A Florida court permitted the model to sue.

c. Keep It Simple

Release agreements do not include many of the legal provisions found in other agreements in this book. Instead, releases are usually "stripped down" to pose less likelihood of triggering a discussion or negotiation. Keep your release short and simple (see tip below).

 You may find it easier to obtain a signed release if you shrink the release information to the size of a 3x5 or 5x7 card. Photographers have found that photo subjects find the smaller documents less intimidating. Some photographers reduce the material to a font size that fits on the back of a business card. However, if the contract is difficult to read, it will be less likely to be enforceable.

d. Get the Right Signatures

There are two requirements for the signature on a release: it must be "informed consent," which means that the person signing the release understood it; and the person signing the release must have the authority to grant the release.

In the majority of states, a minor is any person under 18 years of age, although in some states, the age may be 19 or 21. Since a minor may not understand the terms of a release, the signature of a parent or guardian is required before using a minor's name or image.

> EXAMPLE: A 16-year old boy who was photographed on the beach at Cape Canaveral signed a release; his parents did not. The photo was later used on the cover of a novel about a gay adolescent. His father sued the publisher and settled out of court.

In some cases, an agent representing the person may have the authority to sign a release. For example, an agent signed a release granting an unlimited time period for use of a model's image in a

Nintendo advertisement. The model had intended that the image only be used for one year. A court held that the agent had the authority to sign the release on behalf of the model and the release was binding.

It is always preferable to have a release signed by the subject, not an agent. When dealing with an agent, seek an assurance that the agent has the legal authority to sign. This can be done by including the statement, "I am the authorized agent for [name of model]" above the agent's signature line.

Get a release signed ASAP. It is sometimes difficult to track down a subject after a photo has been taken and there is less incentive for the subject to sign a release. Therefore, most photographers obtain releases prior to or directly after a photo session or when the model is paid.

Consideration: Paying for a Release

A contract is legally binding only if each party obtains something of value (referred to as "consideration") in return for performance of the contract obligations. For this reason, releases traditionally stipulated payment of a nominal amount such as one dollar. However, most courts now take a modern approach to contract law and accept the fact that consideration can be implied and an actual payment is not mandatory. Each release in this chapter establishes that the contract has met the consideration requirement by beginning with the statement, "For consideration which I acknowledge..." However, to fortify this position, you may wish to make a payment—even if nominal—to the person signing the release and indicate the amount of the payment somewhere in the release.

---

2. Unlimited Personal Release Agreement

The following form is an unlimited or blanket release agreement. It permits you to use the model's image and name in all forms of media throughout the world forever.

A tear-out copy of this form is provided in the Appendix. A digital version is included on the forms CD.

Unlimited Personal Release Agreement

Grant

For consideration which I acknowledge, I irrevocably grant to _____ ("Company") and Company's assigns, licensees, and successors the right to use my image and name in all forms and media including composite or modified representations for all purposes, including advertising, trade, or any commercial purpose throughout the world and in perpetuity. I waive the right to inspect or approve versions of my image used for publication or the written copy that may be used in connection with the images.

Release

I release Company and Company's assigns, licensees, and successors from any claims that may arise regarding the use of my image including any claims of defamation, invasion of privacy, or infringement of moral rights, rights of publicity, or copyright. Company is permitted, although not obligated, to include my name as a credit in connection with the image.

Company is not obligated to utilize any of the rights granted in this Agreement.

I have read and understood this agreement and I am over the age of 18. This Agreement expresses the complete understanding of the parties.

Name: _____ Date: _____

Signature: _____

Address: _____

Witness Signature: _____

Parent/Guardian Consent [include if the person is under 18]

I am the parent or guardian of the minor named above. I have the legal right to consent to and do consent to the terms and conditions of this release.

Parent/Guardian Name: _____ Date: _____

Parent/Guardian Signature: _____

Parent/Guardian Address: _____

Witness Signature: _____

3. Limited Personal Release Agreement

The following form is a limited personal release agreement. It allows you to use the model's name or image only for the purposes specified in the agreement.

 A tear-out copy of this form is provided in the Appendix. A digital version is included on the forms CD.

Limited Personal Release Agreement

Grant

For consideration which I acknowledge, I grant to _____("Company") and Company's assigns, licensees, and successors, the right to use my image for the following purposes:

_____

_____ in the following

territory _____ for a period of _____ year(s) (the "Term").

I grant the right to use my name and image for the purposes listed above in all forms and media including composite or modified representations and waive the right to inspect or approve versions of my image used for publication or the written copy that may be used in connection with the images.

Payment

(select if appropriate)

☐   For the rights granted during the Term, Company shall pay $_____ upon execution of this release.

Renewal

(select if appropriate)

☐   Company may renew this agreement under the same terms and conditions for _____ year(s) provided that Licensee makes payment of $ _____ at the time of renewal.

Release

I release Company and Company's assigns, licensees, and successors from any claims that may arise regarding the use of my image including any claims of defamation, invasion of privacy, or infringement of moral rights, rights of publicity, or copyright. Company is permitted, although not obligated, to include my name as a credit in connection with the image.

Name: _____ Date: _____

Signature: _____

Address: _____

Witness Signature: _____

Parent/Guardian Consent [include if the person is under 18]

I am the parent or guardian of the minor named above. I have the legal right to consent to and do consent to the terms and conditions of this release.

Parent/Guardian Name: _____   Date: _____

Parent/Guardian Signature: _____

Parent/Guardian Address: _____

Witness Signature: _____

4. Explanation for Limited and Unlimited Personal Releases

- The **Grant** section establishes the rights granted by the person. In the unlimited agreement, a "blanket" grant is used. This grant is broad and intended to encompass all potential uses whether informational, commercial, or other. In the limited agreement, the uses must be listed—for example, "For use on the cover of trade book and for related advertisements." This release also has limitations regarding territory and term. Insert the appropriate geographic region and term—for example, "North America for a period of two years."
- The **Release** section is the person's promise not to sue the company for legal claims such as libel and invasion of privacy.
- If the person is a minor, the parent or guardian should sign where it is marked **Parent/Guardian Consent** (see Section C1). Since issues about release authenticity often crop up many years after a photo was made, a witness should sign the agreement to verify the person's signature or the signature of the parent. The witness should be an adult. An employee or assistant is suitable.

D. Interview and Property Releases

There are occasions when a release is required for a purpose other than using someone's name or image. Below are two other forms of release: a release to use statements from an interview; and a release permitting use of photos of a building.

1. Interview Releases

Most reporters and writers do not obtain signed interview releases because they presume that by giving the interview, the subject has consented to the

interview and, therefore, cannot claim invasion of privacy. In addition, many interview subjects don't have the ability or inclination to execute a written release—for example, a person interviewed by telephone for a newspaper story on a deadline.

Nevertheless, a written interview release can be useful. It can help avoid lawsuits for libel, invasion of privacy, or even copyright infringement (since the speaker's words may be copyrightable). It's wise to obtain a signed release if the interview is lengthy, will be reprinted verbatim (for example, in a question and answer format), or if the subject matter of the interview is controversial.

It is common for an interview subject to ask to read or edit the interview or to have some comments removed or kept "off the record." Any agreement that is made with the interview subject (including an agreement for anonymity) should be documented. Failure to honor the arrangement may give rise to a lawsuit for monetary damages.

If the interview subject is willing to proceed with the interview but does not want to sign a release, ask if he or she will make an oral consent on audio- or videotape. Although not as reliable as a written release, a statement such as "I consent to the use of my statements in the *Musician's Gazette*" will provide some assurance of your right to use the statement.

a. Interview Release Agreement

An interview release is a hybrid agreement, part release and part license. The release below is suitable if you are seeking permission to use an existing interview or to conduct a new interview.

 A tear-out copy of this form is provided in the Appendix. A digital version is included on the forms CD.

Interview Release Agreement

Grant

For consideration which I acknowledge, I consent to the recording of my statements and grant to _____ ("Company") and Company's assigns, licensees, and successors the right to copy, reproduce, and use all or a portion of the statements (the "Interview") for incorporation in the following work _____ (the "Work").

I permit the use of all or a portion of the Interview in the Work in all forms and media including advertising and related promotion throughout the world and in perpetuity. I grant the right to use my image and name in connection with all uses of the Interview and waive the right to inspect or approve use of my Interview as incorporated in the Work.

Release

I release Company and Company's assigns, licensees, and successors from any claims that may arise regarding the use of the Interview including any claims of defamation, invasion of privacy, or infringement of moral rights, rights of publicity, or copyright. I acknowledge that I have no ownership rights in the Work.

Company is not obligated to utilize the rights granted in this Agreement.

I have read and understood this agreement and I am over the age of 18. This Agreement expresses the complete understanding of the parties.

Name: _____ Date: _____

Signature: _____

Address: _____

Witness Signature: _____

Parent/Guardian Consent [include if the person is under 18]

I am the parent or guardian of the minor named above. I have the legal right to consent to and do consent to the terms and conditions of this release.

Parent/Guardian Name: _____ Date: _____

Parent/Guardian Signature: _____

Parent/Guardian Address: _____

b. Explanation for Interview Release Agreement

- It's possible that the interview may already have been recorded, in which case the language "consent to the recording of my statements and" can be stricken from the **Grant** section. If the interview will be included in more than one work, list all works and change the term "Work" to "Works" throughout the agreement. Unlimited or blanket releases for interviews are not common, partly because subjects usually are not prepared to relinquish unlimited rights.
- If seeking unlimited rights (the interview can be used for any purpose) substitute the following **Grant** section:

Grant

For consideration which I acknowledge, I consent to the recording of my statements and grant to

_____ ("Company") and Company's assigns, licensees, and successors the right to copy, reproduce, and use all or a portion of the statements (the "Interview") for all purposes, including advertising, trade, or any commercial purpose throughout the world and in perpetuity.

I grant the right to use my image and name in connection with all uses of the Interview and waive the right to inspect or approve any use of my Interview.

- If the interview subject does not wish to waive the right to inspect the final work, strike that sentence and arrange for the interview subject to provide approval.
- If the release is executed after the interview has been transcribed, it is helpful to attach a transcription of the interview to the release agreement. This provides an assurance that the interview subject has notice of what was said in the interview. Add a sentence to the **Grant** section such as, "A complete transcription of the interview is attached and incorporated in this Agreement." The **Release** section provides protection against subsequent legal claims.
- If the interview subject is under 18, a parent or guardian's consent is required (see Section C1).

2. Property Releases

In some cases, you'll need to obtain a release for using pictures of places. You may find this odd—after all if a building can be viewed publicly why is permission required to use an image of it? Over the last few decades some buildings have earned protection under both trademark or copyright laws or both. Trademark law will protect a building's appearance under very limited circumstances. If a distinctive-looking building is used to signify a business's services, you cannot use an image of that building in a manner that will confuse consumers. For example, the Sears Tower in Chicago functions as a trademark; if you intend to use it in the foreground of an advertisement, you must obtain permission from the Sears Company. Use of the building's image for informational purposes, such as in magazine article, does not require permission.

Is permission needed to use the image of a trademarked building on a postcard or poster? That issue arose when a photographer sold images of the Rock and Roll Hall of Fame. A federal court of appeals permitted the use of the trademarked building on posters and did not consider it to be a trademark infringement. (*Rock and Roll Hall of Fame v. Gentile*, 134 F.3d 749 (6th Cir. 1998).)

Copyright protection also extends to architectural works, specifically for architectural works created after March 1, 1989. However copyright protection also has limitations. You do not need a release to photograph a building or property visible from a public place, but you do need permission to photograph and reproduce images of a building protected by copyright and not visible from a public place. Entering private property to photograph a building or property may also trigger a claim of trespass. To avoid such claims, photographers, publishers, and filmmakers use a property release, sometimes known as a "location release."

a. Property Release Agreement

This form may be used as a property release.

 A tear-out copy of this form is provided in the Appendix. A digital version is included on the forms CD.

Property Release Agreement

The Property: _____

Grant

For consideration which I acknowledge, I irrevocably grant to _____ ("Company") and Company's assigns, licensees, and successors the right to enter onto the property listed above and to photograph, copy, publish, display, and use images of the property in all forms and media including composite or modified representations throughout the world and in perpetuity for the following purposes: _____

I waive the right to inspect or approve the manner in which the images of the property are used and waive the right to inspect any text that is used in connection with the images of the property.

Dates of Use

Company shall enter onto the property on the following dates and times: _____

In consideration for the rights granted under this Agreement, Company shall pay me $ _____ upon execution of this Agreement.

Company is not obligated to utilize any of the rights granted in this Agreement.

Warranty, Indemnity, & Release

I warrant that I am the owner of the property and have the authority to grant the rights under this agreement and agree to indemnify Company from any claims regarding my ownership of the property. I release Company and Company's assigns, licensees, and successors from any claims that may arise regarding the use of the images of the property.

I have read and understood this agreement. This Agreement expresses the complete understanding of the parties.

Owner's Signature: _____

Owner's Name: _____

Owner's Address: _____

Date: _____

b. Explanation for Property Release

- The **Grant** section allows access to photo-graph the property (on the dates provided in the **Dates of Use** section) and the right to use the photographs for the purposes listed in the agreement.
- If payment is required for the release, indicate the amount in the paragraph after the **Dates of Use** section.
- The owner provides an assurance of owner-ship in the **Warranty, Indemnity, & Release** section and agrees to defend the Company from anyone else with a property ownership claim.

■

13

Copyright Research

Most of the chapters in this book discuss when and how to seek permission from a copyright owner when using a copyrighted work. But what if you don't know who owns the copyright or how to find the owner? This chapter explains how to conduct a very specific type of research: finding information about copyright ownership and validity. This information is usually contained in U.S. Copyright Office and Library of Congress records, on copyright registrations, assignments, renewals, and related documents. This chapter explains how to search these documents, including how to gather information to prepare for your searches.

It's possible you may not have to perform copyright research. You may be able to locate all the copyright information you need through other sources. However, if you seek permissions on a regular basis, there may come a time when you will have to trace copyright ownership (known as "the chain of title"), determine the first date of publication, or find out if copyright for a work has been renewed.

Before walking you through the basics of copyright research and approaches, this chapter begins with answers to some common questions regarding copyright ownership and transfers.

⚠ **This chapter does not cover other types of research such as locating stock photos or private databases of art or music.** For more media-specific research, review the relevant chapter that covers the type of media you seek (see Table of Contents).

⚠ **Copyright Office records are not always conclusive.** Records of the Copyright Office and Library of Congress are helpful for locating ownership information and determining copyright status. Unfortunately, these records don't always show the whole picture because filing copyright registration and assignment (transfer of copyright ownership) documents is not mandatory. Because you don't have to file these documents to own a copyright, there may not be a Copyright Office record regarding a particular work.

Despite this fact, it is still worth your while to search the Copyright Office and the Library of Congress—the largest repositories of copyrighted materials in the United States. In addition, even if you can't find records of ownership, your research will demonstrate that you acted in good faith and are an "innocent infringer" in the event that you are later sued for an unauthorized use, which will limit any damages you may have to pay.

A. Copyright Ownership and Transfers FAQ

When performing copyright research, you may have questions about copyright rules or terminology. For example, you may uncover a registration indicating the work is "made for hire" or you may find a document indicating that the copyright has been "reclaimed" by the author. Below are some answers to frequently asked questions (FAQs) about copyright ownership and transfers.

📖 For a more detailed discussion of these copyright issues, refer to *The Copyright Handbook,* by Stephen Fishman (Nolo).

1. What Is a Work Made for Hire?

Usually, the person who creates a work is also the initial owner of the copyright in the work. But this isn't always the case. Under some circumstances, a person who pays another to create a work becomes the initial copyright owner, not the person who actually created it. The resulting works are called "works made for hire" (or sometimes simply "works for hire"). There are two distinct types of work that will be classified as made for hire:

- a work created by an employee within the scope of employment, or
- a commissioned work that falls within a certain category of works and that is the subject of a written agreement. (The types of works

that qualify and other relevant requirements are explained in more detail in Chapter 15.)

If the work qualifies under one of these two methods, the person paying for the work (the hiring party) is the author and copyright owner. If you want to use the work, you should seek permission from the employer or hiring party, not the person who created the work. If in doubt, you may be able to determine work-for-hire status by examining the copyright registration, as explained in Section C.

2. What Is a Transfer of Title?

The person who owns a copyright is sometimes referred to as having "title" to the copyright. A "title" is the document that establishes ownership to property, like the title to your car or house. But even in the absence of an official document, the owner of a copyright is often said to have title to it.

Just like title to your car or house, title to a copyright can be sold or otherwise transferred. A person or company can have ownership (title) of a copyright transferred to it by means of an assignment (a sale in which all or part of a copyright is transferred) or through a will or bankruptcy proceedings. Since title to a copyright can be transferred, you may have to search copyright records to determine the current owner of a work you want to use.

There are two ways to determine if copyright ownership has been transferred: by reviewing the copyright registration certificate issued by the Copyright Office or by locating an assignment or transfer agreement. By reviewing the copyright registration certificate, you can find out who currently claims copyright and on what basis. For example, if a publisher has been assigned copyright to a work, it will file a copyright registration in its own name and indicate on the registration that it acquired copyright through a legal transfer. Also, many companies file the agreement that establishes the assignment, license, or transfer with the Copyright Office. For example, if an artist assigned his work to a company, the company could file the assignment document with the Copyright Office. (See Section C for guidance on how to check these records.)

3. What Is a Termination of a Transfer?

Sometimes an author transfers copyright to someone and then later the author reacquires it through a process known as "terminating a transfer." Copyright laws provide a method by which authors can reclaim rights after a number of years. This termination and reclamation process is complex, and the rules differ depending on when the work was first published. As a very general rule, transfer terminations occur between 28 and 56 years after the first publication. Terminations are filed with the Copyright Office and can be located by researching Copyright Office records.

> EXAMPLE: In June of 1996, the author J.D. Salinger terminated his transfer to the publisher Little, Brown, and Company and reacquired ownership rights to the story, "A Perfect Day for Bananafish." The termination notice was filed with the Copyright Office (and located through Internet research).
>
> Below is the information from the termination notice as displayed in the Copyright Office's online records.
> RECORDED: 11Jun96
> PARTY 1: Phyllis Westberg, as agent for J. D. Salinger.
> PARTY 2: Little, Brown, and Company.
> NOTE: A perfect day for bananafish & 5 other titles; stories.
> From Nine stories. By J. D. Salinger. Notice of termination of grant under 17 U.S.C. sec. 304; date & manner of service of the notice: 6Jun96, by certified mail, return receipt requested.

For more information on terminations of transfers, see Chapter 9 of *The Copyright Handbook* by attorney Stephen Fishman (Nolo).

4. What If More Than One Person Owns a Copyright?

A common question is whom to ask for permission if several people jointly own a copyright. Co-ownership of copyright can occur in various ways. For example if:

- two people jointly create a work
- the author transfers portions of the rights to different people (for example, giving half to each child), or
- the author sells a portion of the copyright to someone and keeps the remainder.

Co-owners of copyright have a legal status known as "tenants in common." When a co-owner dies, his or her share goes to his or her beneficiaries or heirs, not to the other co-owner. Each co-owner has an independent right to use or nonexclusively license the work—provided that he or she accounts to the other co-owners for any profits. What this means for our purposes is that if you obtain the permission of any one co-owner, you can use the work. However, there are a few exceptions to this rule, as explained in the next section.

You can determine whether there is co-ownership of a certain work by reviewing Copyright Office documents as described in Section B. For example, a registration for a song might indicate that a composer and a lyricist co-own a song.

5. When Must You Get Multiple Permissions?

There are several situations in which you must obtain permission from all the co-owners of a work instead of just one. All co-owners must consent to an assignment of the work (a transfer of copyright ownership) or to an exclusive license (an agreement granting rights solely to one person).

EXAMPLE: Two programmers create a software program. Company A wants an exclusive license to distribute the program, which means that Company A is the only company that can distribute the program. Since the desired license is an exclusive one, Company A must obtain the consent of both programmers.

In addition, you must obtain the consent of all co-owners if:

- the co-owners have an agreement amongst themselves prohibiting any individual owner from granting a license and you are aware of this agreement
- you want to use the text on a worldwide non-exclusive basis (and some countries require consent of all co-owners even for nonexclusive uses)
- you want to use the text for a commercial purpose, such as to sell a service or product, or
- the desired license is for the first public release of a song.

6. Is There a Difference Between an Author and a Copyright Owner?

The author is the first owner of copyright. The author is either the creator of the work or the person who employs someone to create the work (see work-for-hire rules discussed above). Many authors do not retain their copyright ownership; they sell or transfer it to someone else in return for a lump sum payment or periodic payment known as a royalty. In this way, the author and copyright owner (sometimes referred to as "copyright claimant") may be two different people. Even if you do not know the name of the current copyright owner, knowing the name of the author will help you find the owner in the Copyright Office records.

7. What If a Work Does Not Contain a Copyright Notice?

It's common to start copyright research by examining the copyright notice. However, in some cases, the notice may be missing from the work. One reason you may not find a notice is because notice is not required on works first published after March 1, 1989. In addition, for works published prior to that date, notice is required only on visually perceptible copies—that is, copies that can be seen directly or with the aid of a device such as a film projector. Printed books, paintings, drawings, films, architecture, and computer programs are all visually perceptible. However, some works are not visually perceptible, such as a song on a compact disc. But copyright notice would be required if the song lyrics were printed on the album cover.

Another reason that a work may not include notice is that the owner failed to affix it, which may result in the loss of copyright. For works first published before 1978, for example, the absence of a copyright notice from a published copy generally indicates that the work is not protected by copyright. The absence of notice on works published between January 1, 1978 and March 1, 1989 may or may not result in the loss of copyright, depending on whether the owner corrected the error within five years of the publication and met other copyright law requirements.

8. What If There Is a Copyright Notice for an Entire Magazine but Not for the Specific Article You Want to Use?

If a story or a photograph is used in a magazine, there may be a copyright notice for the magazine but not for the specific story or photo that you want to use. That's because the owners of magazines, anthologies, or greatest hits collections in which many different copyrighted works are collected (referred to as "collective works") can use one copyright notice to protect all the works in the collection. This does not necessarily mean that the magazine owns the copyright in all of the works. It may or may not, depending on the contract with the author or photographer. Copyright Office research may not necessarily help you locate copyright information for these works because they may not be listed separately by title in the records. You may be better off contacting the owner of the collective work directly. The principles for contacting copyright owners are explained in the chapters dealing with specific media (text, artwork, photographs, and so on).

B. Starting Your Copyright Research

There are three parts to copyright research. First, you must isolate elements that are necessary to perform your research. For example, you must examine the work for clues such as copyright notice or publication date that will help your research. Second, you must define a method for searching copyright records. You may choose to have the Copyright Office perform the research or you may attempt to search copyright records on the Internet. Finally, you must initiate the search and examine the documents it retrieves. This section discusses the first step—examining the work for clues.

Your first step is to physically examine the work you want to use for information that will help you locate copyright documents in the Copyright Office records. Check the work for the following information:

- **Copyright notice.** The copyright notice is usually on or near the title page of a book; visible at the end of a movie; printed on a compact disc cover or video box; or stamped on the back of a photograph or artwork. For computer programs, it may be located in the Help File under "About this Program." The copyright notice has three parts: the "c" in a circle (©) or the word "copyright," the date of first publication (or, in rare cases, the date of registration), and the name of the copyright owner.

- **Title of the work.** Because Copyright Office records are indexed by title, the title of the work is one of the most important elements in copyright research. Alternative titles may also be helpful (both main and alternative titles are usually listed on the copyright registration).
- **Name(s) of author(s).** Like the title, the name of the author(s) is helpful when searching Copyright Office records because it is usually listed on every copyright document pertaining to that work. Pseudonyms are also traceable in the Copyright Office. Even "Anonymous," as a listing for an author, when cross-referenced with the title, can be helpful in locating a work.
- **The name of the copyright owner.** This may be the author, publisher, or producer of a work. The likely name of the owner is listed in the copyright notice—"likely" because you can never rely solely on the copyright notice for determining the current copyright owner. If you're dealing with an older work, for example, it's possible that ownership may have been transferred or reclaimed since publication. However, the name of the owner listed in the copyright notice is a helpful starting point for your research.
- **Year of publication or registration.** The date of publication is ordinarily listed in the copyright notice. This date usually indicates when copyright protection began, though it may be the year that particular version of the work was first published.

EXAMPLE: Bruce first publishes a book on guitar repair in 1980. He updates it in 1998. The copyright notice on the new version states 1998, so the notice refers only to the new material in the update. The publication date for the earlier material is still 1980.

What If the Copyright Notice Does Not Include the Date?

Because certain industries successfully lobbied Congress for the right to omit the year on copyright notices, the copyright notice may not include the date of first publication. The date can be omitted on greeting cards, stationery, jewelry, toys, or useful articles on which a photograph, graphic, or sculptural work (and accompanying text) appears. For example a greeting card may include the notice "© Hallmark Greetings," with no date. Where no date is provided, you may need to research Copyright Office records to verify the date of first publication.

- **Title, volume, or issue of serialized publication.** If the work you want to use was originally published as a part of a periodical or collection, the title of the publication and other information, such as the volume or issue number, may be useful in searching the Copyright Office records.
- **Underlying works and works contained within works.** Many works, referred to as "derivatives," are based upon other works. For example, motion pictures are often based on books or plays. The work upon which another is based is referred to as the "source" or "underlying" work. For instance, the movie *Jurassic Park* is based on the novel of the same name. Copyright information about a source work such as its title or author can often be found within the derivative work. For example, the motion picture *Jurassic Park* indicates in its opening credits, "Based upon the novel *Jurassic Park,* by Michael Crichton."
- **Identifying numbers.** Identifying numbers, particularly the registration number or other indexing data, may help in your copyright search. Many media industries have a system of cataloguing works. For example, publishers use ISBNs (International Standard Book

Numbers) for books or ISSNs (International Standard Serial Numbers) for serial publications. The Library of Congress has its own catalogue system known as the LCCN (Library of Congress Catalog Number). These numbers, which are usually located on the same page as the copyright notice, may prove helpful in identifying works when performing copyright research.

C. Searching the Copyright Office and Library of Congress Records

Now that you have isolated the information necessary for searching, you can begin examining the records at the Copyright Office and at the Library of Congress. Each of these databases has valuable information about public domain status and copyright ownership:

- Think of the Copyright Office as the source for copyright records. Search this database if you want specific information about copyright ownership, publication, transfers, and derivative works.
- Consider the Library of Congress as a 200-year-old library catalogue. Search the catalogues if you want general information about a work such as the author, date of publication, subject matter, and publisher.

One common search strategy is to use Library of Congress files to identify an author, title, or publisher and then use that information to search the Copyright Office records online, as described below. If you are uncomfortable searching online, consider hiring the Copyright Office to perform the search on your behalf.

1. Defining Your Search

Your search of Copyright Office records will vary depending on your goal. Most likely, you have one of two goals: you want to find the current owner of a copyright or you want to know whether the work has fallen into the public domain. Methods for achieving each goal are described below.

a. Ownership Searching

When trying to determine the owner of copyright, review:

- certificates of registration, and
- assignments or other transfer documents.

Both of these documents are issued by and recorded with the Copyright Office. The registration will indicate who initially acquired ownership. The assignment will indicate if the registration has been transferred to another party.

The certificate of registration is issued by the Copyright Office and is the basic copyright document establishing date of publication, author, source of underlying material, contact person, and initial owner of copyright. The owner's name is listed in the space in Section 4 entitled "Copyright Claimant." If the owner is a different person than the author, the method of acquiring ownership (for example, "by written contract") is indicated in the space in Section 4 entitled "Transfer."

Assignments are transfers of copyright ownership. For example, an author may transfer rights to a publisher by signing an assignment of copyright, often included as part of a publishing agreement. Filing an assignment with the Copyright Office is not mandatory, but many copyright owners do so. When searching online at the Copyright Office, the person acquiring rights (the assignee) is usually listed as PARTY2 or PTY2 and the person transferring rights (the assignor) is usually listed as PARTY1 or PTY1.

b. Public Domain Searching

When researching whether a work is in the public domain, review:

- copyright registrations or other records containing the date of first publication, and
- renewal notices.

Both registrations and renewal notices are issued by and recorded with the Copyright Office. The registration is the initial statement of copyright information about a work and indicates the author, date of registration, copyright claimant (at the time of filing the registration), and date of first publication. A renewal must be filed in order to extend the length of protection for works published or registered before 1964. Although a renewal is no longer required for works published or registered after 1963, many copyright owners still file it.

Works published in the years 1923 through 1963 receive 95 years of protection if they were renewed during their 28th year. If not, they are in the public domain. Works published in the years 1963 through 1977 receive 95 years of protection. Works created after 1977 and all unpublished works are protected for the life of the author plus 70 years.

You may be able to determine if a work was published before 1923 (and is in the public domain) by examining the date in the work's copyright notice. For example, James Joyce's *Dubliners* is in the public domain because the Library of Congress database indicated that *Dubliners* was first published before 1923.

Note that copyright notice dates included in a book are not always accurate because many public domain works are often republished with new dates in their copyright notices. For example, current editions of James Joyce's *Dubliners* have copyright notices with dates after 1980. These "new" dates reflect the fact that the work contains some new material such as a preface, notes, or previously unpublished material. Only this new material is protected under the copyright claim. The public domain part of the work remains in the public domain.

> **EXAMPLE:** To determine if the James Joyce short story collection *Dubliners* is in the public domain (that is, was published before 1923), I reviewed the Library of Congress records. The Library of Congress record, below, indicates that the work was first published in 1916. Information about researching Library of Congress records is provided in Section C4.

Title Search For: Dubliners /
ITEM 1.CALL NUMBER: Microfilm 76492 PZ
AUTHOR: Joyce, James, 1882-1941
TITLE: Dubliners,
PUBLISHED: New York, B. W. Huebsch, 1916.
DESCRIPTION:2 p.l., 7-278 p. 20 cm.
LCCN NUMBER:17-24698

Works published in the United States after 1922 and before 1964 are also in the public domain if the owner failed to file a renewal during the 28th year after first publication. Unlike copyright registrations or assignments, renewal notices for works published before 1964 had to be filed with the Copyright Office. If a work published after 1922 and before 1964 was not renewed, it fell into the public domain. According to Copyright Office surveys, the great majority of pre-1964 works were never renewed and, therefore, are in the public domain. Unfortunately, the Copyright Office does not maintain lists of public domain materials. You must search Copyright Office records to determine whether a renewal was filed on time for each work.

2. Searching Copyright Office Records

Once you have all the available information about your work and know what you're searching for, you need to choose the search method that best suits your purposes. You can either hire a search firm or work directly with the Copyright Office, which will do your search for a fee. Another option is searching the Copyright Office online, discussed in the next section.

What Else Can You Get From the Copyright Office?

Besides copyright research, the Copyright Office offers the following:

- information circulars
- answers to common questions
- announcements of changes in federal regulations
- compulsory licensing guidelines, and
- information on pending legislation.

These materials can be obtained by writing to the Copyright Office or by visiting the Copyright Office website at www.copyright.gov. You can also order circulars and publications by calling the Forms and Publications 24-Hour Hotline. (Copyright Office information is provided in Chapter 16, "Help Beyond This Book.")

Frequently requested Copyright Office circulars and announcements are also available via the Copyright Office's Fax-on-Demand service. The procedure is simple: call the fax-on-demand number (202-707-9100) and enter the document numbers you wish to receive. If you don't have an index of document numbers, you can have one faxed to you. Once you've entered the document numbers, enter the phone number to which you want the documents faxed. You can order up to three items at one time. You usually receive the fax within minutes of your phone call to the Copyright Office. Note that copyright application forms are not available by fax.

a. Hire a Private Search Company

For a fee, you can hire a private company to search Copyright Office records for you. These companies provide additional services such as tracing the copyright history of a fictional character or locating similarly titled works. These companies may be able to determine if a work is in the public domain or whether you can obtain the rights to use the work. The advantage of using these companies is their speed and thoroughness. Search companies compile comprehensive reports using Copyright Office and other database records and can deliver the materials within two to ten days. The disadvantage is the cost, ranging from $75 to $300 per search. The largest and best known copyright search company is Thomson & Thomson Copyright Research Group (www.thomson-thomson.com).

b. Pay the Copyright Office to Perform the Search

Upon request, the Copyright Office staff will search its records at the statutory rate of $80 for each hour or fraction of an hour consumed. You can initiate a search by submitting a Search Request Form (below) or by calling the Copyright Office at 202-707-6850. The Copyright Office will quote you a fee for your job.

Although the cost of a Copyright Office search is much lower than a private search company, the disadvantage is that it may take one or two months to receive a response. The Copyright Office will conduct an expedited search if you pay a higher fee. For more information, see Copyright Circular 22. Also, note that the search fee does not include the cost of additional certificates or photocopies of deposits or other Copyright Office records. For information concerning these services, request Copyright Office Circular 6. (See Chapter 16, Section A1, for information on how to obtain Copyright Office publications.)

Below is an example of the Copyright Office's Search Request Form. You can use this form to have the Copyright Office locate registrations, renewals, assignments, and addresses of copyright owners.

 A tear-out copy of the form is provided in the Appendix. A digital version is included on the forms CD.

Search Request Form

TYPE OF WORK:

☐ Book   ☐ Music   ☐ Motion Picture   ☐ Drama   ☐ Sound Recording
☐ Photography / Artwork   ☐ Map   ☐ Periodical   ☐ Contribution
☐ Computer Program   ☐ Mask Work

SEARCH INFORMATION YOU REQUIRE:

☐ Registration   ☐ Renewal   ☐ Assignment   ☐ Address

SPECIFICS OF WORK TO BE SEARCHED:

TITLE: _____

AUTHOR: _____

COPYRIGHT CLAIMANT (if known): _____ (name in copyright notice)

APPROXIMATE YEAR DATE OF PUBLICATION/CREATION: _____

REGISTRATION NUMBER (if known): _____

OTHER IDENTIFYING INFORMATION: _____

If you need more space please attach additional pages.

YOUR NAME: _____

DATE: _____

ADDRESS: _____

DAYTIME TELEPHONE NO.: _____

Convey results of estimate/research by telephone?   ☐ Yes   ☐ No

Fee Enclosed?   ☐ Yes. Amount $ ____   ☐ No

If You Only Need a Certificate of Registration

It's possible that all you need is the certificate of registration—the document recorded at the Copyright Office indicating who owns the work. You can use the search form above to obtain a copy or simply furnish a letter to the Copyright Office with the following information:

- title of the work
- type of work involved (for example, novel, lyrics)
- registration number, including the preceding letters (for example, TX000-000)
- year of registration or publication
- author(s), including any pseudonym by which the author may be known, and
- any other information needed to identify the registration.

If you do not have all this information, you can furnish what you have. If the information furnished is insufficient for locating the certificate, you may need to pay for a copyright search as outlined above in Section C2.

There is a $30 fee for the certificate. Your check or money order payable to the Register of Copyrights should accompany the request.

All requests for copies of Copyright Office records should be submitted to: Certifications and Documents Section, LM-402, Copyright Office, Library of Congress, Washington, DC 20559; 202-707-6787. It is also possible to go to the office and request records in person (see "Searching in Person," just below).

Searching in Person

It's possible to inspect Copyright Office records by visiting the Library of Congress in Washington DC, at 101 Independence Avenue, SE, on the 4th floor of the James Madison Memorial Building. The building is open on weekdays from 8:30 a.m. to 5 p.m. There is a card catalogue available to the public in Room 459. You can use the catalogue to obtain essential facts about registrations, such as copyright ownership and whether a work was renewed. Alternatively, you may ask the Reference and Bibliography Section in Room 450 to conduct a search for you for an hourly fee. You can get extensive information on the Copyright Office Card Catalog by visiting the Copyright Office website (www.copyright.gov) and downloading Circular 23 or using Fax-on-Demand (explained above).

Another important research tool you can access in person is *The Catalog of Copyright Entries* (CCE). The CCE contains the same information as the Card Catalog, but is in book form (and is actually more complete than the Card Catalog). The CCE is not only available at the Copyright Office but in many libraries throughout the country—typically large university research libraries and city libraries such as the New York Pubic Library. Portions of the CCE are available only in microfiche form (a photographic format requiring a special viewer). The CCE contains essential facts about registrations, such as copyright ownership and whether a work was renewed, but does not include verbatim reproductions of the registration record. In addition there is a time lag, so more recent registrations may not be included. Finally, the CCE cannot be used for researching the transfer of rights, because it does not include entries for assignments or other recorded documents.

3. Searching Copyright Office Records Online

Searching the Copyright Office records online is both free and easy. You can search through copyright files by visiting the Copyright Office at www.copyright.gov/records. All copyright information is located in the following three directories (see Figure 1, below):

- **Books, Music, Etc.:** Contains information about works registered since January 1978. Included are published and unpublished text works, maps, motion pictures, music, sound recordings, works of the performing and visual arts, graphic artworks, and games. Also included are renewals of previous registrations. You can search by author, claimant, title, or registration number. This file is updated weekly. Note that renewal information is only available for works published after 1949.

- **Serials:** Contains information about serial publications (magazine or other periodic publications) and is updated twice yearly.

- **Documents:** Contains legal records maintained by the Copyright Office since January 1, 1978. The file includes transfers of copyright, termination notices, statements that an author is still alive or has died, documents identifying anonymous or pseudonymous authors, and statements identifying an erroneous name in a copyright notice. A typical document contains the names of the parties involved, the date recorded and executed, and the titles of the works involved. The file is updated weekly.

I tested the search system by clicking on "Books, Music, etc." and typing in the title of the book, *Franny and Zooey* (see Figure 2). The resulting search found the record in Figure 3.

Figure 1

Figure 2

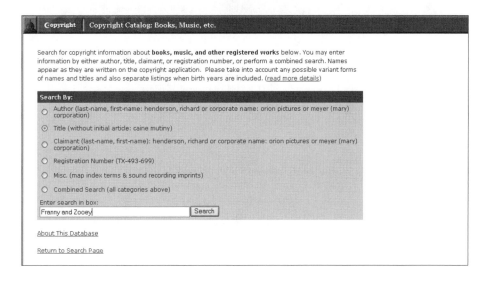

The copyright owner is the author, J.D. Salinger. The date of first publication was August 23, 1961 and the copyright was renewed on October 10, 1989 (indicated by the letters "RE" by the registration number). The original registration number is A591015. Based on this information I can conclude that this work is not in the public domain because the owner filed a timely renewal of copyright after 28 years. (For more information on renewal requirements, see Chapter 8.)

4. Searching Library of Congress Records

In addition to Copyright Office records, there is another catalogue of helpful information at the Library of Congress in Washington, DC. The Library of Congress is the largest library in the world and has been collecting and cataloguing materials for over 200 years. However, contrary to popular belief, the Library of Congress does not contain copies of every work ever published in the United States. The Library's of Congress Online Catalog (www.loc.gov/catalog) includes data for books, serials (magazines and periodicals), music and sound recordings, maps, visual materials (such as photos and graphics), computer files from 1975, and an index of names and subjects. It also includes an incomplete, unedited listing of books catalogued between 1898 and 1975.

Because of the ease of searching and the vast catalogue of materials, use the LOC Catalog for basic research, such as locating the publisher or owner of a work and researching public domain information. Unlike Copyright Office files, the LOC Catalog is searchable by subject matter. Or, you can search by ISBN, ISSN, or LCCN (Library of Congress Catalog Number). You can even limit or define your search by language. For example, you can search for books that are not in English. You may be able to use Library of Congress files to identify an author, title, or publisher and then use that information to search the Copyright Office records.

Figure 3

After Permission Is Granted

Unfortunately, your problems don't necessarily end once you have tracked down a copyright owner and obtained permission to use his or her work. To avoid disputes that could result in lawsuits, you need to keep careful records and manage your permissions process efficiently. However, even a diligent publisher can end up in a dispute with a copyright owner. Common disputes include unauthorized uses or failure to honor the terms of a permission agreement. This chapter addresses potential conflicts and suggests means of minimizing your liability, including the use of business insurance.

A. Permissions Tracking Sheet

The permissions process creates responsibilities. For example, if you fail to make a payment on time or to send a sample for approval, you can lose the right to reproduce the work. If you are managing multiple permissions—for example, reproducing several photographs in a book—you will need to track all the details properly.

A tracking sheet that lists information such as ownership, the rights acquired, and payment arrangements enables the user to keep a running total of fees paid and due, and to keep track of who must receive samples or complimentary copies.

Below is a sample tracking sheet to help you manage the details of multiple permissions. An explanation for each section of the tracking sheet is also provided. This sheet is geared primarily towards copyright permissions, though it can be modified for use with trademark permissions as well. Since the tracking sheet is a modified spreadsheet, you could also prepare it using a computer program such as Excel.

A tear-out copy of this sheet is provided in the Appendix. A digital version is included on the forms CD.

Permissions Tracking Sheet

PTN	Type of Work, Title, Source, and ID Numbers	Author	Owner, Contact Person, Phone, Address, and Email	Payment	Payment Due Date	Date Paid and Form of Payment	Credit	Sample Approval or Comp Copies	Rights Acquired	How the Work is Used

1. PTN (Permission Tracking Number)

Create a number for each permission use, adopting a coding system that reflects the project name. For example, if preparing a text on how to prevent hand injuries, each permission could be consecutively titled as HAND1, HAND2, and so on. The tracking numbers do not have to reflect the order in which the works are used or acquired; what's important is that each permission use has its own PTN.

2. Type of Work

Insert the type of work for which you have acquired permission—for example, photograph, graphic work, text, or trademark.

3. Title

Insert the title of the work—for example, the title of the article, novel, photograph, or graphic image for which you have acquired permission. If there is no title or if the title is not available, create a title that helps to identify the work—for example, "Boy with dog." If the work is a trademark, insert the name or a description of the mark.

4. Source

If you're using a work originally printed in another work—for example, a photograph within a book— insert the title of the source work. For works from serial publications, such as a magazine or journal, insert the title and volume or issue number. If the work is from a website, insert the URL.

5. Identifying Numbers

Many works are identified by code numbers such as the ISBN, ISSN, LCCN, or Dewey Decimal numbers for textual works. Sound recordings also have cata-logue numbers. If the copyright registration number or trademark registration number is available, list it here.

6. Author(s)

Insert the name of the author (the person who created the work). The author may not be the same as the copyright owner. If no author is listed—for example, you're using a newspaper article without a byline or the author is "anonymous" or uses a pseudonym—include that information.

7. Owner and Contact Information

Insert all contact information for the copyright or trademark owner, including the right person to contact (such as a manager or agent, if the owner has one), address, phone number, and email. As indicated in Chapter 15, the author of a copyrighted work is the original owner, but he or she may have transferred rights to a company or another individual.

8. Payments Due

If a payment is required, insert the terms of payment here—for example, "$50 per year"—and list when payment is due.

9. Payments Made

When payment is made, insert the date and the method of payment, such as check or credit card. If paid by check, include the check number.

10. Credit Required

If the copyright owner requires that a credit line be included, insert the type of credit here—for example, "Photograph copyright Prudence O'Neal."

11. Sample Approval/Complimentary Copies

In some cases, the owner has a right to approve samples prior to production or the owner is entitled to complimentary copies. If either samples or complimentary copies are required per your agreement, insert that information and the name of the person who should receive the samples or copies.

12. Rights Acquired

List the rights you acquired under the permission agreement. In general, your primary concerns are exclusivity, territory, language, and term (or length of use). For example, the rights acquired might be stated as: "Nonexclusive English language rights for four years."

13. How the Work Is Used

Indicate where and how the work will be used in your work. For example, if you're creating a book, insert the page number of your book on which you use the work; if the work will be used on a website, insert the URL.

Permissions Calendar

If you're performing a lot of permission work, use a calendaring system to keep track of any renewals, payments, or dates samples must be furnished for approval. If possible, use a computer-based system that can provide timely reminders (known as a "tickler" system).

B. Good Permissions Gone Bad

Regardless of the degree of care the user exercises, not all disputes can be prevented. Two common categories of permission disputes that often arise are contract disputes and intellectual property infringements. Quite often these types of claims overlap. For example, a use that exceeds the written permission agreement may end up as a contract dispute or a copyright dispute. Each type of claim has different remedies and may be brought in different courts. The section below discusses how to approach such disputes.

1. Cease and Desist Letters

The opening salvo in breach of contract or infringement situations is usually a letter from an attorney asking that the user "cease and desist" from using the work further. To minimize any potential damages, you should:

- respond immediately to the owner that you have received the letter and are investigating the claims
- investigate the claims and, if necessary, request further information from the copyright owner, such as proof of ownership
- if possible, stop using or distributing the work (for example, remove the photo from a website or stop selling a book) until the claim has been fully investigated, and
- contact an attorney knowledgeable in copyright law. Information about finding and evaluating an attorney is provided in Chapter 16, "Help Beyond This Book."

Not all legal threats are valid. An attorney's opinion will help you evaluate the claim. As part of the evaluation, seek an estimate of the legal expenses for fighting the dispute.

2. Contract Disputes

A contract dispute can arise if the terms of the permission agreement are broken (or "breached"). The two most common disputes that arise under a license agreement are that the use exceeds the grant of permission or that a payment was not made.

- **The use exceeds the grant.** A dispute might arise if the work is being used in a manner that the copyright owner believes exceeds the rights granted under the agreement. To avoid this type of dispute, monitor the work in all stages of production and review the final product to make sure the use of the work is within the rights granted by the permissions agreement.

- **Payment was not made.** If payment is a condition of permission and payment is not made, the agreement may be terminated by the copyright owner. A prudent approach to avoid this problem is to calendar any dates payments are due and mark payments, you make immediately and clearly. (Note, many companies demand payment before production.)

The permission agreement may provide specific remedies for disputes—for example, arbitration or mediation. In cases of breach, the owner can sue for monetary damages and, if provided under the agreement, attorney fees. Breach of contract claims are usually brought in state courts, but can also be brought in federal court—for instance, as part of a copyright infringement claim.

3. Intellectual Property Infringement

The owner of a work you're using can sue in federal court and seek monetary damages (and in some cases attorney fees) if you infringe on his or her copyright, trademark, or publicity rights.

Infringement claims are typically brought because of unauthorized uses. If the use is not addressed at all in the license agreement (for example, the grant is for use of a photo in a book and you use it on T-shirts), the copyright owner will usually bring the lawsuit under copyright law (although it's possible to bring the claim under contract law in some cases). If the use simply exceeds the dimen-

sions of the grant (for example, you are permitted to reproduce a photograph in a 5,000-print run of a book and you use it in 7,000 copies), a court will probably consider the claim to be a breach of the license (a contract claim as discussed in the previous section) rather than an infringement of copyright. The determinations in these cases—whether copyright law or contract law controls—vary depending on the facts of the case and the judicial district in which the case is filed.

Sometimes a copyright owner files an infringement suit because the user obtained permission from the wrong person, and the correct owner now seeks to assert his or her rights. For example, a magazine claims to own a photograph but, after publication, the photographer claims ownership and sues for infringement. This type of dispute is difficult to predict and equally difficult to prevent. One approach to minimizing liability in this situation is to require that the person signing the permission agreement promise that he or she has authority to grant the permission, and if possible, provide indemnity. (Sample indemnity provisions are provided in many of the permission agreements through this book.)

Libel, Invasion of Privacy, and Other Claims

Unauthorized uses of work may give rise to additional claims such as defamation or invasion of privacy. These claims are discussed in Chapter 12, "Releases." If confronted by a claim of libel or defamation, seek the advice of an attorney knowledgeable in media law.

C. Insurance

Insurance may shield a user from some potential damages. The protection will vary depending on the terms of the insurance policy. Some general business insurance policies contain a provision entitled "advertising injuries" that protect against trademark, copyright, or libel claims. The extent of protection depends upon the wording of the policy and the manner in which insurance policies are interpreted in the state. The model form language used by the insurance industry to define advertising injuries has changed repeatedly over the past two decades as insurers seek ways to avoid paying for claims.

If you are threatened with a claim, examine your business insurance immediately. An attorney should be able to advise you as to whether the insurance company must assume coverage. Publishers and media companies sometimes acquire more comprehensive insurance known as "media perils" policies. Check with your insurance agent for more information.

It is quite common for insurance carriers to attempt to deny coverage to copyright owners. That means that if you assert a claim, the company will look for a way out. One of the most common methods an insurance company uses to avoid payment is to argue that the type of claim raised is not listed explicitly in the policy—for example, the policy does not cover claims from a certain time period or claims involving certain works.

In other situations, the carrier will seek to deny coverage if the insurance company is not informed of the claim promptly. For example, in 1994, the Andy Warhol estate was sued by Time-Life, Inc., and a photographer over Warhol's use of a photograph of Jacqueline Kennedy. The Warhol estate waited until 1996 to notify its insurance company and, on the basis of this late reporting, the insurance company refused to provide coverage. This refusal was upheld by a federal court. (*The Andy Warhol Foundation for the Visual Arts Inc. v. Federal Insurance Co.*, 97 Civ. 2716 (TPG), 1998 U.S. Dist. LEXIS 8094, June 2, 1998 (S.D. N.Y., June 2, 1998).) Therefore, if a claim is made against your company, investigate coverage immediately and report the claim promptly to your carrier.

■

Assignments and Works Made for Hire

Up to this point, the focus of this book has been the rules and process for getting permission from the owner of a work. This chapter, on the other hand, is not about getting permission—it's about acquiring ownership. Once you become the owner of a copyrighted work, you don't need permission from anyone to use it. Instead, others must obtain permission from you.

There are various situations when acquiring ownership may be your best option—for example, when you want an illustration for permanent use at your website. This chapter discusses the two methods of acquiring ownership: by assignment and by commissioning a work for hire.

An assignment is a permanent transfer of ownership, such as acquiring copyright ownership of a photograph from the photographer. A work-for-hire agreement on the other hand, makes the person who pays for the work the owner and author of the work. For example, the Disney Company employs animators who create a cartoon; the Disney Company is the author and owner of the cartoon. The advantages and disadvantages to both approaches are discussed in this chapter. This chapter also provides several model assignments and work-for-hire agreements that can be used with copyright owners, artists, and musicians.

A. Copyright Assignments

When someone who owns a copyrighted work sells all rights in it to another party, the transaction is called an "assignment." Unlike a license agreement in which the licensee obtains only a temporary, conditional right to use a work that is still owned by the licensor, in an assignment, the buyer (assignee) purchases the copyright and the person selling the copyright (the assignor) retains no rights. There are some exceptions, and it is possible to acquire an assignment of a part interest in a copyright, for example, from a co-owner of copyright. In that case, only a part ownership is purchased and the purchaser becomes a co-owner. However, this chapter focuses on acquiring full ownership of a copyrighted work only.

Depending on the terms of the assignment, the assignor may be paid by the assignee with a lump sum or with periodic royalty payments. In addition, an assignment may provide that the rights are assigned back to the assignor in the event of a certain condition—for example, if the assignee stops selling the work.

An assignment is a transfer of ownership, but it may not last for the full term of copyright protection. This is because copyright law permits creators of work transferred after 1977 to recapture all the copyrights that were assigned 35 years from the date of the assignment. (Terminations of transfers for works transferred in or before 1977 are subject to fairly complex rules that are beyond the scope of this book. See *The Copyright Handbook,* by attorney Stephen Fishman (Nolo), for more information.) For example, an author that assigned rights to a book publisher in 2000 can reclaim the rights in 2035. This recapture right is usually not important because few works have a useful economic life of more than 35 years. And this recapture right does not apply to the creator of a work made for hire, as discussed below.

You can use an assignment to acquire a work that already exists, or an artist can agree to assign a work that will be created in the future. An assignment must be in writing. Notarization is not required but is recommended, especially if the assignee is concerned about the assignment's validity. Notarization creates a legal presumption that the transfer is valid. If there are multiple owners of a copyright, the signature of all owners must be obtained to make the assignment valid.

Assignments may be recorded (made into public records) by being filed with the Copyright Office. There is no legal requirement that an assignment be recorded, but recordation provides public notice of the transfer. For information regarding recording assignments, call the Copyright Office's Public Information Office at 202-679-0700 or the Certification and Documents office at 202-707-6850. The assignment and fee should be mailed to: Documents Unit LM-462, Cataloging Office, Library of Congress, Washington, DC 20559.

1. Basic Copyright Assignment

The agreement below is a basic copyright assignment that can be used for any type of work. More specific assignments for musicians and artists are included in Sections A3 and A5.

A tear-out copy of this assignment is provided in the Appendix. A digital version is included on the forms CD.

Basic Copyright Assignment

I, _____ ("Assignor"), am owner of the work entitled _____ (the "Work") and described as follows: _____

_____ .

In consideration of $ _____ and other valuable consideration, paid by

_____ ("Assignee"), I assign to Assignee and Assignee's heirs and assigns all my right, title, and interest in the copyright to the Work and all renewals and extensions of the copyright that may be secured under the laws of the United States of America and any other countries, as such may now or later be in effect. I agree to cooperate with Assignee and to execute and deliver all papers as may be necessary to vest all rights to the Work.

Signature of assignor(s)_____

2. Explanation of Basic Copyright Assignment

- In the first two blanks of the first paragraph, insert the assignor's name (usually the author) and the title of the work. In the next blank space, either describe the work or enter "See attached Exhibit A" and attach a copy of the

work to the assignment. If you attach a copy, be sure to label it "Exhibit A."
- In the next paragraph, insert the amount of the payment and the name of the assignee.
- The assignor must sign the agreement. To have the agreement notarized, the assignor should wait to sign the agreement until in the presence of a notary, who will fill out the rest of the Notarization section, as described below.

Notarization

Notarization for copyright assignments is recommended. The purpose of notarization is to verify the signature and identity of the person executing the agreement. You can usually locate a notary public through your local Yellow Pages. To include notarization, add the following statement at the end of the agreement.

On this ___ day of _____, year ___, before me, _____, the undersigned Notary Public, personally appeared _____ and proved to me based on satisfactory evidence to be the person(s) who executed this instrument.

Witness my hand and official seal.

_____
Notary Public

Sometimes this section does not have to be added, as the notary may have a stamp that includes all such information. Wait to have the assignor sign the agreement until he or she is in the presence of the notary.

- If there is more than one assignor, or if the assignor is married in a community property state, signing the agreement may involve a few more issues.

Multiple Assignors. If there are multiple copyright owners, you will need the signature of all owners for your assignment. There are many ways that a copyright can have co-owners. For example, the work may have been created by joint authors or may have been bequeathed under a will to several children who became co-owners. If you are unsure whether there are multiple co-owners, you can research this using the techniques in Chapter 13.

Spousal Consent in Community Property States. A community property state is one in which any property acquired by either spouse during marriage (other than by gift or inheritance), belongs to the husband and wife equally. Copyrights may be co-owned by a spouse in community property states, though court cases on the subject are conflicting. A court in California has held that a spouse in a community property state has a co-ownership interest in the other spouse's copyrighted work. (*In Re Marriage of Worth*, 195 Cal.App.3d 768, 241 Cal. Rptr. 185 (1987).) The safest route for an assignor who lives in a community property state to obtain his or her spouse's consent to any assignment. The provision below can be added to the assignment and should be notarized.

Spousal Consent Provision

I am the spouse of Assignor and acknowledge that I have read and understand this Agreement. I am aware that my spouse agrees to assign all interest in the Work, including any community property interest or other equitable property interest that I may have in it. I consent to the assignment and agree that my interest, if any, in the Work is subject to the provisions of this Agreement. I will take no action to hinder the Agreement or the underlying assignment of rights.

[Spouse signature] _____

3. Musician Assignment Agreement

If you are hiring a musician to record a composition—for instance, you hire a guitarist to record musical phrases for a video game—you may want to use a more detailed assignment agreement, such as the one offered below. The assignment is for the musician's recorded performance; not for the song. As explained in Chapter 5, there are two separate music copyrights: one in the musical composition or song (musical work) and another in the way in which the song is recorded (sound recording). If the musician has composed the song, you would use the assignment above, in Section 1, in addition to transfer the rights to the composition itself as well as to the sound recordings.

 A tear-out copy of this agreement is provided in the Appendix. A digital version is included on the forms CD.

Musician Assignment Agreement

This Musician Assignment Agreement (the "Agreement") is made between _____ ("Company") and _____ ("Musician").

Grant

Musician has performed or recorded performance(s) for the Company in conjunction with the Company recording under the titles:

_____

_____

_____

In consideration of the payments provided in this Agreement, Musician assigns all rights, including all rights under copyright law, in the recorded performance to the Company, its assigns, licensees, or successors and grants the right to use the recorded performance for any purposes and in all forms and media and waives any claim to moral rights.

Payment

Company shall pay Musician as follows: $ _____ .

Warranty & Release

Musician has the authority to grant the rights under this Agreement and Musician releases Company and Company's assigns, licensees, and successors from any claims that may arise regarding the use of the performance including any claims of infringement of moral rights, rights of publicity, or copyright. Company is permitted, although not obligated, to include musician's name as a credit in connection with the performance.

Company is not obligated to utilize any of the rights granted in this Agreement.

Musician has read and understood this agreement and is over the age of 18. This Agreement expresses the complete understanding of the parties.

Musician Signature: _____

Musician Name: _____

Musician's Address: _____

Date: _____

4. Explanation for Musician Assignment Agreement

- Since the musician is assigning all rights in the performance, the **Grant** section is as broad as possible, and the musician will not retain any rights to the recorded performance.
- The **Warranty and Release** section is an assurance that the musician owns the rights being granted. For example, some musicians are signed to exclusive recording agreements and a record company owns all of their performances, or the musician may be prohibited from recording altogether. The warranty also provides a promise not to sue the company for legal claims such as copyright infringement. The warranty section also includes additional statements that "Company is permitted, although not obligated, to include musician's name as a credit in connection with the performance" and "Company is not obligated to utilize any of the rights granted in this Agreement." These provisions give the company the ability to ditch the performance, if necessary, and to avoid liability in the event that it does not credit the musician.
- It is unusual that the musician would be a minor, but in that event, the musician's parent or guardian should sign a consent similar to the Parent/Guardian Consent in the model release in Chapter 12, "Releases."

Arbitration and Mediation

An arbitration and/or mediation clause provides alternate methods of resolving any disputes that may arise, rather than filing a lawsuit. Although one is not included in the artist or musician assignments, you may, if you wish, include the following provision in either agreement. (For a more detailed explanation of arbitration and mediation, review Chapter 11.)

Mediation; Arbitration. If a dispute arises under this Agreement, the parties agree to first try to resolve the dispute with the help of a mutually agreed upon mediator in the State of _____ . Any costs and fees other than attorney fees shall be shared equally by the parties. If it proves impossible to arrive at a mutually satisfactory solution, the parties agree to submit the dispute to binding arbitration in the same city or region, conducted on a confidential basis pursuant to the Commercial Arbitration Rules of the American Arbitration Association.

5. Artwork Assignment Agreement

The following agreement provides for assignment of artwork, but can be modified for photography as well. The assignment includes optional provisions for payment of expenses and dispute resolution.

 A tear-out copy of this agreement is provided in the Appendix. A digital version is included on the forms CD.

Artwork Assignment Agreement

This Artwork Assignment Agreement (the "Agreement") is made between _____ ("Company") and _____ ("Artist").

Services

Artist agrees to perform the following services: _____ and create the following artwork (the "Art") entitled: _____.

    The Art shall be completed by the following date: _____.

    During the process, Artist shall keep the Company informed of work in progress and shall furnish test prints of the Art prior to completion.

Payment

Company agrees to pay Artist as follows:

$ _____ for performance of the art services and acquisition of the rights provided below.

Grant of Rights

Artist assigns to the Company all copyright to the Art and agrees to cooperate in the preparation of any documents necessary to demonstrate this assignment of rights. Artist retains the right to display the work as part of Artist's portfolio and to reproduce the artwork in connection with the promotion of Artist's services.

Expenses

Company agrees to reimburse Artist for all reasonable production expenses including halftones, stats, photography, disks, illustrations, or related costs. These expenses shall be itemized on invoices and in no event shall any expense exceed $50 without approval from the Company.

Credit

Credit for Artist shall be included on reproductions of the Art as follows:_____

Artist Warranties

Artist is the owner of all rights to the Art and warrants that the Art does not infringe any intellectual property rights or violate any laws.

Artwork Assignment Agreement (cont.)

Artist Signature: _____

Artist Name: _____

Artist Address: _____

Date: _____

Company Authorized Signature: _____

Name and Title: _____

Address: _____

Date: _____

---

6. Explanation of Artwork Assignment Agreement

- Since the artist is assigning all rights in the performance, the **Grant of Rights** section is as broad as possible, and the artist will not retain any rights to the artwork.
- Use the **Services** section if the artist has been hired to perform a specific job. If the artwork has already been completed, this provision is not needed. Strike it or enter "NA" for "not applicable."
- The **Artist Warranties** are promises that the artist owns the rights being granted and will not sue the company for legal claims such as copyright infringement. If you wish, you may include an arbitration or mediation section (see "Arbitration and Mediation" in Section A4).
- It is unusual that the artist would be a minor, but in that event, the artist's parent or guardian should sign a consent similar to the Parent/Guardian Consent in the model release in Chapter 12, "Releases."

B. Works Made for Hire

Sometimes for copyright purposes the author of a work is the person who pays for it, not the person who creates it. The resulting work is called a work made for hire, or often simply a "work for hire." The basis for this principle is that a business that authorizes and pays for a work should own the rights to the work.

There are two distinct types of work that may be classified as "made for hire":

- a work created by an employee within the scope of employment, or
- a commissioned work created by an independent contractor (nonemployee) that is the subject of a written work-for-hire agreement and that falls within a special group of categories.

This section discusses these work-for-hire rules for employees and independent contractors in more detail. First, it explains some general rules regarding copyright ownership and duration for works for hire.

1. Significance of Work-Made-for-Hire Status

If a work qualifies as a work made for hire under one of the two methods described above, the person paying for the work (the hiring party) is both the author and copyright owner. As such, the hiring party must be named as the author on an application for copyright registration.

The work-for-hire status of a work also affects the length of copyright protection and termination rights.

a. Copyright Duration

Works made for hire created after 1977 are protected for a period of 95 years from first publication or 120 years from creation, whichever is shorter. Therefore if a website company created a work made for hire in 2000 but did not publish it until 2001, copyright protection would extend to 2096 (95 years from the date of publication).

b. No Termination Rights

As discussed above, someone who assigns a copyright to someone else may be able to recapture the copyright after 35 years. However, a work made for hire cannot be terminated by the creator. This means that the owner of a work made for hire (the hiring party) is assured that he or she will retain ownership for the full copyright term.

2. Works Created by Employees

Every copyrightable work created by an employee within the scope of employment is automatically a work made for hire. There are no other requirements, no review of the special categories (outlined in Section 3b below), and no need for a written agreement. For this reason, when sorting out ownership issues, a court will first analyze whether an employer-employee relationship exists.

For more information on the law regarding independent contractors, see *Hiring Independent Contractors: The Employer's Legal Guide,* by Stephen Fishman (Nolo).

Whether an employment relationship exists is determined by weighing the following factors:

- **The tax treatment of the hired party.** If the hiring party pays payroll and employment taxes, this factor weighs strongly in favor of an employment relationship. *This factor is virtually determinative by itself.*
- **The provision of employee benefits.** If vacation or health benefits are granted to the worker, this factor weighs in favor of an employment relationship.
- **The hiring party's right to control the manner and means by which the work is accomplished.** If the hiring party exercises control, this factor weighs in favor of an employment relationship.
- **The skill required in the particular occupation.** If the work to be performed requires a unique skill—for example, sculpting—this factor weighs against an employment relationship.
- **Whether the employer or the worker supplies the instrumentalities and tools of the trade.** If the worker supplies his own tools, this factor weighs against an employment relationship.
- **Where the work is done.** If the hiring party determines the location of the work, this factor weighs in favor of an employment relationship.
- **The length of time for which the worker is employed.** The longer the period of work, the more this factor weighs in favor of an employment relationship.
- **Whether the hiring party has the right to assign additional work projects to the worker.** If the hiring party can assign additional tasks—including tasks that do not result in copyrightable works—this factor weighs in favor of an employment relationship.

- **The extent of the worker's discretion over when and how long to work.** If the hiring party controls the working times—particularly if it is a regular work week—this factor weighs in favor of an employment relationship.
- **The method of payment.** If the payment is per job—not per day or week—this factor weighs against an employment relationship.
- **The hired party's role in hiring and paying assistants.** If the worker cannot hire and pay assistants, this factor weighs in favor of an employment relationship.
- **Whether the work is part of the regular business of the hiring party.** If the hiring party does not perform this type of work regularly—for example, taking photographs—this factor weighs against an employment relationship.
- **Whether the worker is in business.** If the worker has a business, this factor weighs against an employment relationship.

3. Works Created by Independent Contractors

A work created by an independent contractor (unlike a work created by an employee) is not automatically classified as a work made for hire. For an independent contractor's work to qualify as a work made for hire, three requirements must be met:

- the work must be specially ordered or commissioned—for example, the hiring party must request the work; it cannot already be in existence
- the work must fall within a group of specially enumerated categories (outlined below), and
- a written agreement must be signed by both parties indicating that it is a work made for hire.

a. Ordering the Work and Executing an Agreement

A work-for-hire agreement with an independent contractor should be signed before the work commences. However, at least one court has held that the agreement can be executed after the work is completed, provided that at the time the work was created, the parties intended to enter into such an agreement. In that case, a magazine paid an artist by check and on the back of each check was a statement that indicated the drawings were works made for hire. A court of appeals ruled that the artist's continued signature on the checks over a seven-year period demonstrated that he was aware of and accepted the arrangement. (*Playboy Enterprises, Inc. v. Dumas*, 53 F.3d 549 (2d Cir. 1995).)

b. Work-Made-for-Hire Categories

An independent contractor's work will be a work for hire only if it falls within one of the following categories:

- a contribution to a collective work (such as a short story for a collection or an introduction to an anthology)
- a part of a motion picture or other audiovisual work
- a translation
- a supplementary work—that is, a work prepared for publication as a supplement to a work by another author for the purpose of introducing, concluding, illustrating, explaining, revising, commenting upon, or assisting in the use of the other work (such as forewords, afterwords, pictorial illustrations, maps, charts, tables, editorial notes, musical arrangements, answer material for tests, bibliographies, appendixes, and indexes)
- a compilation (such as a collection of statistics on stock car racing)
- an instructional text—that is, a literary, pictorial, or graphic work prepared for use in day-to-day instructional activities (such as a

textbook, but not a novel used in a literature class)

- a test or answer material for a test, or
- an atlas.

Any work created by an independent contractor that does not fall within one of the above categories cannot be a work made for hire. This is so even if the parties have signed a written agreement stating that the work is a work made for hire.

EXAMPLE: A painter is commissioned to create a mural for a school. The painter signs an agreement entitled "Work Made for Hire." The painter (not the school) owns the painting because paintings are not included among the enumerated categories of works by independent contractors that can be works made for hire.

4. Work-Made-for-Hire Agreement

Below is a simple work-for-hire agreement. Remember that it is always necessary to use this agreement with an independent contractor. Strictly speaking, it is not necessary to use this agreement when a work is to be created by an employee. The employer automatically owns an employee's work created within the course of employment regardless of whether there is a written agreement. However, employers often prefer to use written agreements to make it clear to employees that the employer owns copyright.

This agreement can be used for other workers besides artists. Simply revise the appropriate sections to describe the worker and the work made for hire.

 A tear-out copy of this agreement is provided in the Appendix. A digital version is included on the forms CD.

Work-Made-for-Hire Agreement

This Work-Made-for-Hire Agreement (the "Agreement") is made between _____ ("Company") and _____ ("Artist").

Services

In consideration of the payments provided in this Agreement, Artist agrees to perform the following services: _____

Payment

Company agrees to pay Artist as follows: _____.

Works Made for Hire—Assignment of Intellectual Property Rights

Artist agrees that, for consideration that is acknowledged, any works of authorship commissioned pursuant to this Agreement (the "Works") shall be considered works made for hire as that term is defined under U.S. copyright law. To the extent that any such Work created for Company by Artist is not a work made for hire belonging to Company, Artist hereby assigns and transfers to Company all rights Artist has or may acquire to all such Works. Artist agrees to sign and deliver to Company, either during or subsequent to the term of this Agreement, such other documents as Company considers desirable to evidence the assignment of copyright.

Artist Warranties

Artist warrants that the Work does not infringe any intellectual property rights or violate any laws and that the work is original to Artist.

Miscellaneous

This Agreement constitutes the entire understanding between the parties and can only be modified by written agreement. The laws of the State of _____ shall govern this Agreement. In the event of any dispute arising under this agreement, the prevailing party shall be entitled to its reasonable attorney fees.

Artist Signature: _____   Company Authorized Signature: _____

Artist Name: _____   Name and Title: _____

Artist Address: _____   Address: _____

Date: _____   Date: _____

5. Explanation of Work-Made-for-Hire Agreement

- In the **Services** section, insert the work that the artist is supposed to perform, for example: "Create a series of photographs for a KeepClean toothbrush advertisement." Insert the amount to be paid to the artist in the payment section.

- The section **Works Made for Hire—Assignment of Intellectual Property Rights** establishes that the work is made for hire. However, if the work does not meet the requirements of copyright law, a backup provision is added that converts the arrangement to an assignment. This type of provision is commonly used by businesses seeking to make sure that ownership rights have been acquired.

- The **Warranty** provision promises that the artist owns the work and that the work is not an infringement. This is necessary to provide an assurance that the work is not taken from another source.

- This agreement includes some **Miscellaneous** provisions. One provision provides that this is the entire agreement and therefore negates any previous oral or written agreements. In addition, any changes to the agreement must be in writing. Insert the home state of the hiring party in the blank space so that that state's law will govern the interpretation of the agreement in the event of a dispute. The attorney provision provides that the winning party in any lawsuit will get attorney fees paid by the loser. For a more detailed explanation of these provisions, read Chapter 11, "Art and Merchandise Agreements."

■

16

Help Beyond This Book

Using the information in this book, you should be able to handle most permission situations yourself. However, it's possible that you could find yourself needing additional information or professional advice from an attorney. For example, if you used material based on a fair use determination and the copyright owner later enters the picture claiming ownership, you should consult an attorney for advice.

The resources provided in this chapter focus primarily on the three areas of law discussed in this book: copyright, trademarks, and the right of publicity. This chapter includes many websites that provide current news on these changing areas of law, as well as links to statutes, cases, and articles.

By educating yourself with this book and the other resources listed in this chapter, you'll be able to work with attorneys more efficiently, keep your costs down, and better evaluate the attorney's services.

Updates and Contacting the Author

Because some of the information in this book may change—website addresses, for example—current update information is provided in the Legal Update section of the Nolo website (www.nolo.com). Also, you can contact the author of this book at rich@nolo.com.

A. Resources for More Detailed Permissions Research

The primary areas of law discussed in this book (copyright, trademark, and the right of publicity) are part of a body of law known as intellectual property law. Most of the resources in this section deal with how to research intellectual property law.

Staying Current

If you'd like to stay current on rights and permission information, check out the leading publication for authors and publishers. The *McHugh Memo on Publishing Management* is published by John B. McHugh, 414-351-3056, email: j.b.mchugh@worldnet.att.net.

---

1. Copyright Information

- The U.S. Copyright Office can provide a broad range of information including circulars, kits, and other publications related to permission issues. Contact the Copyright Office at: Library of Congress, Washington, DC 20559-6000, or visit its website at www.copyright.gov. In addition, the following information will connect you with various services at the Copyright Office:
    - Forms Hotline: 202-707-9100 (24 hours), 202-707-3000 (9 a.m. to 5 p.m.)
    - Fax on Demand: 202-707-2600
    - Publications Sections: LM-455, Copyright Office, Library of Congress, Washington DC 20559
    - Licensing Division Section: LM-458, Copyright Office, Library of Congress, Washington, DC 20559; 202-707-8150.
- The Cornell University law school website at www.law.cornell.edu provides text of copyright statutes and related cases and trademark and right of publicity statutes and cases.
- Stanford University has an excellent resource site devoted to fair use issues at http://fairuse.stanford.edu.

2. Trademark Information

- The U.S. Trademark Office is a division of the U.S. Patent and Trademark Office (USPTO) (www.uspto.gov). The USPTO site includes relevant applications and trademark office forms. You can also write to: P.O. Box 1450, Alexandria, VA 22213.
- The Trademark Blog (http://trademark.blog.us) provides timely news about trademark law and disputes.
- All About Trademarks (www.ggmark.com) offers trademark links and information.

3. General Intellectual Property Resources

- Yahoo! provides a thorough directory of intellectual property resources on the Internet at www.yahoo.com/Government/Law/Intellectual_Property.
- The Intellectual Property Mall (www.ipmall.fplc.edu) provides helpful copyright and trademark links.
- If you would like to better understand the principles of intellectual property, Nolo (www.nolo.com), the publisher of this book, also publishes several titles on intellectual property, including:
  - *The Copyright Handbook,* by attorney Stephen Fishman
  - *Copyright Your Software,* by attorney Stephen Fishman
  - *Patent, Copyright & Trademark: A Desk Reference to Intellectual Property Law,* by attorneys Stephen Elias and Richard Stim
  - *Software Development: A Legal Guide,* by attorney Stephen Fishman
  - *The Public Domain,* by attorney Stephen Fishman, and
  - *Trademark: Legal Care for Your Business & Product Name,* by attorney Stephen Elias.

4. Online Issues

- The Gigalaw website covers online issues at www.gigalaw.com.

B. Conducting Legal Research

Throughout this book are references to legal cases and laws. You may want to read these cases and laws or pursue more detailed legal research on your own. For example, you may want to learn more about defamation law within your state. Finding out more on a specific legal question generally involves reading legal books and finding applicable law and cases.

Conducting legal research is not as difficult as it may seem. Nolo publishes a basic legal research guide called *Legal Research: How to Find & Understand the Law,* written by attorneys Stephen Elias and Susan Levinkind. It walks you through the various sources of law, explains how they fit together, and shows you how to use them to answer your legal questions.

While there are good online sources for basic legal research (see "Nolo's Legal Encyclopedia" below), you may have to visit a local law library for detailed legal research. If there's a public law school in your area, it probably has a law library that's open to the public. Other public law libraries are often run by local bar associations or as an adjunct to the local courts. Law libraries associated with private law schools often allow only limited public access. Call to speak with the law librarian to determine your right to access. You can also call your local bar association to find out about the public law libraries in your area.

C. Working With an Attorney

A number of permission situations may lead you to seek an attorney's advice. Attorneys have various specialties, and you will need to select a lawyer who is qualified to provide the advice you need.

Generally, an attorney knowledgeable in intellectual property law can answer most permission questions. Intellectual property attorneys are familiar with copyrights, trademarks, right of publicity, and, to some extent, media disputes based on defamation and the right of privacy. Don't make the mistake of hiring a lawyer whom you trust but who works in a different field—such as the lawyer who handled your friend's house purchase masterfully.

It's also a good idea to try to find an attorney who has expertise in the particular type of intellectual property that applies to your permission situation. Some intellectual property attorneys specialize in one type of intellectual property, either copyrights, trademarks, or patents. If, for example, you are concerned about a potential trademark dispute, you should seek an intellectual property attorney who specializes in trademarks.

In addition to all these specialties, some intellectual property lawyers focus on litigation (lawsuits), but not all intellectual property attorneys are litigators. If you have a license dispute and want to sue someone (or someone has threatened to sue you), you will need an intellectual property attorney who is an experienced litigator. Litigators usually bill on an hourly basis, though sometimes if you are bringing the suit (rather than being sued) they may take a case on "contingency." Under this arrangement, if you win, the attorney receives a percentage, usually one-third to one-half, of any money you recover in the lawsuit. If you lose, the attorney receives nothing—except for out-of-pocket expenses, which can easily run into the thousands even for relatively simple cases. Read the information on fees in the section below carefully.

The American Intellectual Property Law Association (AIPLA) (www.aipla.org) may be able to help you locate attorneys in your area. The Intellectual Property Law Association of the American Bar Association also has a listing of intellectual property attorneys. You can reach it at 312-988-5000.

Defamation and Invasion of Privacy

If your dispute is based on defamation or invasion of privacy, you may need a media law specialist. In this case, the attorney may not be an intellectual property expert but will be knowledgeable in disputes regarding libel, slander, and other personal claims known as torts, especially as they relate to media industries such as publishing and music. If you are locating an attorney through a bar association referral service, ask for a media law attorney.

1. Finding an Attorney

The best way to locate an attorney is by referrals through friends or others in your field. It is also possible to locate an attorney through a state, county, or city bar association. Check your local Yellow Pages and ask the bar association if they have a lawyer referral service. When interviewing an attorney, ask questions about clientele, work performed, rates, and experience. If you speak with one of the attorney's clients (for example, another website owner), ask questions about the attorney's response time, billing practices, and temperament.

2. How to Keep Your Fees Down

Most attorneys bill on an hourly basis ($150 to $300 an hour) and send you a bill at the end of each month. Some attorneys bill on a fixed fee basis where you pay a set fee for certain services—for example, $5,000 for a license negotiation.

Here are some tips to reduce the size of your bills.

a. Get a Fee Agreement

It's crucial that you get a written fee agreement when dealing with an attorney. The fee agreement is a negotiated arrangement that establishes fixed fees for certain work rather than hourly billings. Read it and understand your rights as a client. Make sure that your fee agreement includes provisions that require an itemized statement along with the bill detailing the work done and time spent and that allow you to drop the attorney at any time. If you can't get fixed billings, ask your attorney to estimate fees for work and ask for an explanation if the bill exceeds the estimates.

b. Keep It Short

If your attorney is being paid on an hourly basis, keep your conversations short (the meter is always running) and avoid making several calls a day. Consolidate your questions so that you can ask them all in one conversation.

Mad at Your Lawyer?

In many states, such as California, a client always has the right to terminate the working relationship with his or her attorney—although this does not terminate the obligation to pay the attorney. If you don't respect and trust your attorney's professional abilities, you should find a new attorney and terminate the relationship. Beware, though: switching attorneys is a nuisance and may cost you time and money.

c. Review Bills Carefully

Your legal bill should be prompt and clear. Do not accept summary billings such as the single phrase "litigation work" used to explain a block of time for which you are billed a great deal of money. Every item should be explained with the rate and hours billed. Late billings are not acceptable, especially in litigation. When you get bills you don't understand, ask the attorney for an explanation—and ask the attorney not to bill you for the explanation.

d. Watch Out for Hidden Expenses

Find out what expenses you must cover. This is especially important if you're hiring a lawyer on contingency, since you must often pay the lawyer's costs even if you lose the case, which can come as a nasty surprise. Watch out if your attorney wants to bill for services such as word processing or administrative services. This means you will be paying the secretary's salary. Also beware of fax and copying charges. Some firms charge clients per page for incoming and outgoing faxes. Other firms charge a per page copy fee which surpasses any commercial copy center. Look out for these hidden expenses in your fee agreement.

What Is a Retainer?

A retainer is an advance payment to an attorney. The attorney places the retainer in a bank account (in some states, this must be an interest-bearing account) and then deducts money from the retainer at the end of each month to pay your bill. When the retainer is depleted, the attorney may ask for a new retainer. If the retainer is not used up at the end of the services, the attorney must return what's left. The amount of the retainer usually depends on the project. Retainers for litigation, for instance, are often between $2,000 and $5,000.

e. Don't Take Litigation Lightly

As a general rule, beware of litigation! If you are involved in a lawsuit, it may take months or years to resolve. Some go on for decades. It often costs $10,000 or more, and the lawyers often profit the most. If you're in a dispute, ask your attorney about dispute resolution methods such as arbitration and mediation. Often these procedures can save money and are much faster than litigation.

If those methods don't work or aren't available, ask your attorney for an assessment of your odds and the potential costs before filing a lawsuit. Get this assessment in plain English. If a lawyer can't explain your situation to you clearly, he or she probably won't be able to explain it to a judge or jury clearly either.

■

How to Use the CD-ROM

The tear-out forms in Appendix B are included on a CD-ROM in the back of the book. This CD-ROM, which can be used with Windows computers, installs files that can be opened, printed, and edited using a word processor or other software. It is *not* a stand-alone software program. Please read this Appendix and the README.TXT file included on the CD-ROM for instructions on using the Forms CD.

Note to Mac users: This CD-ROM and its files should also work on Macintosh computers. Please note, however, that Nolo cannot provide technical support for non-Windows users.

How to View the README File

If you do not know how to view the file README.TXT, insert the Forms CD-ROM into your computer's CD-ROM drive and follow these instructions:

- Windows 9x, 2000, Me, and XP: (1) On your PC's desktop, double click the My Computer icon; (2) double click the icon for the CD-ROM drive into which the Forms CD-ROM was inserted; (3) double click the file README.TXT.
- Macintosh: (1) On your Mac desktop, double click the icon for the CD-ROM that you inserted; (2) double click on the file README.TXT.

While the README file is open, print it out by using the Print command in the File menu.

A. Installing the Form Files Onto Your Computer

Word processing forms that you can open, complete, print, and save with your word processing program (see Section B, below) are contained on the CD-ROM. Before you can do anything with the files on the CD-ROM, you need to install them onto your hard disk. In accordance with U.S. copyright laws, remember that copies of the CD-ROM and its files are for your personal use only.

Insert the Forms CD and do the following:

1. Windows 9x, 2000, Me, and XP Users

Follow the instructions that appear on the screen. (If nothing happens when you insert the Forms CD-ROM, then (1) double click the My Computer icon; (2) double click the icon for the CD-ROM drive into which the Forms CD-ROM was inserted; and (3) double click the file WELCOME.EXE.)

By default, all the files are installed to the \Licensing Forms folder in the \Program Files folder of your computer. A folder called "Licensing Forms" is added to the "Programs" folder of the Start menu.

2. Macintosh Users

Step 1:   If the "Licensing Forms CD" window is not open, open it by double clicking the "Licensing Forms CD" icon.

Step 2:   Select the "Licensing Forms" folder icon.

Step 3:   Drag and drop the folder icon onto the icon of your hard disk.

B. Using the Word Processing Files to Create Documents

This section concerns the files for forms that can be opened and edited with your word processing program.

All word processing forms come in rich text format. These files have the extension ".RTF." For example, the form for the Artwork Assignment Agreement discussed in Chapter 15 is on the file ArtAssign.rtf. All forms and their filenames are listed at the beginning of Appendix B.

RTF files can be read by most recent word processing programs including all versions of MS Word for Windows and Macintosh, WordPad for Windows, and recent versions of WordPerfect for Windows and Macintosh.

To use a form from the CD to create your documents you must: (1) open a file in your word processor or text editor; (2) edit the form by filling in the required information; (3) print it out; (4) rename and save your revised file.

The following are general instructions on how to do this. However, each word processor uses different commands to open, format, save, and print documents. Please read your word processor's manual for specific instructions on performing these tasks.

Do not call Nolo's technical support if you have questions on how to use your word processor.

Step 1: Opening a File

There are three ways to open the word processing files included on the CD-ROM after you have installed them onto your computer.

- Windows users can open a file by selecting its "shortcut" as follows: (1) Click the Windows "Start" button; (2) open the "Programs" folder; (3) open the "Licensing Forms" subfolder; and (4) click on the shortcut to the form you want to work with.
- Both Windows and Macintosh users can open a file directly by double clicking on it. Use My Computer or Windows Explorer (Windows 9x, 2000, Me, or XP) or the Finder (Macintosh) to go to the folder you installed or copied the CD-ROM's files to. Then, double click on the specific file you want to open.

- You can also open a file from within your word processor. To do this, you must first start your word processor. Then, go to the File menu and choose the Open command. This opens a dialog box where you will tell the program (1) the type of file you want to open (*.RTF); and (2) the location and name of the file (you will need to navigate through the directory tree to get to the folder on your hard disk where the CD's files have been installed). If these directions are unclear, you will need to look through the manual for your word processing program—Nolo's technical support department will *not* be able to help you with the use of your word processing program.

Where Are the Files Installed?

Windows Users
- RTF files are installed by default to a folder named \Licensing Forms in the \Program Files folder of your computer.

Macintosh Users
- RTF files are located in the "Licensing Forms" folder.

Step 2: Editing Your Document

Fill in the appropriate information according to the instructions and sample agreements in the book. Underlines are used to indicate where you need to enter your information, frequently followed by instructions in brackets. *Be sure to delete the underlines and instructions from your edited document.* If you do not know how to use your word processor to edit a document, you will need to look through the manual for your word processing program—Nolo's technical support department will *not* be able to help you with the use of your word processing program.

Editing Forms That Have Optional or Alternative Text

Some of the forms have check boxes before text. The check boxes indicate:

- Optional text, where you choose whether to include or exclude the given text.
- Alternative text, where you select one alternative to include and exclude the other alternatives.

If you are using the tear-out forms in Appendix B, you simply mark the appropriate box to make your choice.

If you are using the Forms CD-ROM, however, we recommend that instead of marking the check boxes, you do the following:

Optional text

If you **don't want** to include optional text, just delete it from your document.

If you **do want** to include optional text, just leave it in your document.

In either case, delete the check box itself as well as the italicized instructions that the text is optional.

Note: if you choose not to include an optional numbered clause, be sure to renumber all the subsequent clauses after you delete it.

Alternative text

First delete all the alternatives that you do not want to include.

Then delete the remaining check boxes, as well as the italicized instructions that you need to select one of the alternatives provided.

Step 3: Printing Out the Document

Use your word processor's or text editor's "Print" command to print out your document. If you do not know how to use your word processor to print a document, you will need to look through the manual for your word processing program—Nolo's technical support department will *not* be able to help you with the use of your word processing program.

Step 4: Saving Your Document

After filling in the form, use the "Save As" command to save and rename the file. Because all the files are "read-only," you will not be able to use the "Save" command. This is for your protection. *If you save the file without renaming it, the underlines that indicate where you need to enter your information will be lost, and you will not be able to create a new document with this file without recopying the original file from the CD-ROM.*

If you do not know how to use your word processor to save a document, you will need to look through the manual for your word processing program—Nolo's technical support department will *not* be able to help you with the use of your word processing program.

Forms

All of the following forms are provided as tear-out forms in this Appendix. All of the forms are also provided in digital form on the CD-ROM that accompanies this book, except where noted.

Chapter	Section	Form	File Name
2	H1	Text Permission Worksheet	TextWorksheet.rtf
2	H4	Text Permission Letter Agreement	TextLetter.rtf
2	H4	Text Permission Agreement	TextAgreement.rtf
3	E1	Photo Permission Worksheet	PhotoWorksheet.rtf
3	F3	Photo Permission Agreement	PhotoAgreement.rtf
4	G1	Artwork Permission Agreement	ArtAgreement.rtf
4	G3	Agreement to Use Artwork in Motion Picture	ArtFilm.rtf
5	C3	Lyric Permission Letter Agreement	LyricAgreement.rtf
5	E1	Notice of Intention to Obtain Compulsory License for Making and Distributing Sound Recordings	SoundNotice.rtf
5	G1	Music Synchronization and Videogram License Agreement	SynchAgreement.rtf
5	G2	Master Use and Videogram License	MasterUse.rtf
6	C2	Linking Agreement	LinkAgreement.rtf
7	A3	APS/CCC Coursepack Agreement	CCCAgreement.rtf
7	A4	Coursepack Permission Request Form	CoursepackRequest.rtf
7	A4	Coursepack Permission Agreement	CoursepackAgreement.rtf

Chapter	Section	Form	File Name
10	B9	Basic Permission to Use a Trademark in a Book or Magazine	TrademarkBook.rtf
10	B9	Basic Permission to Use a Trademark in a Movie	TrademarkMovie.rtf
10	B9	Basic Permission to Use a Trademark in a Photograph or Artwork	TrademarkPhoto.rtf
10	D3	Trademark License Agreement	TrademarkLicense.rtf
11	B	Merchandise License Agreement	MerchLicense.rtf
11	D	Merchandise License Worksheet	MerchWorksheet.rtf
11	E	Short-Form Merchandise License Agreement	ShortMerch.rtf
12	C2	Unlimited Personal Release Agreement	UnlimitedRelease.rtf
12	C3	Limited Personal Release Agreement	LimitedRelease.rtf
12	D1	Interview Release Agreement	InterviewRelease.rtf
12	D2	Property Release Agreement	PropertyRelease.rtf
13	C2	Search Request Form	Search.rtf
14	A	Permissions Tracking Sheet	Tracking.rtf
15	A1	Basic Copyright Assignment	CopyrightAssign.rtf
15	A3	Musician Assignment Agreement	MusicAssign.rtf
15	A5	Artwork Assignment Agreement	ArtAssign.rtf
15	B4	Work-Made-for-Hire Agreement	WorkAgreement.rtf

Text Permission Worksheet

MATERIAL YOU WANT TO USE: THE "SELECTION"	
Title of text you want to use:	
Name of author:	
Source publication or product from which it came:	
If from a periodical, indicate the ISSN, volume, issue, and date:	
If from a book, indicate the ISBN:	
If from the Internet, indicate the entire URL address (the website address that starts with "http") as it appears when viewing the document:	
Number of pages or segments to be used (actual page numbers are helpful). If you can, provide a word count, since some permission fees are based on word use:	

YOUR INTENDED USE: THE "WORK"	
Title of your publication, program, product, or website:	
Name of publisher or sponsor:	
Type of publication in which the selection will appear (book, periodical, handout, diskette, electronic program, or website):	
If a website, the average number of visitors to the site per month:	
Estimated number of copies to be printed or produced. If a book, include the estimated first print run:	
If copies are to be sold, indicate the price. If copies are free to attendees of an event, indicate the cost of event:	
The date the material will be distributed (for example, the estimated publication date of your book):	
Rights needed (for example, right to reproduce a work, translate a work, or modify the agreement):	

Text Permission Letter Agreement

To _____ ("Licensor"):

I am writing to you to request permission to use the following material.

Licensor Information

Title of Text (the "Selection"): _____

Author: _____

Source publication (or product from which it came): _____

If from a periodical, the ISSN, volume, issue, and date. If from a book, the ISBN:_____

If from the Internet, the entire URL: _____

Number of pages (or actual page numbers) to be used: _____

If you are not the copyright holder or if worldwide rights must be obtained elsewhere, please indicate that information: _____

Licensee Publication Information

The Selection will appear in the following publication(s) (the "Work"): _____

Title: _____

Name of publisher or sponsor ("Licensee"): _____

Author(s): _____

Type of publication: _____

If print publication, estimated print run: _____

If print publication, projected publishing date: _____

If print publication, expected price: $ _____

If website, the URL: _____

If website, estimated monthly hits: _____

If website, the posting date: _____

Rights needed: _____

Fee

Licensee shall pay a fee of $_____ to Licensor at the following address:

_____ upon publication of the Work or within 6 months of executing this agreement, whichever is earlier.

Credit

A standard credit line including your company name will appear where the Selection is used. If you have a special credit line you would prefer, indicate it below:

_____

Samples

Upon publication, Licensee shall furnish _____ copies of the Work to Licensor.

Signed by Licensee: _____

Name: _____

Title: _____

Address: _____

Date: _____

Licensor's Approval of Request

I warrant that I am the owner of rights for the Selection and have the right to grant the permission to republish the materials as specified above. I grant to Licensee and Licensee's successors, licensees, and assigns the nonexclusive worldwide right to republish the Selection in all editions of the Work.

Permission Granted By: _____

Signed by Licensor: _____

Name: _____

Title: _____

Address: _____

Date: _____

Text Permission Agreement

_____ ("Licensor") is the owner of rights for certain textual material defined below (the "Selection"). _____ ("Licensee") wants to acquire the right to use the Selection as specified in this agreement (the "Agreement").

Licensor Information

Title of Text (the "Selection"): _____

Author: _____

Source publication (or product from which it came): _____

If from a periodical, the ISSN, volume, issue, and date. If from a book, the ISBN:_____

If from the Internet, the entire URL: _____

Number of pages or actual page numbers to be used: _____

Licensee Publication Information

The Selection will appear in the following publication(s) (the "Work"): _____

(check if applicable and fill in blanks)

☐ book—title: _____

☐ periodical—title: _____

☐ event handout—title of event: _____

☐ website—URL: _____

☐ diskette—title: _____

Name of publisher or sponsor: _____

Author(s): _____

Estimated date(s) of publication or posting: _____

Estimated number of copies to be printed or produced (if a book, the estimated first print run): _____

If for sale, the price: $ _____

If copies are free to attendees of a program, the cost of program: _____

If a website, the average number of visitors per month: _____

Grant of Rights

Licensor grants to Licensee and Licensee's successors and assigns, the:

(select one)

| | nonexclusive |
| | exclusive |

right to reproduce and distribute the Selection in:

(select all that apply)

	the current edition of the Work.
	all editions of the Work.
	all foreign language versions of the Work.
	all derivative versions of the Work.
	all media now known or later devised.
	promotional materials published and distributed in conjunction with the Work.
	other rights _____

Territory

The rights granted under this Agreement shall be for _____ (the "Territory").

Fees

Licensee shall pay Licensor as follows:

(select one and fill in appropriate blanks)

| | **Flat Fee.** Licensee shall pay Licensor a flat fee of $_____ as full payment for all rights granted. Payment shall be made: |

      ☐ upon execution of this Agreement

      ☐ upon publication

☐ **Royalties and Advance.** Licensee agrees to pay Licensor a royalty of _____ % of Net Sales. Net Sales are defined as gross sales (the gross invoice amount billed customers) less quantity discounts and returns actually credited. Licensee agrees to pay Licensor an advance against royalties of $_____ upon execution of this Agreement. Licensee shall pay Licensor within 30 days after the end of each quarter. Licensee shall furnish an accurate statement of sales during that quarter. Licensor shall have the right to inspect Licensee's books upon reasonable notice.

Credit & Samples

(check if applicable and fill in blanks)

☐ **Credit.** All versions of the Work that include the Selection shall contain the following statement: _____

☐ **Samples.** Upon publication, Licensee shall furnish _____ copies of the Work to Licensor.

Warranty

Licensor warrants that it has the right to grant permission for the uses of the Selection as specified above and that the Selection does not infringe the rights of any third parties.

Miscellaneous

This Agreement may not be amended except in a written document signed by both parties. If a court finds any provision of this Agreement invalid or unenforceable, the remainder of this Agreement shall be interpreted so as best to effect the intent of the parties. This Agreement shall be governed by and interpreted in accordance with the laws of the State of _____. This Agreement expresses the complete understanding of the parties with respect to the subject matter and supersedes all prior representations and understandings.

Licensor	Licensee
By: _____	By: _____
Name: _____	Name: _____
Title: _____	Title: _____
Address: _____	Address: _____
Date: _____	Date: _____
	Tax ID # _____

Photo Permission Worksheet

PHOTOGRAPHIC USE		
Title of publication, program, product, or website in which the photograph will appear:		
Name of publisher or sponsor:		
Type of publication (book, periodical, annual report, handout, diskette, or electronic program):		
Estimated number of copies to be printed or produced. If a book, include the estimated first print run:		
If copies are to be sold, indicate the price. If copies are free to attendees of an event, indicate the cost of event:		
The date the material will be distributed (for example, the estimated publication date of a book or the posting date of a website):		
Will the publication be in any language other than English?	no	yes
If yes, identify which language:		
Website uses:		
Does the site include advertising?	no	yes
Is the site commercial or editorial?	commercial	editorial
Will the photo be used on a home page or an internal page?	home page	internal page
The number of visitors or hits per day:		
Will the photograph be used in both a print publication and a related website (for example, in a magazine and in the magazine's website)?		
If using in a presentation, the sponsor of the presentation, the number of attendees, and the cost of attendance:		
Rights needed:		
(1) reproduction of the photograph		
(2) display of the photograph		
(3) modification of the photograph		

PHOTOGRAPHIC USE (cont.)	
Territory (for example, North American or world rights):	
The format in which you will need the photograph: scan, print, transparency, or digital (if digital, what DPI and file format):	
The date you need the photo:	
If for a film or TV show, the context of the use (supply a synopsis of the plot):	

Photo Permission Agreement

_____ ("Licensor") is the owner of rights for the photograph described below (the "Selection"). _____ ("Licensee") wants to acquire the right to use the Selection as specified in this agreement (the "Agreement").

Licensor Information

Title of work (the "Selection"): _____

Catalogue number (if applicable): _____

Photographer: _____

Licensee Publication Information

The Selection will appear in the following publication(s) (the "Work"):

(check if applicable and fill in blanks)

☐   book—title: _____

☐   periodical—title: _____

☐   event handout—title of event: _____

☐   diskette–title: _____

☐   website—URL: _____

If to be used on a website, the Selection will appear on:

(check if applicable)

☐   home page

☐   internal page

Name of publisher or sponsor (if different from Licensee): _____

Estimated date(s) of publication or posting: _____

If applicable, the estimated number of copies to be printed or produced (if a book, the estimated first print run): _____

If for sale, the price: $ _____

If copies are free to attendees of a program, the cost of program: _____

If a website, the average number of visitors per month: _____

Grant of Rights

Licensor grants to Licensee and Licensee's successors and assigns, the:

(select one)

☐ nonexclusive

☐ exclusive

right to reproduce and distribute the Selection in:

(select all that apply)

☐ the current edition of the Work.

☐ all editions of the Work.

☐ all foreign language versions of the Work.

☐ all derivative versions of the Work.

☐ all media now known or later devised.

☐ promotional materials published and distributed in conjunction with the Work.

☐ other rights _____

Territory

The rights granted under this Agreement shall be for _____ (the "Territory").

Fees

Licensee shall pay Licensor as follows:

(select payment option and fill in blanks)

☐ **Flat Fee.** As full payment for all rights granted, Licensee shall pay Licensor a flat fee of:

$ _____ . Payment shall be made:

☐ upon execution of this Agreement.

☐ upon publication.

☐ **Royalties and Advance.** Licensee agrees to pay Licensor a royalty of____% of Net Sales. Net Sales are defined as gross sales (the gross invoice amount billed to customers) less quantity discounts and returns actually credited. Licensee agrees to pay Licensor an advance against royalties of $_____ upon execution of this Agreement. Licensee shall pay Licensor within thirty

(30) days of the end of each quarter. Licensee shall furnish an accurate statement of sales during that quarter. Licensor shall have the right to inspect Licensee's books upon reasonable notice.

Credit & Samples

(check if applicable and fill in blanks)

[ ] **Credit.** All versions of the Work that include the Selection shall contain the following statement: _____

[ ] **Samples.** Upon publication, Licensee shall furnish _____ copies of the Work to Licensor.

Warranty

Licensor warrants that it has the right to grant permission for the uses of the Selection as specified above and that the Selection does not infringe the rights of any third parties.

(check if applicable)

[ ] Licensor warrants that a model release is on file for the Selection.

Miscellaneous

This Agreement may not be amended except in a written document signed by both parties. If a court finds any provision of this Agreement invalid or unenforceable, the remainder of this Agreement shall be interpreted so as best to effect the intent of the parties. This Agreement shall be governed by and interpreted in accordance with the laws of the State of _____. This Agreement expresses the complete understanding of the parties with respect to the subject matter and supersedes all prior representations and understandings.

Licensor	Licensee
By: _____	By: _____
Name: _____	Name: _____
Title: _____	Title: _____
Address: _____	Address: _____
Date: _____	Date: _____
	Tax ID # _____

Artwork Permission Agreement

_____ ("Licensor") is the owner of rights for the artwork described below (the "Selection"). _____ ("Licensee") wants to acquire the right to use the Selection as specified in this agreement (the "Agreement").

Licensor Information

Title of work (the "Selection"): _____

Catalogue number (if applicable): _____

Artist: _____

Licensee Publication Information

The Selection will appear in the following publication(s) (the "Work"):

(check if applicable and fill in blanks)

☐ book—title: _____

☐ periodical—title: _____

☐ event handout—title of event: _____

☐ diskette–title: _____

☐ website—URL: _____

If to be used on a website, the Selection will appear on:

(check if applicable)

☐ home page

☐ internal page

Name of publisher or sponsor (if different from Licensee): _____

Estimated date(s) of publication or posting: _____

If applicable, the estimated number of copies to be printed or produced (if a book, the estimated first print run): _____

If for sale, the price: $ _____

If copies are free to attendees of a program, the cost of program: _____

If a website, the average number of visitors per month: _____

Grant of Rights

Licensor grants to Licensee and Licensee's successors and assigns, the:

(select one)

☐   nonexclusive

☐   exclusive

right to reproduce and distribute the Selection in:

(select all that apply)

☐   the current edition of the Work.

☐   all editions of the Work.

☐   all foreign language versions of the Work.

☐   all derivative versions of the Work.

☐   all media now known or later devised.

☐   promotional materials published and distributed in conjunction with the Work.

☐   other rights _____

Territory

The rights granted under this Agreement shall be for _____ (the "Territory").

Fees

Licensee shall pay Licensor as follows:

(select payment option and fill in blanks)

☐   **Flat Fee.** As full payment for all rights granted, Licensee shall pay Licensor a flat fee of:

    $ _____ . Payment shall be made:

    ☐   upon execution of this Agreement.

    ☐   upon publication.

☐   **Royalties and Advance.** Licensee agrees to pay Licensor a royalty of____% of Net Sales. Net Sales are defined as gross sales (the gross invoice amount billed to customers) less quantity discounts and returns actually credited. Licensee agrees to pay Licensor an advance against royalties of $_____ upon execution of this Agreement. Licensee shall pay Licensor within thirty

(30) days of the end of each quarter. Licensee shall furnish an accurate statement of sales during that quarter. Licensor shall have the right to inspect Licensee's books upon reasonable notice.

Credit & Samples

(check if applicable and fill in blanks)

☐   **Credit.** All versions of the Work that include the Selection shall contain the following statement: _____

☐   **Samples.** Upon publication, Licensee shall furnish _____ copies of the Work to Licensor.

Warranty

Licensor warrants that it has the right to grant permission for the uses of the Selection as specified above and that the Selection does not infringe the rights of any third parties.

(check if applicable)

☐   Licensor warrants that a model release is on file for the Selection.

Miscellaneous

This Agreement may not be amended except in a written document signed by both parties. If a court finds any provision of this Agreement invalid or unenforceable, the remainder of this Agreement shall be interpreted so as best to effect the intent of the parties. This Agreement shall be governed by and interpreted in accordance with the laws of the State of _____. This Agreement expresses the complete understanding of the parties with respect to the subject matter and supersedes all prior representations and understandings.

Licensor	Licensee
By: _____	By: _____
Name: _____	Name: _____
Title: _____	Title: _____
Address: _____	Address: _____
Date: _____	Date: _____
	Tax ID # _____

Agreement to Use Artwork in Motion Picture

_____ ("Licensor") is the owner of rights for the artwork described below (the "Selection"). _____ ("Licensee") wants to acquire the right to use the Artwork as specified in this agreement (the "Agreement").

Use of the Artwork

The Artwork will appear in:

(choose one)

☐ motion picture

☐ television program

☐ music video

☐ other:

☐ entitled _____ (the "Picture").

Grant of Rights

Licensor grants to Licensee and Licensee's successors and assigns the nonexclusive worldwide right (but not the obligation) to include the Artwork in the Picture for the unlimited distribution, advertising, and promotion of the Picture in all languages and in all forms or devices now known or later devised. This use includes, but is not limited to, use of the Artwork in foreign language versions of the Picture, advertising, publicity or trailers of the Picture, and music videos derived from the Picture.

Limitations on Use

Licensee will use the Artwork in a manner that is consistent with the general practices of the television and motion picture industry. Licensee will not materially alter the Artwork or depict it in any manner that conflicts with the restrictions below, without the consent of Licensor.

Restrictions: _____

Fees

As full payment for all rights granted, Licensee shall pay Licensor a flat fee of $_____. Payment shall be made upon execution of this agreement.

Credit

The Picture shall include the following credit for the Artwork: _____

Warranty & Release

Licensor warrants that it has the right to grant permission for use of the Artwork as specified above and that the Artwork does not infringe upon the rights of any third parties. Licensor waives any claims, known or unknown, arising out of Licensee's use of the Artwork. In the event that Licensee breaches this agreement, Licensor's relief shall be limited to damages and Licensor shall not be entitled to injunctive or equitable relief.

Miscellaneous

This Agreement may not be amended except in a written document signed by both parties. If a court finds any provision of this Agreement invalid or unenforceable, the remainder of this Agreement shall be interpreted so as best to effect the intent of the parties. This Agreement shall be governed by and interpreted in accordance with the laws of the State of _____ . This Agreement expresses the complete understanding of the parties with respect to the subject matter and supersedes all prior representations and understandings.

Licensor	Licensee
By: _____	By: _____
Name: _____	Name: _____
Title: _____	Title: _____
Address: _____	Address: _____
Date: _____	Date: _____
	Tax ID # _____

Lyric Permission Letter Agreement

To _____ ("Music Publisher"):

I am writing to you to obtain permission to reprint portions of the lyrics (the "Lyrics") from the song

_____ , written by _____ on behalf of _____ ("Licensee").

The lyrics will appear in the following publication(s) (the "Work"):

(check if applicable and fill in blanks)

[ ]   Book Use

Book title: _____

Name of publisher or sponsor: _____

Author(s): _____

ISBN: _____

Estimated date(s) of publication: _____

Estimated number of copies to be printed or produced (if a book, the estimated first print run): _____

Language editions: _____

Territory of publication: _____

Estimated price: $ _____

[ ]   Magazine

Magazine title: _____

Volume, issue, ISSN: _____

Estimated date of publication: _____

Circulation: _____

[ ]   Website

URL: _____

Name of publisher or sponsor: _____

Estimated dates of use: _____

Estimated visitors per day: _____

[ ]   Other (describe): _____

_____

Fee

Licensee shall pay a fee of $ _____ to Music Publisher at the following address: _____ upon publication of the Work or within 6 months of executing this Agreement, whichever is earlier.

Samples

Upon publication, Licensee shall furnish _____ copies of the Work to Music Publisher.

Credit

The following credit shall be included with the Work: _____

Signed by Licensee _____

Name: _____

Title: _____

Address: _____

Date: _____

Music Publisher's Approval of Request

Music Publisher warrants that it is the owner of rights for the lyrics and has the right to grant the permission to republish the lyrics as specified above. This license is for the nonexclusive worldwide right to republish the lyrics in all editions of the Work.

Signed by Music Publisher _____

Name: _____

Title: _____

Address: _____

Date: _____

Notice of Intention to Obtain Compulsory License for Making and Distributing Sound Recordings

To _____ , the copyright owner of _____ , written by _____ :

Pursuant to the compulsory license provisions of the U.S. Copyright Act (17 U.S.C. § 1115), we apply

for a license to make and distribute phonorecords of _____ and provide the following

information:

Legal name or entity seeking the compulsory license:	
Fictitious or assumed names used for making and distributing phonorecords:	
Address:	
Business organization:	☐ corporation ☐ LLC ☐ partnership ☐ sole proprietor
Name of individuals who own a beneficial interest of 25% or more in the entity:	
If a corporation, names of the officers and directors:	
Configuration(s) to be made under the compulsory license (check all that apply):	☐ 7- or 12-inch vinyl single ☐ 12-inch long-playing vinyl record ☐ cassette ☐ compact disc ☐ minidisc ☐ digital cassette recording
Catalogue number(s):	
Label name(s):	
Principal recording artists:	
Anticipated date of initial release:	
We agree to pay the copyright owner royalties at the statutory rate provided by the Copyright Act. Date:_____ By:_____ Name/Title:_____	

Music Synchronization and Videogram License Agreement

Music Synchronization and Videogram License Agreement (the "Agreement") is made between:

_____ ("Publisher") and _____ ("Producer").

Publisher is the owner of rights for the compositions listed below:

_____

_____

(the "Compositions").

Producer is the owner of rights for the Motion Picture tentatively entitled _____

(the "Motion Picture"). Producer desires to license the Compositions for use in the Motion Picture and in audiovisual devices for home use such as videotapes and DVDs ("Videograms"). The parties agree as follows:

Grant

(select one or more Grant provisions)

☐ **Grant of Audiovisual License.** Publisher grants to Producer and Producer's successors and assigns the nonexclusive right to record the Compositions solely in synchronization with the Motion Picture (in any medium, now known or later created) within the Territory. Publisher grants to Producer the right to publicly perform the Compositions solely in synchronization to the Motion Picture within the Territory. These public performance rights include public exhibitions of the Motion Picture in theaters and other public places where motion pictures are customarily exhibited, provided that performances outside the United States are cleared by performing rights societies in accordance with customary practice and customary fees. The public performance rights also include television exhibition of the Motion Picture within the Territory, including all methods of television reproduction and transmissions, provided that the entities broadcasting those performances have licenses from the appropriate performing rights societies. Any television performance not licensed by performing rights societies must be cleared directly by the Publisher.

☐ **Grant of Videogram License.** Publisher grants to Producer and his successors and assigns the nonexclusive right to record, copy, and synchronize the Composition, solely as part of the Motion Picture, on audiovisual devices including, but not limited to, video cassettes, DVDs, and similar compact audiovisual devices that reproduce the entire Motion Picture in substantially its original form ("Videogram"). This Videogram license is solely for the distribution of Videograms intended primarily for home use in the Territory.

☐ **Use in Trailers.** Publisher grants to Producer and his successors and assigns, the nonexclusive right to record, copy, synchronize, and perform the Composition in connection with trailers used for the advertising and exploitation of the Motion Picture.

Reservation of Rights

Publisher reserves all rights not granted in this Agreement.

Modifications to Composition

Producer shall not make any change in the original lyrics, if any, or in the fundamental character of the music of the Composition or use the title or any portion of the lyrics of the Composition as the title or subtitle of the Motion Picture without written prior authorization from Publisher.

Territory

The rights granted in this Agreement are for the following: _____ (the "Territory").

Audiovisual License Payments

As payment for the rights granted for the Audiovisual License, Producer shall pay Publisher as follows:

(select payment option and fill in blanks)

☐ **One-Time Payment.** Producer shall pay Publisher a one-time payment of $ _____ upon first public performance of the Motion Picture or within nine (9) months of signing this agreement, whichever is earlier.

☐ **Advance and Royalties.** Producer shall pay Publisher a nonrefundable advance ("Motion Picture Advance") in the sum of $ _____ recoupable against royalties derived from the Audiovisual License ("Audiovisual Royalties"). Producer shall pay Publisher Audiovisual Royalties of ___% of net profits from the public exhibition and public performance of the Motion Picture.

☐ **Royalties.** Producer shall pay Publisher _____ % of the net profits from the public exhibition and public performance of the Motion Picture.

Videogram License Payments

As payment for the rights granted for the Videogram License, Producer shall pay Publisher as follows: (select payment option and fill in blanks)

☐ **One-Time Payment.** Producer shall pay Publisher a one-time payment of $_____ within nine (9) months of signing this agreement.

☐ **Advance and Royalties.** Producer shall pay Publisher a nonrefundable advance ("Videogram Advance") in the sum of $ _____ recoupable against royalties derived from the Videogram License ("Videogram Royalties"). Videogram Royalties for Videogram copies of the Motion Picture shall be paid as follows:

☐ **Net Profits.** Producer shall pay Publisher_____% of the Producer's net profits for all Videogram revenues including all sales, licenses, or other sources of revenue for Videogram distribution (not including shipping charges or taxes).

☐ **Pro Rata Option.** Producer shall pay Publisher_____% ("Publisher's Pro-Rata Portion") of_____% of the net revenue for all Videogram income including all sales, licenses, or other sources of revenue for Videogram distribution. Publisher's Pro-Rata Portion represents the proportion the Composition bears to the total number of Royalty-bearing compositions contained in the Motion Picture.

Payments & Statements

Within forty-five (45) days after the end of each calendar quarter (the "Royalty Period"), Producer shall furnish an accurate statement of net revenues derived from the licenses granted in this agreement along with any royalty payments. Producer may withhold a reasonable reserve for anticipated returns, refunds, and exchanges of Videograms, and this reserve shall be liquidated no later than twelve (12) months after the respective accounting statement.

Favorable Rates

If a higher royalty rate than set forth in this Agreement becomes payable by operation of law with respect to Videograms sold in a particular country within the Territory, Producer shall either pay the higher royalty to Publisher with respect to that country or delete the Compositions from the Motion Picture with respect to this country. In the event that a musical composition is licensed for a substantially similar use in connection with the Videogram exploitation of the Motion Picture on a more favorable rate, Producer agrees that such favorable rate shall also be granted to Publisher for the licensing of the Composition.

Audit

Producer shall keep accurate books of account and records covering all transactions relating to the licenses granted in this Agreement, and Publisher or its duly authorized representatives shall have the right upon five (5) days prior written notice, and during normal business hours, to inspect and audit these accounts and records.

Warranty

Publisher warrants that it has the power and authority to grant the rights in this Agreement and that the Compositions do not infringe any third-party rights. In no event shall Publisher's liability for a breach of this Warranty exceed the amount of payments received under this Agreement.

Credits

Publisher shall receive credit in the following form: _____

This credit shall be provided as follows:

(select all that apply)

☐ similar to all other musical compositions used in the Motion Picture.

☐ a single card in the main titles on all prints of the Motion Picture and Videograms.

☐ in all paid advertising similar to all other musical compositions used in the Motion Picture.

Samples

Producer shall promptly furnish Publisher with _____ copies of each format of Videogram release.

Cue Sheets

Producer agrees to furnish Publisher a cue sheet of the Motion Picture within thirty (30) days after the first public exhibition of the Motion Picture.

Term

The term of this Agreement is for the term of United States copyright in the Composition including renewal terms, if any.

Termination & Breach

In the event that Producer (or Producer's assigns or licensees) breach this Agreement and fails to cure such breach within thirty (30) days after notice by Publisher to Producer, this license will automatically terminate and all rights granted under this Agreement shall revert to Publisher. Failure to make timely payments or to provide credit as provided in this Agreement shall be considered a material breach of this Agreement.

Miscellaneous

This Agreement may not be amended except in a writing signed by both parties. If a court finds any provision of this Agreement invalid or unenforceable, the remainder of this Agreement shall be interpreted so as best to effect the intent of the parties. This Agreement shall be governed by and interpreted in accordance with the laws of the State of _____ . This Agreement expresses the complete understanding of the parties with respect to the subject matter and supersedes all prior representations and understandings. Any controversy or claim arising out of or relating to this Agreement shall be settled by binding arbitration in accordance with the rules of the American Arbitration Association, and judgment upon the award rendered by the arbitrator(s) may be entered in any court having jurisdiction. All notices provided for under this Agreement must be in writing and mailed to the addresses provided in the signature portion of this Agreement.

_____

PUBLISHER

_____

PRODUCER

Master Use and Videogram License

This Master Use and Videogram License Agreement (the "Agreement") is made between:

_____ ("Owner") and _____ ("Producer").

Owner is the owner of rights for the master recordings: _____

_____

_____

(the "Masters").

Producer is the owner of rights for the Motion Picture tentatively entitled _____

(the "Motion Picture").

Producer desires to license the Masters for use in the Motion Picture and in audiovisual devices for home use such as videotapes and DVDs ("Videograms"). The parties agree as follows:

Grant

(select one or more Grant provisions if applicable)

☐ **Grant of Audiovisual License.** Owner grants to Producer and Producer's successors and assigns the nonexclusive right to use and reproduce the Masters solely in synchronization with the Motion Picture in any medium, now known or later created within the Territory. Owner grants to Producer the right to publicly perform the Masters solely in synchronization to the Motion Picture within the Territory. These public performance rights include the public exhibitions of the Motion Picture in theaters and other public places where motion pictures are customarily exhibited and for television exhibition of the Motion Picture including all methods of television reproduction and transmissions within the Territory.

☐ **Grant of Videogram License.** Owner grants to Producer and Producer's successors and assigns the nonexclusive right to record, copy, and synchronize the Masters, solely as part of the Motion Picture, on audiovisual devices including, but not limited to video cassettes, DVDs, and similar compact audiovisual devices that reproduce the entire motion picture in substantially its original form ("Videogram"). This Videogram license is solely for the distribution of Videograms intended primarily for home use in the Territory.

☐ **Use in Trailers.** Owner grants to Producer and Producer's successors and assigns, the nonexclusive right to record, copy, synchronize, and perform the Masters in connection with trailers used for the advertising and exploitation of the Motion Picture.

Reservation of Rights

Owner reserves all rights not granted in this Agreement.

Modifications to Masters

Producer shall not make any change in the Masters without written prior authorization from Owner.

Territory

The rights granted in this Agreement are for the following: _____
(the "Territory").

Union Reuse Fees

Owner agrees to provide Producer with all information regarding any reuse fees required by unions or guilds as a result of this license. Producer agrees to pay all such reuse payments including related pension or welfare payments and to indemnify Owner from claims arising from such payments.

Musical Works Synchronization Rights

Producer agrees to obtain all appropriate synchronization, performance, and reproduction rights for the musical compositions embodied on the Masters and to indemnify Owner for any claims arising from such rights.

Audiovisual License Payments

As payment for the rights granted for the Audiovisual License, Producer shall pay Owner as follows:
(select payment option and fill in blanks)

☐ **One-Time Payment.** Producer shall pay Owner a one-time payment of $ _____ upon first public performance of the Motion Picture or within nine (9) months of signing this agreement, whichever is earlier.

☐ **Advance and Royalties.** Producer shall pay Owner a nonrefundable advance ("Motion Picture Advance") in the sum of $ _____ recoupable against royalties derived from the Audiovisual License ("Audiovisual Royalties"). Producer shall pay Owner Audiovisual Royalties of __% of net profits from the public exhibition and public performance of the Motion Picture.

☐ **Royalties.** Producer shall pay Owner _____% of the net profits from the public exhibition and public performance of the Motion Picture.

Videogram License Payments

As payment for the rights granted for the Videogram License, Producer shall pay Owner as follows: (select payment option and fill in blanks)

☐ **One-Time Payment.** Producer shall pay Owner a one-time payment of $_____ within nine (9) months of signing this agreement.

☐ **Advance and Royalties.** Producer shall pay Owner a nonrefundable advance ("Videogram Advance") in the sum of $ _____ recoupable against royalties derived from the Videogram License ("Videogram Royalties"). Videogram Royalties for Videogram copies of the Motion Picture shall be paid as follows:

☐ **Net Profits.** Producer shall pay Owner _____% of the Producer's net profits for all Videogram revenues including all sales, licenses, or other sources of revenue for Videogram distribution (not including shipping charges or taxes).

☐ **Pro Rata Option.** Producer shall pay Owner _____% ("Owner's Pro-Rata Portion") of _____% of the net revenue for all Videogram income including all sales, licenses, or other sources of revenue for Videogram distribution. Owner's Pro-Rata Portion represents the proportion the Composition bears to the total number of Royalty-bearing compositions contained in the Motion Picture.

Payments & Statements

Within forty-five (45) days after the end of each calendar quarter (the "Royalty Period"), Producer shall furnish an accurate statement of net revenues derived from the licenses granted in this agreement along with any royalty payments. Producer may withhold a reasonable reserve for anticipated returns, refunds, and exchanges of Videograms, and this reserve shall be liquidated no later than twelve (12) months after the respective accounting statement.

Audit

Producer shall keep accurate books of account and records covering all transactions relating to the licenses granted in this Agreement, and Owner or its duly authorized representatives shall have the right upon five (5) days prior written notice, and during normal business hours, to inspect and audit these accounts and records.

Warranty

Owner warrants that it has the power and authority to grant the rights in this Agreement and that the Masters do not infringe any third-party rights. In no event shall Owner's liability for a breach of this warranty exceed the amount of payments received under this Agreement.

Credits

Owner shall receive credit in the following form: _____

This credit shall be provided as follows:

(select one or more if appropriate)

☐   similar to all other Masters used in the Motion Picture.

☐   in all paid advertising similar to all other musical Masters used in the Motion Picture.

Samples

Producer shall promptly furnish Owner with ___ copies of each format of Videogram release.

Cue Sheets

Producer agrees to furnish Owner a cue sheet of the Motion Picture within thirty (30) days after the first public exhibition of the Motion Picture.

Term

The term of this Agreement is for the term of United States copyright in the Masters including renewal terms, if any.

Termination & Breach

In the event that Producer (or Producer's assigns or licensees) breach this Agreement and fails to cure such breach within thirty (30) days after notice by Owner to Producer, this license will automatically terminate and all rights granted under this Agreement shall revert to Owner. Failure to make timely payments or to provide credit as provided in this Agreement shall be considered a material breach of this Agreement.

Miscellaneous

This Agreement may not be amended except in a writing signed by both parties. If a court finds any provision of this Agreement invalid or unenforceable, the remainder of this Agreement shall be interpreted so as best to effect the intent of the parties. This Agreement shall be governed by and interpreted in accordance with the laws of the State of _____ . This Agreement expresses the complete understanding of the parties with respect to the subject matter and supersedes all prior representations and understandings. Any controversy or claim arising out of or relating to this Agreement shall be settled by binding arbitration in accordance with the rules of the American Arbitration Association, and judgment upon the award rendered by the arbitrator(s) may be entered in any court having jurisdiction. All notices provided for under this Agreement must be in writing and mailed to the addresses provided in the signature portion of this Agreement.

_____

OWNER
_____

PRODUCER

Linking Agreement

This Agreement (the "Agreement") is made between _____ ("Source Site"), with its home page URL of_____, and _____ ("Destination Site"), with its home page URL of_____ .

The parties agree as follows:

The Link

Source Site will provide a link to the Destination Site as follows:_____

_____ (the "Link")

The Link includes Destination Site's URL and:

(select if appropriate)

☐   Hypertext link—the words: _____ .

☐   Image link: _____ .

☐   Framed link:_____ .

Grant

Destination Site grants the right to display the Link at Source Site and the nonexclusive right to display publicly the trademarks or images in the Link. Source Site obtains no trademark rights under this Agreement other than the right to display the marks. Any goodwill associated with Source Site's trademarks automatically vests in Destination Site.

Standards and Notifications

(select if appropriate)

☐   Source Site shall maintain its site in accordance with industry standards and, upon notice from Destination Site, shall promptly remove the Link if required. Source Site shall promptly notify Destination Site of any change to the Link or to Source Site that affects the Link.

By: _____

Date: _____

Source Site Title:_____

Source Site Mailing Address: _____

_____

email: _____

By: _____

Date: _____

Destination Site Title: _____

Destination Site Mailing Address:_____

_____

email: _____

APS/CCC Coursepack Agreement
(courtesy Copyright Clearance Center)

PERMISSIONS AGREEMENT made this ———— day of ———————— , ———— , between the Copyright Clearance Center, Inc. ("CCC") and ————————————————————— ("User").

1. Nature and Form of Program. This Agreement provides for participation by User in CCC's Academic Permissions Service ("APS"). The APS grants authorizations to photocopy and to create photocopy anthologies for sale and/or distribution to students and other academic customers. The copies and anthologies may be made and assembled by faculty members individually or at their request by on-campus bookstores or copy centers, or by off-campus copy shops and other similar entities. It does not permit "publishing ventures" where any particular anthology would be systematically marketed at multiple institutions. User acknowledges that the holders of copyright rights have complete discretion under the United States Copyright Act, 17 United States Code, whether to grant any permission, and whether to place any limitations on any grant, and that CCC has no right to supersede or to modify any such discretionary act by a rightsholder.

2. Grant of Permissions. In order to receive a permission to photocopy a portion of a printed publication, User must first submit to CCC a form as prescribed in CCC's published APS Guidelines. CCC shall not accept any form that is not complete. Within CCC's published response time (measured from CCC's receipt of a completed form), CCC shall notify User whether or not a permission has been granted and the royalty fee due, if any. CCC shall notify User of any limitations imposed by a rightsholder on that permission and, unless User notifies CCC of its intention to decline any particular permission, User shall pay the amount due as set forth in the notification and shall be bound by any such limitation. Any act by User that involves copying beyond that set forth in the notification shall be deemed in its entirety to be an unpermitted act of copying. Separate portions of a work, even if they are to be included in the same anthology, shall require a separate permission under the APS.

3. Payment for Permissions. User shall pay to CCC the amount set forth in the permissions notification in full payment for any permission set forth therein (which will include both the amount due to the rightsholder and the service fee payable to CCC), within the time set forth therein. In the event of a failure by User to pay any such amount by the due date, the applicable permission shall be null and void. In the event that User sells fewer copies than the number for which permissions were granted, User shall pay CCC only for the total number of copies sold, and permissions for the unsold copies shall be null and void.

4. General Terms and Conditions of the Program. Subject to any further limitations determined by any particular rightsholder, the copying permitted under the APS is limited as follows:

(i)   no more than 25% of the text of a book or of the items in a published collection of essays, poems, or articles may be copied;

(ii)   no more than the greater of (A) 25% of the text of an issue or of a journal or other periodical, or (B) two articles from such an issue, may be copied;

(iii)   no User may sell or distribute any particular anthology at more than one institution of learning;

(iv)   each copy sold by User must contain a proper copyright notice, identifying the copyright rightsholder in whose name CCC has granted permission and a statement to the effect that such copy was made pursuant to permission; and

(v)   no materials may be entered into electronic memory by User except in order to produce an identical copy of a work before or during the academic term (or analogous period) as to which any particular permission is granted.

In the event that User shall choose to retain the materials in electronic memory for purposes of producing identical copies more than one day after such retention (but still within the scope of any permission granted), User must notify CCC of such fact in the applicable permission request form and such retention shall constitute one copy actually sold for purposes of calculating permissions fees. No permission granted under the APS shall in any way include any right by User to create a non-identical copy of the work or to edit or in any other way modify the work (except by means of deleting material immediately preceding or following the entire portion of the work copied).

5. Term and Termination. This Agreement shall be in force beginning as of the date hereof and shall continue for an initial period of one year. This Agreement is automatically renewable for subsequent one-year periods in the absence of timely notice of termination. Either party may terminate this Agreement for any reason by giving 90 days' prior written notice thereof to the other party. In the event of termination of this Agreement for any reason, any permissions the periods of which have not yet ended shall remain in effect until their respective terminations. Termination of this Agreement shall have no effect on any party's obligation to pay money to the other party.

6. Warranty. Each copyright rightsholder which has granted CCC the right to grant permission under the APS to use any particular Work has warranted that it has all rights necessary to authorize CCC to act on its behalf.

7. Books and Records; Right to Audit. As to each permission granted under the APS, User shall maintain for at least four full calendar years books and records sufficient for CCC to determine the numbers of copies made by user under such permission. CCC and any representatives it may designate shall have the right to audit such books and records at any time during User's ordinary business hours, upon two days' prior notice. If any such audit shall determine that User shall have underpaid for, or underreported, any copies sold by three percent (3%) or more, then User shall bear all the costs of any such audit; otherwise, CCC shall bear the costs of any such audit. Any amount determined by such audit to have been underpaid by User shall immediately be paid to CCC by User, together with interest thereon at the rate of 10% per annum from the date such amount was originally due. The provisions of this paragraph shall survive the termination of this Agreement for any reason.

8. Notices. All notices and communications under this Agreement shall be in writing addressed, in the case of User, to the person designated below, and in the case of CCC, its President, and shall be deemed to have been given on the day of delivery or transmission if delivered by hand or if sent by electronic mail or facsimile transmission (with receipt confirmed), or on the fifth business day following the day of mailing if mailed, postage prepaid:

Person and/or title: _____

Address: _____

(if different from that set forth at end of Agreement)

Telephone Number: _____

Facsimile Number: _____

Email Address: _____

9. No Assignment; Integrated Agreement; Governing Law. Neither party to this Agreement shall have the right to assign or sublicense any of its rights or obligations hereunder without the prior written consent of the other party. This agreement constitutes the entire agreement between the parties with respect to the subject matter hereof and may not be modified or amended except in a writing signed by the parties hereto. This Agreement shall be interpreted, construed, governed, and enforced in accordance with and under the laws of the State of New York, without giving effect to the principles thereof of conflicts of law.

User's Name: _____

Address: _____

Signature: _____

Printed Name: _____

Title: _____

Copyright Clearance Center, Inc.

222 Rosewood Drive

Danvers, Massachusetts 01923 USA

Signature: _____

Coursepack Permission Request Form
(Association of Academic Publishers)

To:

Publisher Contact: _____

Publisher: _____

Fax Number: _____

Date of Request: _____

From:

Your Name: _____

Department: _____

School name: _____

Address: _____

City: _____

State: _____

Zip code: _____

Phone #: _____

Fax #: _____

Course name and number: _____

Number of copies needed: _____

Instructor: _____

Semester and year: _____

ISBN/ISSN number: _____

Book or journal title: _____

Author: _____

Translator: _____

Editor: _____

Edition: _____

Volume: _____

Copyright year: _____

Publication year: _____

Chapter/article title: _____

Chapter/article author: _____

Page numbers: _____

Total pages: _____

Is it an out-of-print work? _____

Have you included a copy of the material with this request? _____

Are you the author? _____

Permission is requested for use during one term only. _____

Coursepack Permission Agreement

_____ ("Licensor")

_____ ("User")

Department: _____

School Name: _____

Course name and number: _____ ("the Course").

Date when Course starts: _____ (the "Course date").

Authorization

Licensor authorizes User to photocopy the Selection, as defined below, for purposes of creating a photocopy anthology (the "Coursepack") for sale or distribution to students and academic customers in the Course.

Number of Copies & Assembly

_____ copies of the Coursepack shall be assembled and distributed for the Course:

☐ by User

☐ by on-campus bookstores or copy centers, or

☐ by off-campus copy shops.

Number of pages (or actual page numbers) to be used _____ .

The permission granted in this Agreement is limited to the Course and institution listed above and to be used for one semester only. Any further rights must be negotiated separately.

Material for Which Permission Is Sought

Title of text or artwork: _____ (the "Selection").

Author: _____

Source publication (or product from which it came): _____ .

If from a periodical, the ISSN, volume, issue, and date. If from a book, the ISBN:_____ .

If from the Internet, the entire URL address: _____ .

Credit

A standard credit line including Licensor's name will appear where the Selection is used. If you have a special credit line you would prefer, indicate it here: _____ .

Fee

User shall pay a fee of $ _____ to Licensor at the following address: _____

_____ within 30 days of commencement date, listed above.

Warranty

Licensor warrants that it is the owner of rights for the Selection and has the right to grant the permission to republish the materials as specified above.

_____ (User signature)

Name: _____

Title: _____

Address: _____

Date: _____

Permission Granted By:

_____ (Licensor signature)

Name: _____

Title: _____

Address: _____

Date: _____

Basic Permission to Use a Trademark in a Book or Magazine

_____ ("Owner") is the owner of rights in the trademark_____ (the "Trademark"). Owner grants permission to reproduce the Trademark in the format indicated below in the publication _____ and in any subsequent editions or derivative versions in any media. Any goodwill associated with the Trademark vests in Owner.

Owner Name: _____

Signature: _____

Date: _____

[Insert Sample of Trademark]

Basic Permission to Use a Trademark in a Movie

_____ ("Owner") is the owner of rights in the trademark _____ (the "Trademark"). Owner grants permission to reproduce the Trademark in the format indicated below in all versions of the film _____ (the "Film") and any derivative versions in any media. Any goodwill associated with the Trademark vests in Owner.

Owner Name: _____

Signature: _____

Date: _____

[Insert Sample of Trademark]

Basic Permission to Use a Trademark in a Photograph or Artwork

_____ ("Owner") is the owner of rights in trademark _____

(the "Trademark"). Owner grants permission to reproduce the Trademark in the format indicated

below in all versions of the artwork _____ (the "Artwork") and any derivative versions

in any media. Any goodwill associated with the Trademark vests in Owner.

Owner Name: _____

Signature: _____

Date: _____

[Insert Sample of Trademark]

Trademark License Agreement

Introduction

This Trademark License Agreement (the "Agreement") is made between _____
(referred to as "Licensor") and _____ (referred to as "Licensee").

The parties agree as follows:

The Trademarks

The "Trademarks" refer to any trademark, service mark, trade name, logo, or other device and its
associated goodwill used to identify and distinguish Licensor's products and services as included in
Exhibit A. Licensor is the owner of all rights to the Trademarks, and Licensee shall not claim any right
to use the Trademarks except under the terms of this Agreement.

Licensed Products

Licensed Products are defined as Licensee's products incorporating the Trademarks specifically
described in Exhibit A (the "Licensed Products").

Grant of Rights

Licensor grants to Licensee:

(select one)

☐   an exclusive license

☐   a nonexclusive license

to reproduce and distribute the Trademarks on the Licensed Products.

Sublicense

(select one)

☐   **Consent required.** Licensee may sublicense the rights granted pursuant to this Agreement
provided: Licensee obtains Licensor's prior written consent to such sublicense; and Licensor
receives such revenue or royalty payment as provided in the Payment section below. Any
sublicense granted in violation of this provision shall be void.

☐ **No sublicensing permitted.** Licensee may not sublicense the rights granted under this Agreement.

Reservation of Rights & Assignment of Goodwill

Licensor reserves all rights other than those being conveyed or granted in this Agreement. Licensee assigns to Licensor any goodwill from the Trademarks that may accrue under this Agreement or from the distribution of the Licensed Products and agrees that all uses of the Trademarks shall inure to Licensor. Licensee's rights to the Trademarks are only in connection with the Licensed Products and Licensee shall not assert any other association with Licensor or the Trademarks. Licensee acknowledges the validity of the Trademarks and agrees not to challenge Licensor's ownership of the Trademarks or their validity.

Territory

The rights granted to Licensee are limited to _____ (the "Territory").

Term

The "Effective Date" of this Agreement is defined as the date when the agreement commences and is established by the latest signature date.

(select one)

☐ **Specified term with renewal rights.** This Agreement shall commence upon the Effective Date and shall extend for a period of _____ years (the "Initial Term"). Following the Initial Term, Licensee may renew this Agreement under the same terms and conditions for___ consecutive _____ periods (the "Renewal Terms"), provided that Licensee provides written notice of its intention to renew this Agreement within thirty (30) days before the expiration of the current term.

☐ **Term with renewal based upon sales.** This Agreement shall commence upon the Effective Date and shall extend for a period of _____ years (the "Initial Term") and may be renewed by Licensee under the same terms and conditions for consecutive _____ year periods (the "Renewal Terms"), provided that:

(a) Licensee provides written notice of its intention to renew this Agreement within thirty days before the expiration of the current term; and

(b) Licensee has met the sales requirements as established in Exhibit A.

☐   **Indefinite term.** This Agreement shall commence upon the Effective Date and shall continue until terminated pursuant to a provision of this Agreement.

☐   **Fixed term.** This Agreement shall commence upon the Effective Date and shall continue for _____ unless sooner terminated pursuant to a provision of this Agreement.

☐   **Term for as long as Licensee sells Licensed Products.** This Agreement shall commence upon the Effective Date as specified in Exhibit A and shall continue for as long as Licensee continues to offer the Licensed Products in commercially reasonable quantities or unless sooner terminated pursuant to a provision of this Agreement.

Approval of Samples & Quality Control

Preproduction. Licensee shall submit to Licensor a reasonable number of preproduction designs and prototypes at no cost prior to production, as well as production samples of every Licensed Product to assure that the product meets Licensor's quality standards. Licensee agrees not to distribute any Licensed Product until receipt of Licensor's written approval of such Licensed Product.

Production and Promotion. At least once every six (6) months, Licensee shall submit to Licensor two (2) production samples of each Licensed Product for review. Licensee shall pay all costs for delivery of these materials. In the event that any production sample does not meet Licensor's quality standards, Licensee agrees to immediately correct such deficiencies. Licensor shall have the right to inspect Licensee's premises upon reasonable notice for purposes of observing the manufacturing process. Licensee shall submit all advertising and promotional materials to Licensor and shall not distribute such materials until receipt of written approval from Licensor.

Royalties

All royalties ("Royalties") provided for under this Agreement shall accrue when the respective Licensed Products are sold, shipped, distributed, billed, or paid for, whichever occurs first.

Net Sales

"Net Sales" are defined as Licensee's gross sales (the gross invoice amount billed to customers) less quantity discounts or rebates and returns actually credited. A quantity discount or rebate is a discount made at the time of shipment. No deductions shall be made for cash or other discounts, commissions, manufacturing costs, uncollectible accounts, or for fees or expenses of any kind that the Licensee may incur in connection with the Royalty payments.

Fees

(select one or more provisions)

☐   **Advance Against Royalties.** As a nonrefundable advance against royalties (the "Advance"), Licensee agrees to pay to Licensor upon execution of this Agreement the sum of $_____ .

☐   **Licensed Product Royalty.** Licensee agrees to pay a Royalty of____ % percent of all Net Sales revenue of the Licensed Products ("Licensed Product Royalty").

       Per Unit Royalty. Licensee agrees to pay a Royalty of $___ for each unit of the Licensed Product that is ☐ manufactured ☐ sold [select one].

☐   **Guaranteed Minimum Annual Royalty Payment.** In addition to any other advances or fees, Licensee shall pay an annual guaranteed royalty (the "GMAR") as follows: $_____ . The GMAR shall be paid to Licensor annually on_____ . The GMAR is an advance against royalties for the twelve-month (12-month) period commencing upon payment. Royalty payments based on Net Sales made during any year of this Agreement shall be credited against the GMAR due for the year in which such Net Sales were made. In the event that annual royalties exceed the GMAR, Licensee shall pay the difference to Licensor. Any annual royalty payments in excess of the GMAR shall not be carried forward from previous years or applied against the GMAR.

☐   **License Fee.** As a nonrefundable, nonrecoupable fee for executing this license, Licensee agrees to pay to Licensor upon execution of this Agreement the sum of $_____ .

☐   **Sublicensing Revenues.** In the event of any sublicense of the rights granted pursuant to this Agreement, Licensee shall pay to Licensor _____% percent of all sublicensing revenues.

Payments and Statements to Licensor

Within thirty (30) days after the end of each calendar quarter (the "Royalty Period"), an accurate statement of Net Sales of Licensed Products along with any royalty payments or sublicensing revenues due to Licensor shall be provided to Licensor, regardless of whether any Licensed Products were sold during the Royalty Period. All payments shall be paid in United States currency drawn on a United States bank. The acceptance by Licensor of any of the statements furnished or royalties paid shall not preclude Licensor questioning the correctness at any time of any payments or statements.

Audit

Licensee shall keep accurate books of account and records covering all transactions relating to the license granted in this Agreement, and Licensor or its duly authorized representatives shall have the right upon five days prior written notice, and during normal business hours, to inspect and audit Licensee's records relating to the Licensed Products under this Agreement. Licensor shall bear the cost of such inspection and audit, unless the results indicate an underpayment greater than $ _____ for any six-month (6-month) period. In that case, Licensee shall promptly reimburse Licensor for all costs of the audit along with the amount due with interest on such sums. Interest shall accrue from the date the payment was originally due and the interest rate shall be 1.5% per month, or the maximum rate permitted by law, whichever is less. All books of account and records shall be made available in the United States and kept available for at least two years after the termination of this Agreement.

Late Payment

Time is of the essence with respect to all payments to be made by Licensee under this Agreement. If Licensee is late in any payment provided for in this Agreement, Licensee shall pay interest on the payment from the date due until paid at a rate of 1.5% per month, or the maximum rate permitted by law, whichever is less.

Licensor Warranties

Licensor warrants that it has the power and authority to enter into this Agreement and has no knowledge as to any third-party claims regarding the proprietary rights in the Trademarks that would interfere with the rights granted under this Agreement.

Indemnification by Licensor

(select one if appropriate)

☐ **Licensor indemnification without limitations.** Licensor shall indemnify Licensee and hold Licensee harmless from any damages and liabilities (including reasonable attorney fees and costs) arising from any breach of Licensor's warranties as defined in Licensor's Warranties, above.

☐ **Licensor indemnification limited to amounts paid.** Licensor shall indemnify Licensee and hold Licensee harmless from any damages and liabilities (including reasonable attorney fees and costs) arising from any breach of Licensor's warranties as defined in Licensor's Warranties, above. Licensor's maximum liability under this provision shall in no event exceed the total amount earned by Licensor under this Agreement.

Licensee Warranties

Licensee warrants that it will use its best commercial efforts to market the Licensed Products and that sale and marketing of the Licensed Products shall be in conformance with all applicable laws and regulations, including but not limited to all intellectual property laws.

Indemnification by Licensee

Licensee shall indemnify Licensor and hold Licensor harmless from any damages and liabilities (including reasonable attorney fees and costs) arising from any breach of Licensee's warranties and representation as defined in the Licensee Warranties above or arising out of any alleged defects of the Licensed Products, any product liability claims, or any claims arising out of advertising, distribution, or marketing of the Licensed Products.

Intellectual Property Rights

The license granted in this Agreement is conditioned on Licensee's compliance with the provisions of the intellectual property laws of the United States and any foreign country in the Territory.

Proprietary Notices

Licensee shall identify Licensor as the owner of rights to the Trademarks and shall include the notices provided in Exhibit A on all copies of the Licensed Products.

Infringement Against Third Parties

In the event that either party learns of imitations or infringements of the Trademarks or Licensed Products, that party shall notify the other in writing of the infringements or imitations. Licensor shall have the right to commence lawsuits against third persons arising from infringement of the Trademarks or Licensed Products. In the event that Licensor does not commence a lawsuit against an alleged infringer within sixty (60) days of notification by Licensee, Licensee may commence a lawsuit against the third party. Before filing suit, Licensee shall obtain the written consent of Licensor to do so, and such consent shall not be unreasonably withheld. Licensor will cooperate fully and in good faith with Licensee for the purpose of securing and preserving Licensee's rights to the Trademarks.

Any recovery (including, but not limited to a judgment, settlement, or licensing agreement included as resolution of an infringement dispute) shall be divided equally between the parties after deduction and payment of reasonable attorney fees to the party bringing the lawsuit.

Exploitation Date

Licensee agrees to manufacture, distribute, and sell the Licensed Products in commercially reasonable quantities during the term of this Agreement and to commence such manufacture, distribution, and sale by _____ . This is a material provision of this Agreement.

Advertising Budget

(select if appropriate)

☐ Licensee agrees to spend at least _____% of estimated annual gross sales for promotional efforts and advertising of the Licensed Products.

Licensor Copies and Right to Purchase

Licensee shall provide Licensor with _____ copies of each Licensed Product. Licensor has the right to purchase from Licensee, at Licensee's manufacturing cost, at least _____ copies of any Licensed Product, and such payments shall be deducted from royalties due to Licensor.

Confidentiality

The parties acknowledge that each may have access to confidential information that relates to each other's business (the "Information"). The parties agree to protect the confidentiality of the Information and maintain it with the strictest confidence, and no party shall disclose such information to third parties without the prior written consent of the other.

Insurance

(select if appropriate)

☐ Licensee shall, throughout the Term, obtain and maintain, at its own expense, standard product liability insurance coverage, naming Licensor as an additional named insured. Such policy shall provide protection against any claims, demands, and causes of action arising out of any alleged defects or failure to perform of the Licensed Products or any use of the Licensed Products. The amount of coverage shall be a minimum of $_____ , with no deductible amount for each single occurrence for bodily injury or property damage. The policy shall provide for notice to the Licensor from the insurer by Registered or Certified Mail in the event of any modification or termination of insurance. The provisions of this section shall survive termination for three (3) years.

Licensor's Right to Terminate

Licensor shall have the right to terminate this Agreement in the following situations:

(select one or more provisions)

☐ **Failure to Make Timely Payment.** Licensee fails to pay Royalties when due or fails to accurately report Net Sales, as defined in the Payment Section of this Agreement, and such failure is not cured within thirty days after written notice from the Licensor.

☐ **Failure to Introduce Product.** Licensee fails to introduce the product to market by the date set in the Exploitation section of this Agreement or to offer the Licensed Products in commercially reasonable quantities during any subsequent year.

☐ **Assignment or Sublicensing.** Licensee assigns or sublicenses in violation of the Agreement.

☐ **Failure to Maintain Insurance.** Licensee fails to maintain or obtain product liability insurance as required by the provisions of this Agreement.

☐ **Failure to Meet Quality Standards or Submit Samples.** Licensee fails to provide Licensor with samples for approval or fails to meet the quality standards established by Licensor.

Licensor shall have the right to terminate the grant of license under this Agreement with respect to any country or region included in the Territory in which Licensee fails to offer the Licensed Products for sale or distributions or to secure a sublicensing agreement for the marketing, distribution, and sale of the product within two years of the Effective Date.

Effect of Termination

Upon termination of this Agreement, all Royalty obligations as established in the Payments Section shall immediately become due. After the termination of this license, all rights granted to Licensee under this Agreement shall terminate and revert to Licensor, and Licensee will refrain from further manufacturing, copying, marketing, distribution, or use of any Licensed Product or other product which incorporates the Trademarks. Within thirty (30) days after termination, Licensee shall deliver to Licensor a statement indicating the number and description of the Licensed Products that it had on hand or is in the process of manufacturing as of the termination date.

Sell-Off Period

Licensee may dispose of the Licensed Products covered by this Agreement for a period of ninety (90) days after termination or expiration, except that Licensee shall have no such right in the event this agreement is terminated according to the Licensor's Right to Terminate, above. At the end of the post-termination sale period, Licensee shall furnish a royalty payment and statement as required under the Payment Section. Upon termination, Licensee shall deliver to Licensor all original designs or reproductions of Trademarks used in the manufacture of the Licensed Products. Licensor shall bear the costs of shipping for these materials.

Attorney Fees and Expenses

The prevailing party shall have the right to collect from the other party its reasonable costs and necessary disbursements and attorney fees incurred in enforcing this Agreement.

Dispute Resolution

(select one if appropriate)

☐ **Mediation & Arbitration.** The Parties agree that every dispute or difference between them, arising under this Agreement, shall be settled first by a meeting of the Parties attempting to confer and resolve the dispute in a good faith manner. If the Parties cannot resolve their dispute after conferring, any Party may require the other Parties to submit the matter to nonbinding mediation, utilizing the services of an impartial professional mediator approved by all Parties. If the Parties cannot come to an agreement following mediation, the Parties agree to submit the matter to binding arbitration at a location mutually agreeable to the parties. The arbitration shall be conducted on a confidential basis pursuant to the Commercial Arbitration Rules of the American Arbitration Association. Any decision or award as a result of any such arbitration proceeding shall be in writing and shall provide an explanation for all conclusions of law and fact and shall include the assessment of costs, expenses, and reasonable attorney fees. An arbitrator experienced in trademark and merchandising law shall conduct any such arbitration. An award of arbitration may be confirmed in a court of competent jurisdiction.

☐ **Arbitration.** If a dispute arises under or relating to this Agreement, the parties agree to submit such dispute to binding arbitration in the State of_____ or another location mutually agreeable to the parties. The arbitration shall be conducted on a confidential basis pursuant to the Commercial Arbitration Rules of the American Arbitration Association. Any decision or award as a result of any such arbitration proceeding shall be in writing and shall provide an explanation for all conclusions of law and fact and shall include the assessment of costs, expenses, and reasonable attorney fees. An arbitrator experienced in trademark and merchandising law shall conduct any such arbitration. An award of arbitration may be confirmed in a court of competent jurisdiction.

Governing Law

This Agreement shall be governed in accordance with the laws of the State of _____ .

Jurisdiction

The parties consent to the exclusive jurisdiction and venue of the federal and state courts located in _____ in any action arising out of or relating to this Agreement. The parties waive any other venue to which either party might be entitled by domicile or otherwise.

Waiver

The failure to exercise any right provided in this Agreement shall not be a waiver of prior or subsequent rights.

Invalidity

If any provision of this Agreement is invalid under applicable statute or rule of law, it is to be considered omitted, and the remaining provisions of this Agreement shall in no way be affected.

Entire Understanding

This Agreement expresses the complete understanding of the parties and supersedes all prior representations, agreements, and understandings, whether written or oral. This Agreement may not be altered except by a written document signed by both parties.

Attachments & Exhibits

The parties agree and acknowledge that all attachments, exhibits, and schedules referred to in this Agreement are incorporated in this Agreement by reference.

No Special Damages

Licensor shall not be liable to Licensee for any incidental, consequential, punitive, or special damages.

Notices

Any notice or communication required or permitted to be given under this Agreement shall be sufficiently given when received by certified mail or sent by facsimile transmission or overnight courier.

No Joint Venture

Nothing contained in this Agreement shall be construed to place one of the parties in the relationship of agent, employee, franchisee, officer, partner, or joint venturer to the other party. Neither party may create or assume any obligation on behalf of the other.

Assignability

(select one)

☐ **Assignment Requires Licensor Consent.** Licensee may not assign or transfer its rights or obligations pursuant to this Agreement without the prior written consent of Licensor. Any assignment or transfer in violation of this section shall be void.

☐ **Licensor Consent Not Required for Assignment to Parent or Acquiring Company.** Licensee may not assign or transfer its rights or obligations pursuant to this Agreement without the prior written consent of Licensor. However, no consent is required for an assignment or transfer that occurs: (a) to an entity in which Licensee owns more than fifty percent of the assets; or (b) as part of a transfer of all or substantially all of the assets of Licensee to any party. Any assignment or transfer in violation of this Section shall be void.

Each party has signed this Agreement through its authorized representative. The parties, having read this Agreement, indicate their consent to the terms and conditions by their signature below.

By: _____   By: _____

Date: _____   Date: _____

Licensor Name: _____   Licensee Name/Title: _____

Exhibit A

The Property _____

_____

Licensed Products _____

_____

Sales Requirements

$ _____ in Gross Sales per year.

Proprietary Notices

All licensed products shall bear the following proprietary notice: _____

_____

Merchandise License Agreement

Introduction

This License Agreement (the "Agreement") is made between _____ (referred to as "Licensor") and_____ (referred to as "Licensee").

The parties agree as follows:

The Work

The Work refers to the work described in Exhibit A. Licensor is the owner of all rights to the Work and Licensee shall not claim any right to use the Work except under the terms of this Agreement.

Licensed Products

Licensed Products are defined as Licensee's products incorporating the Work specifically described in Exhibit A (the "Licensed Products").

Grant of Rights

Licensor grants to Licensee:

(select one)

☐ an exclusive license

☐ a nonexclusive license

to reproduce and distribute the Work in or on the Licensed Products.

Licensor grants to Licensee:

(select if appropriate)

☐ the right to modify the Work to incorporate it in or on the Licensed Products provided that Licensee agrees to assign to Licensor its rights, if any, in any derivative works resulting from Licensee's modification of the Work. Licensee agrees to execute any documents required to evidence this assignment of copyright and to waive any moral rights and rights of attribution provided in 17 U.S.C. § 106A of the Copyright Act.

☐ the right to publicly display the Work as incorporated in or on the Licensed Products.

☐ the right to publicly perform the Work as incorporated in or on the Licensed Products.

Sublicense

(select one)

| | **Consent required.** Licensee may sublicense the rights granted pursuant to this agreement provided: Licensee obtains Licensor's prior written consent to such sublicense; and Licensor receives such revenue or royalty payment as provided in the Payment section below. Any sublicense granted in violation of this provision shall be void. |

| | **Consent to sublicense not unreasonably withheld.** Licensee may sublicense the rights granted pursuant to this agreement provided: Licensee obtains Licensor's prior written consent to such sublicense. Licensor's consent to any sublicense shall not be unreasonably withheld, and Licensor receives such revenue or royalty payment as provided in the Payment section below. Any sublicense granted in violation of this provision shall be void. |

| | **No sublicensing permitted.** Licensee may not sublicense the rights granted under this agreement. |

Reservation of Rights

Licensor reserves all rights other than those being conveyed or granted in this Agreement.

Territory

The rights granted to Licensee are limited to _____ (the "Territory").

Term

The "Effective Date" of this Agreement is defined as the date when the agreement commences and is established by the latest signature date.

(select one)

| | **Specified term with renewal rights.** This Agreement shall commence upon the Effective Date and shall extend for a period of __ years (the "Initial Term"). Following the Initial Term, Licensee may renew this agreement under the same terms and conditions for__ consecutive _____ periods (the "Renewal Terms"), provided that Licensee provides written notice of its intention to renew this agreement within thirty (30) days before the expiration of the current term. In no event shall the Term extend beyond the period of United States copyright protection for the Work. |

☐ **Term with renewal based upon sales.** This Agreement shall commence upon the Effective Date and shall extend for a period of ___ years (the "Initial Term") and may be renewed by Licensee under the same terms and conditions for consecutive _____ year periods (the "Renewal Terms"), provided that:

(a) Licensee provides written notice of its intention to renew this agreement within thirty days before the expiration of the current term; and

(b) Licensee has met the sales requirements as established in Exhibit A.

☐ **Indefinite term.** This Agreement shall commence upon the Effective Date and shall continue until terminated pursuant to a provision of this Agreement.

☐ **Fixed term.** This Agreement shall commence upon the Effective Date and shall continue for _____ unless sooner terminated pursuant to a provision of this Agreement.

☐ **Term for as long as Licensee sells Licensed Products.** This Agreement shall commence upon the Effective Date as specified in Exhibit A and shall continue for as long as Licensee continues to offer the Licensed Products in commercially reasonable quantities or unless sooner terminated pursuant to a provision of this Agreement. In no event shall the Term extend beyond the period of U.S. copyright protection for the Work.

Payments

All royalties ("Royalties") provided for under this Agreement shall accrue when the respective Licensed Products are sold, shipped, distributed, billed, or paid for, whichever occurs first.

Net Sales

Net Sales are defined as Licensee's gross sales (the gross invoice amount billed to customers) less quantity discounts or rebates and returns actually credited. A quantity discount or rebate is a discount made at the time of shipment. No deductions shall be made for cash or other discounts, commissions, manufacturing costs, uncollectible accounts, or for fees or expenses of any kind that the Licensee may incur in connection with the Royalty payments.

Fees

(select one or more provisions)

☐ **Advance Against Royalties.** As a nonrefundable advance against royalties (the "Advance"), Licensee agrees to pay to Licensor upon execution of this Agreement the sum of $ _____ .

[ ] **Licensed Product Royalty.** Licensee agrees to pay a Royalty of ___% percent of all Net Sales revenue of the Licensed Products ("Licensed Product Royalty").

[ ] **Per Unit Royalty.** Licensee agrees to pay a Royalty of $___for each unit of the Licensed Product that is: (select one)

  [ ] manufactured.

  [ ] sold.

[ ] **Guaranteed Minimum Annual Royalty Payment.** In addition to any other advances or fees, Licensee shall pay an annual guaranteed royalty (the "GMAR") as follows: $ _____. The GMAR shall be paid to Licensor annually on _____ . The GMAR is an advance against royalties for the twelve-month period commencing upon payment. Royalty payments based on Net Sales made during any year of this Agreement shall be credited against the GMAR due for the year in which such Net Sales were made. In the event that annual royalties exceed the GMAR, Licensee shall pay the difference to Licensor. Any annual royalty payments in excess of the GMAR shall not be carried forward from previous years or applied against the GMAR.

[ ] **License Fee.** As a nonrefundable, nonrecoupable fee for executing this license, Licensee agrees to pay to Licensor upon execution of this Agreement the sum of $_____.

[ ] **Sublicensing Revenues.** In the event of any sublicense of the rights granted pursuant to this Agreement, Licensee shall pay to Licensor_____% percent of all sublicensing revenues.

Payments and Statements to Licensor

Within thirty (30) days after the end of each calendar quarter (the "Royalty Period"), an accurate statement of Net Sales of Licensed Products along with any royalty payments or sublicensing revenues due to Licensor shall be provided to Licensor, regardless of whether any Licensed Products were sold during the Royalty Period. All payments shall be paid in United States currency drawn on a United States bank. The acceptance by Licensor of any of the statements furnished or royalties paid shall not preclude Licensor questioning the correctness at any time of any payments or statements.

Audit

Licensee shall keep accurate books of account and records covering all transactions relating to the license granted in this Agreement, and Licensor or its duly authorized representatives shall have the right upon five days prior written notice, and during normal business hours, to inspect and audit

Licensee's records relating to the Work licensed under this Agreement. Licensor shall bear the cost of such inspection and audit, unless the results indicate an underpayment greater than $ _____ for any six-month (6-month) period. In that case, Licensee shall promptly reimburse Licensor for all costs of the audit along with the amount due with interest on such sums. Interest shall accrue from the date the payment was originally due and the interest rate shall be 1.5% per month, or the maximum rate permitted by law, whichever is less. All books of account and records shall be made available in the United States and kept available for at least two years after the termination of this Agreement.

Late Payment

Time is of the essence with respect to all payments to be made by Licensee under this Agreement. If Licensee is late in any payment provided for in this Agreement, Licensee shall pay interest on the payment from the date due until paid at a rate of 1.5% per month, or the maximum rate permitted by law, whichever is less.

Licensor Warranties

Licensor warrants that it has the power and authority to enter into this Agreement and has no knowledge as to any third-party claims regarding the proprietary rights in the Work that would interfere with the rights granted under this Agreement.

Indemnification by Licensor

(select one if appropriate)

☐ **Licensor indemnification without limitations.** Licensor shall indemnify Licensee and hold Licensee harmless from any damages and liabilities (including reasonable attorney fees and costs) arising from any breach of Licensor's warranties as defined in Licensor's Warranties, above.

☐ **Licensor indemnification limited to amounts paid.** Licensor shall indemnify Licensee and hold Licensee harmless from any damages and liabilities (including reasonable attorney fees and costs), arising from any breach of Licensor's warranties as defined in Licensor's Warranties, above. Licensor's maximum liability under this provision shall in no event exceed the total amount earned by Licensor under this Agreement.

☐ **Licensor indemnification with limitations.** Licensor shall indemnify Licensee and hold Licensee harmless from any damages and liabilities (including reasonable attorney fees and costs) arising from any breach of Licensor's warranties as defined in Licensor's Warranties, above, provided that:

(a) such claim, if sustained, would prevent Licensee from marketing the Licensed Products or the Work;

(b) such claim arises solely out of the Work as disclosed to the Licensee and not out of any change in the Work made by Licensee or a vendor;

(c) Licensee gives Licensor prompt written notice of any such claim;

(d) such indemnity shall only be applicable in the event of a final decision by a court of competent jurisdiction from which no right to appeal exists; and

(e) the maximum amount due from Licensor to Licensee under this paragraph shall not exceed the amounts due to Licensor under the Payment Section from the date that Licensor notifies Licensee of the existence of such a claim.

Licensee Warranties

Licensee warrants that it will use its best commercial efforts to market the Licensed Products and that sale and marketing of the Licensed Products shall be in conformance with all applicable laws and regulations, including but not limited to all intellectual property laws.

Indemnification by Licensee

Licensee shall indemnify Licensor and hold Licensor harmless from any damages and liabilities (including reasonable attorney fees and costs):

(a) arising from any breach of Licensee's warranties and representation as defined in the Licensee Warranties, above;

(b) arising out of any alleged defects or failures to perform of the Licensed Products or any product liability claims or use of the Licensed Products; and

(c) any claims arising out of advertising, distribution, or marketing of the Licensed Products.

Intellectual Property Registration

Licensor may, but is not obligated to, seek in its own name and at its own expense, appropriate copyright registrations for the Work. Licensor makes no warranty with respect to the validity of any copyright that may be granted. Licensor grants to Licensee the right to apply for registration of the Work or Licensed Products provided that such registrations shall be applied for in the name of

Licensor and licensed to Licensee during the Term and according to the conditions of this Agreement. Licensee shall have the right to deduct its reasonable out-of-pocket expenses for the preparation and filing of any such registrations from future royalties due to Licensor under this Agreement. Licensee shall obtain Licensor's prior written consent before incurring expenses for any foreign copyright applications.

Compliance With Intellectual Property Laws

The license granted in this Agreement is conditioned on Licensee's compliance with the provisions of the intellectual property laws of the United States and any foreign country in the Territory. All copies of the Licensed Product as well as all promotional material shall bear appropriate proprietary notices.

Licensor Credits

Licensee shall identify Licensor as the owner of rights to the Work and shall include the following notice on all copies of the Licensed Products: "_____. All rights reserved."

Licensee may, with Licensor's consent, use Licensor's name, image, or trademark in advertising or promotional materials associated with the sale of the Licensed Products.

Infringement Against Third Parties

In the event that either party learns of imitations or infringements of the Work or Licensed Products, that party shall notify the other in writing of the infringements or imitations. Licensor shall have the right to commence lawsuits against third persons arising from infringement of the Work or Licensed Products. In the event that Licensor does not commence a lawsuit against an alleged infringer within sixty days of notification by Licensee, Licensee may commence a lawsuit against the third party. Before filing suit, Licensee shall obtain the written consent of Licensor to do so, and such consent shall not be unreasonably withheld. Licensor will cooperate fully and in good faith with Licensee for the purpose of securing and preserving Licensee's rights to the Work. Any recovery (including, but not limited to a judgment, settlement, or licensing agreement included as resolution of an infringement dispute) shall be divided equally between the parties after deduction and payment of reasonable attorney fees to the party bringing the lawsuit.

Exploitation Date

Licensee agrees to manufacture, distribute, and sell the Licensed Products in commercially reasonable quantities during the term of this Agreement and to commence such manufacture, distribution, and sale by _____ . This is a material provision of this Agreement.

Advertising Budget

(select if appropriate)

☐   Licensee agrees to spend at least _____ % of estimated annual gross sales for promotional efforts and advertising of the Licensed Products.

Approval of Samples & Quality Control

Licensee shall submit a reasonable number of preproduction designs, prototypes, and camera-ready artwork prior to production as well as preproduction samples of the Licensed Product to Licensor to assure that the product meets Licensor's quality standards. In the event that Licensor fails to object in writing within ten (10) business days after the date of receipt of any such materials, such materials shall be deemed to be acceptable. At least once during each calendar year, Licensee shall submit two (2) production samples of each Licensed Product for review. Licensee shall pay all costs for delivery of these approval materials. The quality standards applied by Licensor shall be no more rigorous than the quality standards applied by Licensor to similar products.

Licensor Copies and Right to Purchase

Licensee shall provide Licensor with ____ copies of each Licensed Product. Licensor has the right to purchase from Licensee, at Licensee's manufacturing cost, at least _____ copies of any Licensed Product, and such payments shall be deducted from royalties due to Licensor.

Confidentiality

The parties acknowledge that each may have access to confidential information that relates to each other's business (the "Information"). The parties agree to protect the confidentiality of the Information and maintain it with the strictest confidence, and no party shall disclose such information to third parties without the prior written consent of the other.

Insurance

Licensee shall, throughout the Term, obtain and maintain, at its own expense, standard product liability insurance coverage, naming Licensor as an additional named insured. Such policy shall provide protection against any claims, demands, and causes of action arising out of any alleged defects or failure to perform of the Licensed Products or any use of the Licensed Products. The amount of coverage shall be a minimum of $ _____ , with no deductible amount for each single occurrence for bodily injury or property damage. The policy shall provide for notice to the Licensor from the insurer by Registered or Certified Mail in the event of any modification or termination of insurance. The provisions of this section shall survive termination for three years.

Licensor's Right to Terminate

Licensor shall have the right to terminate this Agreement for the following reasons:

(select one or more provisions)

☐   **Failure to Make Timely Payment.** Licensee fails to pay Royalties when due or fails to accurately report Net Sales, as defined in the Payment Section of this Agreement, and such failure is not cured within thirty (30) days after written notice from the Licensor.

☐   **Failure to Introduce Product.** Licensee fails to introduce the product to market by the date set in the Exploitation section of this Agreement or to offer the Licensed Products in commercially reasonable quantities during any subsequent year.

☐   **Assignment or Sublicensing.** Licensee assigns or sublicenses in violation of this Agreement.

☐   **Failure to Maintain Insurance.** Licensee fails to maintain or obtain product liability insurance as required by the provisions of this Agreement.

☐   **Failure to Submit Samples.** Licensee fails to provide Licensor with preproduction samples for approval.

☐   **Termination as to Unexploited Portion of Territory.** Licensor shall have the right to terminate the grant of license under this Agreement with respect to any country or region included in the Territory in which Licensee fails to offer the Licensed Products for sale or distribution or to secure a sublicensing agreement for the marketing, distribution, and sale of the product within two (2) years of the Effective Date.

Effect of Termination

Upon termination of this Agreement ("Termination"), all Royalty obligations as established in the Payments Section shall immediately become due. After the Termination of this license, all rights granted to Licensee under this Agreement shall terminate and revert to Licensor, and Licensee will refrain from further manufacturing, copying, marketing, distribution, or use of any Licensed Product or other product which incorporates the Work. Within thirty (30) days after Termination, Licensee shall deliver to Licensor a statement indicating the number and description of the Licensed Products that it had on hand or is in the process of manufacturing as of the Termination date.

Sell-Off Period

Licensee may dispose of the Licensed Products covered by this Agreement for a period of 90 days after Termination or expiration except that Licensee shall have no such right in the event this agreement is terminated according to the Licensor's Right to Terminate, above. At the end of the post-Termination sale period, Licensee shall furnish a royalty payment and statement as required under the Payment Section. Upon termination, Licensee shall deliver to Licensor all original artwork and camera-ready reproductions used in the manufacture of the Licensed Products. Licensor shall bear the costs of shipping for the artwork and reproductions.

Attorney Fees and Expenses

The prevailing party shall have the right to collect from the other party its reasonable costs and necessary disbursements and attorney fees incurred in enforcing this Agreement.

Dispute Resolution

(select one if appropriate)

☐ **Mediation & Arbitration.** The Parties agree that every dispute or difference between them, arising under this Agreement, shall be settled first by a meeting of the Parties attempting to confer and resolve the dispute in a good faith manner. If the Parties cannot resolve their dispute after conferring, any Party may require the other Parties to submit the matter to nonbinding mediation, utilizing the services of an impartial professional mediator approved by all Parties. If the Parties cannot come to an agreement following mediation, the Parties agree to submit the matter to binding arbitration at a location mutually agreeable to the Parties. The arbitration shall be conducted on a confidential basis pursuant to the

Commercial Arbitration Rules of the American Arbitration Association. Any decision or award as a result of any such arbitration proceeding shall include the assessment of costs, expenses, and reasonable attorney's fees and shall include a written record of the proceedings and a written determination of the arbitrators. An arbitrator experienced in copyright and merchandising law shall conduct any such arbitration. An award of arbitration shall be final and binding on the Parties and may be confirmed in a court of competent jurisdiction.

☐ **Arbitration.** If a dispute arises under or relating to this Agreement, the parties agree to submit such dispute to binding arbitration in the state of_____or another location mutually agreeable to the parties. The arbitration shall be conducted on a confidential basis pursuant to the Commercial Arbitration Rules of the American Arbitration Association. Any decision or award as a result of any such arbitration proceeding shall be in writing and shall provide an explanation for all conclusions of law and fact and shall include the assessment of costs, expenses, and reasonable attorney fees. An arbitrator experienced in copyright and merchandising law shall conduct any such arbitration. An award of arbitration may be confirmed in a court of competent jurisdiction.

Governing Law

This Agreement shall be governed in accordance with the laws of the State of _____.

Jurisdiction

The parties consent to the exclusive jurisdiction and venue of the federal and state courts located in _____ in any action arising out of or relating to this Agreement. The parties waive any other venue to which either party might be entitled by domicile or otherwise.

Waiver

The failure to exercise any right provided in this Agreement shall not be a waiver of prior or subsequent rights.

Invalidity

If any provision of this Agreement is invalid under applicable statute or rule of law, it is to be considered omitted, and the remaining provisions of this Agreement shall in no way be affected.

Entire Understanding

This Agreement expresses the complete understanding of the parties and supersedes all prior representations, agreements, and understandings, whether written or oral. This Agreement may not be altered except by a written document signed by both parties.

Attachments & Exhibits

The parties agree and acknowledge that all attachments, exhibits, and schedules referred to in this Agreement are incorporated in this Agreement by reference.

No Special Damages

Licensor shall not be liable to Licensee for any incidental, consequential, punitive, or special damages.

Notices

Any notice or communication required or permitted to be given under this Agreement shall be sufficiently given when received by certified mail or sent by facsimile transmission or overnight courier.

No Joint Venture

Nothing contained in this Agreement shall be construed to place one of the parties in the relationship of agent, employee, franchisee, officer, partner, or joint venturer to the other party. Neither party may create or assume any obligation on behalf of the other.

Assignability

(select one)

☐   **Assignment Requires Licensor Consent.** Licensee may not assign or transfer its rights or obligations pursuant to this Agreement without the prior written consent of Licensor. Any assignment or transfer in violation of this section shall be void.

☐   **Licensor Consent Not Unreasonably Withheld.** Licensee may not assign or transfer its rights or obligations pursuant to this Agreement without the prior written consent of Licensor. Such consent shall not be unreasonably withheld. Any assignment or transfer in violation of this section shall be void.

☐ **Licensor Consent Not Required for Assignment to Parent or Acquiring Company.** Licensee may not assign or transfer its rights or obligations pursuant to this Agreement without the prior written consent of Licensor. However, no consent is required for an assignment or transfer that occurs: (a) to an entity in which Licensee owns more than fifty percent of the assets; or (b) as part of a transfer of all or substantially all of the assets of Licensee to any party. Any assignment or transfer in violation of this Section shall be void.

Each party has signed this Agreement through its authorized representative. The parties, having read this Agreement, indicate their consent to the terms and conditions by their signature below.

By: _____

By: _____

Date: _____

Date: _____

Licensor Name: _____

Licensee Name/Title: _____

Exhibit A

The Property _____

_____

Licensed Products _____

_____

Sales Requirements

$ _____ in Gross Sales per year.

Merchandise License Worksheet

Licensor	Name of licensor business: _____
	Licensor address: _____
	Licensor business form:
	☐ sole proprietorship
	☐ general partnership
	☐ limited partnership
	☐ corporation
	☐ state of incorporation _____
	☐ limited liability company
	☐ state of organization _____
	Name and position of person signing for licensor:
	_____
The Work(s)	Source: _____
	Description: _____
	Page number: _____
	Relevant data (e.g., ISBN, copyright notice): _____
Licensed Product(s)	Tentative title: _____
	Format: _____
Grant of Rights (check those rights needed)	☐ reproduce
	☐ distribute
	☐ modify, adapt
	☐ display
	☐ perform
Market and Format Limitations	☐ specific market: _____
	☐ specific format: _____
Territory	☐ worldwide
	☐ countries or states (name which): _____
Exclusivity	☐ exclusive
	☐ nonexclusive

Term	
	☐ no time limits
	☐ fixed term (how long: _____)
	☐ unlimited term until one party terminates
	☐ an initial term with renewals (see below)
	☐ other _____

Renewals	
	If the parties have agreed upon an initial term with renewals: _____
	How many renewal periods? _____
	How long is each renewal period? _____
	What triggers renewal? _____

Fee	
	☐ one time fee $ _____
	date due: _____
	☐ recurring fee $ _____
	date due/trigger: _____
	☐ advance against royalties $ _____
	date due: _____
	☐ royalty rate(s): _____% of
	☐ net sales
	☐ gross sales
	☐ If royalty payments, are there any
	☐ deductions: _____
	☐ audits (how many per year: _____)

Warranties	
	☐ licensor warranty conditions: _____
	☐ licensee warranty conditions: _____

Indemnity	
	☐ licensor indemnity conditions: _____
	☐ licensee indemnity conditions: _____

Credit	
	☐ licensor credit: _____

Furnished Samples	
	☐ licensor samples required (how many: _____)
	(when: _____)

Miscellaneous	
	☐ jurisdiction state: _____
	☐ governing law state: _____
	☐ arbitration

Termination	
	☐ conditions: _____

Short-Form Merchandise License Agreement

Introduction

This License Agreement (the "Agreement") is made between _____(referred to as "Licensor") and _____ (referred to as "Licensee").

The parties agree as follows:

Grant of Rights

The "Work" is defined as follows: _____ .

Licensed Products are Licensee's products incorporating the Work, specifically_____ (the "Licensed Products").

Licensor is the owner of all rights to the Work, and Licensee shall not claim any right to use the Works except under the terms of this Agreement. Licensor grants to Licensee:

(select one)

☐   an exclusive license

☐   a nonexclusive license

to reproduce and distribute the Work in or on the Licensed Products.

Sublicense

Licensee may sublicense the rights granted pursuant to this agreement provided: Licensee obtains Licensor's prior written consent to such sublicense, and Licensor receives such revenue or royalty payment as provided in the Payment section below. Licensor's consent to any sublicense shall not be unreasonably withheld. Any sublicense granted in violation of this provision shall be void. Licensor reserves all rights other than those being conveyed or granted in this Agreement.

Territory

The rights granted to Licensee are limited to _____ (the "Territory").

Term

This Agreement shall commence upon the "Effective Date," established by the latest signature date, and shall extend for a period of ____ years (the "Initial Term"). Following the Initial Term, Licensee may renew this agreement under the same terms and conditions for _____ consecutive _____ periods (the "Renewal Terms") provided that Licensee provides written notice of its intention to renew this agreement within thirty (30) days before the expiration of the current term.

Royalties

All royalties ("Royalties") provided for under this Agreement shall accrue when the respective Licensed Products are sold, shipped, distributed, billed, or paid for, whichever occurs first.

Net Sales

Net Sales are defined as Licensee's gross sales (the gross invoice amount billed to customers) less quantity discounts or rebates and returns actually credited. A quantity discount or rebate is a discount made at the time of shipment. No deductions shall be made for cash or other discounts, commissions, manufacturing costs, uncollectible accounts, or for fees or expenses of any kind which the Licensee may incur in connection with the Royalty payments.

Advance Against Royalties

As a nonrefundable advance against royalties (the "Advance"), Licensee agrees to pay to Licensor upon execution of this Agreement the sum of $ _____ .

Licensed Product Royalty

Licensee agrees to pay a Royalty of _____% percent of all Net Sales revenue of the Licensed Products ("Licensed Product Royalty").

Sublicensing Revenues

In the event of any sublicense of the rights granted pursuant to this Agreement, Licensee shall pay to Licensor _____% percent of all sublicensing revenues.

Payments and Statements

Within thirty (30) days after the end of each calendar quarter (the "Royalty Period"), an accurate statement of Net Sales of Licensed Products along with any royalty payments or sublicensing revenues shall be due to Licensor. The acceptance by Licensor of any of the statements furnished or royalties paid shall not preclude Licensor from questioning the correctness at any time of any payments or statements.

Audit

Licensee shall keep accurate books of account and records covering all transactions relating to the license granted in this Agreement, and Licensor or its duly authorized representatives shall have the right upon five (5) days prior written notice, and during normal business hours, to inspect Licensee's records relating to the Work licensed under this Agreement.

Late Payment

If Licensee is late in any payment provided for in this Agreement, Licensee shall pay interest on the payment from the date due until paid at a rate of 1.5% per month, or the maximum rate permitted by law, whichever is less.

Warranties

Licensor warrants that it has the power and authority to enter into this Agreement and has no knowledge as to any third-party claims regarding the proprietary rights in the Work that would interfere with the rights granted under this Agreement.

Licensee warrants that it will use its best commercial efforts to market the Licensed Products and that sale and marketing of the Licensed Products shall be in conformance with all applicable laws and regulations, including but not limited to all intellectual property laws.

Licensor Credits

Licensee shall identify Licensor as the owner of rights to the Work and shall include the following notice on all copies of the Licensed Products:

"_____ . All rights reserved."

Licensee may, with Licensor's consent, use Licensor's name, image, or trademark in advertising or promotional materials associated with the sale of the Licensed Products.

Exploitation

Licensee agrees to manufacture, distribute, and sell the Licensed Products in commercially reasonable quantities during the term of this Agreement and to commence such manufacture, distribution, and sale by _____ . This is a material provision of this Agreement.

Approval of Samples & Quality Control

Licensee shall submit a reasonable number of preproduction samples of the Licensed Product to Licensor to assure that the product meets Licensor's quality standards. In the event that Licensor fails to object in writing within ten (10) business days after the date of receipt of any such materials, such materials shall be deemed to be acceptable.

Licensor Copies and Right to Purchase

Licensee shall provide Licensor with copies of each Licensed Product. Licensor has the right to purchase from Licensee, at Licensee's manufacturing cost, at least _____ copies of any Licensed Product, and such payments shall be deducted from royalties due to Licensor.

Licensor's Right to Terminate

Licensor shall have the right to terminate this Agreement for the following reasons:

(select one or more provisions)

☐ **Failure to Make Timely Payment.** Licensee fails to pay Royalties when due or fails to accurately report Net Sales, as defined in the Payments and Statements section of this Agreement, and such failure is not cured within thirty (30) days after written notice from the Licensor.

☐ **Failure to Introduce Product.** Licensee fails to introduce the product to market by the date set in the Exploitation section of this Agreement or to offer the Licensed Products in commercially reasonable quantities during any subsequent year.

Effect of Termination

After the termination of this license, all rights granted to Licensee under this Agreement shall terminate and revert to Licensor, and Licensee will refrain from further manufacturing, copying, marketing, distribution, or use of any Licensed Product or other product which incorporates the Work. Licensee may dispose of the Licensed Products covered by this Agreement for a period of 90 days after termination or expiration, except that Licensee shall have no such right in the event this agreement is terminated according to the Licensor's Right to Terminate, above.

Miscellaneous

The prevailing party shall have the right to collect from the other party its reasonable costs and attorney fees incurred in enforcing this Agreement. This Agreement expresses the full, complete, and exclusive understanding of the parties with respect to the subject matter and supersedes all prior proposals, representations, and understandings. If a dispute arises between the parties arising under or relating to this Agreement, the parties agree to submit such dispute to arbitration conducted under the rules of the American Arbitration Association. An arbitration award may be confirmed in a court of competent jurisdiction. The waiver or failure of any party to exercise in any respect any right provided for in this Agreement shall not be deemed a waiver of any further right under this Agreement. No party shall represent themselves to be the employee, franchisee, franchiser, joint venturer, officer, or partner of the other party, and nothing in this Agreement shall be construed to place the parties in the relationship of partners or joint venturers. If any provision of this Agreement is invalid under any applicable statute or rule of law, it is to that extent to be deemed omitted and the remaining provisions of this Agreement shall in no way be affected or impaired. Licensee may not assign or sublicense the rights granted under this Agreement without the written consent of Licensor. Such consent shall not be unreasonably withheld. Each party has signed this Agreement through its authorized representative. The parties, having read this Agreement, indicate their consent to the terms and conditions by their signature below.

By: _____   By: _____

Date: _____   Date: _____

Licensor Name: _____   Licensee Name/Title: _____

Unlimited Personal Release Agreement

Grant

For consideration which I acknowledge, I irrevocably grant to _____ ("Company") and Company's assigns, licensees, and successors the right to use my image and name in all forms and media including composite or modified representations for all purposes, including advertising, trade, or any commercial purpose throughout the world and in perpetuity. I waive the right to inspect or approve versions of my image used for publication or the written copy that may be used in connection with the images.

Release

I release Company and Company's assigns, licensees, and successors from any claims that may arise regarding the use of my image including any claims of defamation, invasion of privacy, or infringement of moral rights, rights of publicity, or copyright. Company is permitted, although not obligated, to include my name as a credit in connection with the image.

Company is not obligated to utilize any of the rights granted in this Agreement.

I have read and understood this agreement and I am over the age of 18. This Agreement expresses the complete understanding of the parties.

Name: _____ Date: _____

Signature: _____

Address: _____

Witness Signature: _____ ____

Parent/Guardian Consent [include if the person is under 18]

I am the parent or guardian of the minor named above. I have the legal right to consent to and do consent to the terms and conditions of this release.

Parent/Guardian Name: _____ Date: _____

Parent/Guardian Signature: _____

Parent/Guardian Address: _____

Witness Signature: _____

Limited Personal Release Agreement

Grant

For consideration which I acknowledge, I grant to _____ ("Company") and Company's assigns, licensees, and successors, the right to use my image for the following purposes:

_____

_____ in the following

territory _____ for a period of _____ year(s) (the "Term").

I grant the right to use my name and image for the purposes listed above in all forms and media including composite or modified representations and waive the right to inspect or approve versions of my image used for publication or the written copy that may be used in connection with the images.

Payment

(select if appropriate)

☐ For the rights granted during the Term, Company shall pay $_____upon execution of this release.

Renewal

(select if appropriate)

☐ Company may renew this agreement under the same terms and conditions for _____ year(s) provided that Licensee makes payment of $ _____ at the time of renewal.

Release

I release Company and Company's assigns, licensees, and successors from any claims that may arise regarding the use of my image including any claims of defamation, invasion of privacy, or infringement of moral rights, rights of publicity, or copyright. Company is permitted, although not obligated, to include my name as a credit in connection with the image.

Name: _____ Date: _____

Signature: _____

Address: _____

Witness Signature: _____

Parent/Guardian Consent [include if the person is under 18]

I am the parent or guardian of the minor named above. I have the legal right to consent to and do consent to the terms and conditions of this release.

Parent/Guardian Name: _____ Date: _____

Parent/Guardian Signature: _____

Parent/Guardian Address: _____

Witness Signature: _____

Interview Release Agreement

Grant

For consideration which I acknowledge, I consent to the recording of my statements and grant to
_____ ("Company") and Company's assigns, licensees, and successors the right to
copy, reproduce, and use all or a portion of the statements (the "Interview") for incorporation in the
following work _____ (the "Work").

I permit the use of all or a portion of the Interview in the Work in all forms and media including
advertising and related promotion throughout the world and in perpetuity. I grant the right to use my
image and name in connection with all uses of the Interview and waive the right to inspect or
approve use of my Interview as incorporated in the Work.

Release

I release Company and Company's assigns, licensees, and successors from any claims that may arise
regarding the use of the Interview including any claims of defamation, invasion of privacy, or
infringement of moral rights, rights of publicity, or copyright. I acknowledge that I have no ownership
rights in the Work.

Company is not obligated to utilize the rights granted in this Agreement.

I have read and understood this agreement and I am over the age of 18. This Agreement expresses
the complete understanding of the parties.

Name: _____ Date: _____

Signature: _____

Address: _____

Witness Signature: _____

Parent/Guardian Consent [include if the person is under 18]

I am the parent or guardian of the minor named above. I have the legal right to consent to and do
consent to the terms and conditions of this release.

Parent/Guardian Name: _____ Date: _____

Parent/Guardian Signature: _____

Parent/Guardian Address: _____

Property Release Agreement

The Property: _____

Grant

For consideration which I acknowledge, I irrevocably grant to _____
("Company") and Company's assigns, licensees, and successors the right to enter onto the property
listed above and to photograph, copy, publish, display, and use images of the property in all forms
and media including composite or modified representations throughout the world and in perpetuity
for the following purposes: _____

I waive the right to inspect or approve the manner in which the images of the property are used
and waive the right to inspect any text that is used in connection with the images of the property.

Dates of Use

Company shall enter onto the property on the following dates and times: _____

In consideration for the rights granted under this Agreement, Company shall pay me $ _____
upon execution of this Agreement.

Company is not obligated to utilize any of the rights granted in this Agreement.

Warranty, Indemnity, & Release

I warrant that I am the owner of the property and have the authority to grant the rights under this
agreement and agree to indemnify Company from any claims regarding my ownership of the
property. I release Company and Company's assigns, licensees, and successors from any claims that
may arise regarding the use of the images of the property.

I have read and understood this agreement. This Agreement expresses the complete understanding
of the parties.

Owner's Signature: _____

Owner's Name: _____

Owner's Address: _____

Date: _____

Search Request Form

TYPE OF WORK:

☐ Book ☐ Music ☐ Motion Picture ☐ Drama ☐ Sound Recording
☐ Photography / Artwork ☐ Map ☐ Periodical ☐ Contribution
☐ Computer Program ☐ Mask Work

SEARCH INFORMATION YOU REQUIRE:

☐ Registration ☐ Renewal ☐ Assignment ☐ Address

SPECIFICS OF WORK TO BE SEARCHED:

TITLE: _____

AUTHOR: _____

COPYRIGHT CLAIMANT (if known): _____ (name in

copyright notice)

APPROXIMATE YEAR DATE OF PUBLICATION/CREATION: _____

REGISTRATION NUMBER (if known): _____

OTHER IDENTIFYING INFORMATION: _____

If you need more space please attach additional pages.

YOUR NAME: _____

DATE: _____

ADDRESS: _____

DAYTIME TELEPHONE NO.: _____

Convey results of estimate/research by telephone? ☐ Yes ☐ No

Fee Enclosed? ☐ Yes. Amount $ ____ ☐ No

Permissions Tracking Sheet

PTN	Type of Work, Title, Source, and ID Numbers	Author	Owner, Contact Person, Phone, Address, and Email	Payment	Payment Due Date	Date Paid and Form of Payment	Credit	Sample Approval or Comp Copies	Rights Acquired	How the Work is Used

Basic Copyright Assignment

I, _____ ("Assignor"), am owner of the work entitled _____

(the "Work") and described as follows: _____

_____ .

In consideration of $ _____ and other valuable consideration, paid by _____

 ("Assignee"), I assign to Assignee and Assignee's heirs and assigns all my right, title, and interest in
the copyright to the Work and all renewals and extensions of the copyright that may be secured
under the laws of the United States of America and any other countries, as such may now or later be
in effect. I agree to cooperate with Assignee and to execute and deliver all papers as may be
necessary to vest all rights to the Work.

Signature of assignor(s) _____

Musician Assignment Agreement

This Musician Assignment Agreement (the "Agreement") is made between _____
("Company") and _____ ("Musician").

Grant

Musician has performed or recorded performance(s) for the Company in conjunction with the
Company recording under the titles:

_____

_____

_____

   In consideration of the payments provided in this Agreement, Musician assigns all rights,
including all rights under copyright law, in the recorded performance to the Company, its assigns,
licensees, or successors and grants the right to use the recorded performance for any purposes and in
all forms and media and waives any claim to moral rights.

Payment

Company shall pay Musician as follows: $ _____ .

Warranty & Release

Musician has the authority to grant the rights under this Agreement and Musician releases Company
and Company's assigns, licensees, and successors from any claims that may arise regarding the use
of the performance including any claims of infringement of moral rights, rights of publicity, or
copyright. Company is permitted, although not obligated, to include musician's name as a credit in
connection with the performance.

   Company is not obligated to utilize any of the rights granted in this Agreement.

   Musician has read and understood this agreement and is over the age of 18. This Agreement
expresses the complete understanding of the parties.

Musician Signature: _____

Musician Name: _____

Musician's Address: _____

Date: _____

Artwork Assignment Agreement

This Artwork Assignment Agreement (the "Agreement") is made between _____
("Company") and _____ ("Artist").

Services

Artist agrees to perform the following services: _____
and create the following artwork (the "Art") entitled: _____.

    The Art shall be completed by the following date: _____ .

    During the process, Artist shall keep the Company informed of work in progress and shall furnish
test prints of the Art prior to completion.

Payment

Company agrees to pay Artist as follows:

$ _____ for performance of the art services and acquisition of the rights provided below.

Rights

Artist assigns to the Company all copyright to the Art and agrees to cooperate in the preparation of
any documents necessary to demonstrate this assignment of rights. Artist retains the right to display
the work as part of Artist's portfolio and to reproduce the artwork in connection with the promotion
of Artist's services.

Expenses

Company agrees to reimburse Artist for all reasonable production expenses including halftones, stats,
photography, disks, illustrations, or related costs. These expenses shall be itemized on invoices and
in no event shall any expense exceed $50 without approval from the Company.

Credit

Credit for Artist shall be included on reproductions of the Art as follows: _____

Artist Warranties

Artist is the owner of all rights to the Art and warrants that the Art does not infringe any intellectual
property rights or violate any laws.

Artist Signature: _____

Artist Name: _____

Artist Address: _____

Date: _____

Company Authorized Signature: _____

Name and Title: _____

Address: _____

Date: _____

Work-Made-for-Hire Agreement

This Work-Made-for-Hire Agreement (the "Agreement") is made between _____ ("Company") and _____ ("Artist").

Services

In consideration of the payments provided in this Agreement, Artist agrees to perform the following services: _____

Payment

Company agrees to pay Artist as follows: _____

Works Made for Hire—Assignment of Intellectual Property Rights

Artist agrees that, for consideration that is acknowledged, any works of authorship commissioned pursuant to this Agreement (the "Works") shall be considered works made for hire as that term is defined under U.S. copyright law. To the extent that any such Work created for Company by Artist is not a work made for hire belonging to Company, Artist hereby assigns and transfers to Company all rights Artist has or may acquire to all such Works. Artist agrees to sign and deliver to Company, either during or subsequent to the term of this Agreement, such other documents as Company considers desirable to evidence the assignment of copyright.

Artist Warranties

Artist warrants that the Work does not infringe any intellectual property rights or violate any laws and that the work is original to Artist.

Miscellaneous

This Agreement constitutes the entire understanding between the parties and can only be modified by written agreement. The laws of the State of _____ shall govern this Agreement. In the event of any dispute arising under this agreement, the prevailing party shall be entitled to its reasonable attorney fees.

Artist Signature:_____   Company Authorized Signature: _____

Artist Name: _____   Name and Title: _____

Artist Address: _____   Address: _____

Date: _____   Date: _____

Index

M

Magazines
  interview from, 2/9–10
  ISSN, 2/12, 7/4, 13/7
  locating publisher, 2/5–6
  online, 2/5
  out-of-print, 2/11–12
  reprint rights, 2/7
  trademarks and, 10/11
Markwatch, 6/5
Marvel Entertainment Group, Inc., 4/21
Master use license, 5/6, 5/22, 5/31–38
Mattel, Inc. v. MCA Records, Inc., 10/13
Matthew Bender & Co. v. West Publishing Co., 8/8
McGraw-Edison Co. v. Walt Disney Productions, 10/11
Mechanical rights, 5/45
Mechanical royalty, 5/5, 5/15, 5/17, 5/18
Media law specialist, 16/4
Mediation, 11/28
Mediclip service, 4/8, 4/21
Merchandise
  artwork on, 4/3
  licensable, 11/3
  trademark licensing, 10/15–29
Merchandise licensing, 11/3–40
  fees, 10/16, 11/3
  royalties for, 10/16, 11/3, 11/6, 11/24–25
  sample agreements, 11/6–32, 11/35–40
  sample worksheets, 11/6, 11/32–34
  trademark, 10/15
Merchandising, 4/9
Merger doctrine, 2/15, 8/7
Micropatent, 10/15
MIDI software, 5/39
Mirroring (website), 6/11
MMERL license, 5/40
Model release, 3/15
Monster Communications, Inc. v. Turner Broadcasting System, Inc., 9/7
Montana v. San Jose Mercury News, 12/5
Moral rights, 4/12
Motion pictures, using artwork in, 4/17–20
Movies
  music in, 5/6, 5/24–38
  public domain and, 8/9

trademark and, 10/11–12
MP3s, 5/41
Multimedia programs
  educational fair use, 7/17–18
  music used in, 5/39–40
Multimedia synchronization license, 5/40
Music, 5/3–48. *See also* Songs
  assignment agreement, 15/4–6
  audio streaming, 5/6, 5/40, 5/41–43
  background music, 5/21
  blanket licenses, 5/14
  in commercial radio show, 5/21–22
  compulsory license, 5/17–20
  digital, 5/6, 5/16, 5/40–41
  educational fair use, 7/15–16
  electrical transcription licenses, 5/21
  fees, 1/6, 5/4, 5/5, 5/7, 5/10, 5/15, 5/21, 5/39–42
  grand rights, 5/21
  lawsuits, 5/45, 9/7–8
  lyrics, 1/4
  master use license, 5/6, 5/22, 5/31, 5/40
  mechanical rights, 5/45
  mechanical royalty, 5/5, 5/15, 5/17–18
  movie use, 5/22–38
  multimedia master use license, 5/40
  multimedia synchronization license, 5/40
  music, 5/13, 5/24–31, 15/4–6
  musical arrangements, 5/13
  nonprofit and charitable businesses, use by, 5/16–17
  on-hold music, 5/16
  orchestrations, 5/13
  out-of-print, 7/16
  performance rights, 1/4, 5/8, 5/14
  performance royalties, 5/5
  played at a business, 5/14–16
  production music libraries (PMLs), 5/3, 5/7, 5/22, 5/47
  public performance, 5/5
  recorded, 1/4, 5/3–8, 5/17–21
  resources, 5/47–48
  in software or multimedia programs, 5/39–40
  sound recording copyrights, 5/6–8
  synchronization license, 5/6, 5/22–32
  television use of, 5/24–38

P

CATALOG

...more from Nolo

	PRICE	CODE

BUSINESS

	PRICE	CODE
Buy-Sell Agreement Handbook: Plan Ahead for Changes in the Ownership of Your Business (Book w/CD-ROM)	$49.99	BSAG
The CA Nonprofit Corporation Kit (Binder w/CD-ROM)	$59.95	CNP
Consultant & Independent Contractor Agreements (Book w/CD-ROM)	$29.99	CICA
The Corporate Minutes Book (Book w/CD-ROM)	$69.99	CORMI
Create Your Own Employee Handbook	$49.99	EMHA
The Employer's Legal Handbook	$39.99	EMPL
Everyday Employment Law	$29.99	ELBA
Dealing With Problem Employees	$44.99	PROBM
Drive a Modest Car & 16 Other Keys to Small Business Success	$24.99	DRIV
Federal Employment Laws	$49.99	FELW
Form Your Own Limited Liability Company (Book w/CD-ROM)	$44.99	LIAB
Hiring Independent Contractors: The Employer's Legal Guide (Book w/CD-ROM)	$34.99	HICI
How to Create a Noncompete Agreement	$44.95	NOCMP
How to Form a California Professional Corporation (Book w/CD-ROM)	$59.95	PROF
How to Form a Nonprofit Corporation (Book w/CD-ROM)—National Edition	$44.99	NNP
How to Form a Nonprofit Corporation in California (Book w/CD-ROM)	$44.99	NON
How to Form Your Own California Corporation (Binder w/CD-ROM)	$59.99	CACI
How to Form Your Own California Corporation (Book w/CD-ROM)	$34.99	CCOR
How to Get Your Business on the Web	$29.99	WEBS
How to Write a Business Plan	$34.99	SBS
Incorporate Your Business	$49.95	NIBS
The Independent Paralegal's Handbook	$29.95	PARA
Leasing Space for Your Small Business	$34.95	LESP
Legal Guide for Starting & Running a Small Business	$34.99	RUNS
Legal Forms for Starting & Running a Small Business (Book w/CD-ROM)	$29.99	RUNS2
Marketing Without Advertising	$24.00	MWAD
Music Law (Book w/CD-ROM)	$34.99	ML
Nolo's Guide to Social Security Disability	$29.99	QSS
Nolo's Quick LLC	$24.95	LLCQ
Nondisclosure Agreements	$39.95	NAG
The Small Business Start-up Kit (Book w/CD-ROM)	$29.99	SMBU
The Small Business Start-up Kit for California (Book w/CD-ROM)	$34.99	OPEN
The Partnership Book: How to Write a Partnership Agreement (Book w/CD-ROM)	$39.99	PART
Sexual Harassment on the Job	$24.95	HARS
Starting & Running a Successful Newsletter or Magazine	$29.99	MAG
Take Charge of Your Workers' Compensation Claim	$34.99	WORK
Tax Savvy for Small Business	$36.99	SAVVY
Working for Yourself: Law & Taxes for the Self-Employed	$39.99	WAGE
Your Crafts Business: A Legal Guide	$26.99	VART
Your Limited Liability Company: An Operating Manual (Book w/CD-ROM)	$49.99	LOP
Your Rights in the Workplace	$29.99	YRW

CONSUMER

	PRICE	CODE
How to Win Your Personal Injury Claim	$29.99	PICL
Nolo's Encyclopedia of Everyday Law	$29.99	EVL
Nolo's Guide to California Law	$24.95	CLAW
Trouble-Free Travel...And What to Do When Things Go Wrong	$14.95	TRAV

Prices subject to change.

	PRICE	CODE

ESTATE PLANNING & PROBATE

8 Ways to Avoid Probate	$19.99	PRO8
9 Ways to Avoid Estate Taxes	$29.95	ESTX
Estate Planning Basics	$21.99	ESPN
How to Probate an Estate in California	$49.99	PAE
Make Your Own Living Trust (Book w/CD-ROM)	$39.99	LITR
Nolo's Simple Will Book (Book w/CD-ROM)	$36.99	SWIL
Plan Your Estate	$44.99	NEST
Quick & Legal Will Book	$16.99	QUIC

FAMILY MATTERS

Child Custody: Building Parenting Agreements That Work	$29.99	CUST
The Complete IEP Guide	$24.99	IEP
Divorce & Money: How to Make the Best Financial Decisions During Divorce	$34.99	DIMO
Do Your Own California Adoption: Nolo's Guide for Stepparents and Domestic Partners (Book w/CD-ROM)	$34.99	ADOP
Get a Life: You Don't Need a Million to Retire Well	$24.99	LIFE
The Guardianship Book for California	$39.99	GB
A Legal Guide for Lesbian and Gay Couples	$29.99	LG
Living Together: A Legal Guide (Book w/CD-ROM)	$34.99	LTK
Medical Directives and Powers of Attorney in California	$19.99	CPOA
Using Divorce Mediation: Save Your Money & Your Sanity	$29.95	UDMD

GOING TO COURT

Beat Your Ticket: Go To Court and Win! (National Edition)	$19.99	BEYT
The Criminal Law Handbook: Know Your Rights, Survive the System	$34.99	KYR
Everybody's Guide to Small Claims Court (National Edition)	$26.99	NSCC
Everybody's Guide to Small Claims Court in California	$26.99	CSCC
Fight Your Ticket ... and Win! (California Edition)	$29.99	FYT
How to Change Your Name in California	$34.95	NAME
How to Collect When You Win a Lawsuit (California Edition)	$29.99	JUDG
How to Seal Your Juvenile & Criminal Records (California Edition)	$34.95	CRIM
The Lawsuit Survival Guide	$29.99	UNCL
Nolo's Deposition Handbook	$29.99	DEP
Represent Yourself in Court: How to Prepare & Try a Winning Case	$34.99	RYC
Sue in California Without a Lawyer	$34.99	SLWY

HOMEOWNERS, LANDLORDS & TENANTS

California Tenants' Rights	$27.99	CTEN
Deeds for California Real Estate	$24.99	DEED
Dog Law	$21.95	DOG
Every Landlord's Legal Guide (National Edition, Book w/CD-ROM)	$44.99	ELLI
Every Tenant's Legal Guide	$29.99	EVTEN
For Sale by Owner in California	$29.99	FSBO
How to Buy a House in California	$34.99	BHCA
The California Landlord's Law Book: Rights & Responsibilities (Book w/CD-ROM)	$44.99	LBRT
The California Landlord's Law Book: Evictions (Book w/CD-ROM)	$44.99	LBEV
Leases & Rental Agreements	$29.99	LEAR
Neighbor Law: Fences, Trees, Boundaries & Noise	$26.99	NEI
The New York Landlord's Law Book (Book w/CD-ROM)	$39.99	NYLL
New York Tenants' Rights	$27.99	NYTEN
Renters' Rights (National Edition)	$24.99	RENT
Stop Foreclosure Now in California	$29.95	CLOS

IMMIGRATION

Becoming a U.S. Citizen: A Guide to the Law, Exam and Interview	$24.99	USCIT
Fiancé & Marriage Visas	$44.95	IMAR
How to Get a Green Card	$29.99	GRN
Student & Tourist Visas	$29.99	ISTU

ORDER 24 HOURS A DAY @ www.nolo.com
Call 800-728-3555 • Mail or fax the order form in this book

	PRICE	CODE
U.S. Immigration Made Easy	$44.99	IMEZ

MONEY MATTERS

	PRICE	CODE
101 Law Forms for Personal Use (Book w/CD-ROM)	$29.99	SPOT
Bankruptcy: Is It the Right Solution to Your Debt Problems?	$19.99	BRS
Chapter 13 Bankruptcy: Repay Your Debts	$34.99	CH13
Creating Your Own Retirement Plan	$29.99	YROP
Credit Repair (Quick & Legal Series, Book w/CD-ROM)	$24.99	CREP
Getting Paid: How to Collect from Bankrupt Debtors	$24.99	CRBNK
How to File for Chapter 7 Bankruptcy	$34.99	HFB
IRAs, 401(k)s & Other Retirement Plans: Taking Your Money Out	$34.99	RET
Money Troubles: Legal Strategies to Cope With Your Debts	$29.99	MT
Stand Up to the IRS	$24.99	SIRS
Surviving an IRS Tax Audit	$24.95	SAUD
Take Control of Your Student Loan Debt	$26.95	SLOAN

PATENTS AND COPYRIGHTS

	PRICE	CODE
The Copyright Handbook: How to Protect and Use Written Works (Book w/CD-ROM)	$39.99	COHA
Copyright Your Software	$34.95	CYS
Domain Names	$26.95	DOM
Getting Permission: How to License and Clear Copyrighted Materials Online and Off (Book w/CD-ROM)	$34.99	RIPER
How to Make Patent Drawings Yourself	$29.99	DRAW
Inventor's Guide to Law, Business and Taxes	$34.99	ILAX
The Inventor's Notebook	$24.99	INOT
Nolo's Patents for Beginners	$29.99	QPAT
License Your Invention (Book w/CD-ROM)	$39.99	LICE
Patent, Copyright & Trademark	$39.99	PCTM
Patent It Yourself	$49.99	PAT
Patent Pending in 24 Hours	$29.99	PEND
Patent Searching Made Easy	$29.95	PATSE
The Public Domain	$34.95	PUBL
Trademark: Legal Care for Your Business and Product Name	$39.95	TRD
Web and Software Development: A Legal Guide (Book w/CD-ROM)	$44.95	SFT

RESEARCH & REFERENCE

	PRICE	CODE
Legal Research: How to Find & Understand the Law	$39.99	LRES

SENIORS

	PRICE	CODE
Choose the Right Long-Term Care: Home Care, Assisted Living & Nursing Homes	$21.99	ELD
The Conservatorship Book for California	$44.99	CNSV
Social Security, Medicare & Goverment Pensions	$29.99	SOA

SOFTWARE
Call or check our website at www.nolo.com for special discounts on Software!

	PRICE	CODE
LeaseWriter CD—Windows	$129.95	LWD1
LLC Maker—Windows	$89.95	LLP1
PatentPro Plus—Windows	$399.99	PAPL
Personal RecordKeeper 5.0 CD—Windows	$59.95	RKD5
Quicken Legal Business Pro 2004—Windows	$79.95	SBQB4
Quicken WilMaker Plus 2004—Windows	$79.95	WQP4

Order Form

Name

Address

City

State, Zip

Daytime Phone

E-mail

Our "No-Hassle" Guarantee

Return anything you buy directly from Nolo for any reason and we'll cheerfully refund your purchase price. No ifs, ands or buts.

☐ Check here if you do not wish to receive mailings from other companies

Item Code	Quantity	Item	Unit Price	Total Price

Method of payment

☐ Check   ☐ VISA   ☐ MasterCard
☐ Discover Card   ☐ American Express

Subtotal	
Add your local sales tax (California only)	
Shipping: RUSH $9, Basic $5 (See below)	
"I bought 3, ship it to me FREE!"(Ground shipping only)	
TOTAL	

Account Number

Expiration Date

Signature

Shipping and Handling

Rush Delivery—Only $9

We'll ship any order to any street address in the U.S. by UPS 2nd Day Air* for only $9!

* Order by noon Pacific Time and get your order in 2 business days. Orders placed after noon Pacific Time will arrive in 3 business days. P.O. boxes and S.F. Bay Area use basic shipping. Alaska and Hawaii use 2nd Day Air or Priority Mail.

Basic Shipping—$5

Use for P.O. Boxes, Northern California and Ground Service.

Allow 1-2 weeks for delivery. U.S. addresses only.

For faster service, use your credit card and our toll-free numbers

**Call our customer service group
Monday thru Friday 7am to 7pm PST**

Phone   1-800-728-3555
Fax   1-800-645-0895
Mail   **Nolo
950 Parker St.
Berkeley, CA 94710**

Order 24 hours a day @
www.nolo.com

Remember:

Little publishers have big ears.
We really listen to you.

Your comments make a big difference in the development and revision of Nolo books and software. Please take a few minutes and register your Nolo product—and your comments—with us. Not only will your input make a difference, you'll receive special offers available only to registered owners of Nolo products on our newest books and software. Register now by:

PHONE
1-800-728-3555

FAX
1-800-645-0895

EMAIL
cs@nolo.com

or **MAIL** us
this registration card

fold here

- -

Registration Card

NAME _____ DATE _____

ADDRESS _____

_____

CITY _____ STATE _____ ZIP _____

PHONE _____ E-MAIL _____

WHERE DID YOU HEAR ABOUT THIS PRODUCT? _____

WHERE DID YOU PURCHASE THIS PRODUCT? _____

DID YOU CONSULT A LAWYER? (PLEASE CIRCLE ONE)   YES   NO   NOT APPLICABLE

DID YOU FIND THIS BOOK HELPFUL?   (VERY)   5   4   3   2   1   (NOT AT ALL)

COMMENTS _____

_____

_____

WAS IT EASY TO USE?   (VERY EASY)   5   4   3   2   1   (VERY DIFFICULT)

We occasionally make our mailing list available to carefully selected companies whose products may be of interest to you.

❑   If you do not wish to receive mailings from these companies, please check this box.

❑   You can quote me in future Nolo promotional materials.
   Daytime phone number _____.

RIPER 2.0

Nolo in the NEWS

"Nolo helps lay people perform legal tasks without the aid—or fees—of lawyers."

—USA TODAY

Nolo books are ..."written in plain language, free of legal mumbo jumbo, and spiced with witty personal observations."

—ASSOCIATED PRESS

"...Nolo publications...guide people simply through the how, when, where and why of law."

—WASHINGTON POST

"Increasingly, people who are not lawyers are performing tasks usually regarded as legal work... And consumers, using books like Nolo's, do routine legal work themselves."

—NEW YORK TIMES

"...All of [Nolo's] books are easy-to-understand, are updated regularly, provide pull-out forms...and are often quite moving in their sense of compassion for the struggles of the lay reader."

—SAN FRANCISCO CHRONICLE

- - - - - - - - - - - - - - - - - - - fold here -

Nolo
950 Parker Street
Berkeley, CA 94710-9867

Attn: RIPER 2.0